CW01677652

CIMA™

How to access your on-line resources

Kaplan Financial students will have a MyKaplan account and these extra resources will be available to you online. You do not need to register again, as this process was completed when you enrolled. If you are having problems accessing online materials, please ask your course administrator.

If you are not studying with Kaplan and did not purchase your book via a Kaplan website, to unlock your extra online resources please go to www.en-gage.co.uk (even if you have set up an account and registered books previously). You will then need to enter the ISBN number (on the title page and back cover) and the unique pass key number contained in the scratch panel below to gain access.

You will also be required to enter additional information during this process to set up or confirm your account details.

If you purchased through the Kaplan Publishing website you will automatically receive an e-mail invitation to register your details and gain access to your content. If you do not receive the e-mail or book content, please contact Kaplan Publishing.

Your code and information

This code can only be used once for the registration of one book online. This registration and your online content will expire when the final sittings for the examinations covered by this book have taken place. Please allow one hour from the time you submit your book details for us to process your request.

Please scratch the film to access your unique code.

Please be aware that this code is case-sensitive and you will need to include the dashes within the passcode, but not when entering the ISBN.

KAPLAN PUBLISHING

CIMA

Subject BA1

Fundamentals of Business Economics

Study Text

CIMA PUBLISHING

KAPLAN PUBLISHING

KAPLAN PUBLISHING'S STATEMENT OF PRINCIPLES

LINGUISTIC DIVERSITY, EQUALITY AND INCLUSION

We are committed to diversity, equality and inclusion and strive to deliver content that all users can relate to.

We are here to make a difference to the success of every learner.

Clarity, accessibility and ease of use for our learners are key to our approach.

We will use contemporary examples that are rich, engaging and representative of a diverse workplace.

We will include a representative mix of race and gender at the various levels of seniority within the businesses in our examples to support all our learners in aspiring to achieve their potential within their chosen careers.

Roles played by characters in our examples will demonstrate richness and diversity by the use of different names, backgrounds, ethnicity and gender, with a mix of sexuality, relationships and beliefs where these are relevant to the syllabus.

It must always be obvious who is being referred to in each stage of any example so that we do not detract from clarity and ease of use for each of our learners.

We will actively seek feedback from our learners on our approach and keep our policy under continuous review. If you would like to provide any feedback on our linguistic approach, please use this form (you will need to enter the link below into your browser).

https://docs.google.com/forms/d/1YNo3A16mtXGTDIFJzgJhcu377QA4Q4ihUgfYvVKclF8/edit

We will seek to devise simple measures that can be used by independent assessors to randomly check our success in the implementation of our Linguistic Equality, Diversity and Inclusion Policy.

Published by: Kaplan Publishing UK

Unit 2 The Business Centre, Molly Millars Lane, Wokingham, Berkshire RG41 2QZ

Acknowledgements

We are grateful to the CIMA for permission to reproduce past examination questions. The answers to CIMA Exams have been prepared by Kaplan Publishing, except in the case of the CIMA November 2010 and subsequent CIMA Exam answers where the official CIMA answers have been reproduced. Questions from past live assessments have been included by kind permission of CIMA,

British Library Cataloguing in Publication Data

A catalogue record for this book is available from the British Library

ISBN: 978-1-83996-212-7

Printed and bound in Great Britain

Contents

Introduction

How to Use the Materials

These Kaplan Publishing learning materials have been carefully designed to make your learning experience as easy as possible and to give you the best chances of success in your CIMA Cert BA Objective Test Examination.

The product range contains a number of features to help you in the study process. They include:

- a detailed explanation of all syllabus areas
- extensive 'practical' materials
- generous question practice, together with full solutions.

This Study Text has been designed with the needs of home-study and distance-learning candidates in mind. Such students require very full coverage of the syllabus topics, and also the facility to undertake extensive question practice. However, the Study Text is also ideal for fully taught courses.

The main body of the text is divided into a number of chapters, each of which is organised on the following pattern:

- **Detailed learning outcomes.** These describe the knowledge expected after your studies of the chapter are complete. You should assimilate these before beginning detailed work on the chapter, so that you can appreciate where your studies are leading.
- **Step-by-step topic coverage.** This is the heart of each chapter, containing detailed explanatory text supported where appropriate by worked examples and exercises. You should work carefully through this section, ensuring that you understand the material being explained and can tackle the examples and exercises successfully. Remember that in many cases knowledge is cumulative: if you fail to digest earlier material thoroughly, you may struggle to understand later chapters.
- **Activities.** Some chapters are illustrated by more practical elements, such as comments and questions designed to stimulate discussion.
- **Question practice.** The text contains exam-style objective test questions (OTQs).
- **Solutions.** Avoid the temptation merely to 'audit' the solutions provided. It is an illusion to think that this provides the same benefits as you would gain from a serious attempt of your own. However, if you are struggling to get started on a question you should read the introductory guidance provided at the beginning of the solution, where provided, and then make your own attempt before referring back to the full solution.

If you work conscientiously through this Official CIMA Study Text according to the guidelines above you will be giving yourself an excellent chance of success in your Objective Text Examination. Good luck with your studies!

Quality and accuracy are of the utmost importance to us so if you spot an error in any of our products, please send an email to mykaplanreporting@kaplan.com with full details, or follow the link to the feedback form in MyKaplan.

Our Quality Coordinator will work with our technical team to verify the error and take action to ensure it is corrected in future editions.

Icon explanations

Definition – These sections explain important areas of knowledge which must be understood and reproduced in an assessment environment.

Key point – Identifies topics which are key to success and are often examined.

Supplementary reading – These sections will help to provide a deeper understanding of core areas. The supplementary reading is **NOT** optional reading. It is vital to provide you with the breadth of knowledge you will need to address the wide range of topics within your syllabus that could feature in an assessment question. **Reference to this text is vital when self-studying.**

Test your understanding – Following key points and definitions are exercises which give the opportunity to assess the understanding of these core areas.

Illustration – To help develop an understanding of particular topics. The illustrative examples are useful in preparing for the Test your understanding exercises.

Exclamation mark – This symbol signifies a topic which can be more difficult to understand. When reviewing these areas, care should be taken.

Study technique

In this section we briefly outline some tips for effective study during the earlier stages of your approach to the Objective Test Examination. We also mention some techniques that you will find useful at the revision stage. Use of effective study and revision techniques can improve your chances of success in the CIMA Cert BA and CIMA Professional Qualification examinations.

Planning

To begin with, formal planning is essential to get the best return from the time you spend studying. Estimate how much time in total you are going to need for each subject you are studying. Remember that you need to allow time for revision as well as for initial study of the material.

With your study material before you, decide which chapters you are going to study in each week, and which weeks you will devote to revision and final question practice.

Prepare a schedule summarising the above and stick to it!

It is essential to know your syllabus. As your studies progress you will become more familiar with how long it takes to cover topics in sufficient depth. Your timetable may need to be adapted to allocate enough time for the whole syllabus.

Students are advised to refer to the CIMA website, www.cimaglobal.com, to ensure they are up-to-date.

Students are advised to consult the syllabus when allocating their study time. The percentage weighting shown against each syllabus topic is intended as a guide to the proportion of study time each topic requires.

Tips for effective studying

(1) Aim to find a quiet and undisturbed location for your study and plan as far as possible to use the same period of time each day. Getting into a routine helps to avoid wasting time. Make sure that you have all the materials you need before you begin so as to minimise interruptions.

(2) Store all your materials in one place, so that you do not waste time searching for items every time you want to begin studying. If you have to pack everything away after each study period, keep your study materials in a box, or even a suitcase, which will not be disturbed until the next time.

(3) Limit distractions. To make the most effective use of your study periods you should be able to apply total concentration, so turn off all entertainment equipment, set your phones to silent mode, and put up your 'do not disturb' sign.

(4) Your timetable will tell you which topic to study. However, before diving in and becoming engrossed in the finer points, make sure you have an overall picture of all the areas that need to be covered by the end of that session. After an hour, allow yourself a short break and move away from your Study Text. With experience, you will learn to assess the pace you need to work at. Each study session should focus on component learning outcomes – the basis for all questions.

(5) Work carefully through a chapter, making notes as you go. When you have covered a suitable amount of material, vary the pattern by attempting a practice question. When you have finished your attempt, make notes of any mistakes you made, or any areas that you failed to cover or covered more briefly. Be aware that all component learning outcomes are examinable.

(6) Make notes as you study, and discover the techniques that work best for you. Your notes may be in the form of lists, bullet points, diagrams, summaries, 'mind maps' or the written word, but remember that you will need to refer back to them at a later date, so they must be intelligible. If you are on a taught course, make sure you highlight any issues you would like to follow up with your tutor.

(7) Organise your notes. Make sure that all your notes, calculations etc. can be effectively filed and easily retrieved later.

Progression

There are two elements of progression that we can measure: how quickly students move through individual topics within a subject; and how quickly they move from one course to the next. We know that there is an optimum for both, but it can vary from subject to subject and from student to student. However, using data and our experience of student performance over many years, we can make some generalisations.

A fixed period of study set out at the start of a course with key milestones is important. This can be within a subject, for example 'I will finish this topic by 30 June', or for overall achievement, such as 'I want to be qualified by the end of next year'.

Your qualification is cumulative, as earlier papers provide a foundation for your subsequent studies, so do not allow there to be too big a gap between one subject and another. For example, E1 *Managing finance in a digital world* builds on your knowledge of the finance function from certificate level and lays the foundations for E2 *Managing performance* and all strategic papers particularly E3 *Strategic management* and P3 *Risk management*.

We know that exams encourage techniques that lead to some degree of short term retention, the result being that you will simply forget much of what you have already learned unless it is refreshed (look up Ebbinghaus Forgetting Curve for more details on this). This makes it more difficult as you move from one subject to another: not only will you have to learn the new subject, you will also have to relearn all the underpinning knowledge as well. This is very inefficient and slows down your overall progression which makes it more likely you may not succeed at all.

In addition, delaying your studies slows your path to qualification which can have negative impacts on your career, postponing the opportunity to apply for higher level positions and therefore higher pay.

You can use the following diagram showing the whole structure of your qualification to help you keep track of your progress. Make sure you seek appropriate advice if you are unsure about your progression through the qualification.

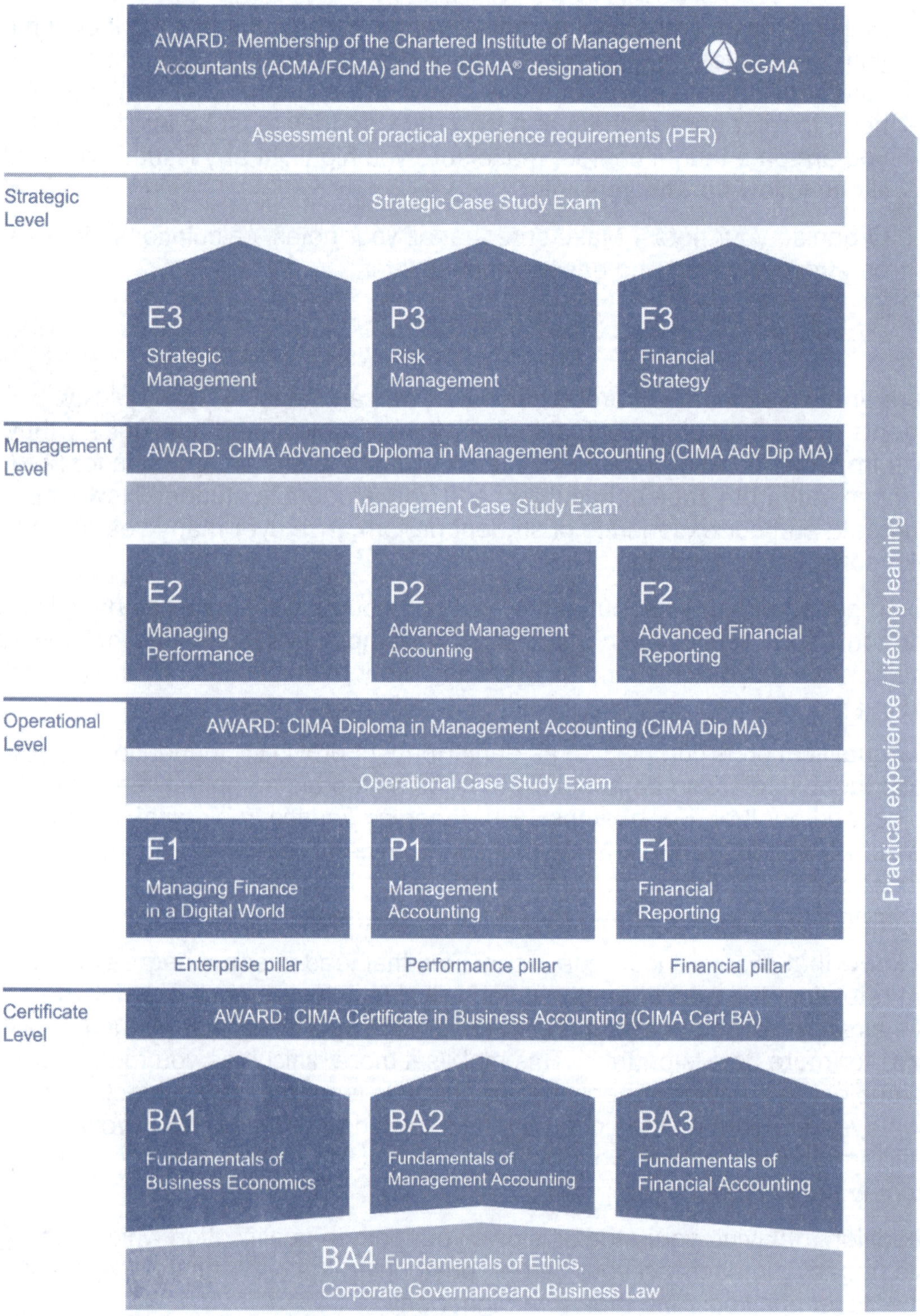

Reproduced with permission from CIMA

Objective Test

Objective Test questions require you to choose or provide a response to a question whose correct answer is predetermined.

The most common types of Objective Test question you will see are:

- multiple choice, where you have to choose the correct answer(s) from a list of possible answers – this could either be numbers or text
- multiple response with more choices and answers, for example, choosing two correct answers from a list of five available answers – this could be either numbers or text
- number entry, where you give your numeric answer to one or more parts of a question, for example, gross profit is $25,000 and the accrual for heat and light charges is $750.
- drag and drop, where you match one or more items with others from the list available, for example, matching several accounting terms with the appropriate definition
- drop down, where you choose the correct answer from those available in a drop down menu, for example, choosing the correct calculation of an accounting ratio, or stating whether an individual statement is true or false
- hot spot, where, for example, you use your computer cursor or mouse to identify the point of profit maximisation on a graph
- other types could be matching text with graphs and labelling/indicating areas on graphs or diagrams.

CIMA has provided the following guidance relating to the format of questions and their marking:

- questions which require narrative responses to be typed will not be used
- for number entry questions, a small range of answers will be accepted. Clear guidance will usually be given about the format in which the answer is required e.g. 'to the nearest $' or 'to two decimal places'
- item set questions provide a scenario which then forms the basis of more than one question (usually 2–4 questions). These sets of questions would appear together in the test and are most likely to appear in BA2 and BA3
- all questions are independent so that, where questions are based on a common item set scenario, each question will be distinct and the answer to a later question will not be dependent upon answering an earlier question correctly
- all items are equally weighted and, where a question consists of more than one element, all elements must be answered correctly for the question to be marked correct.

Throughout this Study Text we have introduced these types of questions, but obviously we have had to label answers A, B, C etc. rather than using click boxes. For convenience we have retained quite a few questions where an initial scenario leads to a number of sub-questions. There will be questions of this type in some Objective Test Examinations but they will rarely have more than three sub-questions.

Guidance re CIMA on-screen calculator

As part of the CIMA Objective Test software, candidates are provided with a calculator. This calculator is on-screen and is available for the duration of the assessment. The calculator is available in Objective Test Examinations for BA1, BA2 and BA3 (it is not required for BA4).

Guidance regarding calculator use in the Objective Test Examinations is available online at: https://planner.cimaglobal.com/

CIMA Cert BA Objective Tests

The Objective Tests are a two-hour assessment comprising compulsory questions, each with one or more parts. There will be no choice and all questions should be attempted. The numbers of questions in each assessment are as follows:

BA1 Fundamentals of Business Economics – 60 questions

BA2 Fundamentals of Management Accounting – 60 questions

BA3 Fundamentals of Financial Accounting – 60 questions

BA4 Fundamentals of Ethics, Corporate Governance and Business Law – 85 questions

All questions are equally weighted. All parts of a question must be answered correctly for the question to be marked correct. Where questions are based upon a common scenario, each question will be independent, and answers to later questions will not be dependent upon answering earlier questions correctly.

Structure of subjects and learning outcomes

Each subject within the syllabus is divided into a number of broad syllabus topics. The topics contain one or more lead learning outcomes, related component learning outcomes and indicative syllabus content.

A learning outcome has two main purposes:

(a) to define the skill or ability that a well prepared candidate should be able to exhibit in the examination

(b) to demonstrate the approach likely to be taken in examination questions.

The learning outcomes are part of a hierarchy of learning objectives. The verbs used at the beginning of each learning outcome relate to a specific learning objective e.g.

Calculate the break-even point, profit target, margin of safety and profit/volume ratio for a single product or service.

The verb **'calculate'** indicates a level three learning objective. The following table lists the learning objectives and the verbs that appear in the CIMA Cert BA syllabus learning outcomes.

CIMA VERB HIERARCHY

CIMA place great importance on the definition of verbs in structuring objective tests. It is therefore crucial that you understand the verbs in order to appreciate the depth and breadth of a topic and the level of skill required. The objective tests will focus on levels one, two and three of the CIMA hierarchy of verbs. However, they will also test levels four and five, especially at the management and strategic levels.

Skill level	Verbs used	Definition
Level 3 Application How you are expected to apply your knowledge	Apply	Put to practical use
	Calculate	Ascertain or reckon mathematically
	Conduct	Organise and carry out
	Demonstrate	Prove with certainty or exhibit by practical means
	Prepare	Make or get ready for use
	Reconcile	Make or prove consistent/compatible
Level 2 Comprehension What you are expected to understand	Describe	Communicate the key features of
	Distinguish	Highlight the differences between
	Explain	Make clear or intelligible/state the meaning or purpose of
	Identify	Recognise, establish or select after consideration
	Illustrate	Use an example to describe or explain something
Level 1 Knowledge What you are expected to know	List	Make a list of
	State	Express, fully or clearly, the details/facts of
	Define	Give the exact meaning of
	Outline	Give a summary of

CIMA Cert BA resources

Access to CIMA Cert BA resources including syllabus information is available online at www.cimaglobal.com.

Additional resources

This Study Text is designed to be comprehensive and therefore sufficient to meet the needs of students studying this subject. However, CIMA recognises that many students also want to read around particular topic(s), either to extend their knowledge and understanding, or because it is particularly relevant to their work environment.

CIMA has therefore produced a related reading list for those students who wish to extend their knowledge and understanding, whether for personal interest or to help support work activities as follows:

BA1 – Fundamentals of Business Economics

Principles of Economics 3rd ed.	McDowell & Thom
Applied Economics 12th ed.	Griffiths & Wall
Mathematics for Economists: An Introductory Textbook 4th ed.	Pemberton & Rau

BA2 – Fundamentals of Management Accounting

Management and Cost Accounting	Colin Drury
Management Accounting	Catherine Gowthorpe

BA3 – Fundamentals of Financial Accounting

Financial Accounting – An Introduction	Pauline Weetman
Frank Wood's Business Accounting 1 & 2	Frank Wood & Alan Sangster

BA4 – Fundamentals of Ethics, Corporate Governance and Business Law

Students can find out about the specific law and regulation in their jurisdiction by referring to appropriate texts and publications for their country.

Managing Responsible Business	CGMA Report 2015
Global Management Accounting Principles	CIMA 2015
Embedded Ethical Values: A guide for CIMA Partners	CIMA Report 2014
Business Ethics for SMEs: A Guide for CIMA Partners	CIMA Report 2014
Ethics: Ethical Checklist	CIMA 2014
Ethics Support Guide	CIMA 2014
Acting under Pressure: How management accountants manage ethical issues	CIMA 2012

SYLLABUS GRIDS

BA1: Fundamentals of Business Economics

Syllabus overview

This subject primarily covers the economic and operating context of business and how the factors of competition, the behaviour of financial markets and government economic policy can influence an organisation. It also deals with the information available to assist management in evaluating and forecasting the behaviour of consumers, markets and the economy in general.

The focus of this syllabus is on providing candidates with an understanding of the areas of economic activity relevant to an organisation's decisions and, within this context, the numerical techniques to support such decisions.

Assessment strategy

There will be a two hour computer based assessment, comprising 60 compulsory objective test questions.

Syllabus structure

The syllabus comprises the following topics and weightings:

Content area		Weighting
A	Macroeconomic and institutional context of business	25%
B	Microeconomic and organisational context of business	30%
C	Informational context of business	20%
D	Financial context of business	25%
		100%

BA1A: Macroeconomic and institutional context of business (25%)

Learning outcomes

On completion of their studies, students should be able to:

Lead	Component	Level	Indicative syllabus content
1. Explain the principal factors that affect the level of a country's national income and the impact of changing economic growth rates and prices on business.	a. Explain determination of macroeconomic phenomena, including equilibrium national income, growth in national income, price inflation, unemployment, and trade deficits and surpluses. b. Explain the stages of the trade cycle and the consequences of each stage for the policy choices of government. c. Explain the main principles of public finance (i.e. deficit financing, forms of taxation) and macroeconomic policy. d. Describe the impacts on business of potential policy responses of government, to each stage of the trade cycle. e. Calculate indices for price inflation and national income growth using either base or current weights and use indices to deflate a series.	2 2 2 2 3	• The causes of changes to the equilibrium level of national income using an aggregate demand and supply analysis and the elements in the circular flow of income. • The trade cycle and the implications for unemployment, inflation and trade balance of each stage and government policy for each stage. • The main principles of public finance: the central government budget and forms of direct and indirect taxation. • The main principles of public finance: fiscal, monetary and supply side policies, including relative merits of each. • The effects on business of changes in the economic growth rate, interest rates, government expenditure and taxation. • Index numbers.
2. Explain the factors affecting the trade of a country with the rest of the World and its impact on business.	a. Explain the concept of the balance of payments and its implications for government policy. b. Identify the main elements of national policy with respect to trade. c. Explain the impacts of exchange rate policies on business.	2 2 2	• The causes and effects of fundamental imbalances in the balance of payments. • Policies to encourage free trade and protectionist instruments. • The effect of changing exchange rates on the profits of business and international competitiveness.
3. Explain the influences on economic development of countries and the effects of globalisation on business.	a. Explain the concept of globalisation and the consequences for businesses and national economies. b. Explain the role of major institutions promoting global trade and development. c. Identify the impacts of economic and institutional factors using the PESTEL framework.	2 2 2	• Nature of globalisation and factors driving it (improved communications, political realignments, growth of global industries and institutions, cost differentials). • Impacts of globalisation on business including off-shoring, industrial relocation, emergence of growth markets, and enhanced competition. • Main trade agreements and trading blocks. • Principal institutions encouraging international trade. • The PESTEL framework (Political, Economic, Social, Technological, Environmental/Ecological, Legal).

BA1B: Microeconomic and organisational context of business (30%)

Learning outcomes

On completion of their studies, students should be able to:

Lead	Component	Level	Indicative syllabus content
1. Distinguish between the economic goals of various stakeholders and organisations.	a. Distinguish between the goals of profit seeking organisations, not-for-profit organisations and governmental organisations. b. Explain shareholder wealth, the variables affecting shareholder wealth, and its application in management decision making. c. Distinguish between the potential objectives of management, shareholders, and other stakeholders and the effects of these on the behaviour of the firm.	2 2 2	• Types of public, private and mutually owned organisations and their objectives. • Types of not-for-profit organisations and their objectives. • Concepts of returns to shareholder investment in the short run and long run (and the cost of capital). • The principal-agent problem, its impact on the decisions of organisations.
2. Demonstrate the determination of prices by market forces and the impact of price changes on revenue from sales.	a. Identify the equilibrium price in product or factor markets. b. Calculate the price elasticity of demand and the price elasticity of supply. c. Explain the determinants of the price elasticities of demand and supply. d. Calculate the effects of price elasticity of demand on a firm's total revenue curve.	2 3 2 3	• The price mechanism: determinants of supply and demand and their interaction to form and change equilibrium price. • The price elasticity of demand and supply. • Influences on the price elasticities of demand and supply. • Consequences of different price elasticities of demand for total revenue.
3. Explain the influence of economic and social considerations on the structure of the organisation and the regulation of markets.	a. Identify the influence of costs on the size and structure of the organisation. b. Explain the sources of market failures and the policies available to deal with them.	2 2	• Sources of internal and external economies of scale and their influence on market concentration. • Impacts of changing transactions costs on the decision to outsource aspects of a business (including network organisations, shared service centres, and flexible staffing). • Positive and negative externalities in goods markets and government responses to them including indirect taxes, subsidies, polluter pays policies, regulation and direct provision. • Impact of minimum price (minimum wages) and maximum price policies in goods and factor markets.

BA1C: Informational context of business (20%)

Learning outcomes

On completion of their studies, students should be able to:

Lead	Component	Level	Indicative syllabus content
1. Apply techniques to communicate business data as information to business stakeholders.	a. Explain the difference between data and information and the characteristics of good information. b. Identify relevant data from graphs, charts and diagrams.	2 2	• Data and information. • Graphs, charts and diagrams: scatter diagrams, histograms, bar charts and ogives.
2. Demonstrate the uses of big data and analytics for understanding the business context.	a. describe the principal business applications of big data and analytics. b. Demonstrate the relationship between data variables. c. Demonstrate trends and patterns using an appropriate technique. d. Prepare a trend equation using either graphical means or regression analysis. e. Identify the limitations of forecasting models.	3 3 3 3 2	• Use of big data and analytics to identify customer value, customer behaviour, cost behaviour and to assist with logistics decisions. • Cross-sectional and time-series analysis. • The correlation coefficient and the coefficient of determination between two variables. • Correlation coefficient: Spearman's rank correlation coefficient and Pearson's correlation coefficient. • Time series analysis – graphical analysis. • Seasonal factors for both additive and multiplicative models. • Predicted values given a time series model. • Seasonal variations using both additive and multiplicative models. • Trends in time series – graphs, moving averages and linear regressions. • The regression equation to predict the dependent variable, given a value of the independent variable. • Forecasting and its limitations.

BA1D: Financial context of business (25%)

Learning outcomes

On completion of their studies, students should be able to:

Lead	Component	Level	Indicative syllabus content
1. Explain the functions of the main financial markets and institutions in facilitating commerce and development.	a. Explain the role of various financial assets, markets and institutions in assisting organisations to manage their liquidity position and to provide an economic return to providers of liquidity. b. Explain the role of commercial banks in the process of credit creation and in determining the structure of interest rates and the roles of the 'central bank' in ensuring liquidity. c. Explain the role of the foreign exchange market in facilitating trade and in setting exchange rates.	2 2 2	• Role and functions of financial intermediaries. • Role of financial assets, markets and institutions in helping institutions regulate their liquidity position. • Role and influence of commercial banks in credit creation. • Role and common functions of central banks including their influence on yield rates and policies of quantitative easing. • Role of foreign exchange markets in facilitating international trade and in determining the exchange rate. • Governmental and international policies on exchange rates (exchange rate management, fixed and floating rate systems, single currency zones).
2. Apply financial mathematical techniques in a business decision-making context.	a. Calculate future values of an investment using both simple and compound interest. b. Calculate the present value of a future cash sum, an annuity and a perpetuity.	3 3	• Simple and compound interest. • Calculate an annual percentage rate of interest given a monthly or quarterly rate. • Annuities and perpetuities. • Discounting to find net present value (NPV) and internal rate of return (IRR).
3. Demonstrate the impact of changes in interest and exchange rates on controlling and measuring business performance.	a. Describe the impact of interest rate changes on market demand and the costs of finance. b. Calculate the impact of exchange rate changes on export and import prices and the value of the assets and liabilities of the business. c. Explain the role of hedging and derivative contracts in managing the impact of changes in interest and exchange rates.	2 3 2	• The impact of interest rates on discretionary spending, borrowing, saving, capital investment, and government borrowing and expenditure. • The impact of a change in the exchange rate on assets and liabilities denominated in a foreign currency. • The effect changing exchange rates has on measures of the economic performance of the business (costs, revenues, profits and asset values). • Forward contracts, futures and options as ways to manage the impact of changes.

Information concerning formulae and tables will be provided via the CIMA website, www.cimaglobal.com.

Chapter

1

Microeconomic and Organisational Context I: The Goals and Decisions of Organisations

Chapter learning objectives

Upon completion of this chapter you will be able to:

- distinguish between the goals of profit-seeking organisations, not-for-profit organisations (NFPs) and governmental organisations
- explain shareholder wealth, the variables affecting shareholder wealth and its application in management decision making
- distinguish between the potential objectives of management, shareholders, and other stakeholders and the effects of these on the behaviour of the firm.

1 The nature of organisations

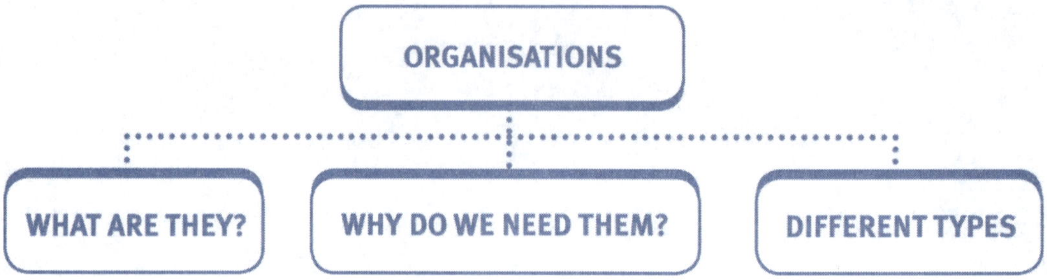

1.1 What is an organisation?

There are many definitions of an organisation. One definition relevant to business is 'organisations are social arrangements for the controlled performance of collective goals.' **(Buchanan and Huczynski)**

The key aspects of this definition are as follows:

(a) 'Collective goals' – organisations are defined primarily by their goals. A school has the main goal of educating pupils and will be organised differently from a company where the main goal is to make profits.

(b) 'Social arrangements' – someone working on their own does not constitute an organisation. Organisations have structure to enable people to work together towards the common goals. Larger organisations tend to have more formal structures in place but even small organisations will divide up responsibilities between the people concerned.

(c) 'Controlled performance' – organisations have systems and procedures to ensure that goals are achieved. These could vary from ad-hoc informal reviews to complex weekly targets and performance reviews.

Illustration 1 – Definition of organisations

For example, a football team can be described as an organisation because:

- It has a number of players who have come together to play a game.
- The team has an objective (to score more goals than its opponent).
- To do their job properly, the members have to maintain an internal system of control to get the team to work together. In training, they work out tactics so that in play they can rely on the ball being passed to those who can score goals.
- Each member of the team is part of the organisational structure and is skilled in a different task: the goalkeeper has more experience in stopping goals being scored than strikers.
- In addition, there must be team spirit, so that everyone works together. Players are encouraged to do their best, both on and off the field.

Test your understanding 1

A queue of people standing at a bus stop is an example of an organisation if they all want to travel to the same place.

True/False.

Defining organisations

As yet, there is no widely accepted definition of an organisation. This is because the term can be used broadly in two ways:

- It can refer to a group or institution arranged for efficient work.
- Organisation can also refer to a process, i.e. structuring and arranging the activities of the enterprise or institution to achieve the stated objectives.

There are many types of organisations, which are set up to serve a number of different purposes and to meet a variety of needs, including companies, clubs, schools, hospitals, charities, political parties, governments and the armed forces.

What they all have in common is summarised in the definition given.

1.2 Why do we need organisations?

Organisations enable people to:

- share skills and knowledge
- specialise and
- pool resources.

The resulting synergy allows organisations to achieve more than the individuals could on their own.

As the organisation grows, it will reach a size where goals, structures and control procedures need to be formalised to ensure that objectives are achieved.

These issues are discussed in further detail below.

Illustration 2 – The nature of organisations

When families set up and run a chain of restaurants, they usually do not have to consider formalising the organisation of their business until they have several restaurants.

After this stage, organisational features can allow more efficient running of the business in some areas. For instance: a new chef in one restaurant may have skills that can be shared across them all. The family management team may naturally start to specialise to run things more efficiently – one may look after operations, another becomes responsible for human resources, etc. The restaurants may also pool resources, such as making bulk orders for supplies in order to get a better price.

1.3 Classifying organisations by profit orientation

Organisations can be classified in many different ways, including the following:

Profit-seeking organisations

Some organisations, such as companies (firms), sole traders and partnerships, see their main objective as maximising the wealth of their owners. Such organisations are often referred to as 'profit-seeking'.

The objective of wealth maximisation is usually expanded into three primary objectives:

- to continue in existence (survival)
- to maintain growth and development
- to make a profit.

Not-for-profit organisations

Other organisations do not see profitability as their main objective. Such not-for-profit organisations ('NFPs' or 'NPOs – non-profit organisations') are unlikely to have financial objectives as their primary ones.

Instead they are seeking to satisfy particular needs of their members or the sectors of society that they have been set up to benefit.

e.g

Illustration 3 – NFP organisations

NFPs include the following:

- museums
- World Bank Group
- schools
- government funded hospitals (e.g. NHS hospitals)
- charities (e.g. Oxfam, Red Cross, Red Crescent, Caritas) and
- clubs
- councils

The objectives of NFPs can vary tremendously:

- Hospitals could be said to exist to treat patients.
- Councils often state their 'mission' as caring for their communities.
- A charity may have as its main objective 'to provide relief to victims of disasters and help people prevent, prepare for, and respond to emergencies'.
- Government organisations usually exist to implement government policy.

NFPs must stay within their budgets to survive. But their stakeholders (those with an interest in the strategy of the organisation) are primarily interested in how the organisation contributes to its chosen field. This can frequently lead to tensions between financial constraints and the NFP's objectives.

Test your understanding 2

Which of the following best completes the statement 'Financial considerations are a constraint in not-for-profit organisations because...'

A they have no profits to reinvest

B they meet the needs of people who cannot afford to pay very much

C they do not have a flow of sales revenue

D their prime objectives are not financial but they still need money to enable them to reach them

Financial objectives in NFPs

Many NFPs view financial matters as constraints under which they have to operate, rather than objectives. For example

- Hospitals seek to offer the best possible care to as many patients as possible, subject to budgetary restrictions imposed upon them.
- Councils organise services such as refuse collection, while trying to achieve value for money with residents' council tax.
- Charities may try to alleviate suffering subject to funds raised.

One specific category of NFPs is a mutual organisation. Mutual organisations are voluntary not-for-profit associations formed for the purpose of raising funds by subscriptions/deposits of members, out of which common services can be provided to those members. They are owned by, and run for, the benefit of their members.

Mutual organisations include:

- building societies
- co-operatives
- credit unions
- trade unions and
- some social clubs.

Test your understanding 3

Which one of the following would not be a stakeholder for a mutual society?

A shareholders

B customers

C employees

D managers

Test your understanding 4

Some building societies have demutualised and become banks with shareholders. Comment on how this may have affected lenders and borrowers.

1.4 Classifying organisation by ownership/control

Public sector organisations

The public sector is that part of the economy that is concerned with providing basic government services and is thus controlled by government organisations.

Illustration 4 – Public sector organisations

The composition of the public sector varies by country, but in most countries the public sector includes such services as:

- police
- military
- public roads
- public transit
- primary education and
- healthcare.

Private sector organisations

The private sector, comprising non-government organisations, is that part of a nation's economy that is not controlled by the government.

Illustration 5 – Private sector organisations

Within these will be profit-seeking and not-for-profit organisations.

This sector thus includes:

- businesses
- charities
- clubs
- community groups

Some of these, for instance charities, clubs and community groups, can be classified as being in the 'third sector'. Organisations in this sector are set up to make a difference to society.

Companies

A company is an organisation where the owners (shareholders) have a limited liability in relation to debts of the company. This is achieved through the process of incorporation, with the company becoming a legal entity in itself, separate from its owners. This distinguishes it from sole traders and simple partnerships, where the owners and the organisation are considered the same from a legal standpoint.

The shareholders buy shares in the company, gaining ownership of the company proportional to their shareholding. The liability of the shareholders in relation to the company is limited to what they have already invested. They cannot be held personally responsible for the company's debts.

Companies can be private (the shares cannot be traded on a stock market) or public (shares are traded on a stock market). Note that these definitions of public and private are different to those of the public and private sectors above.

A company (or any business) can also be referred to as a firm.

Sole traders and partnerships

Sole traders – the organisation is owned and run by one person. In this type of organisation, the owner is not legally separate from the business itself. If a sole trader's business is sued by a customer, the customer is actually suing the owner.

Partnerships – the organisation is owned and run by two or more individuals. Traditionally, partnerships (like sole traders) do not have a separate legal identity from their owners. However, in many countries, there are now alternative structures which mean that the business exists as a separate legal entity (like companies) and the owners' liability is limited to the amount they have invested into the partnership.

Co-operatives and financial sector mutual organisations

A co-operative is an autonomous association of persons united voluntarily to meet their common economic, social and cultural needs and aspirations through a jointly owned and democratically controlled enterprise.

(The International Co-operative Alliance Statement on the Co-operative Identity, Manchester 1995)

Co-operatives are thus businesses with the following characteristics:

- They are owned and democratically controlled by their members – the people who buy their goods or use their services. They are not owned by investors.
- Co-operatives are organised solely to meet the needs of the member-owners, not to accumulate capital for investors.

For example, a retail co-operative could comprise a group of people who join together to increase their buying power to qualify for discounts from retailers when purchasing food.

Co-operatives are similar to mutual organisations in the sense that the organisations are also owned by the members/clients that they exist for. However, they tend to deal primarily in tangible goods and services such as agricultural commodities or utilities rather than intangible products such as financial services. However, such co-operatives as the Co-Op in the UK have diversified into insurance and legal services.

In the financial sector, some asset management organisations, such as The Vanguard Group, are run as mutual organisations, although on a profit-oriented basis.

Building societies, such as Nationwide in the UK, are mutual organisations that offer financial services similar to banks. Many UK building societies demutualised in the 1980s and 1990s to become plcs (public limited companies). For instance, Abbey National converted to a plc, Abbey, and then was taken over and incorporated into Santander.

Credit unions are member-owned financial cooperatives, which offer finance to their members at competitive rates. Members tend to have a 'common bond', such as living in the same area or working in the same industry.

Test your understanding 5

Which one of the following is not a key stakeholder group for a charity that is not a company (such as the Red Cross and Red Crescent)?

A employees and volunteers

B shareholders

C donors

D beneficiaries

Test your understanding 6

Which of the following are usually seen as the primary objectives of profit oriented companies?

(i) To maximise the wealth of shareholders

(ii) To protect the environment

(iii) To make a profit

A (i), (ii) and (iii)

B (i) and (ii) only

C (ii) and (iii) only

D (i) and (iii) only

Test your understanding 7

Many schools run fund-raising events such as fêtes, where the intention is to make a profit. This makes them 'profit-seeking'.

True or False?

2 Shareholder wealth

2.1 Maximising shareholder wealth

As stated above, companies have the primary objective of maximising the wealth of their owners. The owners of companies are shareholders. Achievement of this objective should ultimately be reflected in

- higher share prices
- higher dividend payments.

For those shares that are traded on a market, shareholders will see an increase in the value of their shareholding when prices rise, making them wealthier. This is a notional increase in wealth and would only be crystallised if the shares are sold. Share prices fluctuate over time due to factors both inside and outside of the control of the company managers. The aim of the managers of the company is for the share price to rise consistently over time.

Dividends are distributions of the profit of the company. Company profits can be reinvested to help the company grow or paid out to the shareholders as a reward for share ownership. Managers will aim to have a dividend policy that allows for growth of the company whilst managing shareholder expectations of dividend income.

The role of the managers within the business is to make decisions that will affect the value of the company and therefore increase the value of shareholder wealth.

Attempts to measure and increase shareholder value have focussed on incorporating three key issues:

- Cash is preferable to profit

  Cash flows have a higher correlation with shareholder wealth than profits.

- Exceeding the cost of capital

  The cost of capital represents the cost to the company of providing appropriate returns to the investors. For instance if an equity shareholder requires a 15% return in order to be encouraged to buy shares, the company therefore has a 15% cost of securing equity finance and providing that return (in the form of dividends and growth in share price).

  The return, however measured, must be sufficient to cover the cost of all long-term finance, both equity and debt (for example by exceeding interest payments on the debt). Earnings made above the cost of capital will lead to growth in the business value.

- Managing both long- and short-term perspectives

  Investors are increasingly looking at long-term value. When valuing a company's shares, the stock market places a value on the company's future potential, not only its current profit levels.

Profit versus cash

Profits are calculated as sales less expenses. Net cash flows are cash receipts less cash payments. Profits and net cash flows are not the same.

For instance, if sales of $1,000 are made on credit and only 75% of these have been paid so far then the cash flow in relation to the sales is only $750.

Cash is more important to investors than profits. Their returns are received either in the form of dividends (cash received by the investor from a distribution made by the company) or in the form of a capital gain from a rise in share price (and therefore the potential to earn more cash from sale of the shares).

Share prices themselves are determined by investors' perceptions of how well the company will generate cash in the future.

Profit and shareholder value

Just because a company has made a profit, it does not follow that shareholder wealth has been increased by a level that satisfies the shareholders. Consider the following example.

EVA Co has the following financial structure:

- $100 million debt with an interest rate (pre-tax) of 6%
- $200 million equity where it is estimated that shareholders want a return of 15%.

The company has made a profit before interest and tax of $36 million and pays tax at 30%.

Comment on whether directors have achieved their objective of increasing shareholder wealth.

Solution

Let us determine the profits earned and compare to the return required:

	Working	$m
Profit before interest and tax		36
Interest paid on debt	100 × 6%	(6)
Profit before tax		30
Tax @ 30%		(9)
Profit after tax (available to shareholders)		21
Minimum profit required by shareholders	200 × 15%	30

The company has made a profit.

However, in this example the profit is not enough to cover the "cost of equity" and the company could be said to have reduced shareholder value.

Note also that due to the differences between cash and profit values, earning a profit doesn't necessarily mean that the cash has increased by the same amount.

Profits, and the cash generated, belong to the shareholders, whether or not they are paid out as dividends. Cash not paid out can be reinvested into the business to help it grow and increase the share price (and therefore shareholder value) over the long-term.

2.2 Short-term measures of financial performance

It is quite possible that financial performance of a business in the short-term could be different to its performance in the long-term. Thus measures are needed both of short-term and long-term financial performance.

Profit statement

Here is a basic example of a statement of profit and loss:

	$m
Sales revenue	x
Less: cost of sales	(x)
Gross profit	x
Less: expenses	(x)
Profit before interest and taxation (PBIT)	x
Less: interest	(x)
Profit before taxation	x
Less: taxation	(x)
Profit after taxation (PAT)	x
Preference share dividends	(x)
Earnings	x
Ordinary dividends	(x)
Retained earnings	x

Note that profit before interest and taxation (PBIT) may also be called operating profit or net profit.

The value of 'earnings' is the profit value after all deductions have been made, except for the ordinary dividends, which are a distribution of profits rather than a deduction from them.

As preference share dividends are rare, it is often the case that the profit after tax figure (PAT) represents the earnings figure.

Two standard measures of short-term performance are:

1 return on capital employed

2 earnings per share.

Return on capital employed (ROCE)

$$\text{ROCE} = \frac{\text{profit before interest and tax}}{\text{average capital employed}} \times 100\%$$

Comments:

- Capital represents the funds that have been invested into the business by shareholders and lenders.
- ROCE gives an indication as to how well a business uses its capital (or the assets purchased with the capital) to generate profits.
- Being a percentage makes it easy to compare the ROCE of different companies.

Another similar measure of the return to shareholders' capital is:

$$\text{Return on net assets (RONA)} = \frac{\text{operating profit (before interest and tax)}}{\text{total assets minus current liabilities}} \times 100\%$$

This is very similar to ROCE as net asset values are often used as an approximation to the capital figure.

The higher the figure for ROCE or RONA is, the more profitable the company is. However, ROCE is a measure of the net income generated by the business and not about where that income goes. Shareholders will be more interested in profits after the payment of interest and tax, as it is those profits (earnings) that are earned on behalf of the shareholders.

Earnings per share (EPS)

As its name suggests, EPS determines the profits available to ordinary shareholders, expressed per share.

$$\text{EPS} = \frac{\text{profits after interest, tax and preference share dividends}}{\text{number of ordinary shares issued}}$$

This figure only gives the earnings per share that each owner of ordinary shares might expect to receive. It is up to the Directors (who manage the company) to decide whether/how much to pay out as a dividend.

Furthermore, to calculate a rate of return for the shareholder, the price that the potential shareholder has to pay to acquire a share must be taken into account.

Note that the main weakness of both ROCE and EPS is that they do not correlate directly to the goal of maximising shareholder wealth.

Test your understanding 8

The following is an extract from the accounts of EBG.

	$000
Revenue	500
Cost of sales	200
Gross profit	300
Distribution costs	100
Admin. expenses	50
Operating profit	150
Interest	10
Profit before tax	140
Taxation	30
Profit after tax	110
Capital employed	3,000
Share capital (1 million shares @ $1)	1,000

Calculate

(a) ROCE

(b) EPS

Test your understanding 9

RGP currently has an eps figure of 10c with 1 million shares in issue. A proposed new project will increase profit after tax by $25,000 per annum and will be financed by the issue of a further 400,000 shares.

Calculate the new eps and indicate how shareholders will perceive the change.

2.3 Long-term measures of financial performance

In addition to measuring current financial performance, companies also need to be able to measure longer-term performance, in particular, in relation to investment. In this case, it is important that a business can be sure that returns to shareholders are at least equal to the cost of acquiring the capital required to produce a long-term flow of earnings.

In making these sorts of assessment several problems arise:

- establishing the cost of capital to finance the investment project
- estimating the flow of income derived from the capital investment over the whole life of the investment
- valuing that flow of income.

To solve these problems we calculate the present value of future cash flows by a process of discounting. See later chapter on 'Discounting and Investment Appraisal'.

2.4 Share values

The concept of discounted cash flows (calculations of present values of the cash flows) can be used to explain how press releases and market rumours can affect the share price.

- Suppose the company announces a new project. If the market believes that the project will deliver a positive net present value, then the share price should rise. You will see in more detail in a later chapter that the net present value (NPV) of a project is the sum of the discounted future cash flows minus the capital cost of the project and it represents the value that the project should add to the business.
- Any information that reaches the market that suggests that future cash flows will be higher than previously forecast should result in a share price rise.
- If bad news reaches the market then as well as revising forecast cash flows downwards, investors may reassess the investment as having higher risk. This will result in a higher cost of capital and thus future receipts will be less valuable than previously estimated. The result is a fall in the share price.

Many variables will affect the value of shares. These tend to fall into two groups:

1. factors **external** to the business which may affect a wide range of shares: the onset of a recession would tend to depress share values in general, as would a rise in interest rates
2. factors internal to the business that might affect the future flow of profits such as the failure of a new product, an expected decline in sales, a significant rise in costs or the departure of a key business manager.

Note that share values for different companies will react differently to the same factors. For instance, during the pandemic of 2020, travel firms were more significantly affected than supermarkets. TUI's share price in early 2021 was approximately one third if its pre pandemic level. Tesco plc's share price on 17 Feb 2020 was £2.57 and one year later was £2.37.

Illustration 6 – Share values

TUI

The travel agency company TUI saw its share price fall from a high in May 2018 of £11.34 with an almost continual decline since then, falling to as low as to as low as £1.58 in May 2020. Various factors contributed to this fall:

- In Feb 2019, the company warned of lower sales levels for the coming summer season and of tightening profit margins.
- It also said that previous promises of earnings growth of 10% per annum were unachievable and those targets were to be scrapped.
- In addition, it was explained that the new earnings estimates would only be achievable if the Boeing 737 Max aircraft, which had been taken out of operation after two high profile crashes, became operational again. This statement alone led to an 8% fall in the share price.
- The COVID 19 pandemic severely restricted air travel and reduced significantly the number of holidays taken.

Investors concluded that there would be a reduction in the potential for future positive cash flows for the company and that their investment was now of higher risk (effectively resulting in a higher discount rate being applied to the cash flows, pushing their present values, i.e. the share price, down).

When investors are faced with higher risk, they will demand a higher return as compensation. If an increased return cannot be given in the form of higher business earnings, the share price falls so that the yield (return calculated as income divided by price) improves.

The COVID 19 pandemic continued to affect TUI's share price throughout 2020 and into 2021. In April 2021, TUI resolved to raise finance through the issue of convertible bonds. The bonds would guarantee investors a steady level of interest income (at a rate of 4.5%-5%) for a few years before giving investors the chance to convert them into shares. The issue was to help TUI improve its liquidity position by offering attractive terms on a relatively safe investment to otherwise wary investors. TUI's share price then showed slow overall growth through into 2022.

Test your understanding 10

A company has released a press statement publicising its plans to develop a new product range in order to enter a high growth market.

Consider how the concept of discounted cash flows could be used to determine the likely impact of the announcement on the company's share price.

3 Stakeholders

Stakeholders are "those persons and organisations that have an interest in the strategy of an organisation". Stakeholders normally include shareholders, customers, staff and the local community.

It is important that an organisation understands the needs of the different stakeholders as they have both an interest in the organisation and may wish to influence its objectives and strategy.

Useful definitions:

(a) **Stakeholder interest** – an interest or concern that a stakeholder has in an organisation's actions, objectives or policies.

(b) **Stakeholder influence** – the level of involvement that a stakeholder has in the functions of an organisation and the ability to bring about a desired change.

The degree of interest and influence of different stakeholder groups can vary considerably:

- A well organised labour force with a strong trade union will be able to exercise considerable influence (e.g. through strike action) over directors' plans and will be particularly interested in any plans that relate to jobs, working conditions and the welfare of staff.
- The residents of a small village might have great interest in the plans of a major supermarket chain to close the local village store but would have little power to influence the decision.

Stakeholders can be broadly categorised into three groups: internal (e.g. employees), connected (e.g. shareholders) and external (e.g. government).

3.1 Internal stakeholders

Internal stakeholders are intimately connected to the organisation, and their objectives are likely to have a strong influence on how it is run.

Internal stakeholders include:

Stakeholder	Need/expectation	Example
Employees	pay, working conditions and job security	If workers are to be given more responsibility, they will expect increased pay.
Managers/ directors	status, pay, bonus, job security	If growth is going to occur, the managers will aim for increased profits, leading to increased bonuses.

3.2 Connected stakeholders

Connected stakeholders can be viewed as having a contractual relationship with the organisation.

Profit seeking companies will have shareholders as their most important stakeholder and will aim to satisfy their needs above other stakeholders. However, customer and financiers' objectives must be met if the company is to succeed.

A common misconception is that shareholders, i.e. the owners of a company, are internal stakeholders. However, the shareholder relationship to the business is contractual. The vast majority of shareholders in public companies do not engage in the running of the business. For small companies though, shareholders are often also managers of the business, in which case their relationship to the company is both as internal and connected stakeholders.

Not-for-profit organisations will take more of a balanced view of which stakeholder needs are given the highest priority.

Stakeholder	**Need/expectation**	**Example**
Shareholders	steady flow of income, possible capital growth and the continuation of the business	If capital is required for growth, the shareholders will expect a rise in the dividend stream.
Customers	satisfaction of customers' needs will be achieved through providing value-for-money products and services	Any attempt to, for example, increase the price, may lead to customer dissatisfaction.
Suppliers	paid promptly	If a decision is made to delay payment to suppliers to ease cash flow, existing suppliers may cease supplying goods.
Finance providers	ability to repay the finance including interest, security of investment	The firm's ability to generate cash.

3.3 External stakeholders

External stakeholders include the government, local authority etc. This group will have quite diverse objectives and have varying ability to ensure that the organisation meets their objectives.

Not-for-profit organisations such as charities may put the needs of some external stakeholders, such as the beneficiaries of the charity's work, above those of others.

Stakeholder	Need/expectation	Example
Community at large	The general public can be a stakeholder, especially if their lives are affected by an organisation's decisions.	E.g. local residents' attitude towards out-of-town shopping centres.
Environmental pressure groups	The organisation does not harm the external environment.	If an airport wants to build a new runway, the pressure groups may stage a 'sit in'.
Government	Company activities are central to the success of the economy (providing jobs and paying taxes). Legislation (e.g. health and safety) must be met by the company.	Actions by companies could break the law or damage the environment and governments therefore control what organisations can do.
Trade unions	Taking an active part in the decision-making process.	If a department is to be closed the union will want to be consulted and there should be a scheme in place to help employees find alternative employment.

Stakeholder analysis is a subject that you will learn more about in your later studies, particularly in the enterprise (E) pillar.

Test your understanding 11

Which of the following is not a connected stakeholder?

A Shareholders

B Suppliers

C Employees

D Customers

Test your understanding 12

Rupar is a high-class hotel situated in a thriving city. It is part of a worldwide hotel group owned by a large number of shareholders. Individuals hold the majority of shares, each holding a small number, and financial institutions (e.g. pension funds) own the rest. The hotel provides full amenities, including a heated swimming pool, as well as the normal facilities of bars, restaurants and good quality accommodation. There are many other hotels in the city, all of which compete with Rupar. The city in which Rupar is situated is old and attracts many foreign visitors, especially in the summer season.

Who are the main stakeholders with whom relationships need to be established and maintained by management? Explain why it is important that relationships are maintained with each of these stakeholders.

4 Stakeholder conflict

The needs/expectations of the different stakeholders may conflict. Some of the typical conflicts are shown below:

Stakeholders	Conflict
Employees versus managers	Jobs/wages versus bonus (cost efficiency)
Customers versus shareholders	Product quality/service levels versus profits/ dividends
General public versus shareholders	Effect on the environment versus profit/ dividends
Managers versus shareholders	Revenue growth versus profit growth

Solving such conflicts will often involve a mixture of compromise and prioritisation.

Resolving stakeholder conflict

To help resolve stakeholder conflict, many firms will try to assess both the degree of interest of stakeholders and their power/influence to affect the business.

For example, the government may have high power but may be relatively uninterested in the affairs of a particular company. On the other hand, a major customer may have both influence and interest and so must be incorporated in any significant decisions as a "key player".

With companies, the primary objective of maximising shareholder value should take preference and so decision-making is simplified to some degree. However, this does not mean that other stakeholders are ignored. For example:

- If we do not pay employees a fair wage, then quality will suffer, ultimately depressing profits and shareholder wealth.

Some firms address this by seeing shareholder wealth generation as their primary objectives and the needs of other stakeholders as constraints within which they have to operate:

- We try to increase profit subject to ensuring good working conditions for employees, not polluting the environment, etc.

Stakeholder conflict for NFPs

Unlike firms, NFPs (not-for-profit organisations) may not have one dominant stakeholder group. Consequently, the NFP seeks to satisfy several different groups at once, without having the touchstone of one primary objective, such as profit, to adhere to.

For example, a council may express its mission as 'caring for the community'. Suppose it is considering building a new car park in the city centre where there is currently a small green park. This would affect the community as follows:

- Local businesses would see more trade.
- More jobs would be created for local residents.
- Better parking for shoppers.
- More traffic, congestion and pollution for local residents.
- Loss of a park, thus reducing the quality of life for locals.
- The receipts from the car park could be used to reduce council tax bills and/or fund additional services for the community.

This type of decision is particularly difficult as:

- How do you decide which stakeholder group should take preference?
- Most of the factors being considered are very difficult to quantify (e.g. quality of life) and
- How do you offset different issues measured in different ways (e.g. how many extra jobs justify the extra congestion and pollution?)

Some public sector organisations try to quantify all of the issues financially to see if the benefits outweigh the costs ('cost-benefit analysis').

For example, congestion will delay people, thus adding to journey times. The value of people's time can be estimated by looking at the premium they will pay for quicker methods of transport such as train versus coach.

5 Management objectives

As mentioned above, the role of the managers in a company is to make decisions that ultimately lead to an increase in shareholder wealth, for instance by sourcing and investing in projects whose returns exceed the company's cost of capital. Of course, this may not be achieved due to the managers making poor decisions.

However, another reason for it not being achieved could be due to the managers and shareholders being different types of stakeholders and therefore having different objectives.

An extremely important stakeholder conflict is that between these two stakeholder groups.

5.1 The principal – agent problem

In some, usually small, companies the owners also manage the business.

However, companies that are quoted on a stock market are often extremely complex and require a substantial investment in equity to fund them. They therefore often have large numbers of shareholders.

These shareholders delegate control to professional managers – the board of directors – to run the company on their behalf. Thus, shareholders normally play a passive role in the day-to-day management of the company.

This separation of ownership and control leads to a potential conflict of interests between directors and shareholders. This conflict is an example of the principal – agent problem. The principals (the shareholders) have to find ways of ensuring that their agents (the managers) act in their interests.

The principal – agent problem

In any organisation there are:

- **principals**: in the case of companies the principals are the legal owners of the organisation – the shareholders
- **agents**: those appointed by the principals to act on their behalf such as the board of directors and senior managers in a company.

The problem posed by agency theory is how can the principal ensure that the agent will behave in such a way as to achieve the aims and intentions of the principal? There is clearly the possibility of conflict in that the agent may act to achieve a set of objectives reflecting their self-interest and own objectives rather than those of the principals. In companies, the board of directors and/or senior management may pursue objectives that are not the same as those of the shareholders. In effect, the shareholders may lose control of the companies they legally own.

How might the aims and objectives of management differ from those of shareholders?

- Management will have to balance the interests of different stakeholders in the company. Since these stakeholders have a variety of objectives, profit is unlikely to be the sole aim of management.
- Management may have objectives of its own. These may include salaries, non-salary benefits ('perks'), power, status and prestige, safety and security and a 'quiet life'. The problem with these is that they may conflict with the objective of shareholder wealth generation. For example, many of the management's objectives, such as salary, power and prestige, may be related more strongly to the size of the company (sales, market share, number of employees) than to the underlying value of the company. For example, excessive discounts may be offered to achieve sales growth.
- Focus on short-term objectives at the expense of long-term ones

  Common short term objectives include

  – sales maximisation – this is often simpler than profit maximisation as it excludes costs. Focusing on sales may mean sacrificing profitability, e.g. offering discounts to generate more sales. Proponents would argue that higher sales usually results in greater profit

  – growth maximisation – in the longer term a larger company is likely to be more profitable due to increased revenue and cost economies of scale. But if growth is at the expense of profitability, shareholder wealth can suffer

  – "satisfying" – for example trying to achieve sales growth subject to a minimum increase in profit of 5%. Such targets are often seen as more practical than "maximise profits", which is seen as unachievable. Managers may want to do 'just enough' to achieve their targets (and perhaps their bonuses) in a particular year, rather than strive for maximising shareholder wealth, so that next year's targets will also be achievable.

5.2 Possible areas of conflict

The main areas where managers may not act in the shareholders' best interests are as follows:

- 'Fat cat' salaries and benefits – the media regularly highlight cases where directors are paid huge bonuses despite the company they manage making a loss. In many cases directors deserve their high salaries, but not in all cases.

- Mergers and acquisitions – research suggests that the majority of acquisitions erode shareholder value rather than create it. Some argue that the reasons such takeovers occur is because directors are looking to expand their own spheres of influence rather than focus on shareholder value.
- Poor control of the business – the Enron and WorldCom scandals in the US in 2001/2002 resulted in calls to improve the control that stakeholders can exercise over the board of directors of the company.
- Short-termism – managers may make decisions to maximise short-term profitability to ensure they get bonuses and hit targets, rather than looking at the long-term. For example, a project that creates wealth in the long run but is loss making in the first two years may be rejected.

Attempts to resolve this conflict can take a number of forms:

- Corporate governance (see below) tries to improve ways companies are run through a mixture of principles and regulation.
- A review of the remuneration and bonus schemes given to directors. For example, high bonuses linked to annual profit targets may encourage short-termism that ultimately undermines the long-term prospects of the business. Some firms reward directors using shares (or share options – an option to purchase shares cheaply in the future if business targets are met) to ensure goal congruence. However, these only act as incentives if the share price remains robust over a long period of time.

5.3 The objectives of corporate governance

Corporate governance is defined as 'the systems by which companies and other organisations are directed and controlled'.

As the name suggests, corporate governance is concerned with improving the way companies are governed and run. In particular, it seeks to address the principal – agent problem outlined above.

The main objectives are as follows:

- to control the managers/directors by increasing the amount of reporting and disclosure
- to increase level of confidence and transparency in company activities for all investors (existing and potential) and thus promote growth in the company
- to increase disclosure to all stakeholders
- to ensure that the company is run in a legal and ethical manner
- to build in control at the top that will 'cascade' down the organisation.

Corporate governance should thus be seen as the system used to direct, manage and monitor an organisation and enable it to relate to its external environment.

Illustration 7 – Corporate Governance principles

Corporate governance is one way of trying to manage the principal – agent problem. While rules and principles vary across the world, typical aspects include the following:

- the board of directors should meet on a regular basis and that active responsibilities at board level should be spread over the board and not concentrated in a few hands; in particular, the roles of chairperson and chief executive should be kept separate
- directors should have limited contracts (e.g. 3 years) and all director reward and payments should be publicly disclosed
- there should be three sub-committees of the board: an audit committee, a nominations (to the board) committee and a remunerations (of board members) committee
- greater use should be made of non-executive directors with no direct financial interest in the company in order to provide some independence within the board, especially on the board's sub committees
- the annual accounts should contain a statement, approved by the auditors, that the business is financially sound and is a going concern.

Test your understanding 13

In the case of ALD, a company which makes personalised gifts, which of the following is not a prime objective of corporate governance:

A to control directors' activities

B to improve the way the company is run

C to improve employees' working conditions

D to protect shareholder interests

The UK Corporate Governance Code

The UK Corporate Governance Code represents 'best practice' in corporate governance and what may be seen as a model for companies to adopt. The main features of this model are:

- separation of powers, especially in relation to roles of the chairman and the chief executive
- board membership to include an appropriate balance especially in relation to executive (involved in the management of the business) and non-executive (not involved in the management of the business and hence can take more objective views) directors
- the adoption of the principles of transparency, openness and fairness

- to adopt an approach which reflects the interests of all stakeholders
- to ensure that the board of directors are fully accountable
- detailed disclosure and reporting requirements
- remuneration committees to determine the pay of directors
- nomination committees to oversee appointments to the board
- arrangements for organising the Annual General Meeting (AGM).

Test your understanding 14

Answer the following questions based on the preceding information.

1 What does ROCE mean and what does it measure?

2 Identify four different types of not-for-profit organisations.

3 Explain what is meant by the term stakeholders.

4 Identify five stakeholders for a typical business.

5 Explain what is meant by the principal – agent problem.

6 Give two reasons why shareholders may lose control of the company they own.

7 What is meant by the term corporate governance?

6 Transaction costs

A company has a choice for any economic activity: performing the activity in-house or going to market (outsourcing). In either case, the cost of the activity can be decomposed into production costs, which are direct and indirect costs of producing the good or service, and transaction costs, which are other (indirect) costs incurred in performing the economic activity, for example the expenses incurred through outsourcing.

Managers are faced with a choice as to whether performing an activity in-house or choosing to outsource it will be the better decision from a shareholder wealth point of view.

Outsourcing is where the organisation chooses to contract an outside party to perform work that could be done by the company. Reasons for outsourcing may include cost reduction or to gain access to specialist skills. An example would be the outsourcing of the IT function instead of employing a team of IT specialists.

If an activity is outsourced, it can be difficult to determine the transaction costs. But the decision as to whether or not an economic activity should be outsourced depends critically on transaction costs.

Transaction costs will occur when dealing with an external party.

- Search and information costs – to find the supplier
- Bargaining and decision costs – to determine contractual obligations
- Policing and enforcement costs – to monitor quality.

The way in which a company is organised can determine its control over transactions, and hence costs. It is in the interests of management to internalise transactions as much as possible, to remove these costs and the resulting risks and uncertainties about prices and quality.

The variables that dictate the impact on the transaction costs are:

- Frequency: how often such a transaction is made. The more frequent, the higher the bargaining and decision costs.
- Uncertainty: long-term relationships are more uncertain (due to, for example, changes in the economic environment), lack of trust leads to uncertainty. A higher degree of uncertainty means more needs to be spent on transaction costs to ensure that the supplier will be trustworthy and able to fulfil its contracted obligations.
- Asset specificity: how unique the component is for the business needs. Unique products / services will lead to a greater 'tie-in' between the outsourcer and the supplier. The outsourcer becomes more reliant on the supplier and will spend more on transaction costs to ensure that they are the right supplier for the work.

Small businesses in particular may choose to outsource despite high transaction costs, because they may not have the expertise to perform functions in-house, or because the work is intermittent and does not need a full time member of staff dedicated to it.

6.1 When transaction costs change

If transaction costs reduce, for instance if the drawing up of legal documents is made easier by changes in laws, or if a new supplier is willing to self-regulate to a higher quality level, then the cost of outsourcing will decrease relative to undertaking the activity internally and outsourcing becomes more likely.

On the other hand, if a business is able to reduce its production costs – perhaps by consolidating regional departments into an internal shared service centre, then the decision to outsource may become less likely.

<u>Shared service centres</u>

A shared service centre (SSC) is a business unit that performs business functions on behalf of the other business units. A typical example would be a centralised accounting or IT unit for a multidivisional business. The staff in the SSC are able to consolidate work from across the business in order to perform it more efficiently and at cheaper cost. Because their work is effectively independent from the business's operations, SSC's are often outsourced to specialist firms.

There will be significant transaction costs in relation to SSCs as the business will be entirely reliant on the services provided by the SSC and must ensure that the right supplier is chosen. The business will monitor the SSC regularly to ensure compliance with service level agreements. If these costs rise, the business may consider insourcing the function.

Network organisations

A network organisation, rather than having departments that all report up to board level, has autonomous units that co-ordinate with each other. These units can be departments, divisions or even separate companies. In this kind of organisation, outsourcing is common due to the separable nature of each unit.

For instance, Nike, an American shoe and apparel company, is a network organisation. Instead of engaging in production in-house, it outsources its entire production process to contractors in many different countries.

However, if the transaction costs of the outsourcing arrangements increase so that outsourcing no longer gives Nike a cost advantage, the company may look to bring production back in-house. This could occur, for instance, if wages and salaries in the countries producing the goods rise to a level comparable to those in the USA.

Flexible staffing

Flexible staffing is a convenient way for employers to fill staff vacancies and can involve taking on contracted staff rather than permanent employees. The roles are effectively outsourced. If the costs of outsourcing increase, the employer may consider a move back to permanent staff.

Delivery firms such as Uber Eats and Deliveroo have been criticised for the use of such contracted workers, who do not have the right to earn a minimum wage or to be paid for holidays and sick time. These staff are much cheaper to employ than permanent staff would be. If the companies are forced to spend more on these staff, perhaps through changes in workers' rights legislation, they may consider employing rather than contracting.

Test your understanding answers

Test your understanding 1

False.

Despite having identical individual goals, there is no collective goal that motivates people to work together in any way. For example, passenger A will not be concerned if they get the last available place on a bus while passenger B has to wait for the next one.

Test your understanding 2

D

NFPs are often stopped from realising all their goals by a lack of money. But making money is not their primary goal.

NFPs can earn revenues, such as through donations, subscription fees and from sales in a charity shop. Any surplus of revenues over costs in a period (equivalent to profits) is reinvested in later periods.

Test your understanding 3

A

Response (A) is the correct answer as a mutual society does not have shareholders but is owned collectively by its members, for example a mutual building society is owned by its depositors. Shareholders own shares in a company, a different type of entity described in section 1.4 of the chapter.

Test your understanding 4

Mutual building societies exist for the benefit of their members. This is reflected in setting:

- interest rates for borrowers as low as possible
- interest rates for savers as high as possible.

The aim is not to make a profit, so the borrowing and saving rates are moved as close as possible to each other with a small margin sufficient to cover costs.

Once it becomes a bank the building society must then seek to maximise shareholder wealth and become profit seeking. This is done by increasing borrowing rates and reducing saving rates.

Members will thus find that the terms previously offered by the building society become less attractive when it becomes a company.

However, when demutualising most building societies give their members windfalls of shares so members become shareholders, thus benefiting from dividends and share price increases.

Test your understanding 5

B

Charities, unlike companies, do not have shareholders. Charities could not operate without the work of employees and volunteers, or without donations from their donors, so these are both important stakeholder groups. The objective of a charity is to provide help or support for its beneficiaries. So beneficiaries are also an important stakeholder group.

Test your understanding 6

D

While protecting the environment is to be encouraged and is reinforced within statute to some degree, it is not a primary objective of the company. Companies exist primarily to maximise the return to their owners.

Test your understanding 7

False

Schools run fund-raising activities to help pay for extra books, e.g. to improve the quality of education given to pupils. The primary objective is educational, not profit. The money made at the fête is thus a means not an end.

Test your understanding 8

(a) ROCE = operating profit (PBIT)/capital employed × 100 = $150,000/$3,000,000 × 100 = 5%.

(b) EPS = profit after tax/no of shares in issue = $110,000/1,000,000 = $0.11 (11 cents) per share.

Test your understanding 9

Existing profit after tax = eps × number of shares = $0.10 × 1 million = $100,000

New profit after tax = $100,000 + $25,000 = $125,000

New number of shares = 1 million + 400,000 = 1.4 million

New eps = $125,000/1,400,000 = $0.089, or 8.9 cents

This is lower than before so shareholder reaction will be negative.

Test your understanding 10

Future cash flows

Assuming the markets believe, and have confidence in, the directors' claims, then they should revise their estimates of the company's future cash flows upwards.

Cost of capital/discount rate

The venture into a new product range is likely to be seen as increasing the company's risk – investors are aware that a new product range may fail due to a lack of knowledge / experience – and hence investors will want a higher return to compensate for the higher risk their investment faces. The company therefore faces a higher cost of providing that return. This reduces the value of the project to the company.

Share price

The impact on the share price will depend on the net effect of the above factors. If the shareholders are optimistic about the future growth plans without being overly concerned about the extra risk, then the share price should increase. A fall in share price would indicate more serious concerns over the risks and/or a lack of belief that the high growth in cash flows will materialise.

Test your understanding 11

C

Employees are "internal" stakeholders.

Test your understanding 12

Internal stakeholders

The employees and managers of the hotel are the main link with the guests and the service they provide is vital to the hotel as the quality of the guests' experience at the hotel will be determined by their attitude and approach.

Managers should ensure that employees achieve the highest levels of service and are well trained and committed.

Connected stakeholders (shareholders, guests, suppliers)

The shareholders of the hotel will be concerned with a steady flow of income, possible capital growth and continuation of the business. Relationships should be developed and maintained with the shareholders, especially those operating on behalf of institutional investors who often have large shareholdings, such as pension funds. Management must try to achieve improvements in their return on investment by ensuring that customers are satisfied and willing to return.

Each guest will seek good service and satisfaction. The different types of guest will have different needs (business versus tourist) and management should regularly analyse the customer database to ensure that all customer needs are being met.

Suppliers must be selected very carefully to ensure that services and goods provided (e.g. food/laundry) continue to add to the quality of the hotel and customer satisfaction. They will be concerned with being paid promptly for goods, and maintaining a good relationship with the suppliers will ensure their continued support of the hotel.

External stakeholders (the government and the regulatory authorities)

The management of the hotel must maintain close relationships with the authorities to ensure they comply with all legislation – failure to do so could result in the hotel being closed down.

Test your understanding 13

C

While governance would ensure compliance with relevant legislation concerning employee working conditions, the primary focus is not employees per se.

Test your understanding 14

1 ROCE is the rate of return on capital employed and is a measure of the flow of profits compared to the capital employed in the business. It is thus a measure of the profitability of that capital.

2 Not-for-profit organisations include state-owned (public sector) activities, mutual societies, charities, private clubs, QUANGOs and voluntary organisations.

3 Stakeholders are those persons and organisations that have an interest in the strategy, aims and behaviour of the organisation.

4 Stakeholders may include: shareholders, management, employees, suppliers, customers, the suppliers of financial services and the local community.

5 The principal – agent problem arises when principals (such as shareholders) appoint some agents (such as directors) to act on their behalf (running a company) and cannot be sure that those agents will always act so as to promote the interest of the principals.

6 There may be a divorce of ownership from control because:

- companies may become too big for shareholders to effectively control
- companies may become too complex for shareholders to control
- individual shareholders may lack the power, knowledge, interest or time to control the companies they own.

7 The term corporate governance refers to the systems by which companies and other organisations are directed and controlled. For public companies this means the role of the Board of Directors and its relationship to the shareholders.

Chapter

2

Microeconomic and Organisational Context II: The Market System

Chapter learning objectives

On completion of their studies, students should be able to:

- identify the equilibrium price in product or factor markets
- calculate the price elasticity of demand and the price elasticity of supply
- explain the determinants of the price elasticities of demand and supply
- calculate the effects of price elasticity of demand on a firm's total revenue curve
- identify the influence of costs on the size and structure of the organisation
- explain the sources of market failures and the policies available to deal with them.

1 Introduction

1.1 Different market systems

Given that resources are limited ('scarce'), it is not possible to make everything everyone would want ('unlimited wants'). All societies are thus faced with a fundamental economic problem:

- What goods and services should be produced?
- In what quantities?
- Who should make them?
- Who gets the output?

There are three main economic systems or approaches to solve this problem:

- **A market economy** – interaction between supply and demand (market forces) determines what is made, in what quantity and who gets the output. Patterns of economic activity are determined by the decisions made by individual consumers and producers.
- **A command economy** – production decisions are controlled by the government.
- **A mixed economy** – in reality most modern economies are a mix of free markets and government intervention.

1.2 Market forces

In a free market, the quantity and price of goods supplied in a market are determined by the interaction between supply and demand.

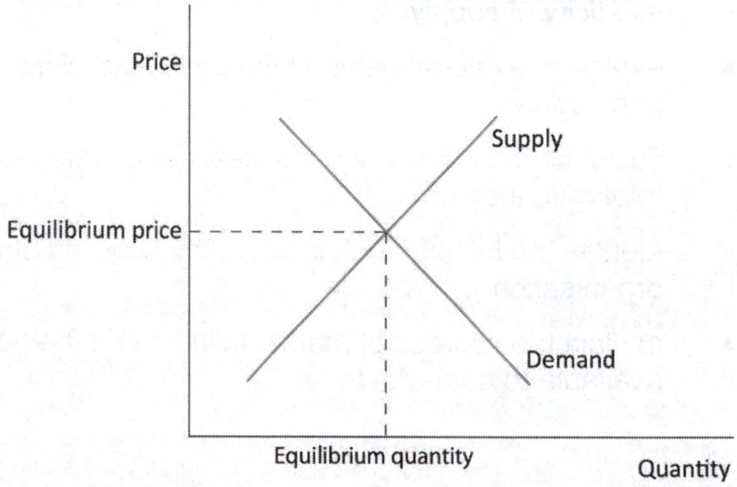

A market price will be set by the 'invisible hand of the market' through the interaction of supply and demand.

In this chapter we will explore this process by looking at demand and supply in detail and at how the price mechanism sets the price. We will then consider the subject of 'market failure' and the reasons why governments are not content to leave everything to market forces.

2 Demand

2.1 Individual demand

Individual demand shows how much of a good or service someone intends to buy at different prices.

This demand needs to be effective in that it is backed by available money, rather than just a general desire without the necessary financial backing.

When considering demand at a price, we assume that the conditions of demand (i.e. other variables – see below) are held constant.

- For most goods, the lower the price, the higher will be its demand.
- When the demand for a good or service changes in response to a change in its price, the change is referred to as:
  - an **expansion** in demand where quantity demanded rises due to a fall in price.
  - a **contraction** in demand where quantity demanded falls due to a rise in price.
- The relationship between demand and price can be shown in a diagram and is referred to as a demand curve. (Note: For such graphs, we plot quantity along the horizontal axis and price on the vertical axis. This may seem the wrong way round to you as we are arguing here that demand depends on price and we normally have the dependent variable on the vertical axis. However, this is the accepted approach for economics.) We show the curve as a straight line, for simplification.
- Thus, in the diagram below, the downward-sloping demand curve D illustrates the demand for a normal good. Movements along this curve as the price changes would be called a contraction in demand (price is rising) or an expansion in demand (price is falling).

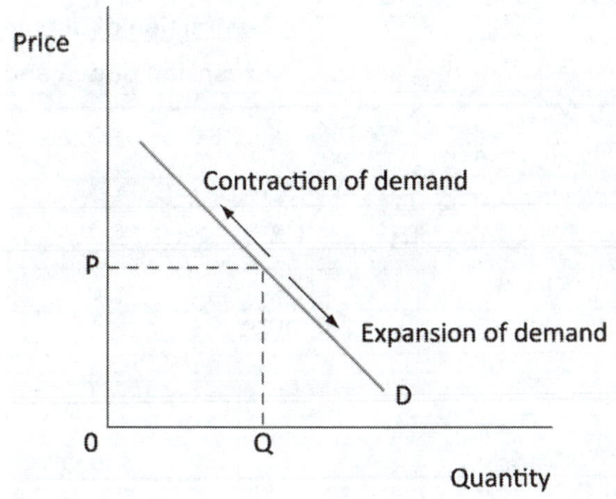

2.2 Market demand

Market demand shows the total amount of effective demand from all the consumers in a market, aggregated together. Market demand is usually shortened to demand and represented by a straight-line curve on a graph. The demand curve for most normal goods is negatively inclined sloping downwards from left to right for reasons explained in the previous section.

2.3 Conditions of demand

So far we have considered exclusively the influence of price on the quantity demanded, assuming other factors to be constant. These factors, termed the conditions of demand, will now be considered, with the price held constant.

Any change in one or more of the conditions of demand will create shifts in the demand curve itself.

- If the shift in the demand curve is outward, to the right, such a shift is called an **increase/rise** in demand.
- If the shift in the demand curve is inward, to the left, such a shift is called a **decrease/fall** in demand.

It is important to distinguish between:

- increases and decreases in demand that result from a shift in the demand curve as a whole
- expansions and contractions in demand that result from price changes leading to movements along the demand curve itself.

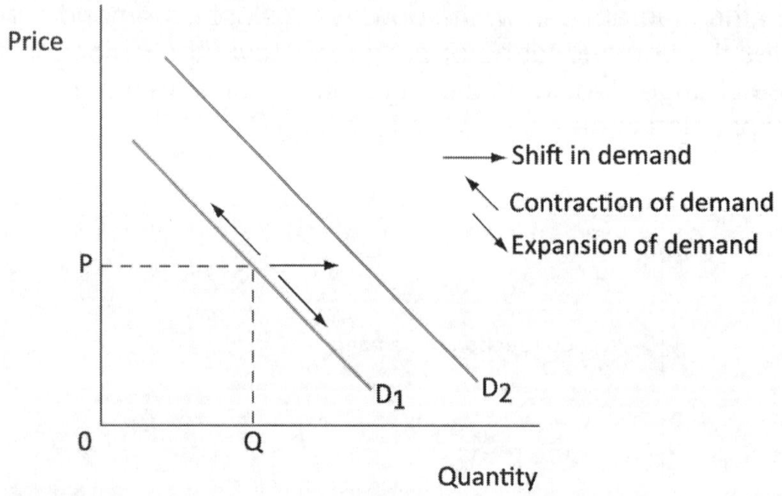

The main conditions of demand are as follows:

- **Income**

  Changes in income often affect demand.

  For example, lower direct taxes would raise disposable incomes and, other things being equal, make consumers better off and so they spend more on discretionary expenditure. For normal goods, an increase in income leads to an increase in demand. Examples could include cars, jewellery, fashion clothing and music streaming services.

  For inferior goods, however, a rise in income leads to a **lower** demand for the product as consumers, now being richer, substitute better quality and preferred goods and services for the original ('inferior') good or service. An example of this is public transport. Here, as incomes rise, the demand for public transport falls as consumers substitute more expensive, private transport such as cars.

- **Tastes**

  Tastes, in particular fashions, change frequently and it may make the demand for certain goods volatile.

  A good example of this was the rapid rise in demand for fidget spinners seen in 2017 followed by a decline as people's attention moved elsewhere.

  Tastes can be manipulated by advertising and producers to try to 'create' markets, particularly for ostentatious goods. For instance, by paying popular social media influencers to positively associate with their brand, producers can stimulate revenue as consumers purchase the brand to emulate the lifestyle of the influencers. An example is BECCA Cosmetics partnering with model and social media star Chrissy Teigen to reach a wider market.

- **The prices of other goods**

  Goods may be unrelated, or they may be complements or substitutes. The former have no effect (a price change in one doesn't affect demand for the other), but the latter two are significant.

  If goods are in joint demand (i.e. complements such as burgers and burger buns), a change in the price of one will also affect the other. Therefore, if the price of burgers falls, there is likely to be an **expansion** of demand for burgers and a related **increase** in demand for burger buns.

  Where goods are substitutes (e.g. Coke and Pepsi, or McDonald's and Burger King), a rise in the price of one will cause an increase in demand for the other (and thus the demand curve for the other will shift to the right).

  Sometimes, technological breakthroughs mean that new products come into the market. For instance, the introduction of affordable streaming services for music and films has reduced the demand for CDs and DVDs (the latter leading to the closure of the Blockbuster chain).

- **Population**

  An increase in population creates a larger market for most goods, thereby shifting demand to the right. For instance, an influx of seasonal workers from other countries will raise the demand for most essential goods during the season in which they are working. Changes in population distribution will also affect demand patterns. If the proportion of old people relative to young people increases, then the demand for products such as false teeth, wheelchairs and old people's homes will increase relative to that of gripe water, nappies and cots.

In the analysis of how the demand and supply model works, the distinctions between increase/decrease in demand and expansion/contraction in demand are very important. Remember:

- If a **price change** occurs, there will be a movement **along** the demand curve and the result will be either an **expansion or a contraction** in demand.
- If the **conditions of demand change**, there will be a **shift in the demand curve** and the result will be either an **increase** (curve moves outward to the right) **or a decrease** (curve moves inward to the left) in demand.

Test your understanding 1

A demand curve is drawn for JMD, a health supplement provider, assuming all but one of the following remains unchanged. Which item can vary?

A The price of competitors' products

B The cost of labour to make the product

C The price of the product

D The level of growth in the economy

Test your understanding 2

Which one of the following would lead to the demand curve for health supplements shifting to the right?

A Adverse publicity that suggests such supplements may be harmful

B A fall in the disposable income of consumers

C A fall in the price of the supplements

D An increase in the size of the population due to people living longer

An understanding of demand will be necessary in later studies, for instance when considering pricing decisions in P2.

Test your understanding 3

Which one of the following would **not** lead to a shift in the demand curve for overseas holidays?

A An advertising campaign by holiday-tour operators

B A fall in the disposable income of consumers

C A rise in the price of domestic holidays

D A rise in the exchange rate for the domestic currency

3 Elasticity of demand

Elasticity, generally, refers to the relationship between two variables and measures the responsiveness of one (dependent) variable to a change in another (independent) variable: There are several types of elasticity that are useful to economists and accountants. Management accountants are particularly interested in knowing price elasticity of demand as this can give a good indication of the optimal price for a good or service.

3.1 Price elasticity of demand (PED)

This concept explains the relationship between changes in quantity demanded and changes in price.

- Price elasticity of demand explains the responsiveness of demand to changes in price.
- The co-efficient of price elasticity of demand (PED) is calculated by:

$$\frac{\text{Percentage change in quantity demanded}}{\text{Percentage change in price}}$$

The formula can be applied either at one point on the demand curve or over part (arc) of it. It is critical that percentage or proportional changes are used rather than absolute ones.

Definitions:

There are two ways of calculating PED using the 'arc method'. Both of these methods are examinable.

– **non-average arc method** – measures % change in quantity demanded / % change in price using the **starting point** of price and quantity as the basis for the % calculation.

– **average arc method** – measures % change in quantity demanded / % change in price using the **average** price and quantity as the basis for the % calculation.

The '**Point method**' is an alternative that requires use of calculus and will not be taught or tested at this level.

Price elasticity of demand levels

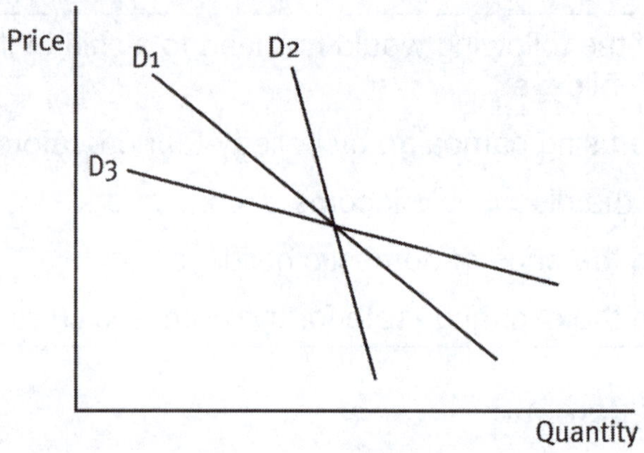

D_1 shows unit elasticity (% change in demand = % change in price).

D_2 shows inelastic demand (% change in demand smaller than % change in price).

D_3 shows elastic demand (% change in demand larger than % change in price).

Note that the value of price elasticity of demand will change as you move along the length of the straight demand curve.

A normal demand curve will always slope downwards from left to right indicating that a price rise will lead to a contraction in demand and a price fall will lead to an expansion in demand.

e.g **Illustration 1 – PED**

Suppose we are currently selling a product at a price of $30 with a resulting demand of 200 units per annum. A marketing manager has suggested raising the price to $60 and claims that demand will fall to 100 units.

Calculate the PED using:

(1) the non-average arc method; and

(2) the average arc method.

Solution (1) the non-average arc method

- Percentage change in price = ($60 – $30)/$30 × 100 = +100%
- Percentage change in demand = (100 – 200)/200 × 100 = –50%
- PED = (–50)/(+100) = –0.5 price inelastic demand

Solution (2) the average arc method

- Average price = ($30 + $60) / 2 = $45
- Average demand = (200 + 100) / 2 = 150 units
- Percentage change in price = ($60 – $30)/$45 × 100 = +66.67%
- Percentage change in demand = (100 – 200)/150 × 100 = –66.67%
- PED = (–66.67)/(+66.67) = –1 unit price elasticity

In exam questions, expect PED to be negative because price and quantity demanded are inversely related. A summary of price elasticity is given below:

Description of curve's elasticity	Coefficient value	Actual examples
Relatively inelastic	Between 0 and –1	Tea, salt
Unit elasticity	–1	–
Relatively elastic	Between –1 and $-\infty$	Cameras, air travel

Note: if demand is completely insensitive to price, then the PED will be 0 and demand would be described as "perfectly inelastic". An example of this would be a vertical demand curve. Similarly a horizontal demand curve would have PED = $-\infty$, "perfectly elastic".

Generally, if the demand curve is fairly steep, a large change in price will cause only a relatively small change in demand, indicating an inelastic demand curve.

Test your understanding 4

A business currently sells 100,000 units of a product per month at a price of $5. The sales manager has suggested dropping the price to $4.90 with the argument that the quantity demanded will rise to 105,000 units.

Calculate the PED using the non-average arc method.

A – 50,000

B – 4

C – 2.5

D – 0.25

Test your understanding 5

A business, currently selling 10,000 units of its product per month, plans to reduce the retail price from $1 to $0.90. It knows from previous experience that the price elasticity of demand for this product is –1.5 (non-average method). Assuming no other changes, the sales the business can now expect each month will be:

A 8,500

B 10,500

C 11,000

D 11,500

PED and gradient

While we might expect a steeper demand curve to be less elastic, elasticity and gradient are not the same thing. It is often wrongly assumed that two demand curves with the same shape will have the same elasticity coefficient. Even for a straight-line demand curve (i.e. constant gradient) the PED will vary depending where exactly you are on the curve.

Consider the following demand curves:

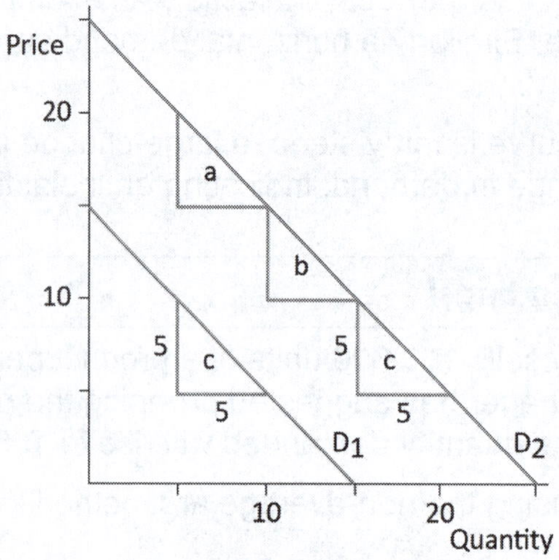

Price	Demand D_1	Demand D_2
5	10	20
10	5	15
15		10
20		5

The PED coefficients for the same range of D1 and D2 are calculated for a price fall (triangle c).

For D_1 (triangle c) the quantity demanded increases from 5 to 10 (i.e. = + 5/5) as the price falls from 10 to 5 (i.e. –½). Elasticity is therefore calculated as (5/5) ÷ (– ½) = –2.

In contrast, D_2 (triangle c) shows that quantity demanded increased from 15 to 20 (i.e. + 1/3) when the price fell from 10 to 5 (i.e. –½). Elasticity is therefore calculated as

1/3 ÷ (–½) = –2/3.

This demonstrates the importance of the position of the demand curve. Generally, a curve further from the origin will tend to be less elastic, as shown above.

The numerical value of the elasticity coefficient also varies according to:

- whether a price fall or price rise is calculated.

  For example, D_2 elasticity = –2/3 when price fell from 10p to 5p. However, a price rise of 5p to 10p gives –1/4 (i.e. –1/4 ÷ 1). This occurs because elasticity shows relative percentage changes and the base from which the calculations are made differs.

- which part of the demand curve is selected. Elasticity varies from point to point on a straight-line demand curve (but not on a rectangular hyperbola). As calculation moves down a linear curve from top left to bottom right the elasticity value falls, that is, the curve becomes relatively more inelastic.

  For example, the price elasticity of demand for a price fall of 5p on D_2 at:

  – a = –4 (i.e. 1 ÷ (–1/4)), whereas at

  – b = –3/2 (i.e. 1/2 ÷ (–1/3)) and at

  – c = –2/3 (i.e. –1/3 ÷ (1/2)).

The point method for calculating PED

So far, we have calculated PED by considering a movement along a demand curve – i.e. we started at one point and then changed both price and quantity. This is known as the arc method.

With a straight-line demand curve, the PED calculated will only depend on where we started (as this determines how we calculate the percentages) but not on how far along the demand curve we move.

Unfortunately if the demand curve is a curve then the PED will depend on both the starting point AND on how far we move. We thus cannot really talk of the elasticity at a point because it depends on our calculation. This is clearly absurd and so we need a more precise method of calculating PED. The solution is the point method and requires a knowledge of the equation of the demand curve and of differential calculus. It is worth being aware that using the point method means that the PED only depends on the point chosen.

3.2 Factors that influence PED

There are several factors that determine the price elasticity of demand:

- **Proportion of income spent on the good**

  Where a good constitutes a small proportion of consumers' income spent, then a small price change will be unlikely to have much impact. Therefore, the demand for low value items such as shoe polish, matches and pencils is likely to be very inelastic. Conversely, the demand for designer clothing, cars or housing will probably be elastic.

- **Substitutes**

  If there are close and available substitutes for a product, then an increase in its price is likely to cause a much greater fall in the quantity demanded as consumers buy suitable alternatives. Thus, the demand for a specific variety box of chocolates may be fairly elastic because there are many competing brands in the market. In contrast, the demand for a unique product such as the Guinness World Records book will tend to be inelastic.

- **Necessities**

  The demand for vital goods such as sugar, milk and bread tends to be stable and inelastic; conversely, luxury items such as foreign skiing holidays are likely to be fairly elastic in demand. It is interesting to note that improvements in living standards push certain commodities such as televisions from the luxury to the necessity category.

- **Habit**

  When goods are purchased automatically, without customers perhaps being fully aware of their price, for example, chocolate bars, the demand is inelastic. This also applies to addictive products such as cigarettes and alcohol, where purchases continue despite a noticeable price rise.

- **Time**

  In the short run, consumers may be ignorant of possible alternative goods in many markets, so they may continue to buy certain goods when their prices rise. Such inelasticity may be lessened in the long run as consumers acquire greater knowledge of markets and of available substitute goods.

- **Definition of market**

  If a market is defined widely (e.g. food), there are likely to be fewer alternatives and so demand will tend to be inelastic. In contrast, if a market is specified narrowly (e.g. orange drinks) there will probably be many brands available, thereby creating elasticity in the demand for the individual brands.

Test your understanding 6

Using the factors above discuss whether you consider the demand for petrol to be price elastic or inelastic.

3.3 The link between PED and total revenue

The PED can also be calculated by examining total revenue. This method is most useful to business people.

- If total revenue increases following a price cut, then demand is price elastic.
- If total revenue increases following a price rise, then demand is price inelastic.

Conversely, if total revenue falls after a price cut, then the demand is inelastic; and after a price rise, it is elastic. If total revenue remains unchanged, then the demand is of unitary elasticity.

Illustration 2 – PED and revenue

Suppose a product is currently priced at $20 with associated demand of 50,000 units per annum. The directors would like to boost revenue and are considering a price cut to $19. Research suggests that the PED is – 0.8, calculated on a non-average basis.

Determine the expected change in demand and total revenue.

Solution

- Suggested % change in price = –5%
- Given a PED of –0.8, the expected % change in demand will be –5% × –0.8 = +4%
- Thus demand will rise to 52,000 units
- Currently revenue = $20 × 50,000 = $1,000,000
- Predicted revenue with price cut = $19 × 52,000 = $988,000

Revenue has fallen. Given inelastic demand, this was expected. A price increase would boost revenue here rather than a price cut.

Note: This illustrates how useful knowledge of elasticity is to managers when making pricing decisions.

Test your understanding 7

If the demand for a good is price elastic, a fall in its price will lead to:

(i) a rise in unit sales.

(ii) a fall in unit sales.

(iii) a rise in total sales revenue.

(iv) a fall in total sales revenue.

A (i) and (iii) only

B (i) and (iv) only

C (ii) and (iii) only

D (ii) and (iv) only

Test your understanding 8

Answer the following questions based on the preceding information.

1 Describe the shape of a typical demand curve.

2 What is the price elasticity of demand?

3 The price of a good falls by 10 per cent but the quantity demanded increases from 100 to 120 units. Calculate the price elasticity of demand using the non-average arc method.

4 List four factors that influence price elasticity of demand.

5 What is the difference between a shift in demand and an expansion of demand?

4 Supply

4.1 The supply curve of a firm

A supply curve shows how much producers would be willing and able to offer for sale, at different prices, over a given period of time.

The supply curve of a firm is underpinned by the desire to make profit. It demonstrates what a firm will provide to the market at certain prices. Given that cost is one of the main determinants of supply, an increase in price will usually result in greater supply. Thus, supply curves are usually upward sloping.

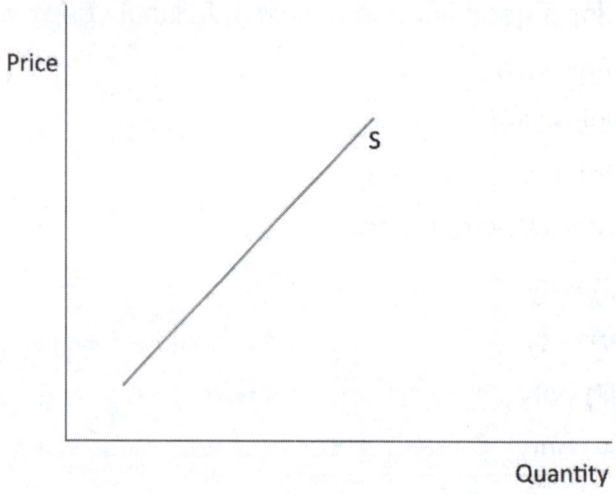

4.2 The supply curve of an industry

Assuming that all the firms in an industry are identical, a market supply curve is composed of all the supply curves of the individual producers in the industry added together. The industry supply curve is an aggregate, which shows what producers are willing to offer for sale at any given price. For example

	Quantity supplied			
Price	Firm A	Firm B	Firm C	Industry
0	0	0	0	0
1	30	15	20	65
2	20	30	25	75
3	30	45	30	105
4	40	60	35	135
5	50	75	40	165

Thus, the supply curve of an industry is similar to that of its individual component firms but at a higher level.

As with the demand curve, changes in price cause movement up and down the supply curve but the supply curve itself is not moving. This is referred to as either a change in the quantity supplied or an expansion/contraction of supply.

4.3 Conditions of supply

A change in factors other than the price will move the supply curve itself.

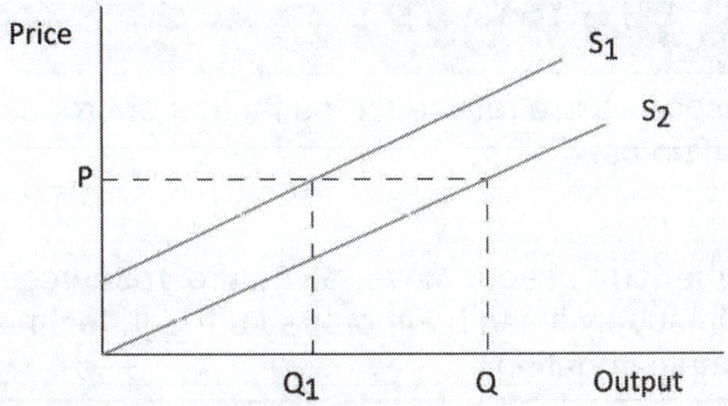

A decrease in supply

At existing prices, **less** will now be supplied, as shown on the upward-sloping, elastic supply curve. At price P, the quantity supplied falls from Q to Q_1 as the supply curve shifts from S_2 to S_1. This means that the cost of supply has increased.

This results from:

- Higher production costs. The costs of production may increase because the factors of production (land, labour, capital and enterprise) become expensive. Thus, conditions such as higher wage costs per unit, higher input prices and increased interest rates will lead to reductions in supply.

- Indirect taxes. The imposition of an indirect tax makes supply at existing prices less profitable. With an indirect tax the costs of production are raised directly because the tax must be paid on each good sold irrespective of how much of the tax can be recouped via a higher price. The profit margin is reduced (by some varying amount) as an indirect effect.

An increase in supply

For example, a shift in the supply curve from S_1 to S_2 illustrates an increase in supply with **more** being supplied at each price, showing that the cost of production has fallen or lower profits are being taken.

Lower unit costs may arise from:

- technological innovations, for example, the advance of microchip technology lowered the cost of computers and led to large increases in supply
- more efficient use of existing factors of production, for example, introduction of a shift system of working might mean fuller use of productive capacity, leading to lower unit costs
- improvements in productivity that may lead to maintaining output levels with fewer workers
- lower input prices, such as cheaper raw material imports and lower-priced components could bring down production costs
- a reduction or abolition of an indirect tax or the application of or increase in subsidies.

Factors of production

Economic resources are referred to as factors of production. These are usually classified as:

- Land

  This is the term used to cover all natural resources. Although largely limited in supply it can be improved through technological advances, for example irrigation.

- Labour

  This is a specific category of human resource. The quality of labour can be raised through education and training. The application of capital, through the use of machinery, will improve labour productivity.

- Enterprise

  This is another human resource but refers to the role played by the organiser of production, including risk-taking, organising and decision-making.

- Capital

  These are man-made resources. Capital may be fixed, for example a factory, or not, for example working capital in the form of raw materials and work-in-progress.

4.4 Elasticity of supply

The elasticity of supply is calculated by the formula:

$$\frac{\text{Percentage change in quantity supplied}}{\text{Percentage change in price}}$$

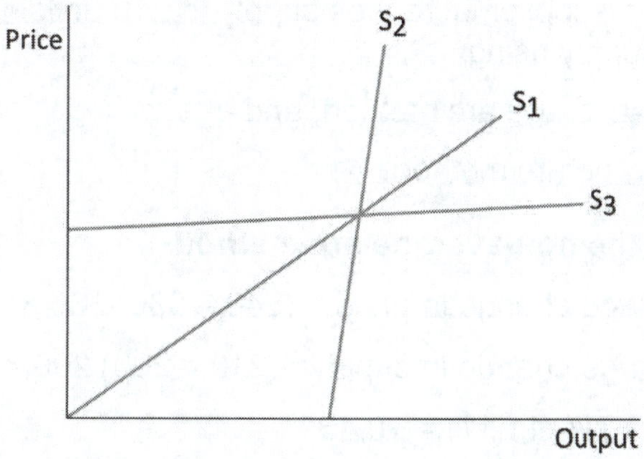

S_1 intersects the origin and shows unit elasticity.

S_2 intersects the output axis and shows inelastic supply.

S_3 intersects the price axis shows elastic supply.

Note that the value of price elasticity of supply will change as you move along the length of the straight supply curve.

A normal supply curve will always slope upwards from left to right indicating that suppliers are willing to supply more when the price they can achieve is higher. Thus, a price rise will lead to an **expansion** in supply and a price fall will lead to a **contraction** in supply.

Therefore, the value of the price elasticity of supply (PES) is always positive.

- If a change in price induces a larger proportionate change in the quantity supplied, the price elasticity of supply will have a value of more than 1 and supply is said to be price elastic.
- If a change in price induces a smaller proportionate change in the quantity supplied, the price elasticity of supply will have a value of less than 1 and supply is said to be price inelastic. The extreme case would be perfectly inelastic where supply is completely unaffected by price.
- If a change in price induces an equally proportionate change in the quantity supplied, the price elasticity of supply will have a value of 1 and supply is said to have unit elasticity.

e.g

Illustration 3 – Price elasticity of supply

As with PED, price elasticity of supply can be calculated by either point or arc methods.

Suppose a supplier is currently supplying 200 units per annum of a product in response to a market price of $36. The market price then rises to $40 and the supplier increases supply to 210 units. Calculate the price elasticity of supply using:

1 the non-average arc method, and

2 the average arc method.

Solution (1) the non-average arc method

- Percentage change in price = ($40 – $36)/$36 × 100 = +11.11%
- Percentage change in supply= (210 – 200)/200 × 100 = +5%
- PES = (+5)/(+11.11) = +0.45

Solution (2) the average arc method

- Average price = ($36 + $40) / 2 = $38
- Average supply = (200 + 210) / 2 = 205 units
- Percentage change in price = ($40 – $36)/$38 × 100= +10.53%
- Percentage change in supply = (210 – 200)/205 × 100 = +4.88%
- PES = (+4.88)/(+10.53) = +0.46

4.5 Factors that influence elasticity of supply

There are several factors that affect the elasticity of supply:

- **Time**. Supply tends to be more elastic in the long run. Production plans can be varied and firms can react to price changes. In some industries, notably agriculture, supply is fixed in the short run and thus perfectly inelastic. However, in manufacturing, supply is more adaptable.
- **Factors of production.** Supply can be quickly changed (elastic) if there are available factors, such as trained labour, unused productive capacity and plentiful raw materials, with which output can be raised. Although one firm may be able to expand production in the short run, a whole industry may not, so there could be a divergence between a firm's elasticity and that of the industry as a whole.
- **Stock levels**. If there are extensive stocks of finished products warehoused, then these can be released onto the market, making supply relatively elastic. Stock levels tend to be higher when business people are optimistic and interest rates are low.

- **Number of firms in the industry**. Supply will tend to be more elastic if there are many firms in the industry, because there is a greater chance of some having the available factors and high stock. Also, it is possible that industries with no entry barriers or import restrictions could expand supply quickly as new firms enter the industry in response to higher prices.

Test your understanding 9

Using the above factors comment on whether the supply of fresh milk is price elastic or inelastic.

Test your understanding 10

Answer the following questions based on the preceding information.

1 Which factors affect the elasticity of supply?

2 What effect will higher wages have on the supply curve?

5 The price mechanism

5.1 Equilibrium

Now we have looked at demand and supply in detail, let us consider how the price mechanism sets a price.

The way to see how market forces achieve equilibrium is to consider what happens if the price is too high or too low:

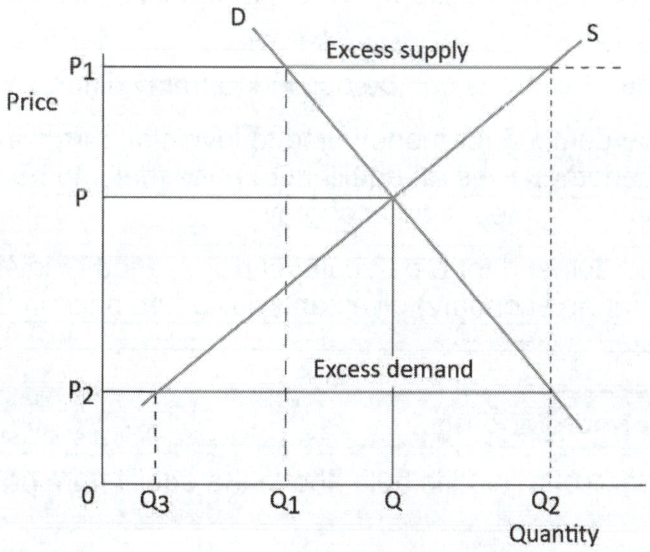

The graph shows the intended demand and planned supply at a set of prices. It is only at price P where demand and supply are the same. If the demand of consumers and the supply plans of sellers correspond, then the market is deemed to be in equilibrium. Only at output Q and price P are the plans of both sellers and buyers realised. Thus, Q is the equilibrium quantity and P is the equilibrium price in this market.

There is only one equilibrium position in a market. At this point, there is no tendency for change in the market, because the plans of both buyers and sellers are satisfied. At prices and outputs other than the equilibrium (P, Q), either demand or supply aspirations could be fulfilled but not both simultaneously.

- For instance at price P_1, consumers only want Q_1 output but producers are making Q_2 output available. There is a **surplus of supply**, the excess supply being the difference between the Q_1 and Q_2 output levels.

  Assuming the conditions of demand and supply remain unchanged, it is likely that the buyers and sellers will reassess their intentions.

  This will be reflected in the short-term by retailers having unwanted goods, returns made to manufacturers, reduced orders and some products being thrown away and so suppliers may be prepared to accept lower prices than P_1 for their goods.

  This reduction in price will lead to a contraction in supply and an expansion in demand until equilibrium is reached at price P.

- Conversely, at a price of P_2, the quantity demanded, Q_2, will exceed the quantity supplied, Q_3. There will be a **shortage of supply** ($Q_2 – Q_3$), demonstrating the excess demand.

  This will be reflected in the short-term by retailers having empty shelves, queues and increased orders. Furthermore, there may be high second-hand values, for example on eBay or Gumtree. The supplier will respond by increasing prices to reduce the shortage.

  This excess demand will thus lead to a rise in the market price, and demand will contract and supply will expand until equilibrium is reached at price P.

A supply and demand analysis can be applied to many different markets:

- Supply of and demand for money (tied to levels of borrowing and saving within the economy) gives an equilibrium price that can be interpreted as the level of interest rates in an economy.

- Supply of and demand for a particular currency (tied to levels of imports and exports for an economy) gives an equilibrium price in the form of an exchange rate.

Test your understanding 11

When the price of a good is held above the equilibrium price, the result will be:

A excess demand

B a shortage of the good

C a surplus of the good

D an increase in demand

Test your understanding 12

When the price of a good is reduced and held below the equilibrium price, the result will be all except one of the following:

A excess demand

B a shortage of the good

C a surplus of the good

D an expansion in demand

5.2 Shifts in supply and or demand

As well as signalling information in a market, price acts as a stimulant. The price information may provide incentives for buyers and sellers. For instance, a price rise may encourage firms to shift resources into one industry in order to obtain a better reward for their use.

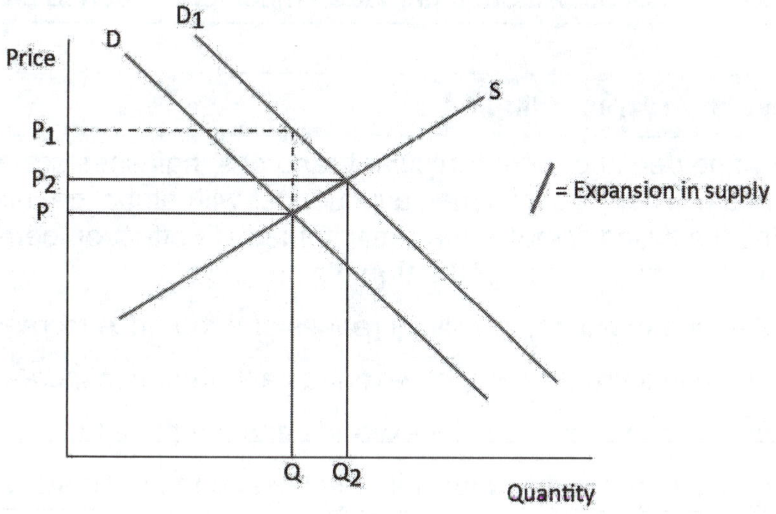

- For example, suppose the equilibrium is disturbed when the conditions of demand change. Consumers' tastes have moved positively in favour of the good and a new curve D_1 shows customers' intentions.
- Supply is initially Q, at the equilibrium, and it is momentarily fixed, so the market price is bid up to P_1.
- However, producers will respond to this stimulus by expanding the quantity supplied, perhaps by running down their stocks.
- This expansion in supply to Q_2 reduces some of the shortage, bringing price down to P_2, a new equilibrium position, which is above the old equilibrium P.

Note that if we had drawn the diagram with steeper supply (and demand curves), then the price fluctuations would have been greater. Thus the more inelastic the demand and supply of a good are, the greater will be price volatility when either demand or supply shifts.

The longer-term effects of these changes in the market depend upon the reactions of the consumers and producers. The consumers may adjust their preferences and producers may reconsider their production plans. The impact of the latter on supply depends upon the length of the production period. Generally, the longer the production period, and the more inelastic the supply is, the more unstable price will tend to be.

- Price acts as a signal to sellers on what to produce.
- Price rises, with all other market conditions unchanged, will act as a stimulus to extra supply.
- Equilibrium price is where the plans of both buyers and sellers are satisfied.

Test your understanding 13

Much of the world's coffee is grown in South America. By use of supply and demand curves explain what would happen to the price of coffee if bad storms in South America damaged much of the coffee crop.

Test your understanding 14

Supply and demand for a particular brand of sunglasses are at equilibrium. Then, a social media influencer with global popularity is seen wearing the brand. What is the likely immediate effect on demand, supply and the equilibrium price of the brand's products?

A demand expands, supply increases and the price increases

B demand increases, supply expands and the price increases

C demand expands, supply expands and the price falls

D demand increases, supply increases and the price stays the same

6 Market failure

6.1 Introduction

In theory, market forces should result in allocation of resources in a way that maximises the utility (benefits) for consumers. However, in some circumstances, markets can lead to sub-optimal allocation of resources, leading to under- or over-production of certain goods and services.

This inability of a market to allocate resources in a way that maximises utility is called market failure. Consumers can lose out when market failure occurs. For example, those on low incomes may be priced out of the market for essential goods.

Government can then have a role to intervene to ensure that a market functions efficiently.

6.2 Public goods

Without government intervention, some goods would not be provided at all by a market economy. These are often referred to as public goods.

Public goods have the following properties:

- **non-excludability** – a person can benefit from the good without having to pay for it (the "free rider" concept). Provision of the good for one member of society automatically allows the rest of society also to benefit.
- **non-rivalry** – consumption of the good by one person does not reduce the amount available for consumption by others.

As a result, a market for public goods does not exist and so must be provided by the state.

e.g

Illustration 4 – Public goods

Imagine you needed a streetlight outside your home. You might ask your neighbours to share the cost, as they too will benefit from its installation. If they refuse and you go ahead, paying for it all yourself, you cannot stop them from benefiting from its presence.

Under such circumstances, in which you have to bear all the costs but benefit no more than any other resident in the street, would you go ahead and buy the light?

In these circumstances consumers are very unwilling to purchase goods and services and there is a role for government to provide them centrally, funded out of general taxation.

Clean air and clean water are also public goods. Should you decide to buy cleaner air or cleaner water in the area you live, say by paying industries to clean up, the services of that cleaner air and water are at the same time available to others, even though they didn't pay anything for them.

Consumers are sometimes unaware of the costs of provision of public goods and that governments work with a limited budget to provide them. Governments may not understand the true benefits of provision. This can lead to underfunding. Governments, underestimating the value of the good/service, may try to reduce their expenditure on it. Consumers, now faced with the prospect of losing the goods or services, respond by petitioning against the cuts. e.g. as part of the UK government's austerity measures (reduction in government spending), a substantial number of public libraries were closed, although some were saved because of public petitioning.

Other public goods include defence, a police force and lighthouses.

Test your understanding 15

The following passage is based on a newspaper article:

British cod – the staple of fish and chips – is on the verge of becoming an endangered species, according to the Worldwide Fund for Nature (WWF), the conservation group. It stressed that the crisis in the fishing industry was due to poor management and to over-fishing. The total weight of cod caught in the North Sea had halved since the 1960s. Similar falls in catches had occurred for other types of fish.

The WWF proposes the establishment of fishing-free zones to protect areas where young fish grow and develop. The WWF said that such a strategy would lead to increased fish stocks and a larger fishing catch for fishermen within five years. However, the problem may become less urgent as consumer demand for this type of fish may decline in the long run. Higher prices themselves may discourage consumers and some observers believe that for many consumers fish and chips may be an inferior good and, in many cases, faces a growing number of alternatives.

Required:

Using both your knowledge of economic theory and material contained in the above passage:

(a) State whether each of the following would lead to a shift in the demand curve for fish or a movement along the demand curve for fish.

(i) An increase in the number of substitutes for fish.

(ii) A rise in the price of fish.

(iii) An outward shift in the supply curve of fish.

(iv) A rise in income of fish consumers. **(4 marks)**

(b) State whether each of the following is true or false.

(i) If the demand for fish is very price elastic a fall in supply will raise prices a great deal. **(1 mark)**

(ii) If the supply of fish is price inelastic, a reduction in supply will have a smaller effect on price than if the supply were price elastic. **(1 mark)**

(iii) Price changes affect demand by leading to a shift in the demand curve for the product. **(1 mark)**

(iv) Effective advertising might raise sales by shifting the demand curve to the right. **(1 mark)**

(v) If the demand for fish were perfectly price inelastic, a change in income would have no effect on demand. **(1 mark)**

(vi) The longer the time period considered, the greater becomes the price elasticity of demand for goods. **(1 mark)**

(Total marks: 10)

As the government is providing public goods on a nationwide basis, it can benefit from economies of scale (see section 8 of this chapter). This could lower costs. There is no allocative efficiency because consumers do not have a choice – the services, such as police, prisons, fire, are provided whether they like it or not. However, a consumer who seeks more protection could buy additions in the marketplace, like burglar alarms, underground concrete bunkers, security staff, etc.

6.3 Externalities

Externalities are social costs or benefits that are not automatically included in the supply and demand curves for a product or service.

Social costs arising from production and consumption of a good or service are described as negative externalities and social benefits as positive externalities.

Supply and demand curves only take into account private costs and benefits, i.e. the costs that accrue directly to the supplier or the benefits that accrue directly to the consumer.

e.g

Illustration 5 – Externalities

If you smoke, drive a car or drink alcohol, who actually pays the cost of the product? In part, you do in the form of the price you pay for each packet of cigarettes, litre of fuel or bottle of wine. These are the private costs.

However, there are other costs. They are social costs that are met by society as a whole – the cost of healthcare for smokers, the environmental damage of burning fossil fuels and the cost of Accident and Emergency treatment for drunk drivers. These could all be described as "negative externalities".

Some would argue that one of the roles of government is to ensure that such externalities get incorporated into decision making, for example by fining polluters ("polluter pays policies"), higher taxes on alcohol or regulation. However, such policies may not always succeed as shown by the car emissions scandal involving Volkswagen in 2015, where government regulations to control diesel particulates were being circumvented by manipulating test results.

e.g

Illustration 6 – Using taxes to control externalities

One way of reducing negative externalities such as pollution would be to tax the supplier concerned, thus adding to their costs.

This would shift the supply curve to the left (S_1 to S_2), resulting in an equilibrium with higher prices (P to P_2) and lower quantity (Q to Q_2):

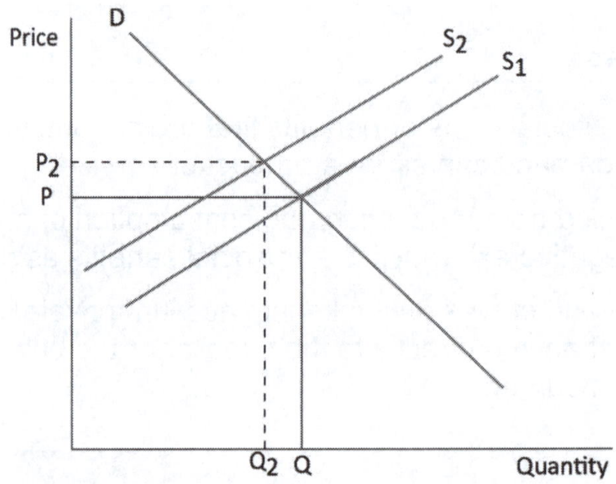

The more significant the tax, the greater the impact.

e.g

Illustration 7 – Reactions to market failures in the modern world

Road traffic congestion charge

Some cities, such as Singapore, London and San Diego, have introduced a congestion charge. The aim of a congestion charge is to reduce congestion on the roads, reduce pollution, make city centres more attractive for pedestrians and cyclists and to raise revenue. It is also to ensure that drivers pay the social cost of driving. Driving in city centres incurs significant external costs on the rest of society. The main external costs include congestion, pollution and accidents. Driving already incurs taxes, most notably petrol tax. However, petrol tax does not discriminate for where congestion is worst. A congestion charge will lead to a contraction in demand for use of the charged roads.

Levy on use of plastic carrier bags

The use of plastic carrier bags has increased massively since they were introduced in the 1950s. As plastic bag use spread globally, their negative externalities began to emerge; reports of littering, lack of biodegradability in landfills, ocean contamination and other environmental pollutants began to crop up. Following a charge for new plastic carrier bags in places such as UK, China and South Africa, as a result of this market failure, reusable bags have been quickly championed as the new right way to transport our goods. A carrier bag levy is charged to consumers, so the price increase will contract demand for the bags and eventually lead to a decrease in production and supply.

Externalities

An externality occurs when the costs or benefits of an economic action are not borne or received by the producer or consumer. Externalities are, therefore, the spill over effects of production and consumption that affect society as a whole rather than just the individual producers or consumers.

- Externalities created by nationalised industries can be good and bad. For example, the railways may be beneficial by relieving roads of congestion and maintaining communications for isolated communities, but may be detrimental in terms of noise and air pollution.
- The pricing policies considered so far have been based purely on private costs. If any pricing policy were to maximise net social benefit (or minimise net social cost), then costs would need to include such externalities.
- Calculate social costs. These would indicate the true cost to society of production to incorporate into decision-making. However, externalities are very difficult to calculate as they are not always attributable, for example noise, and their impact is not universally identical.
- Use indirect taxes and subsidies. Where private costs of production or consumption are below social costs, an indirect tax could be imposed so that price is raised to reflect the true social costs of production. Taxes on alcohol and tobacco can be justified on these grounds. Subsidies to homeowners to install roof insulation will reduce energy consumption and help conserve a scarce resource for wider social benefit.
- Extend private property rights so that firms are still liable for the outputs of their activities even after their product/service has been sold. This is reflected in the way many firms are subjected to compulsory recycling programmes e.g. various waste electronics and waste packaging initiatives, end of lifecycle vehicle directives and so on, as well as noise emission taxes.
- Regulations. A government can set maximum permitted levels of emission or minimum levels of environmental quality. The European Union has over 200 pieces of legislation covering environmental controls. Fines can be imposed on firms contravening these limits.
- Tradable permits. A maximum permitted level of emission is set for a given pollutant, for example, carbon emissions, and a firm or a country is given a permit to emit up to this amount. If it emits less than this amount, it is given a credit for the difference, which it can sell to enable the buyer to go above its permitted level. Thus, the overall level of emissions is set by a government or regulatory body, whereas their distribution is determined by the market.

Despite the many measures to deal with externalities, the issue of achieving the socially optimal level of production remains unresolved. Problems of calculating externalities and the correct level of taxation, issues of avoidance and enforcement and administrative costs can all mean that market failure and how to deal with it has yet to find an optimum solution.

Test your understanding 16

Pure public goods are goods:

A which are produced by the government

B whose production involves no externalities

C whose consumption by one person implies less consumption by others

D where individuals cannot be excluded from consuming them

Test your understanding 17

Which of the following statements are true or false?

A The cost of packaging for cigarettes is a negative externality. TRUE/FALSE

B The benefits to society from education are a positive externality. TRUE/FALSE

C The fine incurred for polluting a watercourse is a negative externality. TRUE/FALSE

D Damage to pine forests from pollution is a negative externality. TRUE/FALSE

6.4 Merit goods

One way of looking at merit goods is in terms of externalities. Merit goods are characterised by external social benefits (i.e. positive externalities) in consumption or by lack of knowledge of the private benefits in consumption. This would lead to under consumption of such services and health and education.

Moreover, merit goods are also ones that it is generally agreed should be available to all, irrespective of the ability to pay. Thus, governments often provide health and education services even though, unlike public goods, these can be provided by the market.

Merit goods may be underprovided by the market because of

- ignorance of consumers of the private benefits
- failure of the market to reflect the social benefits
- excessive prices limiting access to these services.

Furthermore, the private sector often provides alternatives, although these are often seen as different, or even superior goods/services, for example, private school education, private health schemes. These tend to be purchased only by those consumers with the means / willingness to do so. In the case of state-provided merit goods, economies of scale can often be achieved, so the cost of education per student is about three times cheaper in the state sector than in the private sector, for example.

6.5 Demerit goods

A demerit good is a good or service which is considered unhealthy, degrading, or otherwise socially undesirable due to the perceived negative effects on the consumers themselves. The concern is that a free market results in excessive consumption of the goods.

Examples include smoking (tobacco), excessive consumption of alcohol, recreational drugs, gambling and junk food.

While some would argue that the consumption of reasonable amounts of alcohol is acceptable and should not be legislated against by a "nanny state", they would also agree that excessive binge drinking causes significant problems both for the user and others. (Note: With demerit goods, we are particularly looking at the effect on the user in contrast with negative externalities where we considered the impact on society as a whole).

Government responses usually involve regulating or banning consumption, banning advertising of these goods and the use of higher taxes (sometimes known as "sin taxes").

Test your understanding 18

Which of the following are examples of merit goods?

A street lighting TRUE/FALSE

B education TRUE/FALSE

C healthcare TRUE/FALSE

D defence TRUE/FALSE

6.6 Changing transaction costs and market failure

When the transaction costs mentioned in chapter 1 (search and information costs, bargaining and decision costs, policing and enforcement costs) rise in relation to the development of an outsourcing relationship, outsourcing becomes more expensive and therefore less likely. Although outsourcing might provide the best allocation of resources (e.g. through use of a shared service centre or flexible staffing such as contract or temporary workers), companies may choose not to undertake it because of the extra cost.

6.7 Competition policy and fair trading regulations

The final market failure to be addressed is the problem posed by large businesses. The argument is that, unchecked, market forces may result in powerful companies who can abuse their market power and charge excessively high prices to consumers. Government intervention is thus needed to ensure that consumers are protected from such abuses.

Competition policy

As markets have become more heavily concentrated among fewer firms, more controls have been applied to restrictive trade practices and pricing. The economic justifications for such a policy are fairly clear.

- Collusion by suppliers and the operation of cartels usually lead to higher prices and/or monopoly profits and possibly lower output.
- These in turn reduce consumer welfare.
- Furthermore, they are a diminution in allocative efficiency. However, it must be remembered that extra profits may lead to investment in research, which could eventually benefit consumers via new products.

Scope of regulation

There are three aspects to this that involve government regulation:

- **Mergers and acquisitions**

  Many countries have bodies that monitor and assess mergers and acquisitions to see if the resulting organisation has excessive market power that is deemed to be against the public interest.

  In the UK this role is taken by the Competition and Markets Authority (formerly the Competition Commission) and a 25% market share or above is seen as a possible indicator of a "substantial lessening of competition" that may warrant further investigation.

- **Restrictive trade practices**

  Activities such as collusion over price fixing reduce competition within a market and undermine consumer sovereignty.

  In the UK, the Competition and Markets Authority (CMA) investigates anti-competitive behaviour in markets. In the USA, the Federal Trade Commission protects consumers and maintains competition.

- **State created regional monopolies**

  Many countries have gone through a process of privatisation, converting state owned organisations into private companies. In many cases, these result in regional monopolies, for example with water and other utilities.

  To control such monopolies government set up industry regulators, such as OFWAT, which regulates water and sewerage providers in England and Wales.

Regulators will negotiate with firms over key issues of pricing and required investment to leave an appropriate level of return for shareholders, for example, a maximum ROCE.

Regulation in the UK

As examples of how governments regulate markets, we will look at the role of various bodies in the UK.

The Competition and Markets Authority – mergers and acquisitions and restrictive practices

The Competition and Markets Authority (CMA), formerly the Competition Commission, is an independent public body that conducts in-depth inquiries into mergers, markets and the regulation of the major regulated industries, ensuring healthy competition between companies in the UK for the benefit of companies, customers and the economy.

Mergers may be investigated to see whether there is a realistic prospect that they will lead to a substantial lessening of competition (SLC), unless it obtains undertakings from the merging parties to address its concerns or the market is of insufficient importance. In the UK one factor that is considered is whether the combined businesses supply (or acquire) at least 25 per cent of a particular product or service in the UK (or in a substantial part of the UK), and the merger results in an increase in the share of supply or consumption.

The CMA has wide-ranging powers to remedy any competition concerns, including preventing a merger from going ahead and fining businesses for engaging in anti-competitive activities. It can also require a company to sell off part of its business or take other steps to improve competition.

An example of the CMA intervening in the UK was in 2015-2017 when six estate agents in Burnham-on-Sea were investigated for colluding with each other to fix prices in relation to the provision of residential estate agency services, effectively forming an illegal cartel. Four were fined.

The CMA regularly discovers anti-competitive behaviour, particularly when frustrated retailers are threatened by manufacturers that their supplies of products will be curtailed if they continue to sell them at cut prices or as loss leaders (against the maker's wishes). This suggests that competitive policy in the area of restrictive trade practices needed to be strengthened.

In August 2011, eight supermarkets and dairies were fined nearly £50 million after it was discovered they had fixed dairy product prices following a controversial eight-year investigation.

Specific industry regulators

As privatisation of large nationalised industries usually transformed public monopolies into private monopolies, the government accepted the need to create regulatory watchdogs. The role of specific industry regulators (SIRs) is essentially two-fold.

- First, when large state monopolies were privatised, they lacked effective competition. SIRs can introduce an element of competition by setting price caps and performance standards. In this way, consumers can share in the benefits of competitive behaviour even if competition does not actually exist in the market.
- Second, SIRs can speed up the introduction of competition in such markets by reducing barriers to entry for new firms.

Regulation in the EU

The European Commission

The Commission of the European Union can use its powers, directly derived from the Treaty of Rome, to control the behaviour of monopolists and to increase the degree of competition across the European Union.

For example, in 2016, the EU Commission prevented the merger of mobile operators O2 and Three. This decision was reversed by the European Court of Justice in 2020, although)2 has since moved on to target a merger with Virgin Media's fixed line broadband and TV business instead.

Test your understanding 19

Which one of the following is **not** a valid economic reason for producing a good or service in the public sector?

A The good is a basic commodity consumed by everyone

B It is a public good

C There is a natural monopoly in the production of the good

D It is a merit good

7 Interference with market prices

There may be occasions when the equilibrium price established by the market forces of demand and supply may not be the most desirable price. With such cases, the government might wish to set prices above or below the market equilibrium price.

7.1 Minimum price

In certain markets, government may seek to ensure a minimum price for different goods and services. It can do this in a number of ways such as providing subsidies direct to producers (e.g. the EU Common Agricultural Policy). Alternatively, it can set a legal minimum price (e.g. a statutory minimum wage). To be effective, legal minimum prices must be above the current market price.

If the government sets a minimum price above the equilibrium price (often called a price floor), there will be a surplus of supply created.

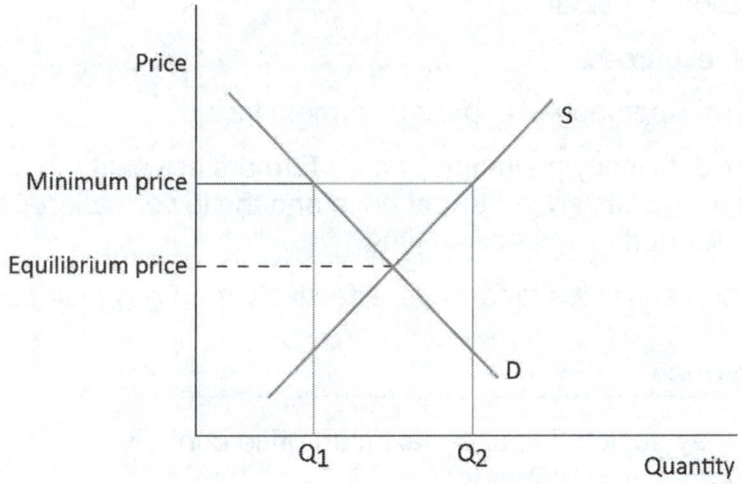

In the diagram this surplus is the difference between Q_2 and Q_1.

If this minimum price was applied in the labour market, it would be known as a minimum wage and the surplus would be the equivalent of unemployment, which would be a waste of a factor of production.

If applied to physical goods, then price floors cause surpluses of products, which have to be stored or destroyed. With the EU Common Agricultural Policy (CAP) this, for many years, resulted in the EU storing large quantities of food ("butter mountains"), selling the surplus to countries outside the EU (such as Russia) and even paying farmers not to grow the product in the first place but to remove land from agricultural use (so called "set aside" conditions). These have now largely disappeared as a result of the reform of CAP (driven in part by the surpluses).

Many argue, however, that CAP has given farmers stability. For example, direct payments provide farmers with a steady income and reward. Left to the mercy of the market, they would be unlikely to be able to invest in improvements to productivity, food safety or environmental protection. CAP ensures that Europeans have stable food supplies at reasonable prices. Increasingly, CAP is used to protect the rural environment. Farmers get more if they sign up to agro-environmental commitments – using fewer chemicals, leaving boundaries uncultivated, maintaining ponds, trees, hedges and protecting wildlife.

Another way of looking at the same problem is to state that it leads to a misallocation of resources both in the product and/or the factor market, which causes lower economic growth. There also may be the temptation for firms to attempt to ignore the price floor, for example, by informal arrangements with workers, which would lead to a further waste of resources in implementing such arrangements as well as raising issues of fair treatment for the workers involved.

In summary, government-imposed minimum prices may cause:

- Excess supply
- Misallocation of resources
- Waste of resources.

Note: Alternative approaches to protect farmers include

- the use of deficiency payments, where farmers are paid the difference between a legislatively set target price and the lower national average market price during a specified time
- payments of subsidies to farmers, effectively reducing their costs.

7.2 Maximum price

Governments may seek to impose maximum price controls or price ceilings on certain goods or services, either to:

- benefit consumers on low incomes, so that they can afford the particular good, or to
- control inflation.

To be effective, a legal maximum price must be set below the equilibrium price. The effect will be to create a shortage of supply.

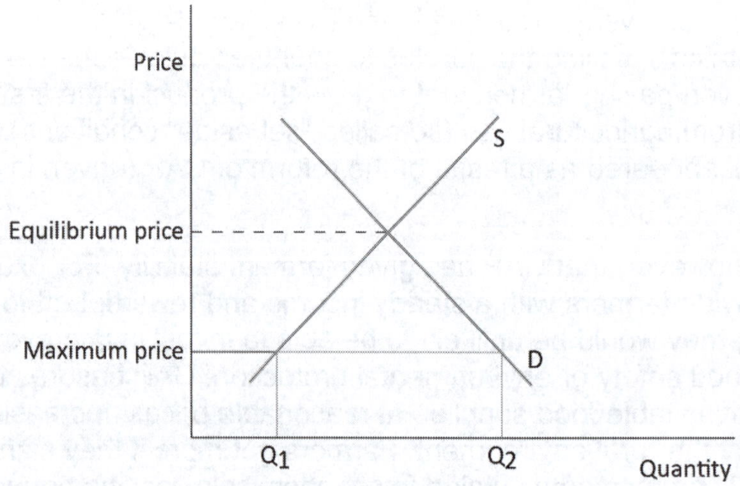

This shortage is the difference between Q_2 and Q_1. If the shortages of supply persist then problems can arise. The limited supply has to be allocated by some means other than by price.

This can be done by queuing, by rationing or by some form of favouritism, for example, by giving preference to regular customers. The difficulty with any of these alternative mechanisms is that they can be considered arbitrary and unfair by those who fail to secure the product. A consequence of the shortage can be the emergence of black markets. This is where buyers and sellers agree upon an illegal price, which is higher than that which has been officially sanctioned as the maximum price.

Maximum prices can also lead to a misallocation of resources. Producers will reduce output of those products subject to price controls, as these products are now relatively less profitable than those products where no price controls exist. In the housing market, this may lead to fewer apartments for rent as landowners develop office blocks rather than residential houses. Alternatively, the quality of the product may be allowed to drop as a way of reducing costs when profits are constrained by price controls. This failure to maintain property can mean that apartments fall into disrepair.

In summary, government-imposed maximum prices may cause:

- Shortages of supply
- Arbitrary ways of allocating a product
- Misallocation of resources.

Test your understanding 20

A government introduces a minimum price below free market price. Which one of the following describes the consequences of this?

A There will be no effect on market price or producer incomes

B Suppliers will withdraw from the market due to falling incomes

C Unsold surpluses of the product will build up

D Demand for the product will contract

8 Economies of scale

Economies of scale (also known as increasing returns to scale) are defined as reductions in unit average costs caused by increasing the scale of production in the long run.

For example, a larger firm may be able to gain greater discounts when purchasing raw materials.

Diseconomies of scale (also known as decreasing/diminishing returns to scale) are defined as increases in unit average costs caused by increasing the scale of production in the long run.

Diseconomies can arise as a firm grows very large. These often reflect the difficulty of communicating within a large organisation, together with a decline in management control.

8.1 Implications for businesses

- Economies and diseconomies of scale

  Managers need to understand whether economies of scale exist or are possible in their industry and the extent and nature of such economies.

  If such economies exist, then firms will need to achieve 'critical mass' in order to be competitive on cost. The low costs that result allow the firm to set its prices below those of smaller competitors and can act as a serious barrier to new firms trying to enter the industry. Obtaining such scale of production can result from organic growth and/or acquisition. While this results in larger firms, it often means fewer firms in the market as well.

  This explains why many industries are dominated by large players. However, the firm should not simply grow for growth's sake, as diseconomies of scale will erode its cost advantage.

The existence of significant economies of scale can be expected to lead to:

- costs and therefore prices falling as firms increase their scale of output
- barriers to entry for newer smaller firms; and
- industries dominated by a small number of large firms.

e.g

Illustration 8 – Economies of scale

Motor industry

The motor manufacturing industry is dominated by global firms. This is due to significant economies of scale such as

- purchasing discounts – e.g. steel
- use of large automated production lines
- marketing economies
- ability to have global supply chains benefiting from lower costs in certain countries.

Estate agencies

However, if you are trying to buy a house, then you will most likely find yourself dealing with small local firms of estate agents. This is because economies of scale are less significant and local expertise and local presence is deemed to be more important.

8.2 Internal economies of scale

When the advantages of expanding the scale of operation accrue to just one firm, these economies are termed **internal**. They can be obtained in one plant, within a division, or across the whole company. The main internal economies are as follows:

- **Technical economies.** These relate to the scale of the production and are usually obtained in one plant. Large-scale operations may make greater use of advanced machinery. Some machines are only worth using beyond a minimum level of output which may be beyond the capacity of a small firm, for example, robots used in car assembly. Such equipment may facilitate the division of labour. In addition, more resources can be devoted to research in large firms, because the cost is borne over more units of output, and this may lead to further technical improvements and subsequent cost reductions for the whole company.
- **Financial economies.** It is usually easier for large firms with household names to borrow money from commercial banks and raise funds on the Stock Exchange. Similarly, their loans and overdrafts will probably be charged at lower interest rates because of their reputation and assets.
- **Trading economies.** Large firms may be able to secure advantages both when buying inputs and selling their outputs. They could employ specialist buyers and, through the quantity of their purchases, gain significant discounts from their suppliers.

  Similarly, bulk selling enables a large firm to make savings in distribution costs, the time and cost of salespeople and advertising expenses.

  These savings are more marked when many products are sold together in related markets. Thus, one big advantage of Nestlé's takeover of Rowntree Mackintosh was that the goods of each could be marketed together, with little extra total cost, thereby reducing the distribution costs of each product sold.

  If a large firm produces several products in different markets, then one failure is unlikely to cause the closure of the whole conglomerate. Thus, trading risks can be spread when a wide range of products are sold.
- **Managerial economies.** These are the many administrative gains that can be achieved when the scale of production grows. The need for management and supervision does not increase at the same rate as output. Specialists can be employed and their talents can be fully utilised in personnel, production, selling, accountancy and so on. Such organisational benefits may lower the indirect costs of production and lead to the efficient use of labour resources.

8.3 External economies of scale

It is possible for general advantages to be obtained by all of the firms in an industry, and these are classed as **external economies of scale**. Most of these occur when an industry is heavily concentrated in one area. The area may develop a reputation for success, for example, computers and electronics in Silicon Valley in California. There may be a pool of skilled labour that is available, and this may lower training costs for a firm. Specialised training may be provided locally in accordance with the industry's needs. This might be provided by a training board to which firms contribute to gain access to the available expertise. Furthermore, a localised industry may attract to it specialist suppliers of raw materials, components and services, who gain from a large market and achieve their own economies of scale, which are passed on through lower input prices. Occasionally, firms in an industry share their research and development facilities, because each firm individually could not bear the overheads involved but can fund a joint enterprise.

8.4 Diseconomies of scale

These exist when the average cost rises with increased production. If they are specific to one firm, they are categorised as internal.

- **Technical diseconomies.** The optimum technical size of plant may create large administrative overheads in its operation, thereby raising average total costs, even though the production cost is lowered.
- **Trading diseconomies.** With large-scale production, products may become standardised. This lack of individualism may reduce consumer choice and lead to lower sales. In addition, it may be difficult to quickly adapt mass-produced goods to changing market trends.
- **Managerial diseconomies.** As the chain of command becomes longer in an expanding hierarchy (when productive capacity grows), senior management may become too remote and lose control. This may lead to cross-inefficiency (complacency) in middle management and shop floor hostility. A concomitant of this is the generally poor state of labour relations in large organisations, which are more prone to industrial stoppages than small firms. This is partly because the trade unions are better organised. Other administrative weaknesses faced by increasingly large organisations are the prevalence of red tape and the conflict between departmental managers who have different objectives and priorities.

However, there may also be general disadvantages that afflict all firms as the scale of the industry grows. The main external diseconomy is technical. If a resource is over utilised then shortages may arise. A shortage of labour might lead to higher wages in order to attract new recruits, while a shortage of raw materials might lower output. Both changes would raise the average cost of production.

Test your understanding 21

In a company such as ESD, a calculator manufacturer, which of the following is not a source of economies of scale?

A The introduction of specialist capital equipment

B Bulk-buying

C The employment of specialist managers

D Cost savings resulting from new production techniques

Test your understanding answers

Test your understanding 1

C

When drawing a demand curve only the price is allowed to vary but all conditions of demand are kept constant.

Test your understanding 2

D

A larger population would presumably want more supplements, especially if they are older and more health conscious.

A and B would shift the curve to the left. C would result in movement along the curve but not a shift in the curve itself.

Test your understanding 3

D

Correct answer is D since a change in exchange rates effectively changes the price of foreign holidays and leads to a movement along the demand curve, not a shift in the curve itself.

Increased advertising should stimulate demand and lead to a shift to the right of the demand curve. A rise in the price of domestic holidays (a substitute product for overseas holidays) would lead to a contraction of demand for domestic holidays and a shift to the right of the demand curve for the substitute foreign holidays. A fall in disposable income would lead to a decrease in demand for overseas holidays as people have less money to spend on them.

Test your understanding 4

C

- % change in price = ($4.90 – $5)/$5 × 100 = –2%
- % change in demand = (105,000 – 100,000)/100,000 × 100 = +5%
- PED = (+5)/(–2) = –2.5

Test your understanding 5

D

- % change in price = ($0.90 – $1.00)/$1.00 × 100 = –10%
- PED = –1.5
- -1.5 = % change in demand / -10
- % change in demand = –1.5 × –10 = +15
- The price cut will thus raise demand and sales by 15%, that is, from 10,000 per month to 11,500 per month.

Test your understanding 6

The six factors given can be applied as follows:

1 **Proportion of income spent** – high petrol prices mean that petrol expenditure is a high proportion of most people's disposable income, which would suggest demand should be price **elastic**.

2 **Substitutes** – drivers cannot substitute a different fuel for use in their cars and so would not consider petrol to have any close substitutes. This would indicate that demand should be **inelastic**. (Note: you may have considered substitutes to driving here, such as using public transport. How close a substitute you consider this to be will depend on your location and the availability of public transport in your area. Most people would probably conclude that it is not a close substitute).

3 **Necessity** – many drivers consider using a car to be a necessity, suggesting demand will be **inelastic**.

4 **Habit** – many drivers get used to using their cars and would not switch to public transport, even if a good local service were available. This would again indicate **inelastic** demand.

5 **Time** – if a driver wanted to switch from a petrol powered vehicle to electricity or diesel, then they would need to sell their vehicle and buy another. This is unlikely to happen quickly suggesting **inelastic** demand.

6 **Definition of market** – If the demand is defined as petrol in general then the above arguments would indicate that demand would be **inelastic**. However, if we specify a particular brand of petrol, then there will be very close substitutes offered by other suppliers resulting in highly **elastic** demand.

Test your understanding 7

A

Changes in demand and price are inversely related. If the demand for a good is price elastic, the demand for it will change more than proportionately to the change in price. Thus, a price fall will raise unit sales and will increase total sales revenue.

Test your understanding 8

1 Downward sloping from top left to bottom right is the shape of a typical demand curve.

2 Price elasticity of demand shows the responsiveness of demand to a change in price.

3 The price elasticity of demand is –2 (i.e. + 20%/–10%). The demand for the good is therefore price elastic.

4 Income, substitutes, necessities, time, definition of the market.

5 A shift in demand (movement of the demand curve) occurs when the conditions of demand change, whereas an expansion of demand (movement along the demand curve) is the result of a fall in price.

Test your understanding 9

We can assess the elasticity of supply for milk as follows:

1 **Time** – in the short run the number of dairy cows available and their milk output is difficult to increase, indicating **inelastic** supply.

2 **Factors of production** – even though more workers could be employed to milk the cows and more land acquired for them to graze on, the main problem would be the fact that all of the milk of existing cows will be being sold already, so farmers would have to buy new cows from a different market. This would suggest supply was **inelastic**.

3 **Stock levels** – fresh milk cannot be stored for long so there will not be stocks that could be utilised, indicating **inelastic** supply.

4 **Number of firms in the industry** – this will depend on the country concerned and whether or not a system of quotas operates. In some markets, new firms may be able to set up quickly but the barriers in others may be significant.

In summary, one would expect supply to be inelastic, at least in the short run.

Test your understanding 10

1 The elasticity of supply is determined by time, the factors of production, stock levels and the number of firms in the industry.

2 Higher wages will cause the supply curve to shift leftwards (upwards) and parallel to the original supply.

Test your understanding 11

C

When the price of a good is held above the equilibrium price suppliers will be willing to supply more at this higher price. However, consumers will demand less. The combined effect of this is to create a surplus of the goods.

Test your understanding 12

C

When the price of a good is held below the equilibrium price, suppliers will be willing to supply less at this lower price. However, consumers will demand more. The combined effect of this is to create an expansion in demand, a shortage of the goods and excess demand.

Test your understanding 13

In the short term the price would rise:

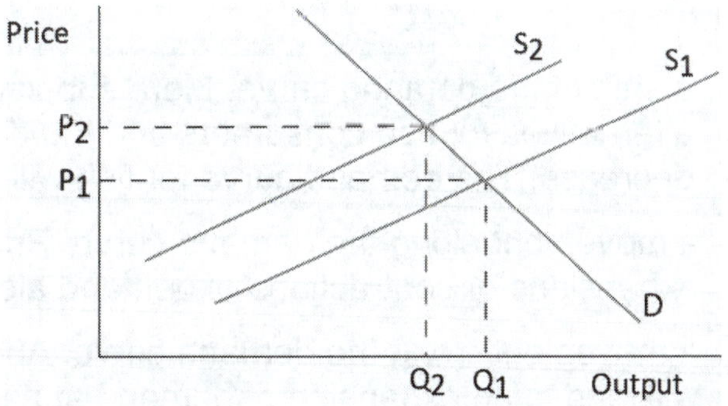

The poor harvest with shift the supply curve to the left but the demand curve is unlikely to move.

The equilibrium will move from P_1, Q_1 to P_2, Q_2, giving a price rise.

In the longer term, the price will fall as supply moves back to the right, either because it is the next harvest or because new suppliers are attracted to the industry by high prices (note this would involve repurposing land to grow coffee that was previously used for something else).

Test your understanding 14

B

The immediate effect will be to increase demand for the product. The demand curve will shift to the right (D_1) and a new equilibrium position will be created (P_2 and Q_2).

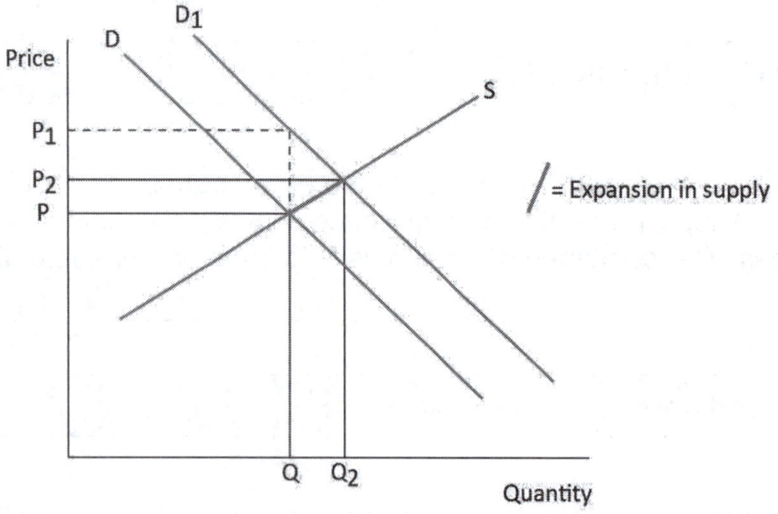

At the new equilibrium point, supply will be expanded and there will be a higher equilibrium price.

Note that if the increase in demand is maintained, the supplier may decide to increase supply to tap into the potential higher sales. This would take time and would mean that in the longer term, the supply curve itself would move and a further new equilibrium point would be created.

Test your understanding 15

(a) (i) a shift of the demand curve. More substitutes means more alternatives for fish consumers and the demand for fish will decrease. The demand curve for fish will shift to the left.

(ii) a movement along the demand curve. Price changes lead to expansions or contractions of demand along the curve.

(iii) a movement along the demand curve. An increase in supply will lead to an expansion of demand at a lower equilibrium price. If in doubt, draw an intersecting demand and supply curve and then draw the supply curve having moved to the right. Note where the new equilibrium point (intersection of demand and the new supply curve) is.

(iv) a shift of the demand curve. Changing income is a change in one of the factors of demand. Rising income will tend to lead to an increase in demand.

(b) (i) False; an elastic demand curve is fairly flat. When the supply curve shifts to the left, the equilibrium price will rise but not by a large amount due to the flatness of the demand curve.

(ii) False; when the supply curve shifts to the left, the impact on the equilibrium price depends on how steep the demand curve is.

(iii) False; price changes lead to movements along the demand curve, not movements of the curve itself.

(iv) True; advertising may get consumers to buy more at every price.

(v) False; a change in income would lead to a shift in the demand curve itself.

(vi) True; the longer the time period, the easier it is to find substitutes and the more likely consumers are to switch.

Test your understanding 16

D

D is the right answer since pure public goods are those that must be provided communally, e.g. defence or public transport.

A is imprecise as the government provides more than just public goods.

B is incorrect as public goods are likely to involve externalities.

C is incorrect since the consumption of a public good by one person must not, by definition, reduce the amount available for another person.

Test your understanding 17

A FALSE – The cost of packaging is paid for by the supplier and is therefore included in the supply curve.

B TRUE – Not only does the individual benefit from education but so does society as a whole through a more productive workforce.

C FALSE – The cost of the fine is met by the company and not by society as a whole. For something to be an externality, it has to be shared by society.

D TRUE – Society as a whole bears the cost of the pollution, in terms of replanting forests, the lost utility of their enjoyment and the negative impact it has on the environment.

Test your understanding 18

A Street lighting FALSE

B Education TRUE

C Healthcare TRUE

D Defence FALSE

Education and healthcare result in positive externalities but can be provided by the private sector are often purchased by individuals – they are merit goods.

Street lighting and defence would not be provided effectively by the private sector due to the problems of charging for them; non-rivalry, non-exclusivity, free rider problem – they would be classified as public goods rather than merit goods.

Test your understanding 19

A

Because a commodity is consumed by everyone (e.g. food), it does not follow that it has any special features such that it cannot be produced efficiently in a competitive market in the private sector. All other responses are valid reasons why a good or service should be produced wholly, or partly, in the public sector.

Test your understanding 20

A

The free market price will not change as it is already above the minimum. B confused a maximum price with a minimum price, and C and D refer to a minimum price set above free market price.

Test your understanding 21

D

Economies of scale are the cost savings resulting from any activity or process that is made possible by increasing the scale of output. This applies to responses (A), (B) and (C), since these are made possible as the size of businesses increases. Response (D), however, is incorrect since it refers to technical change, and this would reduce costs for all producers, large and small.

Chapter

3

Financial Context of Business I

Chapter learning objectives

On completion of their studies, students should be able to:

- explain the role of various financial assets, markets and institutions in assisting organisations to manage their liquidity position and to provide an economic return to providers of liquidity
- explain the role of commercial banks in the process of credit creation and in determining the structure of interest rates and the roles of the 'central bank' in ensuring liquidity.

1 Introduction – The financial system

1.1 The financial system

'The financial system' is an umbrella term covering the following:

- Financial markets – e.g. stock exchanges, money markets.
- Financial institutions – e.g. banks, building societies, insurance companies and pension funds.
- Financial assets and liabilities – e.g. mortgages, bonds, bills and equity shares.

1.2 Financial markets

The financial markets can be divided into different types, depending on the products being issued/bought/sold:

- Capital markets which consist of stock-markets for shares and bond markets.
- Money markets, which provide short-term (< 1 year) debt financing and investment.
- Commodity markets, which facilitate the trading of commodities (e.g. oil, metals and agricultural produce).
- Derivatives markets, which provide instruments for the management of financial risk, such as options and futures contracts.
- Insurance markets, which facilitate the redistribution of various risks.
- Foreign exchange markets, which facilitate the trading of foreign exchange.

1.3 Financial intermediaries

Within each sector of the economy (households, firms and governmental organisations) there are times when there are cash surpluses and times when there are deficits.

- In the case of surpluses, the party concerned will seek to invest/deposit/lend funds to earn an economic return.
- In the case of deficits, the party will seek to borrow funds to manage their liquidity position.

Faced with a desire to lend or borrow, there are three choices open to the end-users of the financial system:

(a) Lenders and borrowers contact each other directly

There are high costs involved with this approach, as well as the risks of default and inherent inefficiencies.

(b) Lenders and borrowers use an organised financial market

For example, an individual may purchase corporate bonds from a recognised bond market. If this is a new issue of bonds by a company looking to raise funds, then the individual has effectively lent money to the company.

If the individual wishes to recover their funds before the redemption date on the bond, then they can sell the bond to another investor.

(c) Lenders and borrowers use intermediaries

In this case the lender obtains an asset which cannot usually be traded but only returned to the intermediary. Such assets could include a bank deposit account, pension fund rights, etc.

The borrower will typically have a loan provided by an intermediary.

Financial intermediaries have a number of important roles.

- Risk reduction

  By lending to a wide variety of individuals and businesses, financial intermediaries reduce the risk of a single default resulting in total loss of assets.

- Aggregation

  By pooling many small deposits, financial intermediaries are able to make much larger advances than would be possible for most individuals.

- Maturity transformation

  Most borrowers wish to borrow in the long-term whilst most savers are unwilling to lock up their money for the long-term. Financial intermediaries, by developing a floating pool of deposits, are able to satisfy both the needs of lenders and borrowers.

- Financial intermediation

  Financial intermediaries bring together lenders and borrowers through a process known as financial intermediation.

Test your understanding 1

Most lenders wish to offer their funds for the short term whereas most borrowers want to borrow over the longer term. Resolving this mismatch is known as:

A risk reduction

B aggregation

C maturity transformation

D pooling

2 Liquidity surpluses and deficits

The lack of synchronisation between payments and receipts has a variety of origins and affects both businesses and governments.

2.1 Business

Businesses may find that flows of payments and flows of receipts rarely match. If payments (e.g. to suppliers for product) tend to occur before the associated receipts (e.g. from customers), this may be referred to as the cash flow problem and can occur in the short, medium and long run.

Receipts

Receipts for the business come mainly from sales revenue. The pattern of receipts will depend on the nature of the business (e.g. whether there is a seasonal aspect to trade), the system of invoicing (e.g. monthly), credit terms and whether customers stick to the payment terms.

Payments

In the short term, businesses have day-to-day costs to meet such as wages and salaries, and buying raw materials. In the medium and longer term, firms need to pay for capital expenditure and research and development.

Dealing with a lack of synchronisation

Deficits – when cash outflows outweigh cash inflows for a period of time, businesses may need to access financing solutions to match the time period of the deficits:

- Short term – e.g. overdraft facility from the bank
- Medium term – e.g. leasing to help acquire a specific asset, usually provided by a finance company that specialises in leasing. For example, Volkswagen financial services can provide lease finance to acquire a Volkswagen car.
- Long term – e.g. equity through the issue of new shares, bank loans.

Surpluses – similarly, when the business has surpluses of cash, they may look to invest the surplus for an appropriate time period.

- Short term – e.g. instant access deposit account with the bank
- Medium term – e.g. purchase medium-term bonds from the bond market. Bonds can be purchased through a broker or directly from companies / governments.
- Long term – e.g. purchase another company.

Matching the time periods of the cash position to the solution is important. For instance, having an overdraft facility that could be taken away at short notice would be a risky method of funding a long-term shortage of cash. Tying up a short-term cash surplus in an investment that cannot be accessed until a long period of time has passed means that cash would not necessarily be available when it is needed.

2.2 Government

Receipts

The government may have some income from profitable state industries or charges made to consumers for state-provided services, but the vast bulk of its income comes from taxation. The main sources of taxation revenue are:

- a range of indirect taxes (sales taxes) such as value added tax and excise duties on alcohol, petrol and tobacco products
- direct taxes on individuals, most importantly income tax and social security taxes
- direct taxes on business organisations such as corporation tax.

Some of these flows of taxation revenue are quite regular, such as income tax paid through the pay-as-you-earn system in the United Kingdom, but many are not. The flow of receipts from corporation tax, for example, can be very uneven with significant payments towards the end of the tax year. This, as with households, implies a problem of synchronisation of payments and receipts.

Payments

In the short term, Governments also have day-to-day costs to meet such as wages and salaries. In the medium and longer term, Governments need to pay for major investment, such as school and hospital building.

Dealing with a lack of synchronisation

The credit and savings needs of government in this respect are often met by the central bank, one of whose functions is to act as banker to the government and to manage the government's finances.

Since it is possible for governments to be net savers or net borrowers over very long periods of time, they may need the services of financial intermediaries over that period.

Governments also have the option, although it is a controversial one, of increasing taxation revenues to help fund higher levels of Government expenditure.

2.3 Linkages

The above inflows and outflows are obviously linked. For example

- In autumn 2021, the UK government announced a 1.25% increase in the rate of National Insurance contributions to be paid to the Government by employees, employers and the self-employed from April 2022.
- This was to help fund increases in the Government provision of social care services.

Further detail on finance for business

Finance for business

There are financial problems for businesses when there is a lack of synchronisation in the flows of payments and receipts. The financial needs of business vary and take a variety of forms. In general their needs can be classified as:

- funds to finance day-to-day business including payments for wages and salaries, raw materials and components – working capital
- funds to finance the purchase of new capital equipment or to finance acquisitions and mergers – investment capital
- suitable instruments for investing any surplus funds as part of the asset management function.

In acquiring funds to finance their activities, businesses have a large range of different types of financial instruments from which to choose. But in making the choice, businesses will follow a general rule that the instrument should be appropriate to the use to which the funds are to be put. Thus:

- short-term instruments (e.g. overdrafts) should be chosen to finance the short-term needs of working capital
- long-term instruments (e.g. corporate debt) should be chosen to finance the long-term needs of investment.

With the investment of surplus funds, a similar rule is generally adopted and the instrument chosen will be balanced between profitability and the needs to match the term of the instrument to the period during which the funds will not be needed.

In most economies and for most businesses, the bulk of the financial needs of those businesses are met by internally generated funds. For the rest of their financial needs, businesses can employ a range of financial instruments.

The most important of these are:

Short- and medium-term instruments

These are typically acquired from the money markets. The most important are:

- short-term certificates of deposit, which are deposits that will be repaid with interest at a predetermined point in time
- bills of exchange, which are typically of 3–6 months duration and are sold with a promise to repay at that date
- commercial papers, which are debt securities issued by the largest companies

- trade credit, which allows business to delay payment for raw materials, components, business services, etc.
- leasing and hire purchase.

Financial intermediaries have thus built up a wide range of instruments to meet the short- and medium-term financial needs of business. However, there has been a persistent complaint in many countries over recent years that the system has been poor at meeting the financial needs of small and newly established businesses. This explains the growth of various government measures designed specifically to help the small business sector and of peer to peer funding (where lenders and borrowers are matched via online services) and crowdfunding (raising small amounts of money from lots of investors, usually via the internet).

Long-term instruments

In meeting their long-term financial needs, businesses have a broad choice between two forms of long-term finance:

- equity finance
- debt finance.

Equity finance is available to limited liability companies through the issue of shares. For publicly quoted companies, additional shares ('rights issues') can be issued via the Stock Market. This is discussed in the next section.

The alternative is long-term borrowing of debt finance. This might be done by issuing long-term corporate bonds. Funds may also be raised by forms of Preference Shares on which fixed rates of interest are paid and mortgaged.

Mezzanine finance, in effect, combines aspects of both debt and equity finance. Although the finance is initially given as a loan (debt capital), the lender has the rights to convert to an equity interest in the company if the loan is not paid back in time and in full.

Test your understanding 2

ABC Chocolate manufactures a range of different chocolate novelties for sale in major supermarkets. It has seasonal trade and finds the period before Christmas difficult from a cash management point of view as it has to pay out wages and for ingredients before the holiday period but often has to wait until the New Year before receiving payment from major customers.

Which of the following would be a suitable way of managing this cash flow problem?

A Issue new equity shares

B Overdraft

C Leasing arrangement

D Mortgage

Test your understanding 3

In recent years FGH, a high-end furniture retailer, has appeared to favour mezzanine finance to alternative forms of finance. What is meant by the term 'mezzanine finance'?

A Short-term loans to help a firm through a cash flow crisis

B Foreign currency loans

C Loans by non-financial institutions

D Finance that is neither pure debt not pure equity

3 Financial products

3.1 Main considerations

There are a wide range of contracts and financial instruments issued by financial institutions for lending/borrowing. (Note that the term 'financial claims' can be used to refer to both).

Whether borrowing or lending the main considerations when choosing which product to use are as follows:

- Yield (return earned) / cost

  For example, investing in certificates of deposit typically gives a lower return than investing in equities. (However, see the comments on risk below.)

  Note that the two parties to a financial instrument will have differing points of view. The party with surplus funds will seek a yield (return), whereas the party with a deficit will pay a cost. For instance, a bank loan provides a yield to the bank and comes at a cost to the lender.

- Risk

  The main determinant of cost (yield) is risk. For example, if a company wishes to raise funds by an issue of bonds, then the yield it must offer to investors (or the cost to the company) must be sufficient to compensate them for the perceived risks of investing in the company bonds relative to a safer investment.

- The amounts involved/divisibility

  For example, the price of an Amazon share in September 2020 was as high as $3,531. An individual investor with only $2,000 to invest would not have been able to purchase even one share at that time.

- The time period the funds are required/available for

  For example, treasury bills usually have an initial maturity of 91 days.

- Liquidity

  This looks at how easy it is to sell the asset to release funds early if required. For example, shares in an unquoted company are much harder to sell to release funds than Treasury bills, which have a recognised market.

- Transaction costs

  For example, the arrangement fees for mortgages.

3.2 Capital and money markets

The time to maturity has traditionally been used to make a distinction between 'capital' markets and 'money' markets:

- Capital markets – maturities > 1 year – examples include equities, bonds and mortgages
- Money markets – maturities < 1 year – examples include certificates of deposit and bills of exchange.

3.3 Ordinary shares ('equity')

Ownership of companies is conveyed via ordinary shares. Ordinary shareholders also have voting rights. Shares have a nominal or par value (e.g. '£1 ords'), which is usually different from the market value (for traded shares). Companies often raise funds through the issue of shares.

Characteristics	
Return	• Potentially very high returns if the company is profitable. • Returns will be in the form of dividends and/or increases in share prices.
Risk	• Shares carry high risk. • If company profits fall, then there is a danger of zero or low dividends, combined with a fall in share value. Furthermore, if, in a worst-case scenario, the company is liquidated, then the shareholders only get paid if there is any money left after settling all other claims. In such situations, the shareholders usually get nothing.
Timescales	• The company usually has no intention of buying back the shares, so equity is considered long-term.
Liquidity	• For unquoted companies it is very difficult to sell the shares but for quoted companies the shares are highly liquid, so investors can "cash in" at any point.

3.4 Bonds

Just as the total equity of a company is split into shares, loans may be broken down into smaller units (e.g. one bond may have a nominal or par value of $100). Different varieties include debentures and loan stock and may be issued by companies, local authorities and governmental organisations.

Bonds will normally have a nominal value (e.g. $100), a coupon (interest) rate (e.g. 5%) and redemption terms (e.g. redeem at nominal value in 2015). The annual interest is the product of the nominal value and the coupon rate (e.g. $100 × 5% = $5 per annum).

Characteristics	
Return	• Typically, bonds have low returns because they are a lower risk investment for the investor. • Returns will be in the form of interest and (possibly) gain on redemption.
Risk	• Bonds are usually lower risk than equity for the investor. • For example, the bonds may be secured (an asset is used as collateral for the bond) and the interest rate fixed. • Note: you can get high-risk, unsecured ("junk") bonds as well.

Characteristics	
Timescales	• The maturity is defined on the bond and varies from very short term (e.g. Treasury Bills) to long term (e.g. 25-year corporate bonds). • Some bonds are redeemable (will be repaid on a fixed date) and some are irredeemable (do not get repaid – instead, interest is paid into perpetuity).
Liquidity	• If the bonds are unquoted then the investor has no choice except to wait for redemption. • However, if quoted, then they will be easier to liquidate by selling on bond markets. • For example, government bonds are usually very liquid. • Note: high risk bonds will be sold at a large discount on face value.

3.5 Certificates of deposit ('CD')

A CD states that a deposit has been made with a bank for a fixed period of time, at the end of which it will be repaid with interest (known as the coupon rate).

Characteristics	
Return	Very low returns (low coupon rate) due to low risk for the investor.
Risk	Very safe.
Timescales	3 and 6 month maturities are the most common.
Liquidity	Can be readily sold on money markets.

3.6 Credit agreements

A credit agreement is an arrangement where one party borrows or takes possession of something in return for future payment. For example – credit cards and store hire purchase contracts.

Characteristics	
Return	• Usually high interest rates. • For example, store cards typically cost around 25 – 30% per annum.
Risk	• The credit card company faces the risk of default – that the cardholder will not repay the amount borrowed as such cards are usually unsecured.

Characteristics	
Timescales	• Usually intended to be short-term, although some individuals can get into financial difficulties by running up large debts on credit cards that they cannot repay.
Liquidity	• The debt cannot be resold by the lender but the borrower may be able to repay early if funds permit.

3.7 Mortgages

A mortgage is a loan to finance the purchase of property, usually with specified payment periods and interest rates.

Characteristics	
Return	• The interest cost is usually relatively low, as the mortgage will be secured on the property bought.
Risk	• As stated above, usually considered low risk. • However, a fall in house prices would reduce the value of security offered. (e.g. in the 1990s this gave rise to 'negative equity' in the UK).
Timescales	• Long-term – e.g. between 10 and 35 years.
Liquidity	• Mortgages can be resold by the lender via Collateralised Debt obligations (CDOs). These CDOs were at the heart of the financial crisis of 2008/09.

3.8 Bills of exchange

A bill of exchange is usually issued by companies to finance trade and promises to pay a certain sum at a fixed future date to the other party. In many respects, it is very similar to a post-dated cheque.

- When a financial intermediary accepts a bill of exchange, it is effectively loaning money to a private trader upon promise of a refund by another trader.
- The bill is a contract between the two traders, with the buyer promising to pay a sum of money in return for goods on a certain date to the seller.
- The seller may sell the bill or cash to a financial intermediary who will discount it. A bank will discount the bill by paying less than the face value, knowing that it will receive the full value at a later date. The difference between the two sums of money is the interest.

Characteristics	
Return	• As stated above there is usually no interest paid but the return is the difference between the discounted amount for which it is sold/bought and the full face value on redemption. • For example, a bill bought for £4,900 is redeemed for £5,000 after three months. Thus, £100 profit is made on an outlay of £4,900 over three months, giving a return of approximately 8.4 per cent per annum.
Risk	• The level of risk varies – some bills may be guaranteed by banks.
Timescales	• Short-term – 3 and 6 month maturities are the most common.
Liquidity	• Can be resold on money markets.

3.9 Inter-relationships

All the markets in a money market closely inter-mesh with each other and in that way the market may be regarded as an entity. The players are the same and they pass the ball between each other.

e.g

Illustration 1 – Inter-relationships within money markets

- A large company might deposit $500,000 with Bull's Bank, which issues it with a CD.
- Bull's Bank then looks at the local authority market, decides that rates there are rather low, and instead lends the money for a week on the inter-bank market to another bank that is short of funds.
- A week later local authority rates have improved and Bull's Bank lends the $500,000 to a big city council.
- Meanwhile, the large company has decided to bring forward an investment project and wants its $500,000 quickly to help pay for some sophisticated new electronic equipment. It sells the CD to a bank, which might either carry it to maturity or sell it to any of the banks – except Bull's Bank.

All these transactions, with the possible exception of the CD deals, will have taken place through a broker who sits at the end of a telephone switching the funds from one market to another as rates move and potential borrowers and lenders acquaint the broker with information about their requirements.

Test your understanding 4

TUL have surplus funds that they wish to invest. Which of the following would be the least risky investment?

A Certificates of deposit from a global bank

B Equity shares in a new growing company

C Unsecured loan stock

D National lottery tickets

4 Calculating yields on financial products

4.1 Equity

The total return to shareholders will incorporate both dividends and growth in the share price.

Dividend yield is measured as:

$$\text{Dividend yield} = \frac{\text{dividend per ordinary share}}{\text{market price of the share}} \times 100\%$$

Thus if a company is paying 30 cents per ordinary share and each share has market price of $7.50 then the dividend yield would be:

$$\frac{30 \text{ cents}}{750 \text{ cents}} \times 100\% = 4\%$$

This figure looks only at the current dividend so does not incorporate future growth expectations.

4.2 Bonds

There are a number of different ways of calculating the yield on bonds:

(a) the bill rate

(b) the running rate or interest yield

(c) the gross redemption yield.

Illustration 2 – Yields on bonds

Consider a bond with characteristics as follows:

- Nominal value $100
- Coupon rate 8%
- Redemption terms – to be redeemed at par in 5 years' time
- Current market value – $108.40

Calculate the following yields:

(a) Bill rate

(b) Running yield

(c) Gross redemption yield.

Solution

(a) The bill rate – this is just another name for the coupon rate, here 8%.

This rate does not consider the market value of the bond or the capital gain/loss on redemption.

(b) The running yield, also known as the "interest yield", given by

Running yield = (annual interest/market value) × 100% = ($8/$108.40) × 100% = 7.38%

If you bought the bond for $108.40, then annual interest of $8 gives a return of 7.38% on your investment each year. Note that this approach takes into account the market value of the bond but ignores the impact of a capital gain or loss on redemption.

(c) The gross redemption yield

The gross redemption yield gives the annualised overall return to the investor and incorporates both interest and capital gains and losses. For the above bond, the gross redemption yield is 6%. Note this is lower than the running yield because it incorporates the loss you would make on redemption – you bought the bond for $108.40 but it gets redeemed at par value (nominal value) of $100.

Calculation of gross redemption yield is outside the syllabus but the principles are still useful to see:

The redemption yield is the required return of investors, which is determined primarily by their perceived risks but also by interest rates.

This then determines the market price as follows:

Market price = Present value of future receipts (interest and redemption proceeds), discounted at the investors' required return

To calculate the redemption yield involves doing this process in reverse – given the market value, what discount rate satisfies MV = PV of future receipts?

Considerations of the use of different financial products for business funding and calculations of their costs / yields form part of your later studies, particularly in F2 Advanced Financial Reporting and F3 Financial Strategy.

4.3 The role of risk

As stated above, the main determinant of the overall yield to an investor is their perceived risk.

This in turn determines the market price for the bond or share.

Suppose a company is currently paying a dividend of 20 cents per share and is expected to do so in the future. If the share price is $1, then the net dividend yield will be 20%. Suppose that adverse environmental factors then cause investors to consider the shares more risky so that they now want a return of 25%. If the company still pays 20 cents per share, then the only way the yield can rise to 25% is if the share price falls:

$$\text{Net dividend yield \%} = \frac{\text{annual dividend}}{\text{market value}} \times 100$$

$$25 = \frac{20}{\text{market value}} \times 100$$

This would give a revised market value of 80 cents.

The order is very important here:

Risk determines required return, which determines the market value.

4.4 The term structure of interest rates and yield curves

Some people believe that the annual interest rate on a loan remains the same regardless of period of the loan. So, if the interest rate charged on a two-year loan was 5% then it would be 5% on a six-year loan of the same risk class.

However, lenders in the financial markets normally demand higher interest rates on loans as the term (i.e. length of time) to maturity increases – that is there is a 'term structure' of the interest rate. The yield curve shows this relationship.

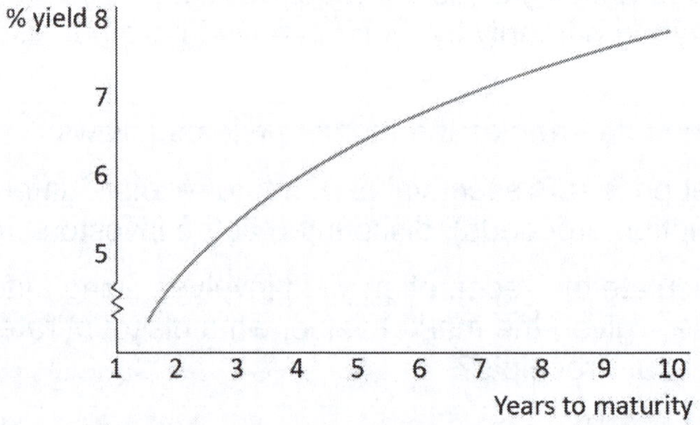

The longer the term of a security, the higher will be its gross redemption yield – the return to the investor.

The normal shape of the yield curve would suggest that it is cheaper to borrow in the shorter term. For example, if a firm wishes to borrow for ten years, then it would be cheaper to take out a five-year loan and then replace it with another five year loan (in five years, time) than to take out a single ten-year loan.

The main reasons why some firms do not do this are:

- Risk – the ten-year loan could be arranged with a fixed rate for the whole term. If two five-year loans are used, then the rate for the second loan would depend on prevailing rates in five years' time, which could be higher than current rates.
- Arrangement fees.

One way of linking risk and yield structures for bonds is through credit rating agencies.

Credit rating agencies

The role of credit rating agencies

If a company wants to assess whether a firm that owes them money is likely to default on the debt, a key source of information is a credit rating agency.

They provide vital information on creditworthiness to:

- potential investors
- regulators of investing bodies
- the firm itself.

The assessment of creditworthiness

A large number of agencies can provide information on smaller firms, but for larger firms credit assessments are usually carried out by one of the international credit rating agencies. The three largest international agencies are Standard and Poor's, Moody's and Fitch.

Certain factors have been shown to have a particular correlation with the likelihood that a company will default on its obligations:

- The magnitude and strength of the company's cash flows.
- The size of the debt relative to the asset value of the firm.
- The volatility of the firm's asset value.
- The length of time the debt has to run.

Using this and other data, firms are scored and rated on a scale, where AAA is the least risky (investment grade, which covers AAA to BBB-) with grades down to C and even D on some scales. The further down the rating, the more risky the investment is considered to be. Any bond with a rating of BB+ or below is considered to be a "junk bond".

Credit spreads

There is no way to tell in advance which firms will default on their obligations and which won't. As a result, to compensate lenders for this risk, firms generally pay a "spread" or premium over the risk-free rate of interest.

The yield on a corporate bond is therefore given by:

Required yield on corporate bond = Yield on equivalent treasury bond + credit spread

Credit rating agencies publish tables of credit spreads detailing the premium for bonds of differing risks and maturities.

For example, suppose a company wants to issue some 5 year bonds with a credit rating of BB. The required yield would be made up of two elements.

- The expected yield on the yield curve for 5 years – suppose this is 4%.
- A premium (the credit spread) to reflect the maturity of 5 years and the credit rating of BB – suppose this is 2.5%.
- The required yield on the new bonds would thus be 4% + 2.5% = 6.5%.

Test your understanding 5

Plantain has $100 stock with a market price of $80 and a dividend of $5. It will generate a yield of:

A 5%

B 8%

C 6.25%

D 12.5%

Test your understanding 6

Suppose a company wants to issue some bonds and is concerned about the level of return it will receive. Which of the following yields does not need knowledge of a bond's market value to calculate it?

A Running yield

B Gross redemption yield

C Bill rate

D Interest yield

5 Understanding interest rates

5.1 A central rate of interest

It is clear that there is no such thing as **the** rate of interest because there are many rates of interest, which reflect varying risk. However, there has always been a central rate around which the others vary and to which governments have paid great attention. This has usually been the rate at which the central bank would lend to the money market (see below for further detail on how central banks set interest rates).

In 2017 in the UK, the "base rate" was moved from 0.25% to 0.5% and in 2018 it rose again to 0.75%. This was reduced back to 0.25% in March 2020 with an aim of stabilising the economy during the coronavirus pandemic and was reduced again to a historic low of 0.1% just over a week later. For comparison, the best fixed mortgage rates available to consumers in April 2021 (while the central rate was still 0.1%) was around 1.7%, reflecting the higher risk of lending to consumers. Rates were increased from late 2021 and through 2022 to curb high inflation levels once the economy started to grow as the pandemic impact reduced.

5.2 Real and nominal interest rates

The real interest rate puts interest rates in the context of inflation. It shows the interest rate, allowing for inflation.

For example, suppose inflation is 3% and you deposit \$100 in a deposit account paying 4% per annum.

- The "nominal" or "money" rate of interest is 4% so you will end up with \$104 in the account.
- However, you are not 4% better off. 3% of the increase merely covers inflation so you will feel that your wealth has only increased by around 1%. This is the "real" rate of interest received.

Note: You will not be expected to do calculations on real and money rates. However, the correct way of determining the real rate in the above example would be

$$1 + r = \frac{1 + m}{1 + i}$$

where r = real rate, m = money rate and i = level of inflation

$1 + r = 1.04/1.03 = 1.0097$, giving $r = 0.0097$ or 0.97% (close to 1%)

When the nominal rate of interest is higher than the rate of inflation there is a positive real rate. This means that borrowers are losing in real terms but savers are gaining.

Conversely, when the rate of inflation exceeds the nominal rate of interest there is a negative real rate of interest. In such a case, borrowers gain and savers lose.

For decision-making by individuals and businesses, it is the real rate of interest that is the important variable.

Test your understanding 7

Daniella has received a salary increase from €30,000 to €36,000 per annum. Given inflation for the next year is expected to be 5%, what percentage increase in salary has Daniella received in ***real*** terms?

Answer _______________% (give your answer as a percentage to one decimal place)

Test your understanding 8

AUSL is considering an investment within the year. They are concerned about interest rate volatility. Which of the following are the likely consequences of a fall in interest rates?

(i) A rise in the demand for consumer goods.

(ii) A fall in investment.

(iii) A rise in government spending.

(iv) A rise in the demand for housing.

A (i) and (ii) only

B (i), (ii) and (iii) only

C (i), (iii) and (iv) only

D (ii), (iii) and (iv) only

Test your understanding 9

The following financial data refer to an economy for the period 2011–2016.

	2011	*2012*	*2013*	*2014*	*2015*	*2016*
Interest rates						
Bank base rate (%)	8.5	7.0	5.5	6.8	5.8	6.0
Instant access account deposit rate (%)	6.3	4.9	3.8	4.2	2.8	2.3
90-day-access account deposit rate (%)	8.8	6.2	4.5	4.9	3.9	3.9
Mortgage rate	11.0	9.4	7.7	8.4	7.0	7.4
Share prices						
Stock market index	2,521	2,900	2,919	2,314	3,711	4,710
Inflation						
Percentage rise in consumer prices	4.0	1.6	2.3	3.5	2.7	2.7

Required:

Using both your knowledge of economic theory and material contained in the table:

(a) With respect to the data given:

(i) using the bank base rate calculate the real rate of interest for 2013

(ii) calculate the real mortgage rate of interest for 2014

(iii) state whether real share prices rose or fell between 2012 and 2013. **(3 marks)**

(b) State whether each of the following are true or false.

(i) Rising real interest rates will encourage savings and investment.

(ii) Interest rates will only affect business investment if that investment is financed by borrowing.

(iii) Rising interest rates in a country tend to raise the exchange rate for that country's currency.

(iv) Producers of consumer durable goods are more sensitive to changes in interest rates than supermarkets.

(v) Central banks would not increase the money supply and raise interest rates at the same time. **(5 marks)**

(c) State whether the effect of a rise in interest rates will be to

(i) increase or decrease government spending

(ii) reflate or deflate the economy. **(2 marks)**

(Total marks = 10)

Note: you will learn more about the effects of interest rate changes in a later chapter.

6 Financial intermediaries

6.1 Introduction

It is common to split financial intermediaries into two types:

1 Deposit-taking institutions (DTIs), such as banks and building societies

2 Non-deposit-taking institutions (NDTIs), such as insurance companies, pension funds, unit trust and investment trusts.

This distinction is made for three reasons:

- The deposit liabilities of DTIs form the bulk of a country's money supply (see below) so DTIs are more important to government economic policy and, hence, Central bank attention.
- DTIs are subject to more regulation.
- The level customers deposit is more discretionary than other products (e.g. once an insurance contract is entered into, the customer is committed to making monthly payments).

6.2 Banks

The main business of banks includes offering financial services, taking deposits and extending credit. In the UK, their activities are regulated by the Financial Conduct Authority (FCA), formerly the Financial Services Authority (FSA)). Global equivalents of such an organisation being e.g. the Securities and Exchange Commission (SEC) in the United States and the China Securities Regulatory Commission (CSRC).

Banking activities are traditionally split between the following:

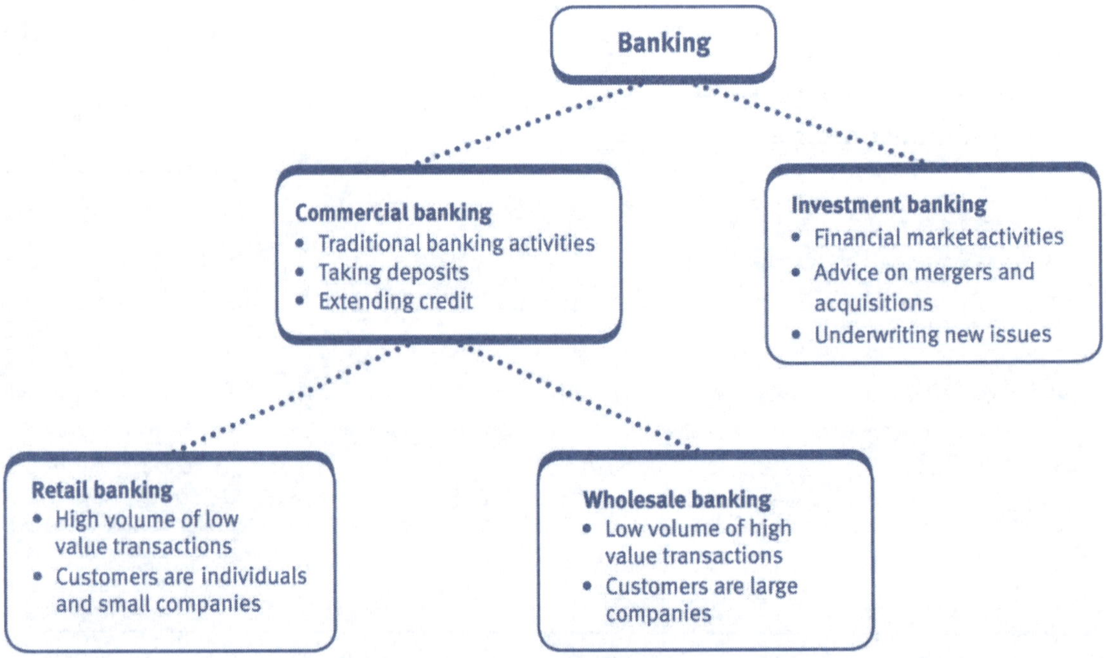

Financial organisations

Retail banks

The retail or commercial banks' main activities are as follows.

Safeguarding money

Customers' deposits are kept in deposit and current accounts.

- Deposit (time) accounts are operated for savers who receive interest for storing their money at the bank. The rate of interest received varies with movements in the bank's base rate. If interest rates in the money market rise, then bank base rate is increased so depositors receive more interest on their deposits.
- Current (sight) accounts do not usually gain significant amounts of interest, although they do provide the holder with instant access to their funds. Customers can settle debts by using debit cards or electronic banking, and also withdraw cash on demand (i.e. no charges) as long as they stay in credit or within an approved overdraft level.
- The distinction between deposit and current accounts is becoming less clear-cut, as banks devise new financial instruments. For example, high interest current accounts continue the traditional features of deposit and current accounts and were invented to attract specific customers.

Transferring money

Banks move cash between their branches when required. In operating the clearing system, they transfer money between accounts within a branch, between different branches and between different banks.

- Each clearing bank has an account at the central bank. In effect, every time one of a bank's customers authorises a payment, which is presented at another bank, the payer's bank has its account at the central bank debited. Conversely, the recipient's bank has its account credited. In practice, at daily clearing, each bank totals up its accounts with every other bank and the net amount owed (or gained) is deducted from (or credited to) its account.
- The introduction of electronic banking has meant that this process has become significantly quicker, with almost instant clearing on many transactions.

Lending money

When goldsmiths realised that only a small proportion of their gold deposits was required daily, they decided to put the gold to work by lending and charging interest. The banks perform a similar profit-earning function by providing loans and overdrafts to customers. Generally, the rates of interest charged to businesses are less than those levied on personal borrowing. Such loans generally take two forms:

- When a customer has a current account, they might seek an overdraft. Usually, overdrafts are for short periods of time, allowing customers to make payments to a value greater than the funds in the current account. Interest is charged on a daily basis on the actual amount by which the customer is overdrawn. This can be a cheaper form of borrowing, if prior authority is given by the bank and the overdraft is used intermittently. Overdrafts are more informal and more flexible than loans, although penalty rates of interest may be charged for unauthorised borrowing.
- Loans. These tend to be for larger amounts and over longer periods of time. They are often tied to particular purchases. Their interest rates may be cheaper than those of overdrafts, especially when the borrowing is secured against an asset, so if the borrowing is needed throughout the time period in question, they should be cheaper than an overdraft.

Facilitating trade

Modern banks provide numerous services, which facilitate easier trading. The accepting of commercial bills and the provision of foreign exchange make international trade smoother in operation. Similarly, the development of advisory services for small firms, the participation in loan guarantee schemes and the giving of financial advice and market information encourage domestic trade.

Wholesale banks

In addition to retail banks there are also wholesale banks. These are also known as investment or secondary banks. The most common of these banks are:

- merchant banks such as J.P. Morgan
- overseas banks operating in countries other than their home country.

Merchant banks are banking brokers who bring together the lenders and borrowers of large sums of money, for example businesses. Merchant banks:

- Operate in a high-risk area and deal in very large deposits and loans primarily from industry and commerce. They often borrow from each other on what is known as the inter-bank market.
- Advise companies on money management.

- Negotiate bills of exchange. A bill of exchange is a trading contract, usually for three months, upon which a trader can usually get credit.
- Underwrite the launching of new shares, for example J.P. Morgan was the underwriter for Zoom shares.
- Supervise company takeovers on the stock market.
- As accepting houses, they guarantee commercial bills for companies.

They are thus wholesalers of money in the system.

Also, overseas banks now operate in most financial centres and their banking activity is mainly related to:

- financing international trade
- international capital movements
- international currency transactions.

In practice, the distinction between retail and wholesale banks has become less clear over time. Many banks that previously operated only as retail banks have taken on many of the functions of wholesale banks, especially in relational to international transactions. They have often achieved this by setting up or acquiring specialist subsidiary companies.

Non-bank financial intermediaries

These institutions are not officially authorised by the Bank of England, although they are informally watched. However, they often perform banking tasks and since financial deregulation in the 1980s, they have competed with banks for business. The best-known type of non-bank in the United Kingdom is the building society, owned by their members ('mutual' building societies). They tend to 'borrow short' and 'lend long' (via mortgages), profiting from interest-rate differentials and fulfilling the function of maturity transformation.

Since the 1980s, building societies have become more independent and competitive. No longer are society interest rates kept in harmony by the Building Societies Association, so there is more competition between them. In addition, competition with banks and other authorised institutions has increased, particularly in home loans and high-interest, instant-access accounts. However, building societies are still constrained by the requirement that they can lend only a maximum of 5 per cent of their assets for personal finance. Many building societies have become banks in recent years.

Another trend has been the growth of financial conglomerates. Formerly, financial institutions tended to specialise, for example building societies and mortgages. Now they are branching out into non-traditional lines of business. The diversification has also brought estate agents, unit trusts and big High Street retailers into financial intermediaries. In the mid-1990s, several building societies decided to 'go public' and become banks. The process takes a while, such that it was not until 1997 that the Halifax, Woolwich and Alliance & Leicester emerged on to the stock market. Thus, the distinction between what banks provide and what building societies provide is now blurred and institutions providing the entire range of financial services are dominating the financial system.

Many other financial institutions exist, mostly providing specialist financial services. The most important of these are:

- Investment and unit trusts, which accept savings by selling shares (or units) and invest these savings, mainly in company shares.
- Pension funds, which accept savings from their customers, both individuals and companies, normally on an ongoing basis, to invest and to provide retirement pensions for their customers.
- Insurance companies, which invest their premium income in a range of assets but mainly long term such as shares and property.
- Finance companies, which provide medium-term credit for business and individual customers. Others act as leasing companies (leasing out capital equipment to businesses) and factoring companies (providing funds for businesses using their receivables as collateral).

6.3 Credit creation

The credit multiplier

Imagine if you made a deposit with a bank and the bank didn't do anything with that money except let it sit there. In order to make money they would have to charge you some kind of fee to make a profit. But through the use of credit creation, they are actually able to pay you a fee, in the form of interest. How do they do this?

For every deposit made, the bank keeps some in reserve, but lends out the rest to borrowers or other users of cash. The amount kept by the bank is known as the cash ratio and is expressed as a percentage of deposited funds.

The rest of the money can be used by the bank to earn money. So if the cash ratio is 5%, then the bank can lend out the remaining 95% of any money deposited. It charges interest on this money lent out. It keeps some of that interest to make a profit and pays some of it over to the initial depositor of money as a reward for putting money with the bank.

So, if 1,000 people all deposited $100 with a bank, totalling $100,000 of deposits and the cash ratio was 5%, the bank would have to keep $5,000 to hand and could lend out the remaining $95,000.

Those who borrow the $95,000 then pay that money into other banks - perhaps those of their suppliers whose bills they are paying with the borrowed money. This then starts another iteration of credit creation. That $95,000 is placed into the various banks used by the suppliers who have just been paid and 5% of that total will be kept in reserve, with the remaining 95% being lent out. That means that another $90,250 (95% of $95,000) becomes available to lend out as credit.

So from deposits totalling $100,000, borrowers have so far been able to get credit of ($95,000 + $90,250) $185,250 - an extra $85,250 appears to have been created from nothing!

This keeps on going and going. Every iteration of credit creation means that more deposits are made and more credit is therefore available for borrowers.

To work out how much ends up being available in total, we use the **credit multiplier**.

Credit multiplier = 1 / cash ratio

In this example, the credit multiplier would be 1 / 5% or 1 / 0.05, which calculates as 20.

This means that the total change in deposits ends up being actually 20 times the value of the initial deposit value. So our $100,000 initial deposits would multiply up to 20 times their value, leading to a total change in deposit values of $100,000 × 20 = $2 million.

Most of the time, this process works very well, but in times of extreme pressure on the economy, it can lead to negative consequences.

At any time in this scenario, the bank will only have 5% of the deposits made by its customers to hand. So as long as the customers in total want no more of that money back, the process works fine. But if, as a whole, the customers want more than that 5% back, the bank won't have the cash available as it has been lent out to borrowers.

During the conflict in Ukraine in 2022, queues formed outside Russian banks as normal Russians worried about the effects of sanctions that their money would no longer be safe. So they went to the bank to withdraw their money, leading to a danger that the banks would run out of cash. This happened to the bank Northern Rock back in 2008 due to the global financial crisis at the time. Once rumours started to circulate that the bank was in trouble, customers queued outside to get their money back and this hastened the demise of the bank.

In practice, banks have discovered that at most 10 per cent of deposited cash will be withdrawn, thereby leaving the remainder for loans and/or investment.

e.g

Illustration 3 – Credit creation

The use of the cash ratio makes possible the multiple creation of credit by banks. Suppose the following sequence occurs.

- A bank opens with a deposit by 'customer A' of $1,000 on day 1.
- On day 2 the bank manager decides, on the basis of the 10 per cent cash ratio, to make a loan to business woman 'B' of $900.
- In the course of their business dealing, 'B' pays $400 to 'C', who banks at the same bank.
- When 'C' pays in $400 on day 3, this raises the cash at the bank to $500 and total liabilities (deposit accounts) to $1,400.
- These liabilities only necessitate $140 in cash (i.e. 10 per cent ratio) which means that the bank can put the 'excess' cash of $360 to work. This is done on day 4 when investments to that account are made. This broadens the bank's asset structure.
- Alternatively, the bank could have lent the $360 to another customer seeking a loan.

This sequence can be shown as follows:

	Liabilities		**Assets**	
Day One	Deposit	A – 1,000	Cash	1,000
Day Two	Deposit	A – 1,000	Cash	100
			B-loan	900
Day Three	Deposit	A – 1,000	Cash	500
		C – 400	B-loan	900
Day Four	Deposit	A – 1,000	Cash	140
		C – 400	B-loan	900
			Investment	360

The process of credit creation can continue as long as the ratio of cash/liquid assets to total deposits is maintained. The term 'deposit multiplier' (or credit multiplier) denotes the amount by which total deposits can increase as a result of the bank acquiring additional cash. This amount equals the reciprocal of the cash ratio:

$$\text{Change in total deposits} = \frac{1}{\text{Cash ratio}} \times \text{the initial cash deposit}$$

Hence, a cash ratio of 10% gives a balance sheet multiplier of 10: the total increase in the money supply is ten times the initial cash deposit. The credit multiplier (the amount by which credit expands in the economy) is, strictly speaking, the balance sheet multiplier –1, since 10% of the rise in the balance sheet consists of the initial cash deposit rather than created credit.

Thus the amount of credit that banks can create depends on two factors:

- the cash and near cash liquid assets they hold.
- the size of the credit multiplier.

6.4 Central banks

All countries have a central bank: in the United Kingdom, the Bank of England; in the USA, the Federal Reserve Board; in the Eurozone, the European Central Bank and in Japan, the Bank of Japan. These are normally government-owned organisations. Although the functions of central banks vary a little from country to country, there are some common functions of these organisations.

The main functions of central banks are as follows.

Banker to the banks

All commercial banks keep accounts at the central bank. These accounts:

- act as a liquid reserve for the commercial banks; thus acting as lender of the last resort
- facilitate transfers from one bank to another arising out of the clearing system.

In most countries, these accounts are compulsory and must be equal to a minimum percentage of the commercial banks' liabilities.

Banker to the government

The central bank provides a range of banking services for the government and for government departments:

- accounts of government departments are held at the central bank and used in the same way as bank accounts in commercial banks; thus, taxation revenue is paid into, and government expenditure paid out of these accounts.
- debt management which involves organising the raising of new borrowing for government when they run budget deficits, redeeming old debts when they run budget surpluses and managing the national debt.
- the central bank operates monetary policy on behalf of the government and is largely concerned with managing the supply of money in the economy, rates of interest and the rate of exchange for the currency.
- it manages the country's reserves of foreign currency; in the United Kingdom, this is done through the Exchange and Equalization account, which may be used to buy and sell sterling on the foreign exchange market in order to smooth out excessive fluctuations in the value of sterling.

Supervision of the banking system

The central bank normally has the duty of supervising the financial system and ensuring that the banks in the system meet the requirements laid down for them. These normally concern:

- Capital adequacy. To ensure that banks have sufficient capital to meet problems arising from business losses or loss of value in their assets, for example losses arising from bad debts.
- Liquidity. To ensure banks can meet the normal day-to-day requirements of their customers for cash.

In order to support the banking system should a problem of liquidity arise, the central bank also acts as lender of the last resort. In this role, the central bank will be willing to rediscount bills or buy bank government stock ('repos') thus providing cash for the banking system.

Note issue

The central bank has the sole right of note issue in an economy. These notes are liabilities on the central bank's balance sheet and the matching assets are largely government securities. Paper currency is no longer backed by gold.

Central banks and monetary policy

The central bank can alter interest rates directly by changing the base rate. This is often done to manage inflation in the economy – higher interest rates curb inflation.

The bank can also sell or buy back ('redeem') government stock. The central bank buys and sells treasury and commercial bills, and government bonds in the money market. This activity is known as 'open market operations'.

- If it seeks a multiple contraction of credit, it will sell bills. The money paying for them will be drawn on the banks, whose deposits will fall and whose balances at the central bank will be lowered. Their cash base will be lowered and their potential to create credit will be limited.
- If it seeks a multiple expansion of credit, it will buy bills. The result will be an increase in the commercial banks' deposits at the central bank and thus their cash base will be increased and their ability to create credit will be raised.

When selling bills in an attempt to restrict credit, the central bank may find that, in practice the commercial banks can restore their cash base by reclaiming money at call from the banks and other financial organisations.

Thus, the central bank can either restrict the credit creating ability of banks by reducing the amount of cash in the financial system or it can force a rise in interest rates through the system. A similar outcome can be achieved by central bank operations in the market for government longer-term securities (in the United Kingdom, 'gilt-edged' securities). If the central bank:

- increases its sales of government bonds, the price will fall and the effective interest rate (the yield) will rise
- decreases its sales of government bonds, the price will rise and the effective interest rate (the yield) will fall.

In addition, the government and central bank might operate rather more directly on the ability of commercial banks to create credit through bank assets ratios. Banks are required to a keep proportion of their total assets in certain specified assets. The basic idea behind these ratios was to ensure prudential standards of liquidity but by varying these required ratios, the central banks could, in principle, affect the credit multiplier. In practice, little use is now made of this and most reliance is placed on open market operations and on interest rate policy.

Monetary policy in the UK

During the first half of 2008, the main concern of the Bank of England was the threat of rising inflation. As a result, the Bank kept interest rates at relatively high levels. By the autumn, the threat of inflation had faded as food & energy prices fell, the price of oil to $40 a barrel in December, & the crisis in the banking system & the onset of a severe recession became the primary problems. The result was a rapid reversal of monetary policy with the Bank cutting its interest rate in a series of steps ending up at 0.5%.

Less than a year later, prices were rising again and by late 2011 the rate of inflation was above 5%, reaching the highest annual rate since June 1991. Since then, inflation fell back again, with inflation in 2015 well below the Bank of England's 2% target rate for the first time since November 2009.

During 2017, inflation levels started to rise and reached a level above the target rate of 2%. The Bank of England's response was to raise the base rate from 0.25% to 0.5% to try and suppress inflation. This policy continued in 2018, with the rate rising to 0.75%.

During the 2020 pandemic, the Bank's policy was reversed as the need to stimulate the economy became the most pressing need, leading to interest rate cuts.

In late 2021 and throughout 2022, as the economy started to recover from the effects of the pandemic, rising inflation again became the key concern and interest rates started to increase.

One of the main tools that a government has to control growth in an economy is raising or lowering interest rates. Lower interest rates encourage people or companies to spend money, rather than save.

But when interest rates are almost zero, central banks need to adopt different tactics – such as pumping money directly into the economy.

This process is known as quantitative easing, or QE.

The central bank buys assets, usually government bonds, with money it has 'printed' – or created electronically these days. It then uses this money to buy bonds from investors such as banks or pension funds, which increases the amount of cash in the financial system and pushes interest rates down. This encourages financial institutions to lend more to businesses and individuals, who also find that borrowing has become cheaper. This, in turn, should allow them to invest and spend more, hopefully increasing growth.

Many central banks engaged in quantitative easing during the COVID 19 pandemic as part of their stimulus packages to support their economies. In March 2022, the European Central Bank announced that it would be discontinuing its emergency pandemic QE programme and wind down (taper) its other asset purchases more quickly than expected. This is partly in response to fast rising inflation.

Test your understanding 10

Which ONE of the following is not a function of a central bank, for example the Bank of Japan?

A Management of the National Debt

B Holder of the foreign exchange reserves

C The conduct of fiscal policy

D Lender of the last resort

(2 marks)

Test your understanding 11

1 What is a cash ratio?

2 What is the relationship between liquidity and profitability of banks assets?

3 How could a central bank reduce the supply of credit in the financial system?

4 How could a central bank reduce the demand for credit in the financial system?

5 What are capital adequacy rules?

7 Financial markets

Financial markets

Financial institutions operate in a range of financial markets. The most important of these are:

- money markets
- capital markets
- international markets.

Money markets

In most economies, the financial markets are dominated by the money market. It is here that banks, companies, local authorities and the government operate via investors in buying and selling short-term debt. Banks and other intermediaries are described as market makers in bills. This is because they will buy (or sell) treasury and commercial bills to enable holders to transform their assets into liquidity (or their cash into paper financial assets).

Treasury bills in the UK are issued at weekly tenders by the Debt Management Office (DMO). Members of the public who wish to invest in them must do so through one of the treasury bill primary participants (various banks and other financial institutions who have agreed to bid at the tenders).

- The price that the investor pays reflects the market rate of interest.
- A high bid price makes a low rate of interest, because the difference between the price paid and the maturity value (usually three months later) is effectively the interest paid on the loan.
- For example, a bill bought for £4,900 is redeemed for £5,000 after three months. Thus, £100 profit is made on an outlay of £4,900 over three months, approximately 8.4 per cent per annum.

The main commercial bill is a bill of exchange (discussed earlier). These treasury and commercial bills are also often resold before maturity, again facilitating liquidity for the seller. The investors, in turn, raise their funds by borrowing 'money at call' from the banks, at very low rates of interest. They make a profit by charging slightly higher rates of interest when buying bills.

The 1970s and 1980s saw enormous financial innovation and the creation of new markets. These are known as parallel money markets. A key characteristic is that transactions are mainly between financial intermediaries, firms and local authorities but not the government. Secondary markets were developed in:

- bank liabilities, such as certificates of deposit
- and in bank assets, such as resaleable bank loans.

Such markets as the inter-bank market evolved to enable banks to accommodate fluctuations in customers' transactions by making loans to one another. With the increase in financial deregulation since the mid-1980s, new parallel markets in local authority debt, inter-company deposits and finance house borrowing have also sprung up.

The stock markets

In the United Kingdom, this encompasses several markets:

- the "full" equities/securities market where ordinary shares, preference shares and debentures are traded
- the Alternative Investment Market (AIM) where smaller companies gain access to capital, under less stringent and less costly entry procedures
- bonds/gilts market where government sells short (up to 5 years), medium (5–15 years), long (over 15 years) and undated stock.

The phrase 'capital instruments' refers to the means (e.g. shares, treasury bonds, etc.) by which organisations raise finance.

The New York stock exchange is by far the world's largest in terms of market capitalisation, followed by the NASDAQ stock market.

In October 1986, the 'Big Bang' occurred and the United Kingdom Stock Exchange radically changed. Its central function as a market for the purchase and sale of second-hand securities remained but its operations and procedures were reformed.

- Previously, an individual bought shares through a stockbroker.
- The broker acted as an adviser and an agent for the client (who was charged a commission) and bought shares from a stockjobber.
- The jobber was a dealer in securities who was willing to buy and sell at a price and hold on to unrequired shares and did not deal with the general public.
- This system of single capacity was ended in October 1986 and the broker and jobbing functions were merged. The new dealer has become known as a market-maker.

Equity market

Transactions in company securities are the most numerous but average only £15,000 per transaction. These can be subdivided into equities (ordinary shares) and loan capital securities.

- Equities bestow full voting rights on the shareholder and an entitlement to dividends, once the preference shareholders and the holders of loan capital have been paid out.

- Preference shareholders receive a fixed dividend and get their capital repaid before ordinary shareholders if a company is wound up.
- Company bonds and debentures do not confer ownership rights but their holders receive a fixed rate of interest over a set period of time. In 1978, 'traded options' were introduced, whereby an option holder can buy/sell a quantity of a company's shares at a fixed price on a specified date.

In 1985, convertible securities became prominent. They combine both debt and equity. The holder of the debt has the option of converting to equity, if desired.

The securities market performs two main functions:

- It is a **primary market** for newly issued shares. Typically, a company's new shares are issued by an issuing house with the help and advice of a stockbroker. There are several possible methods of issuing new shares – by an offer for sale, by placing, by tender and by public issue: issuing a prospectus.
- In addition, existing companies wishing to raise capital may introduce a rights issue. This gives existing shareholders the right to pay to subscribe for more shares in proportion to their existing shareholdings. The stockbroker's involvement is to obtain stock exchange approval for the issue, which a merchant bank usually underwrites.
- A **secondary market** exists for the buying and selling of existing shares. Although this does not contribute to economic production, it has some value. It raises the liquidity of company shares because buyers of new issues know that they can sell in the future. In addition, the worth of a company can be calculated from its share price.
- Furthermore, a company can raise further capital by an issue of extra shares more easily and cheaply if it has a high market share price. This was very clear in the stock market boom of 1986–87.

The stock market is usually given as an example of a perfectly competitive market because there are many buyers and sellers with excellent knowledge and rapid reactions to price changes. Share prices are published daily and they reflect demand changes. For instance, market-makers will 'mark down' the prices of shares for which they have a plentiful supply.

Alternative investment market (AIM)

In the United Kingdom, there exists a market for shares in smaller companies. This was originally the Unlisted Securities Market (USM) set up in 1980. The purpose was to enable smaller companies raise sums up to £250,000 through share issues. The AIM, which replaced the USM, caters for smaller companies with none of the formal requirements regarding the age of the company and its market capitalisation that the main stock market has.

Government bond market

Governments issue bonds as a way of borrowing from investors. There is a wide choice of interest payments and redemption dates to make bonds attractive to buyers. The main buyers are pension funds and life assurance companies who are attracted by a fixed certain income.

- As explained elsewhere the market price varies with the interest payment (called the 'coupon').
- For example, if general market interest rates are around 5 per cent then a bond with a £10 coupon will trade at around £200 (10/200 = 5 per cent). If those market interest rates then rise to 6 per cent, the bond price will move to £166 (10/166 = 6 per cent).

The supply of bonds is determined by the stock of bonds, which basically constitute the national debt. Public sector borrowing, which necessitates debt sales, will increase the supply of bonds.

Test your understanding 12

Which of the following would be expected to lead to a rise in share prices on the Hong Kong stock exchange?

A A fall in interest rates

B A rise in the rate of inflation

C A fall in share prices in other stock markets

D An expected fall in company profits

Test your understanding 13

A 30 year Treasury bond that was issued last year may be sold today in a:

(i) money market

(ii) capital market

(iii) primary market

(iv) secondary market

A Both (i) and (iii)

B Both (i) and (iv)

C Both (ii) and (iii)

D Both (ii) and (iv)

Test your understanding answers

Test your understanding 1

C

The time period money is lent/borrowed is called the maturity.

Test your understanding 2

B

The easiest way to see this is to consider the timescales involved. The shortfall is short-term and relates to the lack of synchronisation between receipts and payments.

Both share issues (A) and mortgages (D) are long-term and more suitable for long-term investments such as buying new premises or buying a competitor.

(C) is a medium-term method of finance more used to acquire plant and machinery or motor vehicles which will last for a medium-term time period.

Test your understanding 3

D

Mezzanine finance is a type of 'middle ground' finance, which has characteristics of both debt and equity.

Test your understanding 4

A

Risk looks at the degree of uncertainty of future cash flows. The CD will be the least risky out of the options given.

(B) – equity is normally considered high risk but may give high returns

(C) – the loan stock is unsecured making it more risky

(D) – Lottery tickets are highly risky and will most likely result in Ian having much less money at the end than he started with.

Test your understanding 5

C

The yield of an asset is the relationship between the income derived from it and the price that has to be paid to acquire it. In this case, the market price is $80 and the income gained is $5. The yield in percentage terms is $5 divided by $80 × 100. This is 6.25%.

Test your understanding 6

C

The bill rate is the same as the coupon (interest) rate

(A) and (D) are the same and can be calculated as (annual interest/market value) × 100%

(B) involves determining the discount rate at which the market value = present value of future receipts (interest and redemption).

Test your understanding 7

Answer = 14.3%

- Increase in money terms = "m" = 20%
- Inflation = "i" = 5%
- 1 + r = (1 + m)/(1 + i) = 1.20/1.05 = 1.143, giving r = 14.3%

Alternatively,

- Inflationary increase at 5% would have given a salary of ($30,000 × 1.05) $31,500
- Real salary increase is ($36,000 – $31,500) $4,500, which is a 14.3% increase on $31,500. ($4,500 / $31,500 × 100 = 14.3%)

Test your understanding 8

C

A fall in interest rates will encourage investment rather than discourage it (as borrowing to pay for investments becomes cheaper). This also applies to consumers in the form of consumption (including on houses as mortgages become cheaper) and to governments in the form of government expenditure.

Test your understanding 9

(a) (i) r = (1+m)/(1+i) – 1 = (1.055/1.023) – 1 = 3.1%

(ii) r = (1+m)/(1+i) – 1 = (1.084/1.035) – 1 = 4.7%

(iii) The share price index represents the change in money values.

% increase in share index 2012–2013 = (2,919 – 2,900)/2,900 = 0.66%. Inflation over same period = 2.3%. As share prices have grown at a lower rate than inflation then in real terms, the prices have fallen.

(b) (i) False. High interest rates encourage savings but discourage business investment.

(ii) False. A rise in interest rates raises the opportunity cost of using internal funds to finance investment.

(iii) True. Higher interest rates encourage capital inflows, which increase the demand for the currency.

(iv) True. Consumer durables are often bought on credit.

(v) True. If the supply of money increases, its price, the rate of interest, will go down. Increasing interest rates would lead to the supply of money falling. Trying to do both at the same time would be counterproductive.

(c) A rise in interest rates would:

raise government spending as the cost of financing government debt would increase.

deflate the economy since it would discourage expenditure.

Note: you will learn more about the effects of interest rate changes in a later chapter.

Test your understanding 10

C

Fiscal policy is concerned with the government budget and the balance of taxation and public expenditure. This is the responsibility of the government, not the central bank.

Test your understanding 11

1 The amount of cash kept by banks in readiness to pay withdrawals as a proportion of their total assets.

2 The most liquid assets, for example cash, are the least profitable; and the least liquid assets, for example advances and loans to customers, are the most profitable.

3 The central bank would need to reduce the liquidity of the financial system, as this is the basis upon which credit is created. It can do this by selling government stocks to financial institutions.

4 The central bank could raise interest rates as interest is the price of credit and a higher price will reduce demand.

5 Capital adequacy rules attempt to ensure that banks have sufficient capital to cover potential bad debts on risk assets.

Test your understanding 12

A

A fall in company profits would clearly discourage the purchase of shares and so share prices would fall. Since stock markets are linked, a fall in one market tends to lead to a fall in share prices in other markets. A rise in inflation would lead to some business pessimism and might be expected to lead to a rise in interest rates. However, since share prices and interest rates move in opposite directions, A is the correct solution.

Test your understanding 13

D

The bond can be sold in a capital market and a secondary market.

As it was issued last year it still has 29 years to run and so will be sold on a capital market. Its initial issue last year would have used the market as a primary market but subsequent transactions will use the market as a secondary one.

Chapter

4

Macroeconomic and Institutional Context I: The Domestic Economy

Chapter learning objectives

On completion of their studies, students should be able to:

- explain determination of macroeconomic phenomena, including equilibrium national income, growth in national income, price inflation, unemployment, and trade deficits and surpluses
- explain the stages of the trade cycle and the consequences of each stage for the policy choices of government
- explain the main principles of public finance (i.e. deficit financing, forms of taxation) and macroeconomic policy
- describe the impacts on business of potential policy responses of government, to each stage of the trade cycle
- explain the role of hedging and derivative contracts in managing the impact of changes in interest rates.

Overview

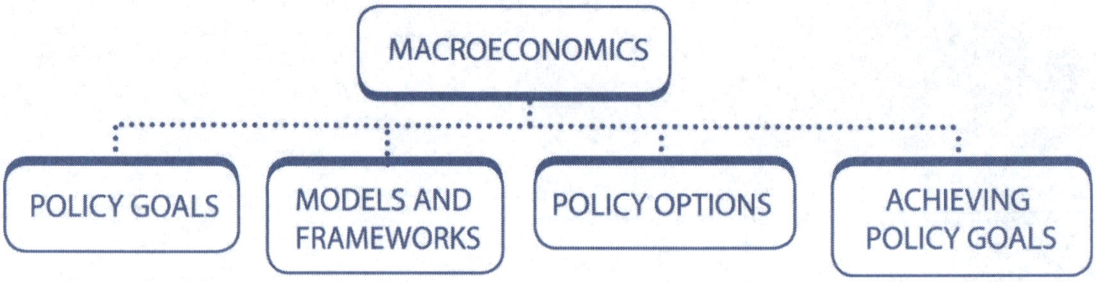

In this chapter, we will look at macroeconomics and the domestic economy by focussing on the following:

- Policy goals – after explaining what is meant by "macroeconomics" we will look at the different policy goals that face all governments:
  - growing the economy,
  - reducing inflation,
  - creating jobs and
  - managing trade with other countries.
- Models and frameworks – to understand how to achieve these goals there are a number of economic models and frameworks you need to understand first. These include:
  - how to measure the size of the economy,
  - the circular flow of funds model and its components,
  - how to apply supply and demand arguments to the whole economy and
- Policy options – next we look at the range of policy options available to governments, including:
  - fiscal and
  - monetary policies.
- Achieving policy goals – finally we consider the range of policies that could be implemented to try to achieve the policy goals we started with and their likely implications.

1 Macroeconomics and government policy goals

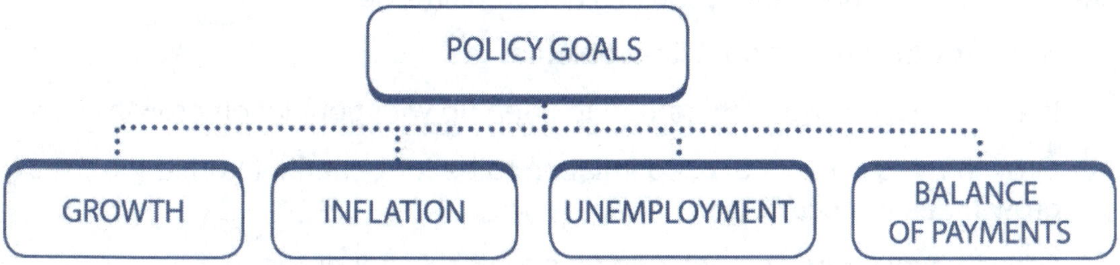

1.1 Macroeconomics

In a previous chapter, we looked at the interaction of supply and demand in individual markets. Macroeconomics focuses on the workings of the economy as a whole, including:

- the overall ('aggregate') demand for goods and services
- the output of goods and services ('national output' or 'national product')
- the supply of factors of production (land, labour, capital and enterprise)
- total incomes earned by providers of factors of production ('national income')
- money spent in purchasing the national product ('national expenditure')
- government policy.

These will be discussed in more detail throughout this chapter.

A general awareness of economic factors will be needed throughout your studies to give context to, for example, strategic decisions made by business managers.

1.2 Government macroeconomic policy

Typically, governments will have four macroeconomic policy objectives:

- Economic growth – how can productive capacity be increased?
- Inflation – how can we ensure that general price levels do not increase?
- Unemployment – how can we ensure that everyone who wants a job has one?
- Balance of payments – how should we manage our financial relationships and trade with other countries?

1.3 Economic growth

Most governments want economic growth. Growth should result in the following:

- more goods being demanded and produced
- people earn more and can afford more goods
- more people should have jobs.

On the face of it, therefore, growth should result in an improved standard of living in a country and higher profitability for businesses.

However, growth is not without its problems.

- Is economic growth fast enough to keep up with population growth?
- Growth rates have to exceed inflation rates for benefits to arise (i.e. "real" growth has to occur).
- Growth may be in 'demerit' goods, such as illegal drugs.
- Growth may be at the expense of the environment or through exploitation of the poor.
- The gap between rich and poor may grow, as the benefits from growth are not evenly distributed.
- Rapid growth means rising incomes and this often 'sucks in' imports, worsening the balance of trade, rather than benefiting domestic producers.

1.4 Inflation

Most governments want stable prices and low inflation. The main reasons given include the following:

- Inflation causes uncertainty and stifles business investment.
- Not all incomes rise in line with inflation – the poor and those on fixed incomes suffer the most.
- In extreme cases of inflation, the function of money may break down, resulting in civil unrest.
- Inflation distorts the working of the price mechanism and is thus a market imperfection.

Note that high inflation can affect savings in different ways:

- inflation erodes the future purchasing power of money so people may decide to save less but spend more now.
- an alternative argument is that higher prices reduce individuals' real wealth and so they spend less. This could result in higher savings (the "real balance" effect).

1.5 Unemployment

Even in a healthy economy, some unemployment will arise as people change jobs. However, mass unemployment is a problem due to the following:

- The government has to pay out benefits to the unemployed at a time when its tax receipts are low. This can result in the government having to raise taxes, borrow money and cut back on services.
- Unemployment has been linked to a rise in crime, poor health and a breakdown in family relationships.
- Unemployment is a waste of human resources and can restrict economic growth.

High unemployment could give firms higher bargaining power allowing them to pay lower wages to prospective employees.

1.6 Balance of payments

In the long-term, governments seek to establish a broad balance between the value of imports into, and exports from, their country.

To run a persistent surplus or deficit can have negative macroeconomic effects.

- A long-term trade deficit (imports > exports with a net position of money leaving the country) has to be financed. The financing costs act as a major drain on the productive capacity of the economy.
- A long-term trade surplus (imports < exports with a net position of money coming into the country) can cause significant inflationary pressures (due to high demand for locally produced goods), leading ultimately to a loss in international confidence in the economy (as prices become too high) and a lack of international competitiveness.

1.7 Trade cycles

Many economies exhibit fluctuations in economic activity over time with an underlying trend of output growth.

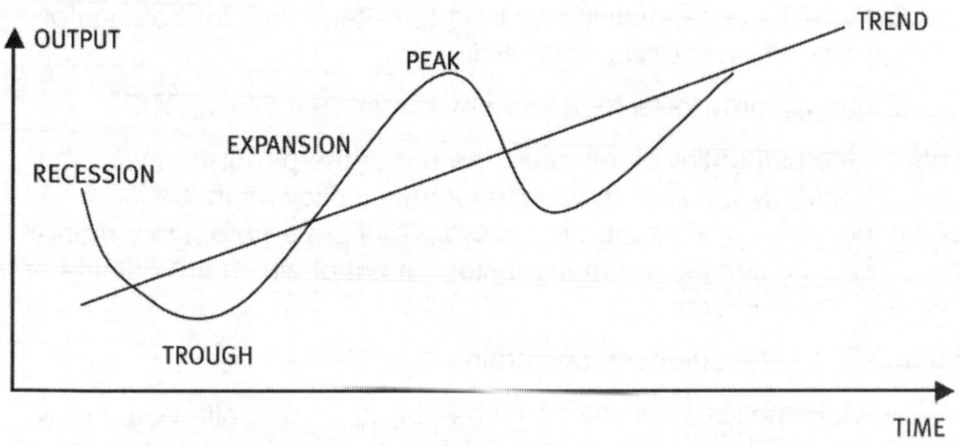

Some economists argue that one role of governments is to smooth out this pattern to avoid 'boom and bust' years.

Illustration 1 – Recession during the COVID 19 pandemic

During the global COVID 19 pandemic, restrictions were put on face to face contact and the movement of people to reduce the level of transmissions of the virus. This immediately reduced global demand levels, particularly for face-to-face services such as those provided by restaurants, hotels, theatres, etc. and for travel services.

Governments across the world introduced stimulus packages with the aim of reducing the economic slowdown as much as possible. Packages were designed differently and multiple different packages were offered in each country with the aim of stimulating different parts of the economy.

Examples include:

- the Eat Out to Help Out Scheme in the UK, offering Government funded discounts for consumers dining out to stimulate demand for restaurant services
- €500 million of repayable advances in France for small and medium sized businesses that may otherwise struggle to find funding
- preferential interest rates for small and medium companies in Argentina to allow them to maintain their salary payments to workers.

The economic diamond

Objectives of economic policy

A useful illustration of the economy's performance and the success of economic policy is the 'economic diamond' showing the main economic objectives of governments. Although the priority among the objectives varies with the government's values and political motives the following four objectives are typical of most governments:

- Price stability. A low annual rate of inflation.
- Full employment.
- External balance implying no long-term tendency for balance of payments current account deficits.
- Economic growth as measured by the annual rise in GDP.

In effect, the bigger the diamond is, the better the performance of the economy and the more successful economic policy might be judged. Of course the conduct of economic policy by any government in a market economy is constrained by many factors, most of which are outside of the control of governments.

The most important of these constraints are:

- previous policies which cannot be abandoned or altered by new governments since there has to be a degree of continuity in policy to ensure a reasonably stable economic environment in which individuals and businesses can work.

- information, which is always limited and imperfect and limits the value of economic predictions upon which economic policymaking must be based.
- time lags between the design and implementation of economic policy and the point at which they start to have an effect on the economy.
- political limitations, which constrain what is possible and acceptable to the electorate and may condition what governments are prepared to do.

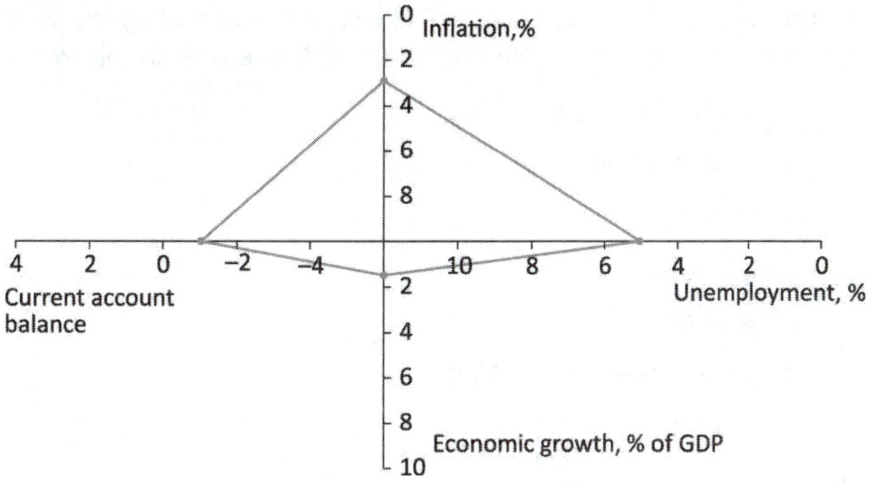

The economic diamond

Test your understanding 1

Which of the following is NOT an objective of macroeconomic policy?

A Economic growth

B Control of Inflation

C Lower levels of taxation

D A balanced balance of payments

Test your understanding 2

Which of the following statements is true?

A Economic growth always brings benefits to all members of a society. TRUE/FALSE

B Economic growth can lead to an increase in imports. TRUE/FALSE

C Inflation does not affect those on fixed incomes as much as those in employment. TRUE/FALSE

D Inflation encourages investment in a national economy. TRUE/FALSE

Test your understanding 3

The Economic boom of the 1920s saw a rapid growth in GDP, production levels and living standards. This boom came to a dramatic collapse with the Wall Street Crash of 1929 on Black Thursday. This led to the Great Depression of the 1930s.

Why is a 'boom and bust' economy a problem?

2 Understanding national income: the circular flow model

Note: In the circular flow model, there is extensive use of symbols to represent variables in the model. The most important of these are as follows:

Y national income

C consumption

S savings

I investment

T taxation

G government expenditure

X exports

M imports

Also, note that the terms companies and firms are used interchangeably.

2.1 The circular flow model

Imagine a simple economy in which there are only producers (firms) and consumers (households). This economy does not have a government and it does not trade with the rest of the world, nor does any private sector investment take place.

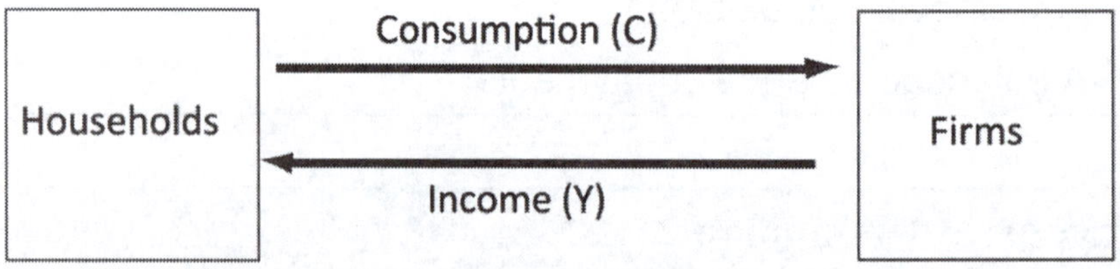

In this scenario, there is a simple circular flow of funds. Households earn factor incomes (Y) by selling their labour to firms. In return, the households buy and consume (C) the goods and services produced by the firms. At this point it is assumed that households spend all that they earn, i.e. income is equal to expenditure (also referred to as demand or aggregate demand) in the home economy.

Note: In all of these models, real things (goods, services and work) go in one direction and payment for these (consumption expenditure, wages) go in the opposite direction.

In this simple economy, equilibrium (when the circular flow is neither increasing nor decreasing) will exist when income equals consumption or aggregate demand and is possible to write:

Consumption = Income

Furthermore, in this simple case total expenditure (E) is made up of consumption only, so we can state that in equilibrium

Expenditure = Income

E = Y

2.2 Injections and withdrawals

The initial model of the circular flow was rather unrealistic as it ignored the possibility of overseas trade, the influence of government, and the fact that households might save some of their income.

A more realistic model would recognise that the circular flow can experience:

- Injections, which are additions to expenditure from outside of the circular flow itself.

  Injections boost the circular flow and include exports (X), government investment (G) and private sector investment (I).

- Withdrawals, which are some element of income in the circular flow that is not passed on as expenditure.

  Withdrawals (also known as leakages) reduce the circular flow and include imports (M), taxation (T) and savings (S).

Remember that with exports goods flow out of the country but money flows into the country; with imports, goods flow into the country and money flows out of the country. It is the flow of money that defines exports as injections and imports as withdrawals.

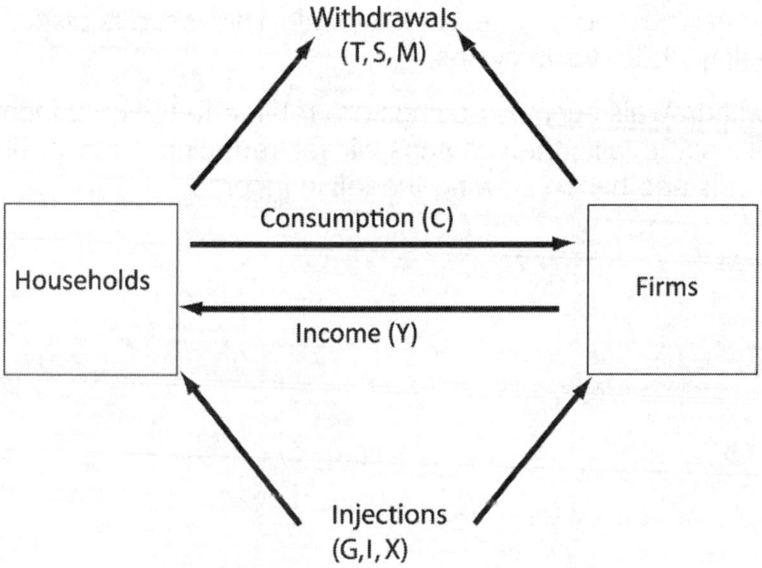

2.3 Equilibrium

An economy making full use of its resources will be moving towards a state of rest, or equilibrium. For equilibrium to be established in the circular flow, planned injections must equal planned withdrawals.

Equilibrium in national income is where

J (injections) = W (withdrawals or leakages)

I + G + X = S + T + M

Where I = investment }
G = government expenditure } injections
X = exports }

And S = savings }
T = taxations withdrawals } withdrawals
M = imports }

It is not necessary that pairs of injections and withdrawals (such as imports and exports or taxation and government expenditure) are equal. Equilibrium only requires that the sum of injections is equal to the sum of withdrawals.

But if:

- J > W, additions to the circular flow exceed withdrawals and so the level of national income will rise
- J < W, additions to the circular flow are less than withdrawals so the level of national income will fall.

Note that in both cases the growth or fall does not continue indefinitely. For example:

- If growth results from additional investment, then further ongoing investment would be required to sustain it. This issue is discussed in more detail below under trade cycles.
- Some withdrawals such as savings are related to national income. If national income falls, then savings will fall reducing the overall level of withdrawals and hence slowing the fall in income.

More complex circular flow of funds

Clearly more complex models can be devised (see diagram below).

- Households may save via financial institutions, which may channel these savings to firms to finance investment.
- Governments tax incomes and may use these revenues either to purchase goods and services from the firms sector or to provide support incomes for certain households.
- International trade occurs. Exports will represent additional spending on the firm sector but imports will represent a diversion of spending away from the firm sector towards firms in other countries.

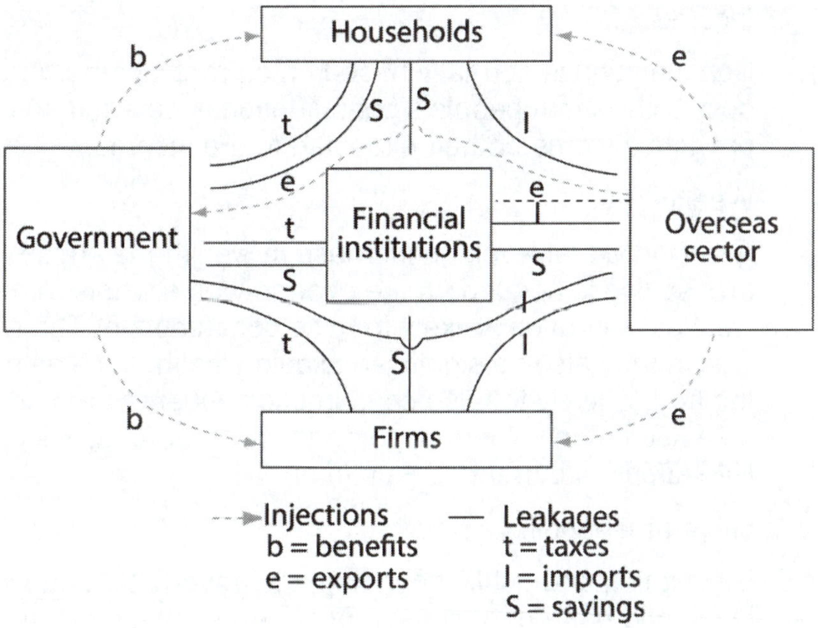

3 Understanding the components of the circular flow of funds

3.1 Consumption (C)

The spending by people, or households, on the circular flow model is termed consumption. The single most important determinant of the level of consumption is the level of income. This is true for both individuals and the economy as a whole.

The extent to which consumption changes with income is termed the marginal propensity to consume (MPC).

The marginal propensity to consume is calculated by the formula:

$$\text{MPC} = \frac{\text{Change in consumption, } \Delta C}{\text{Change in income, } \Delta Y}$$

Thus, if a person's disposable income increases from $100 to $120 per week and their consumption increases from $90 to $105 per week, their MPC would be 0.75 (i.e. 15:20). In other words, 75% of the increase in income has been converted to an increase in consumption. The rest has been saved.

The MPC varies considerably between economies, with some (e.g. Japan), having relatively low MPCs and some (e.g. the USA), having relatively high MPCs. Generally, it is assumed that the MPC is positive but likely to fall as income rises.

Factors affecting consumption

Factors influencing the level of household consumption are:

- Income

  Consumption is normally based on current income. Another possibility is that people's consumption is determined by their previous income or their expected future income.

- Wealth

  At an individual level, an increase in wealth may raise MPC because less saving is needed. In the economy as a whole, a more equal wealth distribution is likely to raise consumption. The nature of wealth may also be significant; liquid wealth, such as savings under the bed, is likely to raise consumption, whereas illiquid wealth, such as a rise in the value of a personal pension fund, will probably have little effect on current consumption.

- Government policy

  By taxation and public spending, the government can influence the level (and pattern) of consumption. An increase in direct taxation lowers disposable incomes and thereby reduces the capacity for consumption. Alternatively, higher government spending, particularly on state benefits, raises incomes and stimulates consumption.

- The cost and availability of credit

  The cheaper the cost (the rate of interest) and the greater the availability of credit, the more likely it is that consumption will occur. Credit is particularly influential when consumer durables are purchased. The United Kingdom has high levels of consumption financed by credit, partly because of the wide range and sophistication of the credit instruments available.

- Price expectations

  In certain circumstances, when price rises are anticipated, consumption might be brought forward. This temporarily raises MPC.

These factors can be described as 'objective' influences. In contrast, there are 'subjective' influences, which determine individual behaviour, irrespective of the other factors. For instance, some cultures encourage high levels of savings (e.g. Japan). It is also usually argued that consumption by individuals in urban areas is higher than in rural areas.

Test your understanding 4

Which of the following is **least** likely to result in a fall in consumption spending in an economy?

A An increase in the rate of income tax

B An increase in interest rates

C An increase in the rate of inflation

D A reduction in the availability of credit

3.2 Savings (S)

Saving is defined as the amount of income not spent. It is therefore sometimes regarded as a residual; the amount of income left after consumption has been determined. Thus the factors determining saving are mainly the mirror image of the factors determining consumption.

Factors affecting savings

The factors influencing saving are as follows.

- Income

  Both for the individual and the economy, the level of saving is determined mainly by income.

- Interest rates

  In theory, an increase in the rate of interest will mean that people need to save less in order to achieve a given target of income earned in interest. However, this income effect can be offset by the substitution effect. With higher interest rates, people might save more and spend less, as saving is now more attractive.

- Inflation

  However, to rational consumers the money (nominal) rate of interest is less important than the real interest rate (i.e. allowing for inflation). Even if the money rate of interest is high, a low real rate of interest might discourage savings. However, consumers might suffer from the 'money illusion' and save more when money interest rates are high even if inflation reduces the real rate of interest.

- Credit

  When credit is easily available, consumers might acquire as much credit as they are saving; in effect, there is no net saving. In some countries, notably the USA and the United Kingdom, the expansion of credit in recent years has meant that net household savings rates have fallen to historic lows.

- Contractual savings

  Most household saving is contractual and regular such as payments into pension schemes. As the need to finance pensions increases, especially in developed economies with ageing populations, this form of saving is expected to increase.

  Most saving is undertaken by households and the company sector. Governments save when they run budget surpluses and dis-save when they run budget deficits. The savings deficits of any one sector of the economy have to be financed by the saving of other sectors. Thus, if the company sector plans to invest more than it is saving, it will have to borrow from other sectors that are net savers. This raises the question of what determines the level of investment in the economy.

3.3 Investment (I)

Expenditure on investment covers:

- fixed capital formation (e.g. plant, machinery, roads, houses)
- the value of the physical increase in stocks of raw materials, work in progress and finished goods.

Investment is undertaken by the public sector and the private sector (the latter featuring firms and households) and it enhances the capacity of the economy.

- The capital stock of the economy is increased by the amount of net investment undertaken each year.
- Net investment is the difference between gross (total) investment and replacement investment (capital consumption), which accounts for the deterioration of the existing capital equipment stock. In other words, some investment expenditure is just to replace worn out assets so does not, in itself, contribute to economic growth.

Note: do not confuse investment (I) and savings (S). Savings are a withdrawal from the circular flow of funds (that can be thought of as investment from a personal point of view but not from an economic one), while investment is an injection.

If we assess investments using discounted cash flow appraisals, then we can say that the main determinants of the level of investment are:

- Expectations about future cash flows

  These expectations will be influenced by the anticipated revenue from the output of the investment compared with the anticipated costs of the investment.

- The business's cost of capital

  This will be affected by the availability and cost of finance, inflation and the perceived risks of the cash flows.

The detail of investment appraisal will be seen in a later chapter.

Additional factors affecting investment

Other factors that influence investment include the following:

- The state of business confidence

  If businesses are optimistic, they are likely to expect greater returns than if they are pessimistic. (Note this will affect estimated cash flows and perceived risk in the NPV approach.) A controlled level of anticipated inflation can lead to increased business confidence.

- Technological innovation

  If capital becomes more productive this is likely to raise the level of investment at any given rate of interest. Note: economists talk about the "marginal efficiency of capital (MEC)" as a way of calculating the return on invested funds. For an investment to be worthwhile, the MEC must exceed the interest rate.

- Government policy

  Inconsistent and varying economic policies might increase business uncertainty and thereby deter investment. In contrast, reductions in corporation tax and improved tax allowances will increase the expected income stream and encourage investment. In addition, changes in interest rates will have direct effects on the profitability of investment.

Test your understanding 5

Hina has decided to spend less but instead invest $100 more in a bank deposit account. This will increase the level of investment in the economy by $100.

True/False

3.4 The government and external sectors

The factors determining the level of government expenditure and taxation and the main influences on the balance of imports and exports will be discussed in later sections.

3.5 Linkages between different elements of the circular flow

There are two key linkages that you need to be aware of:

The accelerator

For growth to occur the economy has to be able to increase output of goods and services. Unless spare capacity exists (where, e.g. national producers are not running their factories at full capacity) this will require additional investment in capital goods.

(**Note:** Failure to increase output at a time of rising demand would simply result in inflation (more money chasing the same amount of goods) or an increase in imports.

The accelerator principle views investment as a function of changes in national income i.e. as national income rises and desired consumption increases, firms will respond, investing in new capital goods to meet this extra demand. This in turn increases aggregate demand further within the economy, increasing pressure for more investment.

Thus, when an economy starts to grow, this in itself can fuel further growth. Unfortunately, the reverse is also true, as a reduction in the size of an economy will result in a cut in investment, accelerating the decline further.

The multiplier

This idea shows the change in national income resulting from a change in planned investment, a change in government spending or a change in the overseas trade sector. It looks at the effect of injections (less withdrawals) into the circular flow of income.

Changes in injections (government expenditure, investment and exports) may cause a more than proportional increase in national income. This is termed the multiplier effect.

Multiplier effects can occur in many ways. When any planned injection into the circular flow increases and other injections and withdrawals remain unchanged, then increased national income will lead to the use of more factors of production whose earnings will be spent, thereby adding to the income of others who may then spend more, and so on... Thus, an initial injection of additional expenditure in the circular flow will lead to a series of additional rounds of expenditure.

Determinants of the multiplier

A simple economy

The increase in national income caused by successive rounds of spending will not go on forever, since with each round some extra income will be lost to the circular flow through the operation of withdrawals. Thus, each succeeding round of spending becomes smaller and smaller. If withdrawals were 20 per cent of income (e.g. a marginal propensity to save of 0.2), the increases in income in each round from an initial increase in spending of $100 would be:

Round 1	$100	
Round 2	$80	($100 minus $20 which is saved)
Round 3	$64	($80 minus $16 which is saved)
Round 4	$51.2	($64 minus $12.8 which is saved)

In a simple economy, the obvious withdrawal is savings. In this simple economy, with no government and no external sector, the value of the multiplier (K) is shown in the following equation.

$$K = \frac{1}{1 - MPC} = \frac{1}{MPS}$$

Where MPC marginal propensity to consume

MPS marginal propensity to save

If one assumed an MPC of 0.8 (or therefore an MPS of 0.2) the multiplier would have a value of 5 and an increased injection of $10 m would increase total national income by $50 m. This is important for government policy making.

e.g **Illustration 2 – Explaining trade cycles**

Although there a number of explanations for trade cycles, attempts have been made to combine the accelerator and multiplier effects to explain the behaviour:

- Something happens to boost Investment – for example, innovation or war.
- The increase in investment triggers the multiplier effect leading to rising incomes.
- Rising incomes increase consumption and therefore demand.
- Higher expected demand triggers the accelerator effect as firms invest further to meet demand.
- The extra investment then triggers the multiplier again leading to rising incomes and so on.

This means that once the economy starts growing it will continue to grow, giving a strong upward swing in the trade cycle.

However, this process cannot continue indefinitely, as the economy will eventually reach full capacity, i.e. all factors of production are employed. As this point is reached, investment tails off and incomes start to fall triggering a reverse multiplier. As incomes fall so does consumption and demand. This is in turn reduces investment and so on, resulting in the downward part of the trade cycle.

Long-term and short-term conflicts

It is clear that if a government wishes to engage in some form of demand management policy, that is using its levels of taxation and expenditure to influence the level of aggregate demand and hence the level of national income, it will need to have some knowledge of the working of the multiplier and its value in their economy.

- The government will also need to be aware that the value of the multiplier can vary not only over time as savings rates and the propensity to import changes, but also between government policy instruments.
- Expenditure tends to have a higher multiplier value than tax cuts since in the first round all public expenditure is 'spent' but some of the tax cuts may be saved.
- Some expenditure has immediate spending effects (e.g. increased pensions) whereas some (e.g. long-term investment projects) may only have their full effect over a period of years.
- Some economists (including monetarist and new classical economists) argue that the multiplier value of government expenditure is zero since an increase has to be financed via government borrowing from the private sector, which 'crowds out' an equivalent amount of private, expenditure.

Test your understanding 6

Which of the following is **least** likely to result in a fall in investment spending in an economy?

A An increase in government expenditure

B An increase in interest rates

C An increase in the rate of inflation

D A reduction in the availability of credit

Test your understanding 7

Answer the following questions based on the preceding information.

1 Name two withdrawals from the circular flow.

2 What is an injection into the circular flow?

3 When, in theory, is an economy in equilibrium?

4 What does the consumption function show?

5 Apart from households and firms, what else is a major consumer of goods and services?

6 Define net investment.

7 What does the accelerator theory show?

8 What does the multiplier show?

9 What is the formula for calculating the multiplier, K?

4 Aggregate supply and demand

The common economic issues facing all economies include the twin problems of inflation and unemployment. Much government economic policy effort is devoted to attempts to prevent either of these undesirable outcomes. In order to understand these economic policies it is first necessary to see how unemployment and inflation might arise in a market economy. The starting point for this understanding is the aggregate demand and aggregate supply model.

4.1 The aggregate demand and aggregate supply model

The circular flow model discussed in Sections 2 and 3 showed how the total demand for goods and services in the economy was made up of several elements: consumption, investment, government expenditure and net exports (i.e. exports minus imports). Together these made up aggregate monetary demand or simply just aggregate demand (AD).

$$AD = C + I + G + (X - M)$$

However, an understanding of how the economy functions and why problems may occur cannot be explained solely in terms of the demand for goods and services; we also need to know about the ability of the economy to produce goods and services. This is known as aggregate supply (AS).

4.2 Aggregate demand (AD)

In the circular flow model, AD was related to the level of national income and the level of expenditure; in the aggregate demand and supply model, it is related to national income and to the price level. This makes possible a discussion of the origin of both unemployment and inflation.

It is assumed that aggregate demand:

- is made up of all components of expenditure in the economy, consumption, investment, government expenditure and net exports
- is inversely related to prices since a price fall would raise everyone's real (purchasing power) wealth and thus tend to raise spending
- may shift if any one component (e.g. investment or exports) changes through the multiplier effect.

Thus, the AD curve (plotted with price on the vertical axis and quantity demanded on the horizontal axis) slopes down from left to right but may shift.

4.3 Aggregate supply (AS)

The aggregate supply in an economy refers to the willingness and ability of producers in an economy, largely the business sector, to produce and offer for sale, goods and services. It is assumed that aggregate supply

- is the collective result of decisions made by millions of business producers, large and small to produce and sell goods and services
- is positively related to the price level since, other things being equal, a rise in the price level will make sales more profitable and thus encourage businesses to expand output
- is limited by the availability of resources (labour, capital, etc.) so that at full employment, output cannot be increased any further
- can only shift in the long run as the result of a change in the costs of production or in the availability of factors of production.

Thus the AS curve slopes upward from left to right and does not shift in the short run.

4.4 Equilibrium

National equilibrium will be where the aggregate demand (AD) curve intersects with the aggregate supply (AS) curve; here, the total demand for goods and services in the economy is equal to the total supply of goods and services in the economy.

The particular value of this model is that it demonstrates the effect of changes in either aggregate demand or aggregate supply on both the level of national income and on the price level. Given the reasonable assumption that the level of employment in an economy in the short to medium run is a function of the level of national income, the model can show how inflation and unemployment might arise in an economy and how governments might respond to these problems.

4.5 Changes in aggregate demand

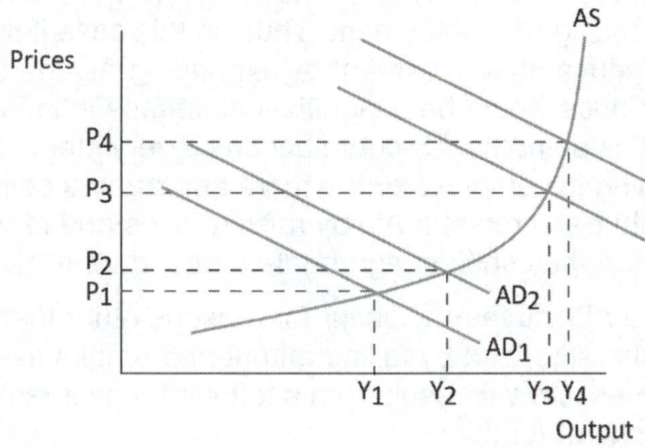

Example 1

Suppose that the economy is initially in equilibrium at a level of national income (equivalent to national output) and employment denoted by Y_1. If there was an increase in aggregate demand from AD_1 to AD_2

- the new equilibrium would be at national income level Y_2
- national income would have risen from Y_1 to Y_2 and unemployment would have fallen
- the price level would have risen from P_1 to P_2.

In this case, most of the effect of an increase in AD is felt in the form of rising income and employment (generated by the increase in national output from Y_1 to Y_2) and there is only a small inflationary impact (a small average price rise from P_1 to P_2). Thus, in this case, if the government wished to reduce unemployment an expansion of AD by reducing taxes or by raising government expenditure would be an appropriate and effective policy.

Example 2

Suppose that the economy is initially in equilibrium at a level of national income and employment denoted by Y_3. If there was an increase in aggregate demand from AD_3 to AD_4

- the new equilibrium would be at national income level Y_4
- national income would have risen from Y_3 to Y_4 and unemployment would have fallen
- the price level would have risen from P_3 to P_4.

In this case, most of the effect of an increase in AD is felt in the form of a rise in the price level (a large increase from P_3 to P_4) and there is only a small effect in raising national income (as generated from the small increase in national output from Y_3 to Y_4) and reducing unemployment. Thus, in this case if the government attempted to further reduce unemployment by expanding AD the effect would be very small and the price would be a significant increase in inflationary pressure. Indeed, at this point the AS curve becomes very steep because the economy is approaching full employment; a more appropriate policy for government here might be to restrain AD by raising taxes and reducing government expenditure thus shifting aggregate demand from AD_4 to AD_3.

Of course, shifts in the AD curve may occur for reasons other than government policy. A recession, characterized by falling output and employment and reduced inflationary pressure will result from a leftward movement in the AD curve caused by, among other things

- a fall in investment if business confidence is damaged
- a fall in consumer expenditure if consumers lose confidence or if they reach the limits of their ability to finance extra credit
- a fall in exports if there is a major loss of competitiveness or there is a recession in the country's major trading partners.

Since 2009, this has been the experience of many developed economies, as declining consumer and business confidence led to falling aggregate demand and contracting national income. The result was a serious recession affecting much of the world economy.

By 2013, however, some countries were seeing renewed growth. The US economy grew at an annual rate of 2.5% in the first three months of the year, helped by the strongest consumer spending figures in two years.

Since then, global growth occurred, albeit at a sluggish rate, until the COVID-19 pandemic.

Likewise, the economy may expand and experience a period of business boom characterised by rising output and employment and increasing inflationary pressures conditions if there is a rightward movement in the AD caused by, among other things

- an investment boom if business is confident and profitable
- a rapid rise in consumer expenditure if consumers are confident and have access to affordable credit
- a rapid rise in exports if there is a major gain in competitiveness (e.g. from a depreciation of the currency) or there is a boom in the country's major trading partners.

4.6 Changes in aggregate supply

It is also possible that, in the long run, the aggregate supply in the economy might change. This is shown as shifts in the aggregate supply curve.

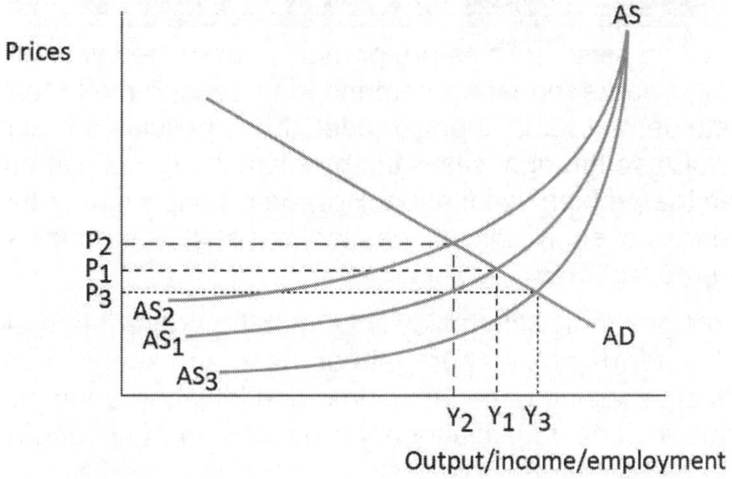

Example 1

The economy might suffer from **supply-side shocks,** which reduce the ability or willingness of productive businesses in the economy to produce and sell goods and services. If this occurred, the AS would shift to the left, for example, from AS_1 to AS_2. The result would be a rise in the price level from P_1 to P_2 and a fall in output from Y_1 to Y_2. This combination of falling output and rising inflation is sometimes referred to as **stagflation**. Such supply-side shocks might arise from:

- a major rise in energy and/or raw material prices such as the oil price rises in the 1970s and early 1980s.
- a major rise in labour costs; the problems of many of the European Union larger economies in past years may be partly the result of social and labour legislation significantly raising the cost of labour for businesses.
- a significant fall in productivity in businesses due to major technological problems; some fear that attempting to deal with global warming by emissions controls may have something of this effect on economies.
- a global pandemic, forcing the closure of businesses and a reduction in national output for a period of time.

Example 2

The economy might also experience a rightward shift in the AS curve such as from AS_1 to AS_3. This would produce a highly beneficial result that national income and employment would expand from Y_1 to Y_3 and the price level would fall from P_1 to P_3. This might be seen as the opposite of stagflation. Such shifts to the right in the aggregate supply curve might arise from:

- favourable developments in the economy reducing costs such as falling energy and raw material prices or big productivity improvements from technological change

- deliberate government supply-side policies designed to shift the AS curve to the right such as privatisation, business tax reductions or labour market reforms.

Further details on supply side policies

Monetary and fiscal policies are primarily concerned with influencing the level of aggregate monetary demand in the economy. In terms of the aggregate demand and supply model, these policies are aimed to shift the AD curve to the right when the problem is unemployment and to the left when the problem is inflation. However, concern over the effectiveness of such policies, has led to a shift of emphasis towards **supply side policies**.

The object of supply side policy is to shift the aggregate supply curve to the right. In terms of the aggregate demand and supply model, this would have effect of raising national income and lowering unemployment at the same time as reducing inflationary pressures in the economy.

Supply side policy typically consists of a wide range of measures, the most important of which are:

- shifting taxation away from direct to indirect taxation and reducing marginal rates of taxation to encourage work and enterprise
- reducing social security payments and tailoring them to encourage the unemployed to seek employment
- an emphasis on vocational education and training to improve work skills in the labour force
- reducing the power of trade unions and employee organisations to limit entry into occupations and to raise wages above equilibrium levels
- deregulation and privatisation to encourage enterprise and risk-taking.

In the longer run, such policies appear to have been successful. In the USA and the UK where such policies have been most widely adopted, both unemployment and inflationary pressures fell significantly in the 1990s and onwards.

However, supply side policies have had other, less desirable consequences. The most significant of these have been:

- making the taxation system much more regressive: in the UK the proportion of income paid in tax (although not on income tax) by the poorest 20% of the population is higher than that paid by the richest 20%
- a more unequal distribution of income
- a greater degree of uncertainty for workers in the labour market and with less employment protection
- a fall in the relative (and sometimes absolute) standard of living of many who are dependent on social security payments.

Test your understanding 8

In an aggregate demand and supply diagram, if the aggregate supply curve shifted to the left, the consequences would be:

A national income and the price level would both fall

B national income and the price level would both rise

C national income would fall and the price level would rise

D national income would rise and the price level would fall

Test your understanding 9

Which one of the following would cause a fall in the level of aggregate demand in an economy?

A A decrease in government expenditure

B A fall in the propensity to save

C A fall in the level of imports

D A decrease in the level of income tax

Test your understanding 10

Which one of the following would cause the aggregate supply curve of an economy to shift to the right?

A A decrease in government expenditure

B Increased investment in new technologies in industry

C A fall in interest rates

D Lower unemployment

Test your understanding 11

State whether each of the following would affect the AD curve or AS curve and state whether the curve would move to the right or to the left.

Factor	AD	AS	Right	Left
A fall in business confidence due to political scandals				
An increase in tariffs on imported goods				
A major increase in world oil prices				
An increase in trade union power and militancy				
An increase in interest rates				
New training initiatives for the unemployed				

5 Trade cycles

The trade cycle and government policy

Aggregate demand and supply analysis has shown how the trade cycle of recessions, recoveries and booms followed by further recession might occur and how government policy might be used to deal with these problems.

Stage of trade cycle	Features	Causes	Policy response
Recession	• falling output/income, • high and rising unemployment, • reduced inflationary pressure, • improving trade balance as imports fall • public finance will be adversely affected due to reduced tax income and increased benefits payments	• falling domestic AD from lower levels of: consumer spending, investment, exports, government expenditure • world recession	• raise AD by reducing taxation, raising public expenditure, lowering interest rates • Note: this will further increase the need for government borrowing
Stagflation: special type of recession	• falling output, income and employment • rising inflationary pressure	• supply-side shocks reducing aggregate supply • could have a recession due to low AD combined with imported cost-push inflation	• supply-side policy to raise aggregate supply

Recovery	• output and income begin to rise • unemployment begins to fall • only moderate inflationary pressure • improving public finances	• returning confidence in business and consumer sectors • effect of government expansionary policy undertaken in recession	• reduction in expansionary policy to prevent too strong a boom
Boom	• high output and employment • rising inflationary pressure • deteriorating trade balance as imports rise • Higher net income for government allows repayment of debt	• high and rising AD from higher levels of: consumer spending, investment, exports, government expenditure	• reduce AD by raising taxation, reducing public expenditure, higher interest rates

Of course, there might be a period of economic growth with all the features of a boom but without undue inflationary pressure, if the aggregate supply of the economy continually increases. The ability of some economies such as the United Kingdom and the USA to maintain steady growth with high levels of employment but without serious inflationary pressures in recent years may have been, at least partly, the result of supply-side reforms in these countries since the 1980s.

Implications for businesses

The main implication of trade cycles will be the impact on likely demand for the firm's products.

- A firm selling staple goods such as milk and bread will be less affected than one selling new cars for example.
- Manufacturers of capital goods such as machinery will see a major downturn in demand in recessions but a large upswing in a growth phase.
- A firm that supplies to the public sector will be particularly concerned with government spending plans. For example, if a government wishes to try to spend their way out of a recession by building new roads and schools, then clearly this would present major opportunities for building contractors.

- A firm may need to consider its portfolio of products to reduce the risk associated with trade cycles, perhaps by diversifying geographically.
- Some firms produce/provide counter-cyclical goods/services. These are firms that provide items that sell well in a recession, such as discount retailers (Lidl, Poundland) and auto repair businesses (car owners are more likely to repair their cars than buy new ones).

Other implications include

- In times of economic downturn, unemployment will be higher, so the firm will have more bargaining power over employees so may be able to pay lower wages than in boom times.
- Success may also be influenced by being able to determine when best to act – for example, increasing production in response to an anticipated upturn in economic activity.
- If the government adjusts interest rates as part of its policies, then this will affect the firm's cost of borrowing.

Trade cycles

- A recession starts when demand begins to fall. Firms respond to the fall in demand by reducing their output, causing a decline in purchases of raw materials and an increase in unemployment, as workers are laid off.
- The reduction in demand will feed through into households' incomes, causing these to fall too, resulting in a further reduction in demand.
- The economy will quickly move into a slump, with low business confidence, depressed 'animal spirits' and little incentive to carry out investment.
- Once in the slump, it can take a long time before the economy begins to recover. One of the most difficult things to restore is business and consumer confidence.
- Eventually, though, economic activity begins to pick up. It may be a new invention that tempts entrepreneurs to invest, it may be that replacement investment can be put off no longer or a war may force the government to inject expenditure into the economy.
- The extra investment will push up incomes, which will persuade consumers to spend and this will induce yet more investment, reducing unemployment.
- The economy will expand, pushing upwards into a boom. After some time, however, full capacity will be reached and demand will become stable. The reduction in investment starts off the downward spiral once again.

6 Fiscal and monetary policy options

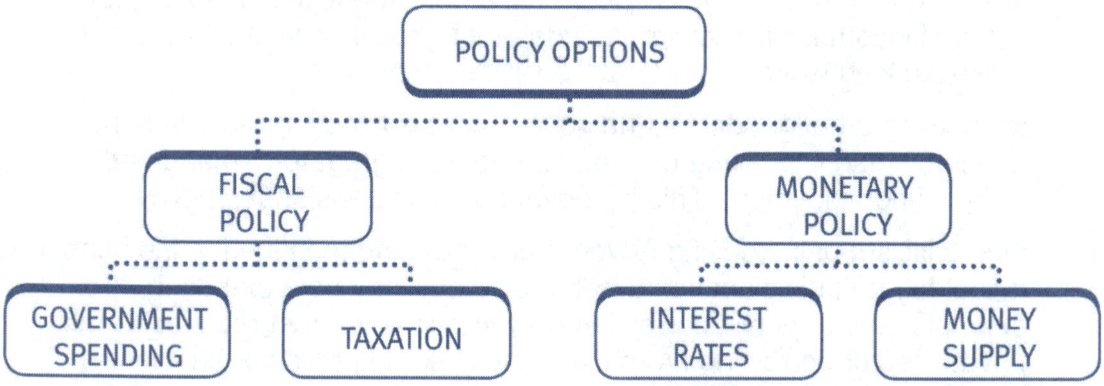

In the previous sections, we looked at policy options for managing trade cycles and the different schools of thought relating to whether governments should focus on demand management or supply side policies. Here we look at fiscal and monetary policy.

6.1 Fiscal policy options

- Fiscal policy refers to a government's taxation and spending plans and is usually understood within the context of demand side policies (see section 4.5 above), known as Keynesian economics.

Government budget

- In the medium- to long-term, it is suggested that a government should aim to achieve a balanced budget, i.e. one in which government expenditure is matched by government income.
- For a number of macroeconomic reasons that are explored in this chapter, governments may decide to run either a budget deficit or a budget surplus.

  Government income < expenditure = budget deficit

  Government income > expenditure = budget surplus

  Government income = expenditure = a balanced budget.

Note: Don't confuse a balanced budget with the balance of payments. The former refers to the relationship between government income (from taxation) and spending, while the latter refers to the flow of funds into and out of a country.

Running a budget deficit

- If a government intends to run a budget deficit, then this has to be financed through borrowing – this borrowing is referred to as the Public Sector Net Borrowing (PSNB).
- Running a budget deficit has frequently been used to promote economic growth and reduce unemployment by closing a 'deflationary gap'.

- A deflationary gap exists if the level of aggregate demand in the economy is less than that required to ensure full employment. The resulting level of national income is too low to provide employment opportunities for all those seeking work.
- By running a budget deficit, the government is injecting more into the economy than it is taking out and can boost aggregate demand and reduce unemployment. This is known as an 'expansionary' policy.
- One criticism of increasing government spending to influence the economy is that higher public spending will "crowd out" private expenditure. For example, higher public borrowing may increase interest rates and make private sector borrowing more expensive, leading to lower business investment levels.

Running a budget surplus

- If aggregate demand lies above the level necessary to generate full employment, this can lead to inflation (too much money chasing too few goods). In this situation, an 'inflationary gap' is said to exist.
- Fiscal policy can also be used to control inflation. If an inflationary gap exists, government can seek to reduce aggregate demand by running a budget surplus, effectively taking money out of the economy. This is known as a 'contractionary policy'.

6.2 Monetary policy options

- Monetary policy refers to the management of the money supply in the economy and is usually understood within the context of monetarism.
- Monetarist economists believe in using monetary policy rather than fiscal policy (as advocated by Keynesian economists to influence demand) to control the economy.
- Monetary policy can involve changing interest rates, either directly or indirectly through open market operations and setting reserve requirements for banks.
- Like fiscal policy, monetary policy can be described as expansionary or contractionary. An expansionary policy increases the total supply of money in the economy, and a contractionary policy decreases the total money supply. Expansionary policy is traditionally used to combat unemployment in a recession by lowering interest rates, while contractionary policy has the goal of raising interest rates to combat inflation.

Money supply

- The term "money supply" refers to the total amount of money in the economy. There are many measures of the money supply, including the following:

  M0 Notes and coins in circulation and balances at the country's Central Bank.

  M4 Notes and coins and all private sector sterling bank/building society deposits (96% of which are deposits).

Reserve requirements

- Typically, banks operate a fractional reserve system, i.e. only a part of their deposits are kept in cash on the assumption that not all customers will want their money back at the same time. The proportion of deposits retained in cash is known as the reserve asset ratio or liquidity ratio.

Open market operations

- By buying and selling its own bonds the government is able to exert some control over the money supply.
- For instance, by buying back its own bonds it will release more cash into circulation. Conversely, when it sells bonds it receives cash in return, reducing the amount of money in circulation thus restricting the ability of banks to lend.

Interest rates

- High interest rates suppress demand for money due to the increased cost of borrowing. Over a period of time, the money supply will then react to this reduced demand for money by contracting. Monetarists view interest rate manipulation as a key control over inflation.
- In some countries, such as India, Singapore, Japan and the UK, the setting of interest rates is the responsibility of the Central Bank. In others, it may be a government minister.
- Interest rates are discussed in more detail below.

The problem of government borrowing

When governments run budget deficits and borrow to finance those deficits a distinction can be made between two elements in those deficits:

- a **cyclical** element in which the deficit arises as a result of the downswing phase of the trade cycle and will decrease or even turn into a surplus in the upswing phase of the trade cycle
- a **structural** element in which the deficit is the result of a permanent imbalance between expenditure and taxation and will not be affected by the trade cycle.

A cyclical deficit is of much less concern since over the whole trade cycle, budget deficits would be broadly balanced by budget surpluses. However, a structural deficit implies continuous borrowing by governments and an increasing total debt ('national debt') owed by the government. There are some reasons to believe that many countries are facing pressures that tend to increase public expenditure on a long-term basis and hence threaten the emergence of structural budget deficits.

These pressures include:

- an ageing population which increases public expenditure on health care for the elderly and on state pensions
- inflation in the prices of public sector goods and services which are mainly labour intensive and thus tend to show the fastest rate of inflation
- spending commitments for public and merit goods, especially social welfare, education and health, which are difficult to decrease in the face of voter opposition
- tax changes as it is always politically much easier to reduce taxes than to raise them thus making raising more tax revenue problematic.

Thus, many governments are faced with the problem of financing budget deficits. The ways in which this might be done can be distinguished by:

- from whom the government borrows; this might be the non-bank private sector such as pension funds or individual households
- the type of liability the government issues where the main distinction is between different degrees of liquidity of those liabilities. Long-term government securities (in the United Kingdom, 'gilts') are the principal liabilities of governments.

For most governments the PSNB arising from the budget deficit is mainly financed by the sale of long-term government debt to the private (non-bank) sector of the economy. This is likely to have some effects on the economy but the nature of those effects is subject to some debate among economists.

- Some believe that the effects are real in that a budget deficit financed in this way will tend to affect the real variables in the economy, raising output and employment via the effect of the deficit on aggregate demand.
- Others, including monetarists and new classical economists, believe that the effects are **monetary** in that government borrowing injects liquid assets into the economy thus boosting the money supply and causing inflation. Moreover, government borrowing may push up interest rates thus reducing private spending. This reduction in private spending will offset the government expenditure financed by borrowing – a process known as 'crowding out'.

The problems of financing budget deficits and the potential problems arising from the need to service (pay interest on) the national debt have led governments across the world to adopt policies designed to control the level of government borrowing, such as austerity measures in the UK.

In the European Union, a condition of joining the single currency (euro) was a maximum size of national debt and of current government borrowing in relation to the national income of the country concerned.

Once a country has joined the single currency and adopted the euro, it is obliged to keep control of its government borrowing via the 'stability and growth pact', which specifies maximum amounts that governments can borrow. The crisis in the Eurozone has shown that these rules were clearly not working in many countries, especially Greece, Spain and Italy. New rules, with real sanctions, were introduced, such as a fine of up to 0.5% of gross domestic product for breaking the rules for three consecutive years.

In the United Kingdom since 1997, the government has tried to adopt the "golden rule" for government finances. This states that over the economic cycle, the Government will borrow only to invest and not to fund current spending.

This rule states that

- over the whole trade cycle, government current expenditure on goods, services and transfer payments should not exceed its taxation income
- only government investment expenditure may be financed by government borrowing
- the overall burden of public debt should not go above sustainable levels, generally taken to mean equal to 40 per cent of GDP.

However, the effect of the recession in the UK from 2008 onwards forced the government to effectively abandon this golden rule.

The current UK Government had intended to generate a surplus over all expenditure and secure a fall in government debt as a % of GDP, which in the 2018-19 fiscal year was at over 80.8%. Due to the impact of the COVID-19 pandemic, this figure had instead risen to 103.7% by March 2021.

Canada

The federal government of Canada projected a deficit of $26.6 billion in the 2019–20 fiscal year, a shortfall that is nearly five times projections from December 2015 and well past the $10 billion limit promised by the Liberal government. This had grown from original predictions, but was predicted to start falling after 2021. However, the impact of the COVID-19 pandemic meant that a historic deficit of $325.5 billion was posted in 2020. As a percentage of GDP, the deficit had risen from 1.8% in 2019 to 14.8% in 2020.

COVID-19

All government targets and measures were obviously significantly impacted by measures introduced in 2020 to protect economies during the COVID-19 crisis.

Test your understanding 12

According to the advocates of supply-side economics, which one of the following measures is most likely to reduce unemployment in an economy?

A Increasing labour retraining schemes

B Increasing public sector investment

C Increasing unemployment benefits

D Decreasing the money supply

7 Interest rate management

Monetary policy is concerned with managing the monetary environment in order to influence the decisions of economic agents including consumers, investors and businesses. It can do this by affecting either the availability of credit or the price of credit. The main feature of monetary policy is the policy of changing interest rates since they are the price of credit.

7.1 The effects of interest rate changes

Changes in interest rates affect the economy in many ways. The following consequences are the main effects of an **increase** in interest rates:

- **Borrowing falls and saving rises.**

  Higher interest rates will affect borrowers (those not already tied into fixed interest rates) adversely as it becomes more expensive to borrow, but will attract savers, who will now see an increased return on their savings.

- **Spending falls.**

  Expenditure by consumers will be reduced. This occurs because the higher interest rates raise the cost of credit and deter spending.

  If we take incomes as fairly stable in the short term, higher interest payments on credit cards/mortgages, etc. leave less income for spending on consumer goods and services. This will lower the demand for individual goods and services as well as lowering overall aggregate demand.

- **Government borrowing becomes more expensive and government expenditure falls.**

  Like consumers and businesses, governments are affected by interest rate changes. Government borrowing will become more expensive and they are less likely to borrow to fund expenditure.

- **Investment falls.**

  A rise in interest rates will reduce the net return to investment and thus discourage businesses from undertaking new investment projects.

- **Asset values fall.**

  The market value of financial assets, such as bonds, will drop, because of the inverse relationship between bond prices and the rate of interest. This, in turn, will reduce many people's wealth.

  It is likely that they will react to maintain the value of their total wealth and so may save, thereby further reducing expenditure in the economy.

Consumer spending and investment are both components of aggregate demand. As a result of the rise in interest rates causing these to fall, the aggregate demand curve shifts to the left (meaning lower demand at the same prices). This will lower inflationary pressures but at the cost of reducing the level of economic activity and raising unemployment.

In addition to these domestic effects, there may be some external effects of a rise in interest rates.

- **Foreign funds are attracted into the country.**

  A rise in interest rates will encourage overseas financial businesses to deposit money in domestic banking institutions because the rate of return has increased, relative to that in other countries.

- **The exchange rate rises, at least in the short term.**

  The inflow of foreign funds raises demand for the currency and so pushes up the exchange rate (which is the price of currency).

  In the longer term, high interest rates can stifle economic growth, potentially making domestic firms less competitive in global markets. This can reduce export demand, resulting in a fall in exchange rates.

The overall effect – and in most cases its intended effect – of a rise in interest rates is to reduce the inflationary pressures in the economy.

7.2 The impact on businesses

Clearly, businesses will be affected both directly and indirectly by changes in interest rates. These effects fall into three categories.

- **Costs**

  Some of the costs of a business, such as the cost of credit and the cost of stockholding, are directly determined by the rate of interest the business has to pay.

- **Investment decisions**

  The rate of interest is the cost of acquiring external investment funds, or the opportunity cost of using internal funds; a change in interest rates will therefore affect the profitability of investment projects.

The connection between interest rates and the cost of debt is easy to see. When a business borrows money, it will pay interest to the lender. If interest rates rise, the business will pay more in interest, and their cost of capital will rise. One mitigating factor with debt financing is the fact that the interest the business pays is a tax-deductible business expense.

As interest rates rise, so will the return the business could have earned if they had invested the money, rather than use it to e.g. finance their expansion. The return they are giving up is known as 'opportunity cost' and it is a real cost that must be figured into their cost of capital.

The business can also try and obtain equity finance from outside investors. These investors will expect a return on investment comparable to what they could get from other investments of equal risk. So if the business has other investors, the cost of equity finance is not just an opportunity cost, it is the return those investors expect to receive. This is another factor that is influenced by the rate of interest.

- **Sales revenue**

  The volume of sales will decrease if interest rates rise: this is partly because this will generate deflationary pressure in the economy and partly because some sales, for example consumer durable goods, are often based on credit.

Of course, the reverse would happen if interest rates were to be reduced. This would be a reflationary policy and appropriate when inflationary pressures are weak and the economy is experiencing low levels of output and high unemployment. In this case, lower interest rates would reduce business costs, raise the profitability of investment projects and thus encourage investment, and raise sales revenue as consumes have access to cheaper credit. Thus, the thrust of monetary policy affects the economy as a whole and impacts in many ways on the businesses that make up the economy.

UK interest rate policy

In the case of the United Kingdom, the government in 1997 established a Monetary Policy Committee at the Bank of England. It gave its members, including external experts, the power to decide the central rate of interest in the United Kingdom.

- The committee has a target rate of inflation of 2.0 per cent.
- Should the rate of inflation vary from this target by 1 per cent or more, the Governor of the Bank of England is required to provide a written explanation to the Chancellor of the Exchequer.
- Despite inflation being above 2% in 2011 and 2012, the MPC kept interest rates at 0.5% to counter the global recession and to boost lending and liquidity in financial markets.

- In 2015 there were fears of deflation and calls by some commentators for the MPC to drop interest rates further, which they did, to 0.25%, although by 2017 inflation was picking up and in response the rate was raised back to 0.75% by 2018.

In the EU, the European Central Bank manages monetary policy for the Eurozone and a similar process operates with the central bank being given an inflation target. Even in those countries where a formal target does not exist, central banks are required to regard the rate of inflation as the main policy target for monetary policy and to conduct interest rate policy accordingly.

In January 2016, Japan dropped interest rates to –0.1 %, meaning that commercial banks would be charged by the central bank for some deposits. This policy is designed to encourage them to use their reserves to lend to businesses in an attempt to counter Japan's economic stagnation.

2020 coronavirus pandemic

During the global coronavirus pandemic in 2020, many countries, including the UK, adopted monetary policy measures, including interest rate cuts to historically low levels, to try and protect their economies, which were in freefall due to disruptions of supply and shrinking of demand. It was hoped that this, along with increases in government spending to protect the incomes of people and businesses, would help businesses avoid bankruptcy and prevent individuals ending up in poverty. The UK MPC allowed rates to fall as low as 0.1%.

Some UK government gilts were issued with negative yields. Investors were willing to accept this instead of earning a positive return as they felt that the safety of lending to the government in this time of uncertainty outweighed the need for a positive return.

From late 2021 and into 2022, as the global economy started to recover from the pandemic, many countries experienced rising inflation due to increased demand and shortages of supply. Out of control inflation became the main issue for interest rate policy to address. As a result, interest rates were increased to combat inflation.

Test your understanding 13

If interest rates in Japan were cut, which of the following would not occur as a result?

A Increase in consumer spending

B Increase in private sector investment

C Decrease in the value of corporate bonds

D Short term drop in the exchange rate

Test your understanding 14

An increase in the money supply in India will cause

A Interest rates to rise, investment spending to rise, and aggregate demand to rise

B Interest rates to rise, investment spending to fall, and aggregate demand to fall

C Interest rates to fall, investment spending to fall, and aggregate demand to fall

D Interest rates to fall, investment spending to rise, and aggregate demand to rise

7.3 Managing interest rate risk

Financial managers face risk arising from changes in interest rates, i.e. a lack of certainty about the amounts or timings of cash payments and receipts. Companies face the risk that interest rates might change between the point when the company identifies the need to borrow or invest and the actual date when they enter into the transaction.

Managers are normally risk-averse, so they will look for techniques to manage and reduce these risks.

Adverse Interest Rate Movements

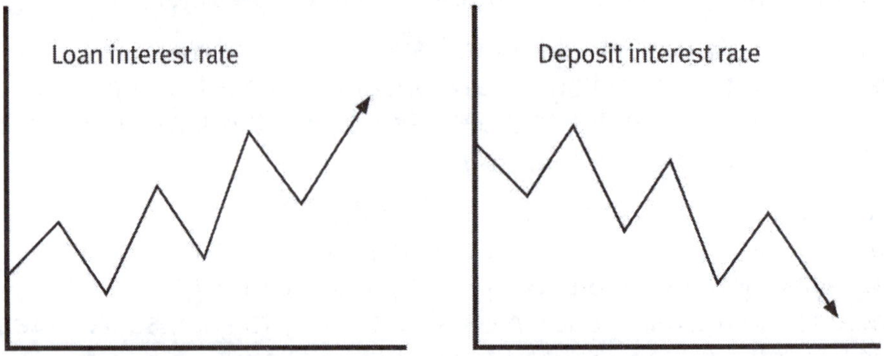

Test your understanding 15

Which of the following best describes interest rate risk?

A The risk from borrowing

B The risk from not being able to meet interest payments on debt obligations

C The risk that interest rates will rise

D The risk to profit, cash flow or a company's valuation from changes in interest rates

The aim of a **forward rate agreement (FRA)** is to:

- lock the company into a target interest rate
- hedge both adverse and favourable interest rate movements.

The company enters into a normal loan but independently organises a forward rate agreement with a bank:

- interest is paid on the loan in the normal way
- if the interest is greater than the agreed forward rate, the bank pays the difference to the company
- if the interest is less than the agreed forward rate, the company pays the difference to the bank.

Test your understanding 16

Company Y enters into a forward rate agreement (FRA) with a bank to borrow $5 million in 6 months' time at a rate of 5%. In 6 months' time, the market borrowing rate is 6%. How much interest is transferred via the FRA and in which direction?

A 5% to the FRA bank

B 5% from the FRA bank

C 1% to the FRA bank

D 1% from the FRA bank

An **interest rate guarantee (IRG)** is an option on an FRA. It allows the company a period of time during which it has the option to buy an FRA at a set price.

IRGs, like all options, protect the company from adverse movements and allow it to take advantage of favourable movements.

Decision rules:

If there is an adverse movement	If there is a favourable movement
↓	↓
Exercise the option to protect	**Allow the option to lapse**

IRGs are more expensive than the FRAs, as one has to pay for the flexibility to be able to take advantage of a favourable movement.

If the company treasurer believes that interest rates will rise:

- they will use an FRA, as it is the cheaper way to hedge against the potential adverse movement.

If the treasurer is unsure which way interest will move:

- they may be willing to use the more expensive IRG to be able to benefit from a potential fall in interest rates.

Interest rate futures work to provide an offsetting contractual position to a move in interest rates. The result of a future is to

- lock the company into the effective interest rate
- hedge both adverse and favourable interest rate movements.

Futures can be used to fix the rate on loans and investments.

Borrowers may additionally buy **options** on futures contracts. These allow them to enter into the future if needed, but let it lapse if the market rates move in their favour.

8 Taxation

There are many aims to taxation and their priority varies with the political complexion of the government. However, all governments are agreed on the need to raise revenue.

Taxation can also be used to:

- **Change markets**.

  Certain potentially harmful goods, such as cigarettes and alcohol, may be heavily taxed, thereby lowering the quantity demanded and reducing consumption levels. Over 75 per cent of the price of cigarettes goes in tax; and at times higher taxes on petrol have been used to deter consumption and induce energy conservation.

- **Influence the level of aggregate monetary demand**.

  AD can be reduced by raising taxation and can be raised by reducing taxation.

- **Finance the provision of public and merit goods**.

  The collective provision of certain public goods, such as defence, paid for from taxation revenue, enables it to be given free to everyone.

  Similarly, the zero price provision of a merit good such as education provides access to everyone, when market-priced supply might lead to under-consumption by many, which society might consider to be undesirable.

- **Change the distribution of income and wealth**.

  Direct taxes and especially progressive direct taxes fall most heavily on upper groups while indirect taxes and regressive taxes in general fall most heavily on lower income groups. Changing the balance between different taxes can thus alter income distribution.

Types of taxation

Taxes can be classified in several ways:

- What is taxed?

  The three main categories are:

Income	**Expenditure**	**Capital**
Income tax	VAT	Inheritance tax
Corporation tax	Excise duties	Capital gains tax
Social security taxes (e.g. National insurance)	Customs duties	

  However, there are also taxes on property ownership (e.g. council tax in the United Kingdom), car use (motor vehicle licence duty), a firm's payroll (employers' social security taxes), and oil royalties (petroleum revenue tax).

- Who is levying the tax?

  Most taxes are imposed by central government but some local government authorities are given the power to raise taxes.

- Who is paying the tax?

  Usually a distinction is made between **direct** and **indirect** taxes. With a direct tax, the person receiving the income pays the tax to the authorities, for example income tax. In contrast, most taxes on expenditure are termed indirect, because the purchaser who benefits from the consumption is charged, usually in the purchase price, but the actual tax revenue is remitted, for convenience, by the seller to the authorities. Although the seller pays in the nominal sense, he/she may be able to pass on the burden of the tax to the purchaser through a higher price.

- What percentage of income is paid in tax? The main categories here are:

  – **progressive**. A larger percentage of income is paid in tax as income rises, e.g. income tax (above a certain minimum).

  – **regressive**. A smaller percentage of income is paid in tax as income rises, e.g. VAT (on most goods and services).

  – **proportional**. The same percentage of income is paid in tax at all income levels.

  Thus, with a progressive tax the average rate of taxation rises with income, whereas with a regressive tax the average rate falls. The average rate of tax is constant with a proportional tax. The marginal rate of taxation (percentage of extra $1 income paid in tax) also varies between these different types of tax. The marginal rate is higher than the average rate with a progressive tax but lower with a regressive tax as income rises. The two rates are equal for a proportional tax.

Example of a regressive tax:

Income tax rates for earnings between £0 and £10,000 are 40% and for earnings above £10,000 are 20%.

This would be an example of a regressive tax, as higher earning people would pay a lower proportion of their overall income as tax. But the monetary (£) amount they pay will still be higher than someone on a lower income:

Annual earnings of £1,000: pay £400 tax - 40% of income

Annual earnings of £10,000: pay £4,000 tax - 40% of income

Annual earnings of £15,000: pay (£10,000 × 40% + £5,000 × 20%) £5,000 - 33.3% of income

Annual earnings of £50,000: pay (£10,000 × 40% + £40,000 × 20%) £12,000 - 24% of income.

So the £ amount of tax paid rises with income but the proportion of tax paid falls with income, making it regressive.

Test your understanding 17

In China, the tax on an individual's income is progressive. A progressive tax is one where the tax payment:

A rises as income increases

B falls as income increases

C is a constant proportion of income

D rises at a faster rate than income increases

Test your understanding 18

The following data refer to the principal sources of taxation revenue for the government of a developed economy.

Government tax revenue: main tax sources as a percentage of total tax revenue.

		200X	200Y
		%	%
1	Income taxes	34.1	30.0
2	Social security taxes	19.2	20.0
3	Corporation tax	6.8	7.9
4	Value added tax	14.7	22.9
5	Excise duties	15.9	14.3
6	Other expenditure taxes*	7.7	3.7
7	Capital gains tax	0.9	0.6
8	Inheritance tax	0.7	0.6

*includes stamp duty and motor vehicle duties.

Required:

Using both your knowledge of economic theory and material contained in the table:

(a) State whether each of the following is a direct tax or an indirect tax:

- (i) income tax
- (ii) corporation tax
- (iii) value added tax
- (iv) excise duties
- (v) social security taxes. **(5 marks)**

(b) State whether each of the following statements is true or false.

- (i) Between 200X and 200Y the burden of taxation this economy shifted from indirect towards direct taxation.
- (ii) Retailers cannot pass all of an indirect tax onto the customer.
- (iii) Most tax revenue is gained when indirect taxes are levied on goods with high price elasticity of demand.
- (iv) Indirect taxes are likely to be more regressive than direct taxes.

(4 marks)

(Total marks = 9)

9 Achieving policy objectives

The above (and other) policy options discussed can be blended to achieve economic objectives as follows.

9.1 Engineering a recovery from a recession

Policies to promote growth in order to get out of a recession include the following:

Cutting interest rates

- This can be interpreted either as part of Keynesian demand management (cutting interest rates should boost aggregate demand) or monetarism (to boost the money supply).

Running a budget deficit

- The classic Keynesian response to a recession.
- Monetarists would argue that the way the government finances the increase will have a negative effect elsewhere (e.g. higher taxation), thus reducing its effectiveness.

9.2 Enabling long term growth

Supply-side policies

Supply side policies attempt to increase the total quantity of factors of production especially capital as well as raise levels of productivity. Such policies should increase the economic capacity of the economy and include:

- Increasing the availability and quantity of skilled labour:
  - Training schemes to increase skills
  - Childcare vouchers to encourage single parents to enter the labour market
  - Using the income tax and benefits systems to encourage workers to work harder and longer hours.
- Encouraging research and development, for example by government sponsorship of university research in cutting edge technologies.
- Modernisation of the transport system, such as the motorway network, to enhance the distribution networks of firms.
- Providing smaller firms with assistance in the form of market information, advice on exporting, management training, technical assistance as well as tax concessions.
- Deregulation of markets.

Other

- Regional development grants and tax incentives to boost investment.
- Protectionist measures to reduce imports (e.g. quotas).
- Creating a stable economy to boost confidence (e.g. by achieving low inflation).

Further details on economic growth

Factors influencing economic growth

The growth potential of an economy is dependent upon two things:

- The amount of economic resources. The more factors of production there are, in the form of land, labour, enterprise and capital, the greater the potential for economic growth.
- The productivity of these factors of production.

Improvements in productivity are important for economic growth, as it will not only increase output from a given stock of factors of production but it will also lower costs and improve the competitiveness of an economy.

Capital can play a major part in economic growth.

- The greater the capital/output ratio, the higher the productivity of labour. The greater the levels of investment, the faster will be the growth in the capital stock.
- The higher the quality of capital, the more advanced will be the technology progress. This will occur when machinery is updated and when investment in research and development is high.

Labour also influences economic growth via its quantity and quality.

- Demographic factors such as the size and gender/age composition of the population determine the size of the work force. The participation rate measures the proportion of any age group that makes itself available for work. The greater this is, the greater the size of the working population.
- Education and training are likely to make a work force more adaptable and enterprising. This in turn will improve mobility of labour and raise its productivity.

Policies to promote economic growth

Due to the importance of economic growth in raising standards of living, governments have always taken an interest in policies to promote it. A necessary condition is that levels of aggregate monetary demand are kept sufficiently high to see that existing productive capacity is fully used and that firms are encouraged to expand potential production by further investment.

- Governments can use fiscal and monetary policy to keep aggregate monetary demand close to its full employment level.
- Tax rates can be cut and interest rates lowered to encourage consumer and investment spending.

However, government policies will also seek to encourage aggregate supply in order to expand production in the economy.

Supply-side policies attempt to increase the total quantity of factors of production especially capital as well as raise levels of productivity. Such policies can be market driven or interventionist in nature. Market driven policies seek to create as free a market as possible within which private enterprise and entrepreneurial activity can thrive. Such policies aim to reduce the role of government in the economy and place a greater emphasis on the role of the individual in driving economic activity.

- This should encourage workers to work harder and longer hours as they will retain a greater amount of their earnings.
- It might also encourage previously non-active persons, such as homemakers, to enter the labour market as the opportunity costs of not doing so has now risen.

Supply-side policies also seek to offer greater incentives in the economy. Marginal rates of taxation can be cut for workers and firms.

- Consequently, the amount of labour as well as its productivity could rise as income tax rates are reduced, thus raising economic growth.
- Cuts in business tax would raise the level of retained profits, providing more funds for firms to reinvest in the business and thus raising the capital stock in the economy.

Finally, market driven policies will seek to reduce the amount of controls in the economy. This could involve regulations that include unnecessary restrictions on business activity, for example, licensing laws, or the amount of bureaucratic form-filling required from small firms.

However not all firms and entrepreneurs automatically thrive in a free market. Consequently, supply-side policies are often interventionist in order to promote further economic growth in an economy. In most developed economies, governments support the infrastructure to give firms a stronger foundation from which to conduct their businesses.

- This can take the form of modernisation of the transport system, such as the motorway network, which will enhance the distribution networks of firms.
- Education and training may be upgraded which will provide firms with potentially a more adaptable and productive supply of labour.
- The government may sponsor research and development in universities in order to provide an economy with an advantage in respect of leading edge technologies.

9.3 Unemployment

Reducing unemployment is not straightforward. At any moment in time, unemployment may have a variety of causes, each of which may require a different and incompatible solution.

Cyclical unemployment

- This is sometimes referred to as demand-deficient, persistent or Keynesian unemployment.
- In this case, unemployment is caused by the fact that aggregate demand in the economy is too small to create employment opportunities for all those willing, and able, to work.
- Keynesian economists refer to this as a deflationary gap and would seek to remove it by boosting aggregate demand.
- Monetarists would seek to reduce cyclical unemployment by appropriate supply-side measures, as they would argue that cyclical unemployment does not really exist.

Frictional unemployment

- This refers to those people who are short-term unemployed as they move from one job to another.
- While not seen as a problem, it can be reduced by the provision of better information through job centres and other supply-side policies.

Structural and technological unemployment

- This is caused by structural change in the economy, leading often to both a change in the skills required and the location where economic activity takes place (e.g. coal miners' skills not being transferable to newer industries).
- Boosting aggregate demand (a demand-side policy) is likely to have little impact on structural unemployment. Supply-side policies are likely to be more effective, including:
  - government funded retraining schemes
  - tax breaks for redevelopment of old industrial sites
  - grant aid to encourage relocation of industry
  - business start-up advice and soft loans
  - help with worker relocation costs
  - improved information on available employment opportunities.

Seasonal unemployment

- Demand for some goods and services is highly seasonal, e.g. demand for fruit pickers. This in turn creates highly seasonal demand for workers. This can create regional economic problems in areas where a significant proportion of the workforce is employed in these seasonal industries.

Real wage unemployment

- This type of unemployment can occur in industries that are highly unionised. By keeping wages artificially high by the threat of strike action and closed shops, the number of people employed in the industry is reduced.
- Monetarists would see this as a prime example of a market imperfection and would address it by reducing union powers and abolishing minimum wage agreements.

Illustration 3 – Unemployment

In the 1980s, the UK experienced a huge decline in its traditional heavy industries in the north. At the same time, new high technology industries were established in the south.

Workers in the former heavy industries were at a double disadvantage. Not only were they in the wrong location but they also had the wrong skills required by the new industries.

A current worry relates to the rise of automation, particularly that driven by artificial intelligence (AI). As computers become more and more able to perform tasks that were previously performed manually in a quicker, more efficient and cheaper way, manual workers will increasingly find that their skillsets are out of date.

Test your understanding 19

Match each of the scenarios given below with one of the following types of unemployment.

- Types
- Cyclical
- Structural
- Seasonal
- Frictional
- Real Wage

Scenarios

A A worker loses their job because of the introduction of new technology.

B After the financial crisis in 2008 and the resulting recession, EU unemployment rose considerably.

C A rise in the minimum wage has resulted in job losses in the retail sector.

D A management accountant has just been made redundant but is due to start a new job in three weeks' time.

E Bar staff are out of work in November in a European holiday resort.

Test your understanding 20

In recent years, a number of skilled workers have left Country A to work in neighbouring countries, because the tax rates in the neighbouring countries are lower than Country A's tax rates. The resulting decrease in the supply of skilled labour in Country A is likely to lead to:

A A lower equilibrium wage and a lower quantity of labour employed.

B Structural unemployment.

C A higher equilibrium wage and a lower quantity of labour employed.

D Frictional unemployment.

9.4 Inflation

Inflation has a number of causes and solutions.

Demand-pull inflation

- If demand for goods and services in the economy is growing faster than the ability of the economy to supply these goods and services, prices will increase – the classic case of too much money chasing too few goods.
- Demand-side policies would focus on reducing aggregate demand through tax rises, cuts in government spending and higher interest rates.
- One type of demand-pull inflation is that due to excessive growth in the money supply.
- Monetarists argue that inflation can result from an over expansion of the money supply. In effect increasing the money supply increases purchasing power in the economy, boosting demand for goods and services. If this expansion occurs faster than expansion in the supply of goods and services inflation can arise.
- The main monetarist tool for controlling such inflation is to reduce the growth in the money supply through higher interest rates.

Cost-push inflation

- If the underlying cost of factors of production increases, this is likely to be reflected in an increase in output prices as firms seek to maintain their profit margins irrespective of the level of aggregate demand.
- Reasons for cost increases include rising factor prices, rising import prices and increases in indirect taxes.
- For example, in an economy in which imports are significant, a weakening of the national currency will increase the cost of imports and could lead to domestic inflation. This can be reduced by policies to strengthen the national currency (see later).

Expectations effect

- If anticipated levels of inflation are built into wage negotiations and pricing decisions then it is likely that the expected rate of inflation will arise. Whilst the expectations effect is not the root cause of inflation it can contribute significantly to an inflationary spiral, particularly when underlying levels of inflation are high and rising.
- This spiral can be managed by a 'prices and incomes' policy where manufacturers agree to limit price rises in response to union agreements to limit wage claims.
- In the 1970s, the UK government sought to control the inflationary effect of rising oil prices by setting ceiling prices for basic goods and services and, through the extensive nationalised industries of the day, wage increases. Ministers specified what the price of bread and milk would be and by how much the wages of workers in specific sectors would be allowed to rise.

Illustration 4 – Inflation

After the collapse of communism in the former Soviet Union, inflation in Russia during the early 1990s reached 5,000%, according to some estimates. This was due to the government policy of financing redevelopment through a rapid growth in the money supply.

Test your understanding 21

Answer the following questions based on the preceding information.

1 What could be the underlying causes of demand-pull inflation?

2 In cost-push inflation, cost rises are 'exogenous'. What does that mean?

3 Suggest four effects of inflation.

4 List three important types of unemployment.

5 Specify three costs of unemployment.

Test your understanding 22

The following data refer to an economy over a period of 13 years. Consider the data and answer the following questions:

Year	Rate of growth of GDP[1] %	Govt. borrowing[2] $bn	Balance of payments[3] $bn
2004	–2.0	+11.8	+2.6
2005	–1.1	+10.5	+6.7
2006	+1.7	+4.8	+4.6
2007	+3.7	+11.5	+3.5
2008	+2.0	+10.3	+1.4
2009	+4.0	+7.4	+2.2
2010	+4.0	+2.5	–0.9
2011	+4.6	–1.4	–5.0
2012	+4.9	–11.9	–16.5
2013	+2.2	–9.3	–22.5
2014	+0.6	–2.1	–18.2
2015	–2.3	+7.7	–7.6
2016	–0.5	+28.9	–8.5

[1] Annual rate of growth of gross domestic product (GDP).

[2] Government borrowing (PSNB) '+' denotes net borrowing, '–' denotes repayment of previous debt.

[3] Balance of payments, current account: '+' denotes surplus, '–' denotes deficit.

Required:

Using both your knowledge of economic theory and the data contained in the table:

(a) With respect to the data in the above table, identify 2 years of economic recession in this economy and state in whether a recession: **(2 marks)**

(i) government borrowing increases or decreases

(ii) the current account of the balance of payments moves towards deficit or surplus. **(2 marks)**

(b) State whether, other things being equal, the following would increase or decrease the level of government borrowing (the PSNB) or have no effect:

(i) a rise in exports

(ii) a fall in unemployment. **(2 marks)**

c) State whether each of the following is true or false.

(i) A current account deficit must be financed by a surplus on the capital and financial accounts.

(ii) If the government has a budget deficit it must borrow from abroad to finance it.

(iii) The national debt is the amount of money owed by the government to other countries.

(iv) The government budget acts as an automatic stabiliser in the trade cycle. **(4 marks)**

(Total marks = 10)

The Phillips Curve

It is generally believed that unemployment and inflation are linked. Phillips correlated changes in United Kingdom money wages and the level of unemployment. The relationships suggested that when unemployment was 2.5%, the rate of change in money wages would be non-inflationary. As wages accounted for 70% of production costs and it was assumed that cost-plus pricing was adopted, it was concluded that prices and unemployment were also correlated. If an economy was run at a 2.5% level of unemployment, it was suggested that the general price level would be stabilised. Thus, the Phillips curve is normally shown as a relationship between the level of unemployment and the rate of inflation.

Thus, the Phillips curve seemed to show a stable relationship between inflation and unemployment.

This means that:

- the lower the rate of unemployment, the higher the rate of inflation
- the higher the rate of unemployment, the lower the rate of inflation
- there was a trade-off between employment and price stability
- governments could not simultaneously achieve price stability and full employment.

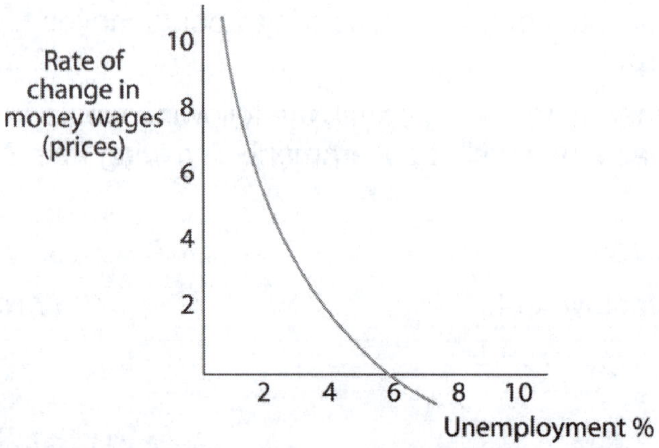

Test your understanding answers

Test your understanding 1

C

Lower taxation is not a policy objective. Rather it is a policy instrument that could be used to encourage economic growth.

Test your understanding 2

A Economic growth always brings benefits to all members of a society. **FALSE**

The benefits of economic growth are often very unevenly spread across a population. Those missing out on growth can experience a relative decline in their standard of living.

B Economic growth can lead to an increase in imports. **TRUE**

Rising incomes that accompany economic growth can lead to an increase in imports as consumers choose to spend their income on foreign rather than domestically produced goods. Also, supply doesn't grow as fast as demand, so it may be that domestic goods aren't immediately available to satisfy the increased demand, hence foreign goods are purchased instead.

C Inflation does not affect those on fixed incomes as much as those in employment. **FALSE**

Fixed incomes do not increase in line with inflation, e.g. 10% on $10,000 savings will not increase if a country is experiencing inflation. Those in employment would expect to receive pay rises broadly in line with inflation ensuring that the spending power of their income is not eroded.

D Inflation encourages investment in a national economy. **FALSE**

Inflation tends to discourage investment in a national economy in a number of ways. High inflation levels make forecasting the results of investment projects more difficult. This leads to a loss of confidence to invest for both domestic and international investors.

Test your understanding 3

The main implications of 'boom and bust' are:

	Boom	Bust
Individuals and households	On the whole a boom time will be good for households: • low unemployment • rising house prices • high levels of confidence • increasing consumer spending. But: • People may be tempted to over-stretch borrowings. • Possible inflation, the main problem with 'boom and bust'.	The main problem with 'boom and bust' is the 'bust': • job losses • people losing their homes when unable to pay mortgages • fall in labour mobility due to negative equity • bankruptcy • low confidence.
Firms	• growth in profitability • extra competition as new firms are established • May be tempted to over-stretch themselves through growing too quickly (which can give cash flow problems) and/or excessive borrowing.	• corporate failures • fall in profits • excess capacity.

Most people and firms would prefer steady growth without the high risks associated with the extremes of 'boom and bust'.

Test your understanding 4

C

Rising prices will generally reduce people's levels of consumption, but in some circumstances, higher inflation can result in an increase in consumption spending as people prefer to spend now while their money has greater purchasing power.

Test your understanding 5

False

Do not confuse investment and savings. What Hina has done is save more, so the level of savings will increase by $100 not the level of investment.

You could argue that the bank, having additional funds, would increase its lending to businesses that could then use it for investment (e.g. building new factories) but it is highly unlikely that investment will rise by exactly $100. The counter argument is that the reduction in consumption demand may result in a fall in investment levels.

Test your understanding 6

A

Excluding any (largely spurious) crowding out effects there is no reason to expect an increase in government expenditure to lead to a fall in investment. Given the impact on GDP, the opposite might be expected.

- B – an increase in interest rates will make fewer projects worth undertaking (higher cost of capital means lower NPVs)
- C – higher inflation creates uncertainty and thus stifles investment
- D – less credit means firms will struggle to raise funds for investment

Test your understanding 7

1 Withdrawals from the circular flow are savings, taxes and imports.

2 An injection into the circular flow is any additional expenditure that does not arise from the circular flow of income itself.

3 At equilibrium, injections and withdrawals are equal.

4 The consumption function shows how the level of consumption changes as the level of income changes.

5 There are two other major consumers of goods and services: the government and overseas consumers (via exports).

6 Net investment is the volume of investment in capital goods over and above that required to replace worn-out capital, that is depreciation.

7	The accelerator theory shows that changes in consumption expenditure may induce much larger proportional changes in investment expenditure and thereby contribute to the trade cycle.
8	The multiplier shows that an increase in expenditure (e.g. investment, government expenditure or exports) will produce a much larger increase in total income and expenditure through successive rounds of spending.
9	The multiplier can be calculated as K= 1/(1 – MPC) where MPC is the marginal propensity to consume or K = 1/MPS where MPC is the marginal propensity to save.

Test your understanding 8

C

On the aggregate supply and aggregate demand diagram AS/AD the horizontal axis is national income and the vertical axis is the price level. If the AS curves shifts to the left then national income must fall. Since the AD curve is normally sloped down left to right, the new AS curve will intersect is a higher point. Thus the price level will rise.

Test your understanding 9

A

(D) would increase consumer incomes and therefore demand. (B) would mean consumers spending a higher proportion of their income. (C) would imply an increase in demand for home-produced goods. A is correct because government expenditure is one component of aggregate demand.

Test your understanding 10

B

(A) and (C) will impact aggregate demand not supply and (D) is a consequence of the supply curve moving to the right not a cause.

Test your understanding 11

Factor	AD	AS	Right	Left
A fall in business confidence due to political scandals	X			X
An increase in tariffs on imported goods	X		X	
A major increase in world oil prices		X		X
An increase in trade union power and militancy		X		X
An increase in interest rates	X			X
New training initiatives for the unemployed		X	X	

Test your understanding 12

A

Supply-side theorists believe unemployment is the result of problems with the supply of labour. (B) and (D) are concerned with aggregate demand and the demand for labour, and are therefore incorrect. (C) is incorrect since supply-side theorists believe that generous unemployment benefits encourage unemployment.

Test your understanding 13

C

The value of bonds is inversely proportional to interest rates. As rates fall, the value will increase.

(A) and (B) could be due to a cut in interest rates, as finance will become cheaper for both individuals and businesses.

(D) is correct as, in the short run, a cut in interest rates will result in funds leaving the country to find higher interest rates elsewhere. This will increase supply of the currency and hence lead to a drop in its price (exchange rate).

Test your understanding 14

D

If the supply of money is increased, then the price of money – in effect, interest rates – will be reduced. Lower interest rates mean the cost of capital used in investment decisions will also be reduced, meaning that the net present value of investment projects will increase. This will lead to an increase in investment spending. Investments represent an injection into the economy, so a growth in investments will lead to an increase in aggregate demand.

Test your understanding 15

D

Interest rate risk arises for investors and lenders, as well as for borrowers, and risk can arise from a fall as well as a rise in interest rates, or from a change in the structure of interest rates.

Test your understanding 16

D

The company will take on a loan at the market rate of 6% and the FRA bank will transfer 1% to the company so that the company's net overall borrowing ends up at the agreed FRA rate of 5%.

Test your understanding 17

D

B refers to a regressive tax and (C) refers to a proportional tax. (A) is insufficient since the tax payment could rise with regressive and proportional taxes. (D) is correct since it identifies a progressive tax as one where the proportion of income taken in tax rises.

Test your understanding 18

(a) (i) direct tax

(ii) direct tax

(iii) indirect tax

(iv) indirect tax

(v) direct tax

Income, corporation and social security taxes are levied on the provider of labour. VAT and excise taxes are levied on the consumer.

(b) (i) False. The burden of taxation shifted towards indirect taxation.

(ii) True. A retailer can only pass on all of a tax onto customers if the demand for the good is perfectly price inelastic. While perfectly price inelastic products are theoretically possible there are no real life examples of them.

(iii) False. Most revenue is gained from taxing goods with very low price elasticity since consumers continue to buy even when the price has risen such as in the case of tobacco, petrol and alcohol.

(iv) True. Indirect taxes are unrelated to income and therefore tend to be strongly regressive.

Test your understanding 19

A Structural

B Cyclical

C Real wage

D Frictional

E Seasonal

Test your understanding 20

C

Workers leaving Country A to work in foreign countries means the labour supply curve in Country A will shift to the left (inwards). This resulting equilibrium between supply and demand now occurs at a higher wage rate but a lower quantity than before.

Test your understanding 21

1 The principal cause is aggregate monetary demand exceeding the supply of goods and services at current prices. This could result from increases in injections into the circular flow when the economy is at or near full employment.

2 Exogenous cost rises are those that occur from outside of the economic system and are not the result of excessive aggregate demand. These could include increases in import prices or wage increases due to trade union pressure rather than the demand for labour.

3 Inflation may: reduce the international competitiveness of the trade sector of an economy; shift wealth from the holders of financial assets to the holders of debts; discourage savings as the value of savings decreases; distort consumer expenditure as consumers attempt to anticipate price changes.

4 The main types of unemployment are: structural, frictional, cyclical, seasonal and voluntary.

5 The costs of unemployment include the loss of output, the loss of tax income to the government, the loss of income to the unemployed and damage to the unemployed's skills and health.

Test your understanding 22

(a) The years of recession are 2004, 2005, 2015 and 2016 and in a recession

(i) government borrowing would increase

(ii) the balance of payments current account would move towards a surplus.

(b) (i) A rise in exports would have no direct effect on the government budget and therefore on government borrowing.

(ii) A fall in unemployment would lead to lower government borrowing as expenditure on unemployment pay fell and tax receipts rose.

(c) (i) True. The balance of payments always balances so a deficit (surplus) on one account is always matched by a surplus (deficit) on the other.

(ii) False. If the government has a budget deficit is must borrow but it can do this domestically as well as internationally.

(iii) False. Most government borrowing is done domestically so the bulk of the national debt is debt owed by the government to individuals and organisations in its own country.

(iv) True. In a recession, taxes fall and expenditure rises thus limiting the recession; the reverse occurs in a boom period.

Chapter

5

Macroeconomic and Institutional Context II: The International Economy

Chapter learning objectives

On completion of their studies, students should be able to:

- explain the concept of the balance of payments and its implications for government policy
- identify the main elements of national policy with respect to trade
- explain the impacts of exchange rate policies on business
- explain the concept of globalisation and the consequences for businesses and national economies
- explain the role of major institutions promoting global trade and development
- identify the impacts of economic and institutional factors using the PESTEL framework.

1 Introduction

In the previous chapter, we looked at the main policy objectives of governments.

- Economic growth – how can productive capacity be increased?
- Inflation – how can we ensure that general price levels do not increase?
- Unemployment – how can we ensure that everyone who wants a job has one?
- Balance of payments – how should we manage our relationship and trade with other countries?

In this chapter, we look in detail at the last of these. We then go on to identify the impacts of economic and institutional factors on the success of a current business or proposed new venture, using the PESTEL framework.

2 International trade

2.1 The benefits of international trade

Ignoring political reasons for trading, it is possible to identify a number of significant advantages relating to international trade:

- World trade allows **specialisation** enabling different nations with differing skills and resources to gain the rewards from the division of labour. In theory, nations specialise in the production of goods for which they have a natural advantage.

  For instance, Saudi Arabia extracts oil, Argentina rears beef and the UK provides financial services.

  Specialisation usually enables an industry to benefit from large-scale production and make the maximum use of resources.

  This also ties into **opportunity costs**. Countries benefit from international trade if they give up less to obtain foreign goods than would be used if the good were produced domestically. For example, growing pineapples in the UK would mean giving up land and resources (e.g. electricity to heat greenhouses) that would otherwise be used to produce other products. If the UK grows pineapples it has lost the opportunity to grow the other products. If the benefit of producing the other product outweighs the benefit of growing pineapples then the pineapples should be imported rather than grown locally.

- The **economies of scale** that can be obtained are determined by the size of the market.

  As international trade opens up new markets, it facilitates economies of scale. Such efficiency has benefits for the trading economies because it should produce lower prices and better products, leading to improvements in general living standards.

- **Competition** should be fostered by world trade, particularly free trade.

  A domestic market that is controlled by a monopolist might be subject to a foreign competitor. Alternatively, the market of a few complacent home suppliers might be revitalised by the entry of foreign firms (e.g. Japanese and American companies in British consumer goods industries).

- **Lower prices and greater choice** should be available to consumers.

  The increased choice that results from international trade is particularly evident in the food industry. Many consumers are now used to being able to eat fruits and vegetables from all over the world and all year round.

Practical limitations on specialisation

The advantages which can be gained from specialisation and international trade may be limited in practice by many of the following:

- Factor immobility

  In the real world, factors (land, labour, capital, enterprise) tend to be fairly immobile in the short run, and over longer periods in some industries. For instance, those who may struggle to find work where they live may find it difficult to move to other areas where they could find employment because of a large increase in house prices. Or they may have strong ties to the local area. However, improved technology has lowered factor costs and thereby facilitated more international trading. For some jobs, the ability to perform the work from home now means that the job can be done from anywhere with a good internet connection.

- Transport costs

  Although the production of certain bulky intermediate goods, such as cement, may be cheaper abroad, the distribution costs are so great that domestic suppliers still have a stranglehold over the market. However, generally transport costs in world trade are falling, thereby stimulating trade.

- The size of the market

  Specialisation and the resultant possible economies of scale are only justified if the production can be sold. No longer can any individual European country support a commercial or military aircraft building industry from the size of its own domestic market. Consequently, pan European production facilities were established to produce the A380 airbus. Production of the Lockheed Martin F35 Lightning II fighter jets was made possible through the participation of nine countries, including Denmark, Turkey and Australia. Sales are expected to all nine countries as well as to Japan, Israel and the Republic of Korea.

  As the standard of living improves around the world so the sizes of markets grow. Generally, the development of new products, particularly in fields such as microelectronics, encourages world trade, as it creates new markets.

- Government policies

  Governments may install barriers to trade for political, economic and social reasons. For example, the United Kingdom imposes sanctions on trade, including arms embargoes, on many countries including Afghanistan, Iran and Venezuela.

2.2 Terms of trade

One way of measuring a country's health in terms of exports and imports is the 'terms of trade', which is the ratio of a country's export prices to its import prices. If a country's export prices increase, perhaps because its exchange rate has strengthened, this leads to an improvement in the terms of trade. The strengthening currency will also reduce the import prices. However, this could then lead to a reduction in exports and an increase in imports, worsening the balance of payments.

Test your understanding 1

The existence of international trade is best explained by the fact that:

A countries use different currencies

B countries have different economic systems

C opportunity costs vary from one country to another

D specialisation enables a country to export certain goods and services

Test your understanding 2

Which of the following is not a benefit of free trade for a country?

A Greater competition

B Greater choice for consumers

C Greater opportunities for specialisation

D More jobs created in that country across all industries

2.3 Protectionism

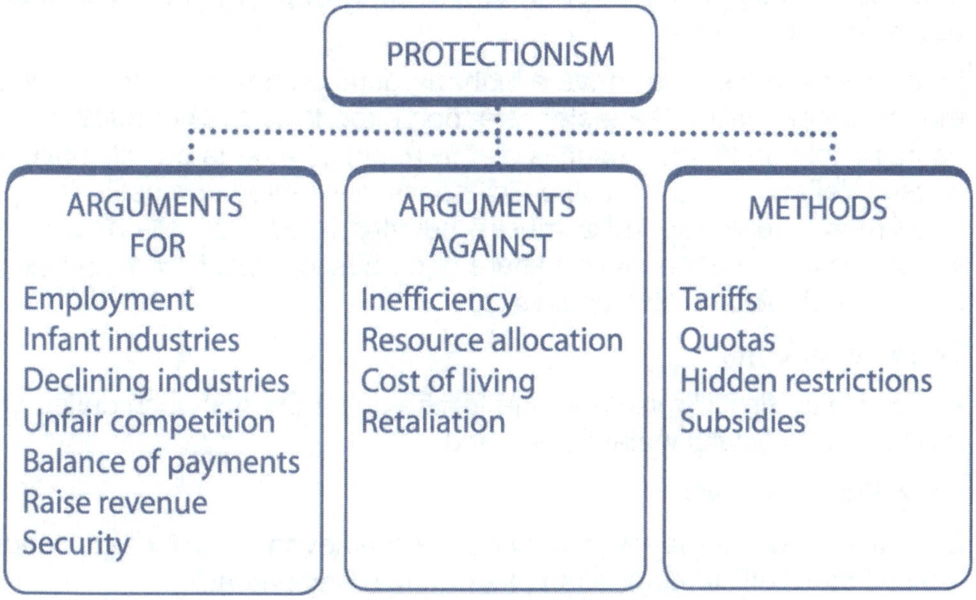

Many countries do not engage in free trade but seek, through a variety of mechanisms, to restrict the flow of imports into the domestic economy, either in total or from specific countries.

The main reason is simply that domestic producers want protection from imports in order to make higher profits at the expense of consumers. However, national governments provide a number of 'justifications' for protectionism.

- **To protect employment**

  For example, if a nation with an advantage successfully exports a good (e.g. Indian textiles), then this may result in redundancies in a recipient nation (e.g. the UK).

- **To help an infant (sunrise) industry**

  The classic argument for protection is that new industries require help during their infancy because of the high initial costs and lack of economies of scale. If this help was not provided and they had to face competition from fully developed similar industries, it is claimed that these industries might not survive.

- **To protect declining industries to buy time for structural readjustment**

  For example, the US government has made various attempts to protect its declining steel industry, including applying tariffs to imported Chinese steel.

- **To prevent unfair competition**

  A government may justify protection by reference to the trading policies of its competitor nations. For instance, certain producers in developing countries may try to sell fake UK goods in the UK. These imitations break the copyright and patent laws in purporting to be of UK origin, and are justifiably banned.

- **To protect the balance of payments**

  One remedy suggested for persistent balance of payments deficit is the use of import controls.

  Many Western countries have a high marginal propensity to import, which means imports grow at a faster rate than exports as the domestic economy expands. The result is that frequent payments deficits have caused deflationary domestic policies, which inhibited domestic investment and weakened domestic industry. In addition, the rise in imports will reduce the market share of domestic firms, thereby making them less viable and less optimistic.

- **To raise revenue**

  Protective tariffs will raise revenue for the government if such duties are levied on goods with inelastic demand.

- **To maintain security**

  Essential products may be produced at home even when foreign goods may be more efficient, for example, defence equipment.

Arguments against protectionism

- **Inefficiency is encouraged**

  If domestic firms are protected from international competition, then they may settle for their existing market share and profits. Such complacency will discourage innovation and risk-taking. New technology may not be introduced and over manning may persist. The protected industry (e.g. the textiles industry) may lobby to make temporary help permanent.

- **Resources are misallocated**

  By maintaining existing patterns of trade, resources do not move from declining industries, which are protected, to expanding industries. In addition, protection for one industry (e.g. steel) may adversely affect another (e.g. buyers of steel) because unit costs are raised.

- **The cost of living is raised**

  Protection will probably raise prices and so domestic consumers have to pay higher prices for (the taxed) imported goods or for (the protected) home-produced goods.

- **Retaliation may occur**

  Protection by one nation may provoke its trading partners to take similar action, and this will reduce the volume of world trade with the attendant consequences outlined above. This may weaken confidence, as the internationally accepted rules for trading are weakened when governments take unilateral action. China and the US engaged in such retaliation measures during Donald Trump's administration, with China imposing tariffs on US cars and auto parts in response to the US taxing Chinese imports at a high level.

The methods of protection

Trade barriers fall into two groups – tariffs and non-tariff barriers (NTBs), which include everything else detailed below.

- **Tariffs**

  The most common import control is the tariff. This tax may be ad valorem – a given percentage of the import price – or specific (a set amount per item).

  It is sensible to levy tariffs on imports with an elastic demand if the objective is to reduce the volume of imports. However, if a tariff is imposed in order to raise revenue, then goods with inelastic demand should be chosen. Tariffs, therefore, act on the price of goods/services.

- **Quotas**

  In contrast, quotas are restrictions on the quantity of imports. The WTO has tried to stop quotas, although it does permit exceptions for nations with severe balance of payments difficulties.

  A more acceptable and modern type of protection (although not in favour with the WTO and therefore rare) which aims to limit the amount of a certain good being imported is the Voluntary Export Restraint Agreement (VERA). For example, in 2018 South Korea agreed to limit its exports of steel to the USA.

  Often, quota restrictions are combined with tariff values, known as Tariff-rate quotas. These allow a certain amount of goods to be imported at a low tariff, but imports above that level will have a higher tariff levied on them. Turkey has such a tariff-rate quota on steel, with the higher rate of duty being an additional 25% above the lower rate. The USA has tariff quotas allocated to various countries for the import of raw cane sugar.

- **Hidden restrictions**

  Also, there are hidden import restrictions and procedures that can be utilised to subtly undermine foreign competition.

  Administrative devices include complicated forms, special testing regulation and safety certification, unusual product specification and the specialisation of customs posts.

  For example, some commentators have claimed that the ban on single-use plastic bags in France in 2016 was less to do with protecting the environment and more concerned with limiting imports of plastic bags. Before the ban, 90% of single-use plastic bags used in France were imported from Asia. Newer biodegradable bags are unlikely to be fit for purpose after a journey of several weeks in a sun-heated shipping container.

  Public procurement can also be used to assist domestic firms. Government departments may deliberately buy goods from domestic firms even though they may not be the 'best on the market'.

- **Subsidies**

  As well as restricting imports, governments often encourage exports by various means. The systematic use of export credits and official support for export deals by departments is increasingly becoming part of the UK's trading strategy. Such measures make exporting cheaper and easier; a theme that is furthered by the government-sponsored international promotions and exhibitions.

  However, the most blatant help given to exporters is the direct subsidy, for example, the subsidies given by both national governments and the European Commission to European steel firms. This is outlawed by the WTO and so done in more subtle ways nowadays. For instance, sales tax on exports is refunded by the British Government to the producers. Similarly, some European governments subsidise domestic producers. For example, Germany gives subsidies on electricity, which indirectly helps German manufacturers' costs of production.

International friction has increased because of the expansion of protectionism. There is friction between governments (e.g. between countries of the EU over beef and livestock movements), and between governments and trading blocs. EU steel manufacturers are currently concerned over "dumping" of cheap steel by Chinese firms.

In 2016 during his campaign to become president of the United States of America, Donald Trump threatened to levy an import tariff of up to 45% on goods from China (with levies at the time standing at an average of 3%) in order to encourage US companies to bring back production to the United States. China's response was that it would defend its rights under the World Trade Organisation (WTO) rules. Trump ended up applying a 25% tariff in 2018 and threatened even more tariffs when China said they would respond in kind. In January 2020, the US and China signed a limited trade deal, reducing tensions somewhat and with the potential for more deals to follow.

Test your understanding 3

Which of the following is not an example of protectionism?

A Subsidy to exporters

B Fixed exchange rate

C VERA

D Import tariff

Test your understanding 4

Which of the following is not an argument in favour of protectionism?

A To protect domestic jobs

B To reduce inflationary pressure

C To raise revenue via tariffs

D To protect declining domestic industries while they restructure

3 Trade agreements

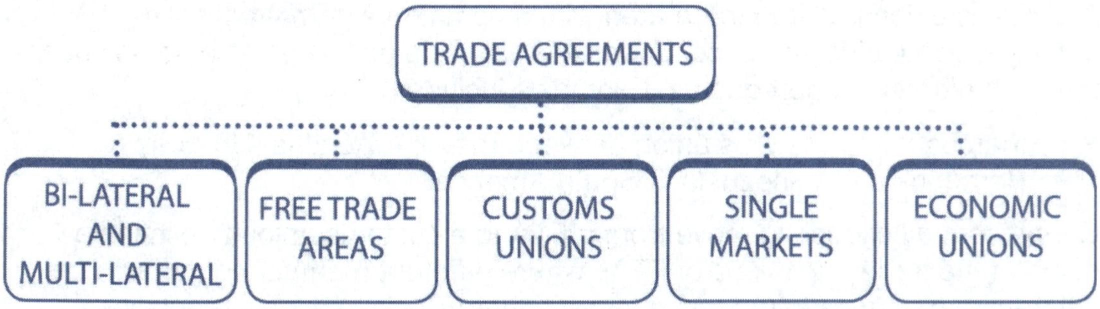

In many parts of the world, governments have created trade agreements and common markets to encourage free trade. However, the World Trade Organisation (WTO) is opposed to these trading blocs and customs unions (e.g. the European Union) because they encourage trade between members but often have high trade barriers for non-members.

From a business perspective, such agreements give major opportunities to firms within the area specified but create barriers to entry for those outside. This is the reason why Japanese car manufacturers have built factories within the EU, so they can avoid quotas.

The different types of agreement are as follows:

3.1 Bi-lateral and multi-lateral trade agreements

These are agreements between two or more countries to eliminate quotas and tariffs on the trade of most (if not all) goods between them. Examples include:

- The Closer Economic Relations (CER) agreement between Australia and New Zealand.
- Costa Rica and South Korea entered into a free trade agreement in November 2019. Other Central American republics have also entered into similar deals with South Korea.

3.2 Free trade areas

If the members of a multi-lateral free trade agreement are all in the same geographical area then it is sometimes described as a free trade area. Examples include

- The North American Free Trade Agreement (NAFTA) between Canada, the United States, and Mexico (which is due to be replaced by the United States – Mexico – Canada agreement (USMCA).
- The ASEAN Free Trade Area (AFTA) is an agreement by the Association of Southeast Asian Nations (Brunei, Indonesia, Malaysia, Philippines, Singapore, Thailand, Vietnam, Laos, Myanmar and Cambodia).
- South Korea and the EU have a free trade agreement that entered into force in December 2015. Trade between South Korea and the EU totalled $100 billion in 2017.

3.3 Customs unions

A customs union is a free trade area with a common external tariff. The participant countries set up common external trade policies, but in some cases they use different import quotas. Examples include:

- Mercosur is a customs union between Brazil, Argentina, Uruguay, Paraguay and Venezuela in South America.

Countries may choose to move from a FTA to a customs union to eliminate some of the trade distortions of FTAs where different member countries have different export rules to the same target country. To avoid local regulations producers may sell to a partner in another member country with less stringent regulations who then sells to the target customer. This results in the need for rules to determine the origin of goods.

3.4 Single markets (economic communities)

A single market is a free trade area with common policies on product regulation and free movement of goods and services to which has been added free movement of factors of production, notably capital and labour.

Advocates argue that this gives a more "level playing field" for producers in different countries, as they all have to meet the same standards.

Examples include

- The Economic Community of West African States (ECOWAS).
- The European Union (EU), which is also a customs union.
- The European Economic Area (EEA). This is not a customs union

Note that a single market can also be a customs union, but does not have to be.

In 2016, during his campaign for election to become president of the U.S.A, Donald Trump stated that he would abandon the Trans-Pacific Partnership (TPP), an attempt by 12 nations (including Japan, Canada and Australia – in total responsible for 40% of world trade) to effectively create a single market between them. Trump called the TPP 'a potential disaster for our country' and prefers to concentrate on protectionism measures. Subsequently the USA did indeed fail to ratify the agreement, so the remaining partners reached a separate agreement, called the Comprehensive and Progressive Agreement for Trans-Pacific Partnership, which came into force in December 2018. In January 2021, the newly 'EU free' UK applied to join the agreement. China also formally applied to join in 2021.

3.5 Economic unions

An economic and monetary union is a single market with a common currency.

The largest economic and monetary union at present is the Eurozone. The Eurozone consists of the European Union member states that have adopted the Euro.

- Another example is the West African Economic and Monetary Union UEMOA), which is a sub block of the ECOWAS single market. The common currency is the CFA Franc.

Arguments abound regarding the effects of regional trading blocs.

- Their supporters say that they encourage trade creation by harmonizing economic policies and standards within member countries and reducing prices as trade restrictions are removed.
- Opponents state that they lead to trade diversion. Member countries buy within the regional trading bloc when cheaper sources are available outside.
- Common external tariffs can encourage a regional fortress mentality, which can lead to conflicts between different regional trading blocs. For example, NAFTA has complained over the EU's agricultural imports while the EU has complained over NAFTA's restrictions on steel imports.
- The fear is that regional trading blocs could lead to the development of protectionism worldwide at a time when the WTO is seeking to create free trade.

Test your understanding 5

Which of the following are necessary characteristics of a single market?

(i) a multi-lateral trade agreement between nearby countries

(ii) a common external tariff

(iii) free movement of factors of production

(iv) a single currency

A (i) only

B (i) and (ii)

C (i), (ii) and (iii)

D (i), (ii), (iii) and (iv)

4 The balance of payments

4.1 Balance of payments

The balance of payments is an account showing the financial transactions of one nation with the rest of the world over a period of time.

The balance of payments is split into three parts:

- current account (goods and services)
- capital account (acquisition and disposal of fixed assets) and
- financial account (e.g. cash flows).

The nature of the accounting system for the balance of payments (similar to double entry book keeping) ensures that the accounts, as a whole, will always balance to zero. However, there may be deficits or surpluses on each of the three accounts that together make up the balance of payments.

4.2 The current account

This is composed of two parts.

Visible trade. This is trade in goods.

Invisible trade. Invisible trade includes trade in services, investment income and transfers of money between individuals and national bodies.

Current account balance

This combines the visible and invisible trade. Generally, a surplus balance is a good sign, and can indicate a prosperous and expanding economy. The UK's current account was in surplus in the early 1980s but has been in deficit ever since.

A deficit (surplus) on the current account will be balanced by a surplus (deficit), that is a net inflow (outflow) on the combined capital and financial accounts. However, as changes in the current account affect national income, a deficit means a decrease in spending power (and a net withdrawal from the circular flow), which is deflationary.

4.3 The capital and financial accounts

These accounts show transactions in the country's external assets and liabilities. It records capital and financial movements by firms, individuals and governments. It also includes the balancing item. A positive balancing item indicates unrecorded net exports, while a negative total shows unrecorded net imports. The figure arises because of the errors and omissions that occur in the collection of such detailed and numerous statistics based on enormous numbers of international transactions.

Types of flow include:

- Real foreign direct investment, such as a UK firm establishing a manufacturing facility in China. Direct investment refers to investment in an enterprise where the owners or shareholders have some element of control over the business.
- Portfolio investment, such as a UK investor buying shares in an existing business abroad. With portfolio investment, the investor has no control over the enterprise.
- Financial derivatives are any financial instrument whose underlying value is based on another asset, such as foreign currency, interest rates, commodities or indices.

- Reserve assets are foreign financial assets that are controlled by monetary authorities – namely Central Banks. These assets are used to finance deficits and deal with imbalances. Reserve assets include gold and foreign exchange held by Central Banks.

4.4 Equilibrium and disequilibrium

The balance of payments accounts always balance for technical reasons:

Current account + capital account + financial account + balancing items = 0

However, economists are concerned with the component parts of the structure. Persistent imbalances in certain sections, such as the visible trade and the current account, indicate **fundamental disequilibrium**.

For example:

- Countries with persistent deficits on their current accounts include the USA, the UK, Spain, Italy and France.
- Countries with persistent surpluses on their current accounts include China, Japan and Germany.

Such disequilibria will induce governments to undertake policy action to create/restore equilibrium. For instance, a persistent balance of payments current account deficit may be covered by substantial capital inflows or by a decrease in official reserves. The former may be achieved by higher interest rates for a short period of time, while the latter similarly cannot be undertaken indefinitely.

However, this temporary expediency may have damaging consequences for the economy, such as higher debt repayments, lower investment and a higher exchange rate. Thus, remedial action to deal with a balance of payments problem may constrain policies that are designed to achieve other economic objectives, such as economic growth via lower interest rates.

Causes

A structural deficit in the balance of payments current account is usually due to a high demand for imports alongside a weak export performance in manufacturing products.

(a) **Import penetration**. This can arise from imports taking larger shares of static markets or from imports maintaining their shares of expanding markets. Import penetration has increased for many reasons.

- Growth in consumer spending is often largely supported by imports.
- Imports may have become more competitive than domestic substitutes.
- Domestic currencies may be overvalued.
- Foreign currencies may be undervalued (a criticism often made of the Chinese Yuan).

- Domestic producers have lacked competitiveness in non-price factors such as design, reliability, delivery and pre and after sales service.

(b) **Export performance**. The factors determining exports are similar to those affecting the demand for imports.

- First, the willingness and ability of domestic producers to supply abroad. For instance, a growing home market and a lack of surplus capacity will inhibit exporting and lead to concentration on home sales.
- Second, the price competitiveness of exports.
- Third, firms in some countries tend to have more surplus capacity, which can be quickly utilised to raise output for domestic consumption when incomes rise.

4.5 Policies

Many policies have been advocated to restore a balance of payments account to equilibrium, usually when deficits have been a regular feature and there is evidence of fundamental disequilibrium.

Do nothing

The primary advantage of a floating exchange rate is that it is claimed to lead to automatic correction of a balance of payments disequilibrium. For example

- If imports exceed exports, then a balance of payments deficit exists.
- In sterling terms, this means that more sterling is being sold to buy imports than is being bought to purchase UK exports.
- This excess of supply of sterling over demand for sterling will lead to a weakening of sterling against other currencies.
- This makes imports into the UK more expensive and exports from the UK cheaper.
- As a result, export volumes should start to rise and import volumes fall, gradually removing the balance of payment deficit.

Deliberate depreciation of the exchange rate

The objective behind depreciation and devaluation has been to induce expenditure-switching by consumers. This occurs in two ways:

- dearer imports hopefully lead domestic consumers to buy domestic goods instead
- while cheaper exports cause foreign consumers to purchase exports rather than foreign products.

With a "dirty floating" exchange rate system, intervention to change the exchange rate will be through the central bank buying or selling currency onto markets.

However, a depreciation/devaluation will not immediately benefit a balance of payments in practice.

- There is an initial worsening of the current account because volumes are fixed and prices adjust automatically. However, eventually demand and supply become more elastic and so consumption and production patterns change, creating an improvement in the accounts.
- Furthermore, there is some evidence that, following a depreciation, exporters maintain their foreign exchange price (i.e. raise their prices measured in the domestic currency) rather than lowering them; this raises their short-run profits at the expense of long-run sales growth.

Deflation

An effective, but generally undesirable, policy used to return a balance of payments deficit to equilibrium has been domestic deflation to induce expenditure-reduction by consumers.

- The government, through either tight fiscal or restrictive monetary policy, curbs demand at home.
- The balance of payments is improved because the growth of import demand is weakened and domestic suppliers, facing a static home market, might switch resources towards export markets in order to fully utilise capacity.
- Additional gains from government deflationary policies can be to weaken trade union bargaining power through the fear of unemployment and by restraining production costs help to reduce inflation.

Although deflation improves the current account of the balance of payments, it has unfortunate costs for the economy.

- The tightening of fiscal policy, by either tax increases or expenditure cuts, and the restrictions on money supply, both reduce the demand for goods.
- Less demand means less supply and so unemployment rises.
- The general effect is to constrain the rate of economic growth, by depressing business optimism, lowering investment and under-utilizing resources.

Deflation is often used in conjunction with depreciation (devaluation) of the currency to improve the current account of the balance of payments.

Import controls

These have the effect of causing expenditure switching rather than expenditure reduction. Quotas prevent the purchase of imports, while tariffs raise import prices and possibly lower outgoings (assuming elastic demand for imports). The advantage gained from implementation will probably only be temporary because the basic weakness of price uncompetitiveness has not been changed. The likelihood would be that a fundamental disequilibrium would return once the import controls were lifted.

In the UK's case, wide-ranging import controls are not a realistic option. As a member of the WTO the UK has disavowed such a policy. There is also the danger of retaliation by trading partners, with the consequent diminution in world trade.

Supply-side policies

These are policies that attempt to improve the efficiency of the supply base of the economy. By freeing up markets, increasing incentives, deregulating and removing the dead hand of the state from economic activity, it is claimed that the economy can be revitalised and achieve noninflationary economic growth. The intention is to transform attitudes and behaviour so that domestic competitiveness re-emerges.

Test your understanding 6

Which of the following might cause a country's exports to fall?

A A fall in the exchange rate for that country's currency

B A reduction in other countries' tariff barriers

C A decrease in the marginal propensity to import in other countries

D A rise in that country's imports

Test your understanding 7

If a country has a floating (flexible) exchange rate, which one of the following would lead to a fall (depreciation) in the rate of exchange for its currency?

A A rise in capital inflows into the economy

B An increase in the country's exports

C An increase in the country's imports

D A fall in the country's rate of inflation

Test your understanding 8

Which of the following would normally result from an increase (appreciation) in a country's exchange rate?

(i) A fall in the country's rate of inflation.

(ii) A rise in the volume of its exports.

(iii) A surplus on its current account.

A (i) and (ii) only

B (ii) and (iii) only

C (i) only

D (ii) only

Test your understanding 9

Sierra Leone operates a floating exchange rate system. The main advantage of a system of flexible (floating) exchange rates, such as that in Sierra Leone, is that it:

A provides certainty for international traders

B provides automatic correction of balance of payments deficits

C reduces international transactions costs

D provides policy discipline for governments

5 Globalisation

5.1 The nature of globalisation

The term 'globalisation' does not have a universally agreed definition. The International Monetary Fund defines globalisation as 'the growing economic interdependence of countries worldwide through increasing volume and variety of cross-border transactions in goods and services, free international capital flows, and more rapid and widespread diffusion of technology'.

It is useful here to make a distinction between globalisation and internationalisation:

Internationalisation

Internationalisation refers to the increasing spread of economic activities across geographical boundaries. For example:

- Many firms are taking advantage of the Internet to sell to new countries overseas.
- Setting up production facilities overseas.

Globalisation

Globalisation, however, refers to a more complex form of internationalisation where much greater integration is seen. For example:

- The erosion of trade barriers is creating a single global market, rather than many different international markets.
- The homogenising of tastes across geographies. Food, once highly local in style, has become more global in many respects.
- Firms selling the same product in every world market rather than tailoring products to local preferences.
- Greater harmonisation of laws in different countries.
- The dilution of traditional cultures in some developing countries as they are replaced by Western value systems.

5.2 The factors driving globalisation

When considering the driving forces of globalisation it can be difficult to distinguish between cause and effect. For example, does the existence of global firms drive globalisation or are they the consequence of it? Both viewpoints have validity. However, for the exam, you should consider the main drivers of globalisation as follows:

Improved communications

Advances in information and communications technology (ICT) over the past ten years have paralleled the emergence of globalisation as a concept.

- Many within developing countries see the internet as an opportunity to gain access to knowledge and services from around the world in a way that would have been unimaginable previously.
- The internet and technologies such as mobile telephony allow developing countries to leapfrog steps in their development of infrastructure. A poor land line telephone system in the Philippines, for example, is being rapidly bypassed by mobile phones with internet access.

The wider access to Hollywood and Bollywood movies has also given rise to greater multiculturalism.

Political realignments

The growth of trade agreements, free trade areas and economic unions, described above, all contribute towards the idea of single markets replacing separate ones.

In addition, political realignments have opened the huge markets of China and the old Soviet Union, both of which used to be closed to Western firms.

- The collapse of communism in the USSR in 1989 (the date of the fall of the Berlin Wall) marked the beginning of new trade opportunities in Russia.
- Political change in China led to the signing of a bilateral trade agreement with the USA in 1979. This has been further reinforced by China joining the WTO.

Growth of global industries and firms

The growth of global firms has been a key driver of globalisation.

- Some would argue that the rapid growth of corporations such as McDonalds and Coca Cola has resulted in pressure on local cultures to accept Western tastes and values.
- Global firms can influence governments to open up markets for free trade.
- Global firms can encourage political links between countries. For example, the entry of Japanese car manufacturers into the United Kingdom fostered a stronger political dialogue between the Japanese and UK governments.

Cost differentials

Most firms' competitive strategy is based on cost and/or quality advantages. Many firms have found that they can manufacture their products at a much lower cost in developing countries rather than in their home markets. This is usually due to much lower labour costs.

For example, most clothing sold in the United Kingdom is manufactured in factories in China, Sri Lanka and India.

A more recent development is that many firms are finding that the goods produced often have higher quality as well as lower cost than using domestic suppliers.

Trade liberalisation

The World Trade Organisation (WTO) is constantly working towards the removal of trade barriers. The role of the WTO is discussed in more detail below.

Liberalisation of international capital markets

The liberalisation of capital controls has encouraged greater freedom in international capital flows. In particular, developing countries have much greater access to capital for funding growth. This has been a mixture of aid and loans, although the distinction between the two is not always clear.

5.3 The impacts of globalisation

Industrial relocation/offshoring

As mentioned above, many firms have relocated their manufacturing base to countries with lower labour costs/more favourable economic conditions. This is known as 'off-shoring' and can entail moving product manufacturing, service centres or operations to a different country.

However, this can give the impression that the only form of expansion is into developing economies. This is not always the case as illustrated by Nissan building a car factory in Sunderland in the United Kingdom to avoid EU import quotas and tariffs. They have continued manufacturing in the UK despite Brexit but have had to move battery production to the UK to avoid tariffs imposed via the UK's new trade deal with the EU. The batteries were previously made in the USA.

Also, the motivation is not always cost. As mentioned before, some non-Western countries are developing regional areas of excellence. For example, Bangalore in India is recognised globally for its expertise in telecommunications.

Managing (often complex) global supply chains has only been made possible by the advances in ICT mentioned above.

Emergence of growth markets

As mentioned above, many previously closed markets, such as China, are opening up to Western firms.

In addition, if tastes are becoming more homogeneous, then this presents new opportunities for firms to sell their products in countries previously discounted.

Access to markets and enhanced competition

The combination of firms' global expansion plans and the relaxation of trade barriers have resulted in increased competition in many markets. This can be seen in:

- greater pressure on firms' cost bases with factories being relocated to even cheaper areas
- greater calls for protectionism.

Developments in ICT have also facilitated greater access to markets, for example by selling via the internet.

Cross-national business alliances and mergers

To exploit the opportunities global markets offer many firms have sought to obtain expertise and greater economies of scale through cross-national mergers and acquisitions.

For example:

- In 2010, Kraft Foods (a US company) acquired Cadbury (a UK company) as part of its strategy to gain economies of scale for its intended global snacks business.
- In 2013, Liberty Global Inc., a multinational telecoms company founded in the US, acquired UK based Virgin Media, which expanded Liberty's reach into the European cable market.

Widening economic divisions between countries

Many opponents of globalisation argue that it is creating new gaps between the rich and the poor. For example:

Rich countries have much greater access to the internet and communications services. In the current information age, wealth is created by the development of information goods and services, ranging from media, to education and software. Not all poor countries are taking part in this information revolution and are falling further behind the "digital divide".

The relentless drive to liberalise trade, i.e. to remove trade barriers, promote privatisation, and reduce regulation (including legal protection for workers), has had a negative impact on the lives of millions of people around the world.

Many poor countries have been pressured to orientate their economies towards producing exports and to reduce already inadequate spending on public services such as health and education so that they can repay their foreign debt. This has forced even more people into a life of poverty and uncertainty.

5.4 Impacts of ICT on international trade and patterns of development

Developments in ICT have accelerated globalisation and the number of global firms. In particular improved ICT makes it much easier for firms to control long, geographically diverse, supply chains.

Test your understanding 10

Few places in the world have seen the dramatic effects of globalisation more than Bangalore, the Silicon Valley of India, which is experiencing an unprecedented IT boom that is transforming the prospects of the Indian economy. Which of the following would hinder rather than drive globalisation?

A Improved communications

B The switch from a command to a market economy

C The growth of multi-lateral trade agreements

D Protectionism

6 Institutions encouraging free trade

6.1 The World Trade Organisation (WTO) and the General Agreements on Tariffs and Trade (GATT)

As trade began to recover after the Second World War, attempts were made to reduce barriers to free trade around the world. The General Agreements on Tariffs and Trade (GATT) came into being in 1948. Regular rounds of talks were held to agree trading patterns around the world and to negotiate removal of trade barriers.

These negotiations have become more prolonged and complex as time has gone on.

In 1995, the World Trade Organisation based in Geneva replaced GATT. It has a number of roles:

- to ensure compliance of member countries with previous GATT agreements
- to negotiate future trade liberalisation agreements
- to resolve trading disputes between nations.

The WTO has much greater authority than GATT as it has the power to police and 'enforce' trade agreements. It faces an increasingly difficult role as the facilitator for global free trade talks.

The WTO is opposed to the development of trading blocs and customs unions such as the EU and NAFTA. Although these promote free trade between members of the union, there are normally high trade barriers for non-members, e.g. the difficulties faced by non-EU food producers when they attempt to export to the EU.

Example

There is growing tension between the developed and the developing world. The developing world regards heavy subsidy of EU and American farmers as a huge barrier to trade for their domestic farmers. At the same time, the developed world complains about export of low cost manufactured goods from the developing world that are not subject to the same health, safety and environmental regulations that they face.

The activities of the WTO

Reviewing members' trade policies

Reviews are conducted on a regular, periodic basis. The four biggest traders – the European Union, the United States, Japan and Canada – are examined approximately once every two years. The next 16 countries in terms of their share of world trade are reviewed every four years; and the remaining countries every six years, with the possibility of a longer interim period for the least-developed countries.

Anti-dumping rules

If a company exports a product at a price lower than the price it normally charges on its own home market, it is said to be "dumping" the product. Is this unfair competition? The WTO agreement does not pass judgement. Its focus is on how governments can or cannot react to dumping – it disciplines anti-dumping actions, and it is often called the "Anti-dumping Agreement".

For example, Turkey expressed concern about the Dominican Republic's decision to impose a country-wide anti-dumping duty on steel rods and bars coming from Turkey.

6.2 The European Union (EU)

The EU is an example of a single market and, within the Euro zone, an economic union (see above). It has its origins in the Treaty of Rome (1957).

The aims of the treaty were as follows:

- the elimination of customs duties and quotas on imports and exports between member states
- the establishment of a common customs tariff and a common commercial policy towards non-member states
- the abolition of obstacles to the free movement of persons, services and capital between member states
- the establishment of common policies on transport and agriculture
- the prohibition of business practices that restrict or distort competition
- the association of overseas countries in order to increase trade and development.

Further details on the EU

The main challenges facing the EU are as follows:

1 Managing the ongoing economic crisis

While many countries have suffered economically as a result of the global banking crisis and credit crunch, four countries within the EU – Spain, Portugal, Ireland and Greece – are still in particularly difficult positions. Some analysts have argued that unless these problems can be dealt with, then the viability of the euro will be in doubt.

2 Enlargement/exit

There are challenges to the EU relating both to the admission of new countries, such as Turkey, and the implications of a country leaving, such as the UK. Both aspects may result in changes being required to the EU constitution.

3 Ongoing reform of the Common Agricultural Policy (CAP)

The Common Agricultural Policy (CAP) is a system of agricultural subsidies, which work by guaranteeing a minimum price to producers and by direct payment of a subsidy for crops planted. This provides some economic certainty for EU farmers and production of a certain quantity of agricultural goods.

Critics of the CAP argue that it increases poverty in developing countries by putting their farmers out of business. This is done by creating an oversupply of agricultural products, which are then sold in the developing countries, and preventing those countries from exporting their agricultural goods to the West.

4 Migration

One of the biggest challenges facing the EU is dealing with a huge influx of refugees and economic migrants.

6.3 The Group of Seven (G7)

The Group of Seven (G7) consists of Canada, France, Germany, Italy, Japan, the United Kingdom, and the United States. Together, these countries represent about 65% of the world economy. Before 2014, Russia was included and it was known as the G8. In 2014, Russia was suspended and has since declared that it will not return.

The agenda of G7 meetings is usually about controversial global issues such as global warming, poverty in Africa, fair trade policies and AIDS but has implications for global trade.

For example, the agenda for the 2019 summit had a mixture of economic issues (global trade, taxing technology companies), political ones such as the Iran nuclear deal, and environmental, particularly in relation to global warming.

The G7 summit has consistently dealt with:

- Macroeconomic management
- International trade
- Energy issues and climate change
- Development issues and relationships with developing countries
- Issues of international concern such as terrorism and organised crime.

The G7 does not have any formal resources or powers, as is the case with other international organisations such as the WTO. However, it provides a forum for the most powerful nations to discuss complex international issues and to develop the personal relations that help them respond in effective collective fashion to sudden crises or shocks. The summit also gives direction to the international community by setting priorities, defining new issues and providing guidance to established international organisations.

It is also important to be aware of the G20. This is an international forum for the governments and central bank governors from 20 major economies. The members include 19 individual countries – Argentina, Australia, Brazil, Canada, China, France, Germany, India, Indonesia, Italy, Japan, South Korea, Mexico, Russia, Saudi Arabia, South Africa, Turkey, the United Kingdom and the United States – along with the European Union. The G20 was founded in 1999 with the aim of studying, reviewing and promoting high-level discussion of policy issues pertaining to the promotion of international financial stability. It seeks to address issues that go beyond the responsibilities of any one organisation.

Test your understanding 11

The main objective of the WTO is:

A to raise living standards in developing countries

B to minimise barriers to international trade

C to harmonise tariffs

D to eliminate customs unions

Test your understanding 12

Answer the following questions based on the preceding information.

1 Why are exchange rates important?

2 What factors inhibit international trade?

3 Give three arguments for trade protection policies.

4 What is a VERA?

5 What does the WTO attempt to do?

6 Why have some companies become multinational in structure?

7 How can multinational companies benefit national economies?

Test your understanding 13

Answer the following questions based on the preceding information. You can check your answers below.

1 Name one invisible earning.

2 What do the capital and financial accounts show?

3 What is 'hot money'?

4 What has caused the UK's balance of payments current account deficit?

5 What is the difference between devaluation and depreciation of the exchange rate?

6 How could a fall in the exchange rate help an economy?

7 How can deflation help the balance of payments deficit?

Test your understanding 14

The following passage is based on an imaginary country – Atlantia – that uses the A$ as its currency:

'Atlantian companies are expressing alarm at the strength of the A$ after seeing the rising exchange rate choke off their exports', industry leaders said yesterday as the A$ rose to €2 in late trading.

The industry leaders said that demand for exports had levelled off for the first time since the autumn of 2003, with optimism and order books hit by the 9 per cent appreciation of the A$ in the final three months of 2016. According to a recent survey, prices were regarded as more of a constraint on exports than at any time since 2009. The picture that emerged was of weakening export orders balanced by the strength of domestic demand for Atlantian-produced consumer goods.

The industry leaders said that the decision on whether the government should raise interest rates was 'finely balanced'. Any rise in interest rates to prevent the very rapid recovery from recession leading to excessive inflation was likely to further strengthen the A$ and have an adverse effect on exporters' order books.

However, the prospects of a rise in interest rates to slow inflation were lessened by the latest figures for the growth of the money supply. They showed that broad money growth fell from an annual rate of 10% in November to 9% in December. However, these were still well above the Atlantian government's target for the growth of the money supply. In response, a Government source pointed out that the rise in the A$ itself would act to reduce the rate of inflation through its effects on costs and on the level of aggregate demand.

Required:

Using both your knowledge of economic theory and material contained in the above passage:

(a) State whether, other things being equal, the effect of each of the following would be to raise the exchange rate for a currency, lower the exchange rate or leave the exchange rate unaffected.

(i) A rise in interest rates in the country.

(ii) A rise in the rate of inflation in a country.

(iii) A surplus on the current account of the balance of payments.

(iv) A government budget deficit.

(v) An increase in the export of capital from the country.

(5 marks)

(b) State whether each of the following is true or false:

(i) A rise in the exchange rate tends to reduce the domestic rate of inflation.

(ii) A rise in the exchange rate tends to reduce domestic unemployment.

(iii) A rise in the exchange rate tends to worsen the terms of trade.

(iv) A rise in the exchange rate tends to worsen the balance of trade.

(v) A rise in the exchange rate tends to raise domestic living standards.

(5 marks)

(Total marks = 10)

7 External analysis of the macro environment

We will now focus our attention on external analysis, which looks at the environment within which the organisation operates.

When establishing its strategy, it is important for an organisation to look at the various factors within its environment that may represent threats or opportunities and the competition it faces.

The analysis requires an external appraisal to be undertaken by scanning the business external environment for factors relevant to the organisations current and future activities.

External analysis can be carried out at different levels. There are a number of strategic management tools that can assist in this process. These include the PESTEL framework, which helps in the analysis of the macro or general environment.

PESTEL analysis

The macro environment consists of factors that cannot be directly influenced by the organisation itself. These include social, legal, economic, political, environmental and technological changes that the firm must try to respond to, rather than control. An important aspect of strategy is the way the organisation adapts to its environment.

PESTEL analysis is an approach to analysing an organisation's environment:

- **political influences and events** – legislation, government policies, changes to competition policy or import duties, etc.
- **economic influences** – a multinational company will be concerned about the international situation, while an organisation trading exclusively in one country might be more concerned with the level and timing of domestic development. Items of information relevant to marketing plans might include: changes in the gross domestic product, changes in consumers' income and expenditure, and population growth.
- **social influences** – includes social, cultural or demographic factors (i.e. population shifts, age profiles, etc.) and refers to attitudes, value and beliefs held by people; also changes in lifestyles, education and health and so on.
- **technological influences** – changes in material supply, processing methods and new product development.
- **ecological/environmental influences** – includes the impact the organisation has on its external environment in terms of pollution etc.
- **legal influences** – changes in laws and regulations affecting, for example, competition, patents, sale of goods, pollution, working regulations and industrial standards.

Some of the **PESTEL** influences may affect every industry, but industries will vary in how much they are affected. For example, an interest rate rise is likely to affect a business selling cars (car purchase can be postponed) more than it will affect a supermarket (food purchase cannot be postponed).

PESTEL analysis will be particularly useful in your later studies on strategy (within the E pillar) and for the case study exams.

e.g

Illustration 1

Oil company BP has explained on its website how it approaches the task of identifying and assessing country risk.

BP carries out a country risk assessment whenever it faces a strategic decision about whether to invest in a new country. Country risk assessments are also made when the political or social environment changes, or if a significant change in the size of investment is under consideration.

This process culminates in an intensive discussion with active participation from outside experts and BP personnel with experience of the region and relevant BP operations. Over two days many strands of thinking and research are brought together to form a view of the country in question, which then informs all major decisions, including investment decisions, relating to BP's involvement in the country. The results of these assessments remain, by their nature, confidential to the business.

e.g

Illustration 2 – The PESTEL model for a newspaper

Illustration – The PESTEL model

A newspaper is planning for the next five years. The following would be some of the **PESTEL** factors it should consider:

- **Political influences:** tax on newspapers – many countries treat newspapers in the same way as books and have no sales tax (or value added tax) on their sales price. If government policies on the classification of newspapers were to change so that sales tax had to be charged, then sales of newspapers are likely to fall.
- **Economic influences:** exchange rates – most newspapers import their raw materials (paper, pulp etc.) and therefore they will suffer when their domestic currency weakens. Recession – in a recession, buyers might move down market, so that cheap tabloids benefit, and more expensive broadsheets suffer. The opposite might apply as the economy recovers.
- **Social influences:** people want more up-to-date information – buyers are less inclined to wait for news than they were 20/30 years ago and may therefore switch to alternative sources of information, such as online ones. Multiple ethnicity in countries – the increased social mobility around the world might actually open new avenues of growth for newspapers through launching, for example, different language versions.
- **Technological influences:** there are many alternative sources of information that are provided through technologies such as the internet, mobile phones and television – this is likely to adversely affect the sales of newspapers. At the same time, e-readers are becoming more popular – this might present an opportunity for newspapers to provide daily downloadable content to these devices.

- **Environmental/ecological influences:** concern about the impact of carbon emissions from the use and production of paper – newspapers may be seen as being harmful to the environment due to their use of natural resources, their high production volumes and large distribution networks. Buyers might abandon newspapers in favour of carbon neutral news via modern technologies.
- **Legal influences:** limits on what can be published – this will make it harder for newspapers to differentiate themselves from each other and therefore harm growth prospects.

Overall, it would appear that growth prospects for newspapers are poor. The industry is more likely to decline than to grow. Existing rivals need to plan ahead for new products and new markets and perhaps focus on new technologies such as the provision of news via e-readers.

Note that it does not matter under which category an influence has been listed. Tax has economic, legal and political dimensions. All that matters is that tax has been considered in the environmental scan.

Test your understanding 15

DM is the world's largest and best-known food service retailing group with more than 30,000 'fast-food' outlets in over 120 countries. Currently half of its restaurants are in the USA, where it first began 50 years ago, but up to 1,000 new restaurants are opened every year worldwide. Restaurants are wholly owned by the group (it has previously considered, but rejected, the idea of a franchising of operations and collaborative partnerships).

As market leader in a fiercely competitive industry, DM has strategic strengths of instant global brand recognition, experienced management, site development expertise and advanced technological systems. DM's basic approach works well in all countries and although the products sold in each restaurant are broadly similar, menus are modified to reflect local tastes. Analysts agree that it continues to be profitable because it is both efficient and innovative.

DM's future plans are to maximise global opportunities and continue to expand markets. DM has long recognised that the external environment can be very uncertain and consequently does not move into new locations or countries without first undertaking a full investigation.

You are part of a strategy steering team responsible for investigating the key factors concerning DM's entry for the first time into the restaurant industry in the Republic of Borderland.

Required:

Discuss some of the main issues arising from each aspect of the framework.

(15 minutes)

Test your understanding 16

Ava is carrying out a PESTEL analysis for her employers. During her research, the aging of Europe's population has become apparent to Ava as a potentially important strategic issue for the company. In which section of her analysis should Ava record this matter?

A P

B S

C T

D L

(2 marks)

Test your understanding answers

Test your understanding 1

C

Opportunity costs represent the value lost from using resources in one area instead of another. In one country, resources may be best suited to production of a particular product. In another, perhaps because worker time is more expensive and the natural resources needed are not so abundant the country's resources are better utilised elsewhere. to make the product themselves they would have to give up the value gained from the better use of the resources.

Value is maintained and costs kept down if they source the product from the first country.

Test your understanding 2

D

International trade may result in some domestic jobs being displaced by more efficient overseas competitors.

Test your understanding 3

B

A fixed exchange rate should bring stability but does nothing to favour domestic firms over foreign ones. All the other options are classic examples of protectionism.

Test your understanding 4

B

If anything, you could argue that protectionism will lead to higher inflation:

- imported goods will be more expensive due to tariffs
- the lack of competition may result in domestic goods being more expensive
- the increase in aggregate demand may result in inflationary pressure.

Test your understanding 5

C

By definition. A single market does not have to have a single currency (that would make it an economic union).

Test your understanding 6

C

A fall in the exchange rate (depreciation or devaluation) or a fall in barriers to trade will be likely to lead to increases in a country's exports. A rise in a country's imports will have no direct effect on its exports, but may indirectly raise them, since it will have increased the level of incomes in trading partners. However, if the propensity to import in the country's trading partners falls, exports would decline.

Test your understanding 7

C

The exchange rate will rise if the demand for the currency increases; this will result from increased inward capital flows and increased exports, especially if lower inflation increases the demand for exports. Increased imports however will increase the supply of the currency to pay for them; the currency will therefore depreciate.

Test your understanding 8

C

A rise in the exchange rate will raise export prices; export volumes will fall, so statement (ii) is false, and the current account will move towards deficit, so statement (iii) is also false.

However, import prices will fall, dampening domestic inflation, so statement (i) is true.

Test your understanding 9

B

A and D are benefits of a fixed exchange rate system since the exchange rate remains fixed and domestic economic policy is constrained by this. Response C is incorrect since transaction costs occur whenever foreign exchange is bought or sold, irrespective of the exchange rate regime. The correct solution is B since a deficit would lead to a fall in the exchange rate, which would improve the country's competitiveness and thus correct the deficit.

Test your understanding 10

D

Protectionism will reduce international trade and hence slow the rate of globalisation.

Test your understanding 11

B

The WTO is an organisation concerned with trade agreements and associated matters, and seeks a reduction in barriers to trade. The minimalisation of trade barriers is its primary aim. The WTO may see the others as desirable, but they are not its direct concerns.

Test your understanding 12

1 Exchange rates facilitate pricing and this enables international comparisons to be made.

2 International trade is inhibited by transport costs, the immobility of factors, market size and protective policies.

3 Protection is used to protect employment, help infant industries, prevent unfair competition and help the balance of payments.

4 Voluntary export restraint agreement.

5 The WTO tries to reduce tariff barriers and other protective measures.

6 To reduce costs and expand markets and sales. This has been helped by the development of appropriate organisational structures and technologies.

7 Direct foreign investment can boost: domestic capital fund; technology transfer; improvement in production processes and organisational structures; employment gains.

Test your understanding 13

1 A dividend from an overseas share.

2 The capital and financial accounts show changes in a country's external assets and liabilities.

3 'Hot money' refers to short-term capital movements of currencies by international financiers/speculators.

4 The UK's current account deficit has been caused by a lack of competitiveness (for many reasons) in trade.

5 A devaluation occurs when a fixed exchange rate is lowered, whereas depreciation refers to a floating exchange rate that is moving downwards.

6 A fall in the exchange rate could help an economy by reducing the price of exports (and increasing the price of imports) and thereby increasing sales, which might lead to increased employment and greater export earnings (if demand is price elastic).

7 Deflation can help the balance of payments by suppressing domestic demand for imports and by releasing goods for export (if home sales are stagnant).

Test your understanding 14

(a) (i) Raise. An interest rate rise encourages the purchase of the local currency to make deposits in that currency. The increased demand for the currency means its price (the exchange rate) rises.

(ii) Lower. Increasing inflation makes domestic goods and services appear more expensive to foreign customers and encourages domestic customers to look for cheaper imports. The increased supply of local currency on imports and reduced demand for it from foreign customers leads to the exchange rate falling.

(iii) Raise. A surplus means that exports are higher than imports. This means that demand for the local currency is high and the supply of it is low, leading to an upward pressure on the exchange rate.

(iv) No effect. The level of government spending and taxation within an economy has no direct effect on the exchange rate.

(v) Lower. The key word here is 'capital'. The overall balance of payments must add up to 0, so if the balance on the capital account is moving towards a surplus, the balance on the current account is moving towards a deficit – the opposite situation to answer iii.

(b) (i) True

A rise in the exchange rate reduces the domestic price of imports.

(ii) False

A rising exchange rate reduces exports and raises imports, thus increasing domestic unemployment.

(iii) False

The terms of trade are a measure of the relative prices of imports and exports; a rising exchange rate raises export prices and reduces import prices.

(iv) True

As export prices rise, total exports tend to fall, but the opposite occurs for imports, thus worsening the trade balance.

(v) True

The rise in exchange rate reduces import prices and thus raises the purchasing power of domestic incomes.

Test your understanding 15

Political factors

- Political stability: Given DM's worldwide penetration (over 120 countries), it is likely that Borderland is in a developing region which may be more politically unstable than many countries in which they currently operate. This may affect the long-term potential in the market.
- Tariffs and other barriers to trade. Tariffs may be imposed on imports into Borderland. This may put DM at a significant disadvantage compared with local competitors if they aim to import a significant number of items (unlikely on food items, more likely on clothing, fittings etc.).

Economic factors

- Economic prosperity: The more prosperous the nation the more money people will have to invest in 'fast-food'. Examining the current and likely future prosperity enables the organisation to understand the potential of this market and the likely future investment required.
- Position in economic cycle: Different countries are often at different positions in the economic cycle of growth and recession. The current position of Borderland will affect the current prosperity of the nation and the potential for business development for DM.

- Inflation rates: High inflation rates create instability in the economy, which can affect future growth prospects. They also mean that prices for supplies and prices charged will regularly change and this difficulty would need to be considered and processes implemented to account for this.

Social factors

- Brand reputation: As a global brand, the reputation of DM might be expected to have reached Borderland. If not, more marketing will be required. If it has, the reputation will need to be understood and the marketing campaign set up accordingly.
- Cultural differences: Each country has its own values, beliefs, attitudes and norms of behaviours, which means that people of that country may like different foods, architecture, music and so on, in comparison with US restaurants. By adapting to local needs DM can ensure it wins local custom and improve its reputation. Different cultures also need to be considered when employing people, especially given the importance to DM of employee relations. People might have different religious needs to be met or may dislike being given autonomy so the management style needs changing.

Technological factors

- DM may need to train people in the use of their technologies if the local population are unfamiliar with them e.g. accounting systems or tills. In addition, technology might have to be adapted to work in local environments, such as different electrical systems.
- Availability of infrastructure within Borderland would have to be considered, ensuring that it is suitable to allow DM's operations.

Environmental factors

- Laws and regulations on emissions and pollution. DM would have to ensure that it could carry out its operations within these guidelines.
- Sustainability of raw materials could be an issue that DM should consider as it could affect how they source their raw materials, which could affect the cost.

Legal factors

- Regulation on overseas companies: There may be regulation on how overseas companies can operate in the market. In China, for instance, it is common for joint ventures with local companies to be a prerequisite for western companies entering the market.
- Employment legislation: Each country will have different employment legislation e.g. health and safety, minimum wages, employment rights. DM may have to change internal processes from the US model to stay within this legislation within Borderland. Being a good employer is also one of DM's specific strategies.

Test your understanding 16

B Age is a demographic factor that falls under the Social aspect of the PESTEL analysis.

P = Political

T = Technological

L = Legal

Chapter

6

Financial Context of Business II: International aspects

Chapter learning objectives

On completion of their studies, students should be able to:

- explain the role of the foreign exchange market in facilitating trade and in setting exchange rates
- calculate the impact of exchange rate changes on export and import prices and the value of the assets and liabilities of the business
- explain the role of hedging and derivative contracts in managing the impact of changes in exchange rates.

1 Introduction

In this chapter, we expand our discussion of the financial system to encompass international aspects, looking in particular at foreign exchange markets and the role of national and international organisations.

2 International money markets

International markets are in broadly two groups.

1 international capital markets

2 the foreign exchange market

2.1 International capital markets

International capital markets have greatly expanded since the 1950s. This has been the result of:

- the progressive abolition of exchange controls limiting the flow of capital in and out of economies
- growth of multinational companies (MNCs) who often do not use capital markets in the 'home' country; by borrowing abroad in different currencies, MNCs can shop around for favourable terms and also avoid any domestic government credit restraints.

The funds available on international capital markets fall into three broad categories:

1 short-term capital (Eurocurrency) borrowed mainly for the purposes of working capital

2 medium-term capital (Eurocredit) borrowed for working capital and investment purposes

3 long-term capital (Eurobonds) borrowed for investment purposes and for financing mergers and acquisitions. Eurobonds are bonds issued by very large companies, banks, governments and supranational institutions, such as the European Commission, to raise long-term finance (typically five years and over). These bonds are denominated in a currency other than that of the borrower, although often US dollars are used. The bonds are bought and traded by investment institutions and banks.

The international capital market is useful not only for business borrowers. It is also used for government borrowers (e.g. United Kingdom local government authorities) and provides a market for lending funds for businesses with surplus cash. Thus, the market performs a useful international element to the financial asset management function of commercial enterprises.

Although these international markets operate in many financial centres, they are dominated by Europe and the USA, and especially London. The term 'euromarket' had its origins in the 1970s. International trading expanded and this led to new foreign currency markets, such as the Eurodollar market. In this market, dollar balances earned by European exporters (to the USA) were held in European banks earning interest on favourable terms because they are offshore (held outside the country of origin and not subject to central bank control).

Note: A market that is 'international' from one business's point of view will be 'domestic' from another's. For instance, if an Indian business obtains credit from its local bank denominated in Indian Rupees, to invest in working capital, this is simply a domestic transaction. If a German business obtains credit from its local bank in Indian Rupees to invest in working capital for an Indian subsidiary, it would be borrowing Eurocurrency or Eurocredit, as rupees are not the national currency of the lending bank.

2.2 Foreign exchange markets

Foreign exchange markets are concerned with the purchase and sale of foreign exchange. This is primarily for four reasons:

1 the finance of international trade

2 companies holding and managing a portfolio of currencies as part of their financial asset management function

3 financial institutions dealing in foreign exchange on behalf of their customers and in order to benefit from changes in exchange rates

4 to manage risks associated with exchange rate movements.

This market enables companies, fund managers, banks and others to buy and sell foreign currencies. Capital flows arising from trade, investment, loans and speculative dealing create a large demand for foreign currency, particularly sterling, US dollars and euros and typically deals worth $2 trillion are traded daily in London, the world's largest foreign exchange centre.

London benefits from its geographical location, favourable time intervals (with the United States and the Far East in particular) and the variety of business generated there – insurance, commodities, banking, Eurobonds, etc.

Foreign exchange trading may be **spot** or **forward**.

- **Spot** transactions are undertaken almost immediately and settled within two days.
- However, **forward** buying involves a future delivery date from three months onward. Banks and brokers, on behalf of their clients, operate in the forward market to mitigate the risk of adverse exchange rate movements occurring in the normal course of international trading transactions.

This risk arises when the prices of imports or exports are fixed in foreign currency terms and there is movement in the exchange rate between the date when the price is agreed and the date when the cash is paid or received in settlement.

The forward price of a currency is normally higher (at a premium) or lower (at a discount) than the spot rate. Such premiums (or discounts) reflect interest rate differentials between currencies and expectations of currency depreciations and appreciations.

The price of currency (the exchange rate) is determined by the operation of currency transactions undertaken in the foreign exchange markets, with high demand or low supply of a currency leading to a rise in its exchange rate and low demand or high supply leading to a fall in the rate.

2.3 Foreign exchange rates

A foreign exchange rate is the price of a currency expressed relative to another currency.

For instance, the price of Japanese Yen relative to US$ may be expressed as 108.21 Yen:US$1, or 108.21 Yen = US$1. This could also be expressed from the point of view of US$ to Japanese Yen as 0.0092 US$ = 1 Yen.

When the exchange rate changes, one of the pair of currencies will appreciate (increase or strengthen in value) relative to the other. The other currency will depreciate (decrease or weaken in value) relative to the first.

If the price of Yen relative to the US$ moves to 105 Yen = US$1, the Yen has appreciated in value (the same US$1 now only purchases 105 Yen instead of 108.21 Yen) and the US$ has depreciated (it now only takes 105 Yen to purchase US$1 instead of 108.21 Yen).

3 Foreign exchange risks

Firms dealing with more than one currency are exposed to risks due to exchange rate movements. There are three main aspects of this.

(i) **Economic risk**

Long-term movements in exchange rates can undermine a firm's competitive advantage.

For example, a strengthening currency will make an exporter's products more expensive to overseas customers. One way of managing this risk would be to set up production facilities in the markets you wish to sell into.

If this risk is not managed then the business's revenues, costs and profits can be affected over the long-term and the overall value of the business could be adversely (or favourably) affected.

(ii) **Transaction risk**

In the time period between an order being agreed and payment received the exchange rate can move causing the final value of the transaction to be more or less than originally envisaged.

This affects the business's cash flows and therefore its ability to forecast and manage its cash position.

Transaction risk can be hedged (minimised) in various ways.

Forward exchange contracts enable the purchase and sale of currencies at a fixed exchange rate for a specified time period. They are a straightforward way to guarantee the value of future transactions.

Transaction risk can also be managed by using derivatives, such as futures and options.

Futures are like a forward contract in that:

- the company's position is fixed by the rate of exchange in the futures contract
- it is a binding contract.

A futures contract differs from a forward contract in the following ways:

- Futures can be traded on futures exchanges. The contract which guarantees the price (known as the futures contract) is separated from the transaction itself, allowing the contracts to be easily traded.
- Settlement takes place in three-monthly cycles (March, June, September or December), i.e. a company can buy or sell September futures, December futures and so on.
- Futures are standardised contracts for standardised amounts. For example, the Chicago Mercantile Exchange (CME) trades sterling futures contracts with a standard size of £62,500. Only whole number multiples of this amount can be bought or sold.
- Because each contract is for a standard amount and with a fixed maturity date, they rarely cover the exact foreign currency exposure.

Transaction risk can also be mitigated using **currency options**.

Options are similar to forward contracts but with one key difference.

They give the right but not the obligation to buy or sell currency at some point in the future at a predetermined rate.

A company can therefore:

- exercise the option if it is in its interests to do so
- let it lapse if:
  - the spot rate is more favourable
  - there is no longer a need to exchange currency.

  The downside risk is eliminated by exercising the option, but there is still upside potential from letting the option lapse. Options are most useful when there is uncertainty about the timing of the transaction or when exchange rates are very volatile.

You will learn more about financial risks and tools to mitigate them, including forwards and futures, in later studies, particularly F3 Financial Strategy.

(iii) **Translation risk**

If a company has foreign assets (e.g. a factory) denoted in another currency, then their value in its home currency will depend on the exchange rate at the time. If its domestic currency strengthens, for example, then foreign assets will appear to fall in value.

This risk, however, is not realised unless the asset is sold, although it can affect investors' perception of the financial statements.

However, if the local currency value of foreign currency denominated assets and liabilities changes, the change in local value could lead to a breach in a debt covenant or a change in the viewpoint of the shareholders, which could then affect the share price. If asset values increase, measures such as return on capital employed will decrease, also potentially affecting the viewpoint of the investors.

Test your understanding 1

Last month the exchange rate between US$ and Euros was US$1.13 = €1. Today it is US$1.15 = €1. In terms of appreciation and depreciation, which currency has experienced which type of movement?

A US$ and Euros have appreciated

B US$ and Euros have depreciated

C US$ have appreciated and Euros have depreciated

D US$ have depreciated and Euros have appreciated

Test your understanding 2

A jeweller who is exporting gold jewellery worth $50,000 is considering a hedging strategy. What is the purpose of hedging?

A To protect a profit already made from having undertaken a risky position

B To reduce costs

C To reduce or eliminate exposure to risk

D To make a profit by accepting risk

Test your understanding 3

A forward exchange contract is

1 an immediately firm and binding contract

2 is for the purchase or sale of a specified quantity of a stated foreign currency

3 is at a rate of exchange fixed at the time the contract is made

4 for performance at a future time which is agreed when making the contract

A 1 and 2 only

B 1, 2 and 3 only

C 2 and 3 only

D All of the above

Illustration 1 – Transaction risk

Suppose a UK Company A contracts to sell a machine to a US Company B for $300,000 payable in three months' time.

If the exchange rate now (the 'spot' rate) is £1 = $2, then the $300,000 is worth £150,000.

However, when the cash is received, suppose the exchange rate has moved to £1 = $2.10. (note: the $ has weakened compared to the £ so £1 buys more $)

The $300,000 will then be worth 300,000/2.10 = £142,857, a fall of £7,143.

Similarly an exchange gain may arise if the exchange rate moves in Company A's favour (here we would want the $ to strengthen compared to the £). The key problem lies in being able to predict future exchange rates.

Illustration 2 – Economic risk

A US exporter sells one product in the UK on a cost-plus basis and invoices in £ to remain competitive in the UK market. The selling price in £ is based on costs of $100 plus a mark-up of 5% to give a sales value of $105.

If the current exchange rate is $1 = £0.85 and the exporter sets the £ price now, the invoice price for the product will be $105 × 0.85 = £89.25.

If the exchange rate moves to $1 = $0.90 then a receipt of £89.25 for the product from the exporter's customers would mean that (£89.25/0.9) $99.17 is received by the exporter once the £ have been converted to $.

This would mean that the exporter would no longer be able to make any profit on this product in the UK market and is in fact not quite covering its costs. The exporter would have to consider raising the price to remain profitable, but this would lead to lower competitiveness.

Conversely, if the exchange rate had moved in the opposite direction, the exporter would be making higher profits on the product in the UK market and could consider lowering the £ price to improve competitiveness.

Importers would feel the effects of exchange rate movements if they are paying for goods and services in a foreign currency.

E.g., if the exporter invoiced in \$ instead of £, pushing the exchange rate risk onto the customer, then the UK importer is invoiced for \$105. This m a payment of £89.25 when the exchange rate is \$1 = £0.85 but this would rise to £94.50 if the exchange rate moves to \$1 = £0.90.

Illustration 3 – Translation risk

A US company has debt denominated in US\$ and its existing debt provider has stipulated in a debt covenant agreement that the company will not take on further debt above a level of US\$1.5 million.

The company then takes out a loan in Euros with a value of €1,000,000. At the time of the loan being taken out the exchange rate between US\$ and € was € = US\$1.3, meaning that it has an effective US\$ value of US\$1.3 million. This would not breach the debt covenant.

However, if the exchange rate moved above € = US\$1.5 then the US\$ value would rise to a higher value than is allowed by the covenant and the company would be in breach of it.

Test your understanding 4

A Euro zone company has agreed to sell a product to a US customer for \$1,200. Suppose that the Euro:\$ exchange rate was €1 = \$1.2 when the deal was agreed but had moved to €1 = \$1.25 when the cash was received. What was the exchange gain or loss on the transaction?

A gain €40

B loss €40

C gain €60

D loss €60

Test your understanding 5

A UK company has agreed to sell a product to a US customer and has raised the invoice in US dollars. If the dollar strengthens against sterling before the funds are received this will lead to an exchange gain.

TRUE/FALSE?

Test your understanding 6

A US company is struggling to compete against imported goods due to a strong dollar making imports cheaper to US consumers. What type of exchange risk is being described here?

A economic risk

B transaction risk

C translation risk

4 Exchange rate systems

4.1 Exchange rates

As shown in section 2.3, the exchange rate of a currency is a price. It is the external value of a currency expressed in another currency, for example

£1 = $1.25

The exchange of currencies is vital for trade in goods and services. UK firms selling abroad will require foreign buyers to exchange their currency into sterling to facilitate payment. Similarly, UK importers will need to pay out in foreign currencies. Also, when funds are transferred between people in different countries, foreign exchange is required.

4.2 Exchange rate systems – floating exchange rates

Exchange rates that float are flexible and free to fluctuate in the light of changes that take place in demand and supply. Such exchange rates are examples of nearly perfect markets.

Demand

Demand for a currency, sterling say, comes from a number of sources:

- It is required to pay for UK exports – for example, a French supermarket buying English food priced in sterling will need to pay its suppliers in sterling.
- Overseas investors making investments in the UK will need sterling – for example, an American property company buying a factory building in the UK will have to pay in sterling.

- Speculators may buy sterling if they feel it is about to increase (appreciate) in value relative to other currencies.
- The government (strictly the central bank) may wish to buy sterling to manipulate the exchange rate.
- For some currencies, there may be a demand for it to be held as an international medium of exchange as is the case with the US dollar.

Supply

Supply of sterling is also derived from a number of sources:

- UK purchasers wishing to buy imports priced in a foreign currency will need to sell sterling and buy foreign currency.
- UK investors making overseas investments will need to sell sterling and buy foreign currency.
- Speculators may sell sterling if they feel its value is about to decrease (depreciate) relative to other currencies.
- The UK government (again, strictly the central bank) may sell currency on the international markets to weaken the currency to improve export performance.

Today, the sale and purchase of currencies for trading purposes is dwarfed by the lending and borrowing of funds.

Impact of different factors on the exchange rate

Putting these issues together, we can comment on how various economic factors affect exchange rates as follows:

- High inflation will weaken a currency as it makes goods more expensive thus dampening export demand and reducing the demand for the currency.
- An increase in interest rates will have a two-fold effect.

  In the short run, "hot money" will be attracted to UK deposits, increasing demand for sterling and a corresponding rise in the exchange rate.

  In the long run, high interest rates will erode the competitiveness of UK businesses reducing the supply of and demand for UK goods. This will reduce the demand for sterling, reducing the exchange rate.
- A trade deficit will result in the demand for sterling to buy exports being lower than the supply of sterling to buy imports. This will result in downward pressure on the exchange rate.
- Speculation can influence the exchange rate up or down. This is usually a short-term factor. In 2016, after the UK's vote to leave the EU the pound depreciated sharply. This was attributed by some as the effect of speculation as to the future stability of the UK economy, with investors switching their capital into traditionally secure currencies such as the yen and the Swiss franc.

Example using a diagram of supply and demand

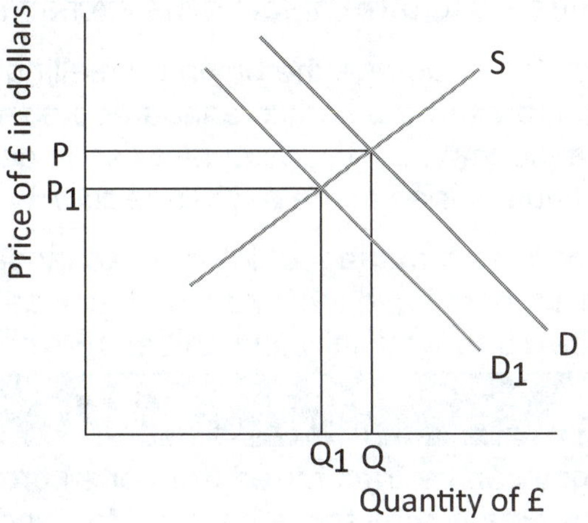

In the diagram, suppose we have a factor that causes British goods to become less competitive on world markets.

- This will result in a fall in the demand for British exports and hence causes a shift in the demand curve for sterling to D1.
- This shift causes a fall in the exchange rate to P1, assuming that the demand for British imports (and hence the supply curve) remains unchanged.
- P_1 Q_1 would be a new equilibrium position at which the demand for pounds and the supply of pounds are equal.

Note: since the demand and supply of a currency for trade purposes is a tiny fraction of all demand and supply for a currency, current account deficits/surpluses are unlikely to have much effect on the exchange rate.

Test your understanding 7

Suppose that demand for imports in the UK is price inelastic. If sterling were to depreciate in value against other currencies, which of the following would happen?

	Imports would become	Total spending by the UK on imports
A	Cheaper in £ sterling	Would rise
B	Cheaper in £ sterling	Would fall
C	More expensive in £ sterling	Would rise
D	More expensive in £ sterling	Would fall

4.3 Exchange rate systems – dirty floating

Governments often intervene in the foreign exchange markets (either by creating demand or supply of their currency as required) in order to maintain or achieve an exchange rate target. The purpose of this normally is to make a country's exports more competitive, by lowering the exchange rate, or to assist in the control of inflation.

The central bank will be instructed to:

- Buy or sell the currency to raise or lower the exchange rate.
- Alter interest rates to encourage the buying or selling of the currency. For example, raising interest rates should encourage speculators to deposit more funds in that country. The subsequent rise in demand for the currency should cause a rise in the exchange rate.

For example, China operates a managed floating exchange rate system for the Yuan and international leaders have criticized the Chinese government for keeping the value of the Yuan artificially low, to boost exports.

'Hot' money

Deposits of money can be transferred from one currency to another at short notice. This clearly affects the demand for, and supply of, currencies. The main factors influencing such transfers of what has been called 'hot money' are:

- relative interest rates – if the differential between nations changes, then capital tends to move towards the nation whose interest rate offers the most lucrative return
- expectations – if the holders of 'hot money' expect a currency to appreciate, they will deposit money in that country, as the appreciation will raise the exchange value of the deposits
- inflation – countries with relatively high rates will find their currency less attractive to depositors because its value is depreciating more than that of other countries.

Test your understanding 8

If a country has a 'floating' (flexible) exchange rate, which one of the following would lead to a fall (depreciation) in the rate of exchange for its currency?

A a rise in capital inflows into the economy

B an increase in the country's exports

C an increase in the country's imports

D a fall in the country's rate of inflation

Test your understanding 9

Which one of the following would be likely to result in a rise in the value of UK sterling against the Euro?

A a rise in interest rates in the UK

B the UK central bank buying Euros in exchange for sterling

C a rise in interest rates in the Euro zone

D increased capital flows from the UK to the Euro zone

Test your understanding 10

All of the following would normally lead to a rise in the exchange rate for a country's currency, except which one?

A an increase in the country's exports

B an increased inflow of foreign direct investment into the country

C a short term rise in interest rates in the country

D an increase in the export of capital from the country

Test your understanding 11

The country of Xanadu has as its currency the Krown and for many years has fixed the exchange rate against the US dollar so

$1 = K10

Recent economic events have made this level harder and harder for the Xanadu central bank to support. A speculator has entered into a forward contract to sell 1 bn Krowns at $1 = K10, on the hope that the additional pressure will force the Xanadu government to devalue the Krown.

Calculate the speculator's profit in $ if the Krown is devalued to a new level of $1 = K12.

Answer = $ __________ (give your answer in billions to 3 decimal places)

4.4 Exchange rate systems – fixed

Some governments will have a policy of fixing the value of their currency against the value of another currency or to another measure of value, such as gold. Known as a fixed exchange rate system, this can operate to stabilise the value of their currency, making international trade easier.

For instance, the Saudi Arabian Monetary Authority has an exchange rate policy of fixing its currency, the riyal, to the US dollar. It can buy and sell the country's reserves of foreign exchange to affect supply and demand for its currency and so maintain its price (exchange rate).The rate is set at 3.75 riyal = US$1.

4.5 Currency substitution

Some countries even allow the use of a foreign currency in addition to the domestic currency (known as currency substitution, or dollarisation when the foreign currency used is US dollars). They may choose to do this in a period of economic uncertainty where the home currency may be subject to significant fluctuation. The use of a stable foreign currency stabilises the value of day to day transactions.

5 Single currency zones

One way of avoiding exchange rate risk is for each country to use the same currency. The best known example of such an arrangement is the plan for Economic and Monetary Union (EMU), which seeks to establish a single currency and monetary authority within the European Union.

Two major components of this integration are:

- A single European currency – the Euro
- The European Central bank.

The Euro

The Euro was launched on 1 January 1999, with 11 of the then 15 members agreeing to participate. National currencies were retained until 2002 to be replaced with Euro notes and coins.

Performance of the Euro against other major world currencies has been patchy. In its first year, the Euro depreciated from $1.19 per Euro to $0.80 per Euro, though it since recovered some of this value.

The European Central Bank (ECB)

The European Central Bank (ECB) began operations in May 1998 as the single body with the power to issue currency, draft monetary policy, and set interest rates in the Euro-zone. The Maastricht Treaty envisaged the ECB as an independent body free from day-to-day political interference, with a principal duty of price stability.

The ECB is the central bank for the Euro currency area and is based in Frankfurt. It is the sole issuer of the Euro. Its main objective, as defined by the Maastricht Treaty, is price stability. It therefore has the power to set short-term interest rates.

The main focus of its activities has been on interest rate policy rather than exchange rate policy. Like the Monetary Policy Committee of the Bank of England, the ECB pursues a policy of controlling interest rates as a means of achieving influence over the long-term rate of inflation.

Test your understanding 12

All of the following are benefits that all countries will gain from the adoption of a single currency such as the Euro, except which one?

A reduced transactions costs

B increased price transparency

C lower interest rates

D reduced exchange rate uncertainty

Test your understanding 13

Which one of the following is not a benefit from countries forming a monetary union and adopting a single currency?

A International transactions costs are reduced

B Exchange rate uncertainty is removed

C It economises on foreign exchange reserves

D It allows each country to adopt an independent monetary policy

Test your understanding answers

Test your understanding 1

D

Prior to the change, 1 Euro could purchase 1.13 US$. It can now buy more US$ (1.15), so the Euro must now be more valuable relative to the US$ - it has appreciated – and the US$ is now less valuable relative to the Euro – it has depreciated.

Test your understanding 2

C

The correct answer is: to reduce or eliminate exposure to risk.

Test your understanding 3

Answer D

A forward exchange contract is a binding contract that specifies in advance the rate at which a specified currency will be bought and sold at a specified future time.

Test your understanding 4

B

- When the deal was agreed, $1,200 would have been worth 1200/1.2 = €1,000
- When the cash was received, $1,200 was worth 1200/1.25 = €960
- Thus, there was an exchange loss of €40.

Test your understanding 5

True

The UK company will be receiving dollars. If the dollar strengthens, then these dollars will become more valuable and can be swapped for more sterling, giving rise to an exchange gain.

Note that if the company had invoiced in sterling, they would not have suffered any transaction risk related to this sale – the risk would have been passed to the US customer.

Test your understanding 6

A

By definition.

Test your understanding 7

C

With a depreciation in the value of sterling, import prices rise, because it costs more in sterling to obtain the foreign currency to pay foreign suppliers for the imported goods. Since demand for imports is inelastic, the fall in demand for imports resulting from an increase in their price will be relatively small, and total spending on imports will rise.

Test your understanding 8

C

Rising imports is the only one that will raise the supply of its currency to the foreign exchange market, depressing the exchange rate. The other three will raise demand, which will push up the exchange rate.

Test your understanding 9

A

If interest rates in the UK rise, this attracts foreign money in to invest here. Pounds sterling are demanded in exchange for the foreign currencies in order to invest, and therefore the 'price' of the £, i.e. the exchange rate, rises.

The other options lead to movement of sterling out of the UK – increasing the supply of sterling – and would lead to a fall in the sterling exchange rate.

Test your understanding 10

D

Capital leaving the country would increase the supply of that country's currency and reduce the exchange rate.

Test your understanding 11

$0.017bn

- The speculator will buy 1 bn Krowns at the new exchange rate of $1 = K12, costing $0.083bn.
- These can then be used to deliver on the forward contract where they can be sold at a rate of $1 = K10, thus realising $0.100bn.
- The net profit will thus be $0.100 – $0.083 = $0.017bn.

Test your understanding 12

C

Interest rates are not directly related to the adoption of a single currency. Instead, the impact would depend on the policy of the central bank administering the single currency. The others should all be benefits.

Test your understanding 13

D

Countries in a monetary union and adopting a single currency cannot have independent monetary policies. In the Euro zone, monetary policy is controlled by the ECB (European Central Bank).

Chapter

7

Financial Context of Business III: Discounting and Investment Appraisal

Chapter learning objectives

On completion of their studies, students should be able to:

- calculate future values of an investment using both simple and compound interest
- calculate the present value of a future cash sum, an annuity and a perpetuity
- calculate the net present value (NPV) and internal rate of return (IRR) of a project and explain whether and why it should be accepted.

1 Introduction

In this chapter, we shall be looking at various techniques of investment appraisal. We introduce the important concept of net present value and to aid your understanding we start by looking at the calculations surrounding interest payments and equivalent rates of interest.

2 The investment decision-making process

- Managers need to decide where they want to 'take' the business
- What investment decision they make is vital to the success and growth of the business
- Investment decision making has a number of distinct stages:

1 **Origination of proposals:** where many different alternatives are introduced and discussed.

2 **Project screening:** where the 'sensible' projects are looked at with the company's long-term aims in mind.

3 **Analysis and acceptance:** where detailed investment appraisal techniques/financial analysis are undertaken, together with qualitative issues being discussed.

4 **Monitor and review:** where progress is monitored, comparison to capital expenditure budgets is made and timing is reviewed.

In this chapter, we will focus on stage 3.

One characteristic of all capital expenditure projects is that cash flows arise over the long-term (a period usually greater than 12 months). Under this situation, it becomes necessary to carefully consider the time value of money.

3 The time value of money

Money received today is worth more than the same sum received in the future, i.e. it has a **time value**.

This occurs for three reasons:

- potential for earning interest/cost of finance
- impact of inflation
- effect of risk.

This is a key concept throughout this chapter.

Discounted cash flow (DCF) techniques take account of this time value of money when appraising investments.

The time value of money

Potential for earning interest

Cash received sooner can be invested to earn interest, so it is better to have $1 now than in one year's time. This is because $1 now can be invested for the next year to earn a return, whereas $1 in one year's time cannot. Another way of looking at the time value of money is to say that $1 on a future date is worth less than $1 now.

Impact of inflation

In most countries, in most years prices rise because of inflation. Therefore, funds received today will buy more than the same amount a year later, as prices will have risen in the meantime. The funds are subject to a loss of purchasing power over time.

Risk

The earlier cash flows are due to be received, the more certain they are – there is less chance that events will prevent payment. Earlier cash flows are therefore considered to be more valuable.

4 Interest

4.1 Simple interest

One of the most basic uses of mathematics in finance concerns calculations of interest, the most fundamental of which is simple interest.

With simple interest the interest is paid only on the original principal (i.e. the original amount borrowed/saved), not on the interest accrued.

Illustration 1 – Simple interest

Suppose I invest $200 for 3 years at an annual interest rate of 5% and that interest is calculated by reference to the original sum invested.

How much will I have at the end of the investment?

- The annual interest will be 200 × 5% = $10
- At the end of three years the total interest will be 3 × 10 = $30
- The final sum will thus be $230

Formula

More generally, suppose $P is invested at a fixed rate of interest of r per annum (where r is a percentage expressed as a decimal). The interest earned each year is calculated by multiplying the rate of interest r by the amount invested, $P, giving an amount $(r × P). After n years the sum of $(r × P × n) will be credited to give a total at the end of the period, $V, of:

$$V = P + r \times P \times n$$

or:

$$V = P(1 + r \times n)$$

This well-known formula is often referred to as the simple interest formula.

Note: this formula can be applied to non-annual time periods as long as an interest rate is used to match the timescales.

Illustration 2 – Simple interest

Suppose I invest $2,000 in a deposit account paying 0.1% per month.

Calculate the final value in the account after two years, assuming simple interest.

- P = 2,000
- r = 0.001 (remember to express the interest rate as a decimal)
- n = 24

V = P(1 + r × n) = 2,000 × (1 + 0.001 × 24) = 2,000 × 1.024 = $2,048

Test your understanding 1

An amount of $5,000 is invested at a rate of 8 per cent per annum. What will be the value of the investment in 5 years' time, if simple interest is added once at the end of the period?

Test your understanding 2

Calculate the value of the following, assuming that simple interest is added:

A $20,000 invested for 5 years at 5 per cent per annum

B $50,000 invested for 3 years at 6 per cent per annum

C $30,000 invested for 6 years with 1 per cent interest per quarter

4.2 Compound interest

In practice, simple interest is not used as often as compound interest.

With compound interest, the interest is paid on both the original principal plus any interest accrued. This means that the interest is calculated on the total balance brought forward rather than on the initial amount.

Illustration 3 – Compound interest

Suppose $200 is invested for 3 years at 5% compound interest – i.e. interest is added at the end of each year based on the brought forward balance and so affects the interest for the next year.

- For year 1 the interest will be 5% × $200 = $10. The total sum carried forward will thus be

  $200 + $10 = $210.

- For year 2 the interest will be 5% × $210 = $10.50. The total sum carried forward will thus be

  $210 + $10.50 = $220.50.

- For year 3 the interest will be 5% × $220.50 = $11.025. The total sum at the end of the investment will thus be

  $220.50 + $11.025 = $231.525.

Notice that each year the sum grows by a factor of (1.05). As a short cut we could calculate the value at the end of year 3 as

$$\$200 \times (1.05) \times (1.05) \times (1.05) = \$200 \times (1.05)^3 = \$231.525$$

Formula

Suppose $P is invested for n years at a fixed rate of interest of r per annum compounded annually. After n years the value, $V, will be given by

$$\mathbf{V = P(1 + r)^n}\text{, where r is expressed as a decimal}$$

This well-known formula is often referred to as the compound interest formula.

As you will see, in financial mathematics we work with an annual ratio denoted by (1 + r) rather than with the rate of interest.

Test your understanding 3

An amount of $5,000 is invested at a fixed rate of 8 per cent per annum. What amount will be the value of the investment in 5 years' time, if the interest is compounded:

A annually?

B every 6 months?

Test your understanding 4

Calculate the value of the following, assuming compound interest

A $20,000 invested for 5 years at 5 per cent per annum

B $50,000 invested for 3 years at 6 per cent per annum

C $30,000 invested for 6 years with 1 per cent interest per quarter

4.3 Equivalent rates of interest

Suppose the rate of interest on a loan was stated to be 8 per cent per annum with payments made every 6 months. This means that 4 per cent would be paid every 6 months.

We can find the effective annual rate of interest by considering the impact of two 4 per cent increases on an initial value of $1:

Value at the end of 1 year = $1 × 1.04 × 1.04 = $1.0816

$0.0816 has been added on to the initial value of $1, or 8.16% of its original value.

Hence, the effective annual rate of interest is 8.16 per cent in this case.

A three step approach can be used to calculate equivalent rates:

1 For the rate given, add 1 to its decimal value.

2 Take this value to the power of the number periods of the rate you're using are in the period of the rate you're looking for

3 Take 1 off the answer

So for the example above, we were given information to know that the rate was 4% every six months. In step 1 we would calculate a value of 1.04.

In step 2, as there are 2 six-month periods in a year and we're looking to calculate the yearly rate, we would take the 1.04 to the power of 2. This calculates as $1.04^2 = 1.0816$.

In the final step we deduct 1 and this gives us 0.0816, or 8.16%.

Illustration 4 – Monthly rate from annual rate

If the annual percentage rate of a deposit is 25% and interest is earned and compounded monthly, what is the equivalent monthly interest rate on the deposit?

Step 1 – take the rate given as a decimal and add 1 to it. 25% is 0.25 as a decimal and if we add 1 we get 1.25

Step 2 – the period of the rate we're looking for is a month and the period of the rate we're using is a year. There is 1/12th of a year in a month, so the power we need to apply to the 1.25 is 1/12.

$1.25^{(1/12)} = 1.0188$

Step 3 – take 1 off this answer and we get 0.0188 which, as a percentage is 1.88%

Note: you can double check this answer by seeing if \$1 earning interest compounded at 1.88% every month for 12 months would earn total interest of 25%, which it does: $\$1 \times 1.0188^{12} = \$1.25$

Note: In some respects, quoting the cost of the loan as 8% per annum is misleading and understates the real effective rate. This is why, in the UK, lenders have to quote the 'APR' of any loans or financing deals they want you to use, as this gives the effective annual percentage rate. This is the most useful figure to use when comparing different financing deals. The same considerations apply to deposit rates. In the illustration above, you might feel that earning 1.88% per month would lead to annual earnings of (1.88% × 12) 22.56%, but in reality, because of compounding, 25% is earned.

Test your understanding 5

An investor is considering two ways of investing \$20,000 for a period of 10 years:

- option A offers 1.5 per cent compounded every 3 months
- option B offers 3.2 per cent compounded every 6 months.

Which is the better option?

Test your understanding 6

Find the effective annual rates of interest corresponding to the following:

A 3 per cent every 6 months

B 2 per cent per quarter

C 1 per cent per month

Test your understanding 7

Over 5 years a bond costing \$1,000 increases in value to \$1,250. Find the effective annual rate of interest.

Test your understanding 8

If house prices rise by 20 per cent per annum, find:

A the equivalent percentage rise per month

B the percentage rise over 9 months

5 Investment appraisal

5.1 Introduction

Firms often have investment appraisal decisions that involve looking at forecast cash flows occurring many years into the future. The long-term nature of such projects raises potential problems when comparing cash flows at different times. Consider the following illustration.

e.g. Illustration 5 – Long-term projects

Suppose you have a very simple project that involves the following:

- Invest $10,000 now
- Based on your best estimates you expect to receive $11,000 in the future.

Would you accept this project?

Even though it gives you a gain of $1,000 and a return of 10%, the answer is not clear cut because it depends on **when** you receive the $11,000 and what else you could do with the $10,000 now.

Suppose the $11,000 is to be received in 2 years' time (t2) and that you could invest your current funds in a deposit account paying interest at 6% per annum.

If you invest your cash for two years, then in two years' time you would end up with

$$\$10,000 \times 1.06^2 = \$11,236$$

This is greater than the $11,000 expected through the project, so you would therefore reject the project and invest the money in the bank instead.

Effectively you are saying that $10,000 now (t0) is worth more to you than $11,000 in two years' time (t2), illustrating the concept that money has a **time value**.

5.2 The time value of money

As mentioned earlier, money received today is worth more than the same sum received in the future, i.e. it has a **time value**.

We said this occurs for three reasons:

- potential for earning interest/cost of finance
- impact of inflation
- effect of risk.

The time value of money can be expressed as an annual interest rate for calculation purposes. Different terminology is used to describe this rate, depending on the exam paper and the context:

- discount rate
- required return
- cost of capital.

Suppose we have a 'required return rate' of 10% per annum:

- If this related just to a deposit rate at a bank, say, then we could invest \$100 now and end up with \$100 × 1.10 = \$110 in one year's time.
- This means that \$100 now and \$110 in one year's time have the **same value to us** for decision-making purposes when assessing other potential projects.
- Equivalently, we could say that the offer of \$110 in a year's time is only worth \$110/1.10 = \$100 in today's terms (or 90.9% of its actual value).

5.3 Discounted cash flows

In a potential investment project, cash flows will arise at many different points in time. To make a useful comparison of the different flows, they must all be converted to a common point in time, usually the present day, i.e. the cash flows are discounted.

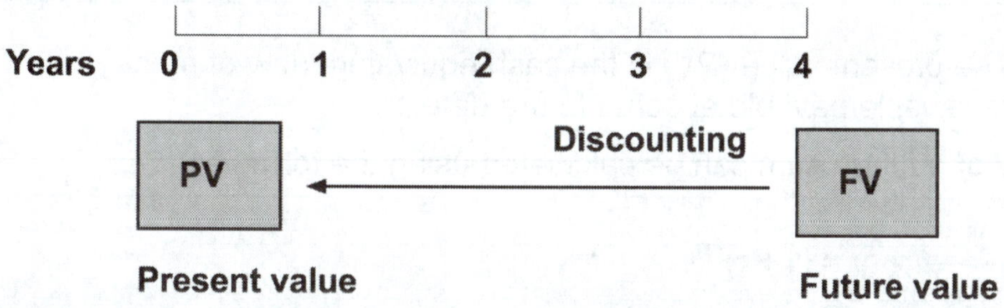

The process of converting future cash flows into present values is known as "discounting" and is effectively the opposite of compounding interest.

e.g Illustration 6 – Discounting

Find the present value of:

(a) \$200 payable in 2 years' time, assuming that an investment rate of 7 per cent per annum, compounded annually, is available

(b) \$350 receivable in 3 years' time, assuming that an annually compounded investment rate of 6 per cent per annum, is available.

Solution

(a) From the definition, we need to find that sum of money that would have to be invested at 7 per cent per annum and have value \$200 in 2 years' time. Suppose this is \$P, then the compound interest formula gives:

$V = P(1 + r)^n$

Thus:

$\$200 = P(1 + 0.07)^2$

$$P = \frac{\$200}{1.1449} = \$174.69$$

Thus, the present value is \$174.69: that is, with an interest rate of 7 per cent, there is no difference between paying \$174.69 now and paying \$200 in 2 years' time.

(b) Using the compound interest formula again:

$\$350 = P(1 + 0.06)^3$

$$P = \frac{\$350}{1.191016} = \$293.87$$

The present value is thus \$293.87.

Discounting a single sum

The present value (PV) is the cash equivalent now of money receivable/payable at some future date.

The PV of a future sum can be calculated using the formula:

$$P = \frac{V}{(1 + r)^n} = V \times (1 + r)^{-n}$$

This is just a re-arrangement of the formula we used for compounding.

$(1 + r)^{-n}$ is called the discount factor (DF). To find the DF, for example if r = 10% and n = 5, you can either use the formula or the tables:

The 5-year DF at 10%

Formula
$1.1^{-5} = 0.621$

or

Tables
(given in examination)

You can simply find the DF from the PV table by locating the DF at the 10% column and the 5-year row, i.e. 0.621

Test your understanding 9

Calculate the present values of the following amounts:

A	$12,000 payable in 6 years' time at a rate of 9 per cent
B	$90,000 payable in 8 years' time at 14 per cent
C	$80,000 payable in 5 years' time at 6.3 per cent
D	$50,000 payable in 4 years and 3 months' time at 10 per cent

6 Net present value (NPV)

In many situations, there are a number of financial inflows and outflows involved, at a variety of times. In such cases, the net present value (NPV) is the total of the individual present values, after discounting each, as above.

The NPV represents the net gain or loss on the project after taking into account the timing of cash flows and the time value of money (i.e. incorporates the cost of finance, investment opportunities, inflation and risk), therefore:

- if the NPV is positive – the project is financially viable
- if the NPV is zero – the project breaks even
- if the NPV is negative – the project is not financially viable
- if the company has two or more mutually exclusive projects under consideration it should choose the one with the highest NPV
- the NPV gives the impact of the project on shareholder wealth.

NPV is a hugely important topic that will be revisited again in later exams. For example, it is used to evaluate capital investment projects in P2 Advanced Management Accounting. The principles are used to calculate the cost of capital in F2 Advanced Financial Reporting and to value businesses in F3 Financial Strategy.

Illustration 7 – Net Present Value

A company can purchase a machine now for $10,000. The company accountant estimates that the machine will contribute $2,500 per annum in positive cash flows for five years, after which time it will have to be scrapped for $500.

Find the NPV of the machine if the interest rate for the period is assumed to be 5 per cent.

(Assume, for simplicity, that all inflows occur at year ends.)

Solution

We set out the calculations in a systematic, tabular form:

Timing	Cash flow ($) ($)	Discount factor @ 5%	Present value ($)
0	(10,000)	1.000	–10,000.00
1	2,500	0.952	2,380.00
2	2,500	0.907	2,267.50
3	2,500	0.864	2,160.00
4	2,500	0.823	2,057.50
5	3,000	0.784	2,352.00
			1,217.00

Hence, the NPV is $1,217.

Test your understanding 10

The cash flows for a project have been estimated as follows:

Year	$
0	(25,000)
1	6,000
2	10,000
3	8,000
4	7,000

The cost of capital is 6%.

Calculate the net present value (NPV) of the project to assess whether it should be undertaken.

Test your understanding 11

Evaluate the net present values of the following potential purchases (figures, all in $000, show net inflows/(outflows)):

		A	B
		r = 6%	r = 8%
After:	Year 0	(35)	(55)
	Year 1	(10)	0
	Year 2	20	15
	Year 3	30	25
	Year 4	40	35

Are either of the above purchases worth making, on financial grounds alone?

Using NPV in practice

Problems using NPV in practice

One of the major difficulties with present values is the estimation of the 'interest rates' used in the calculations. Clearly, the appropriate rate(s) at the start of the time period under consideration will be known, but future values can be only estimates. As the point in time moves further and further into the future, the rates become more and more speculative.

Many situations in which NPV might be involved are concerned with capital investments, with the capital needing to be raised from the market. For this reason, the 'interest rate(s)' are referred to as the cost of capital, since they reflect the rate(s) at which the capital market is willing to provide the necessary money.

Another problem with calculating net present value is the need to estimate annual cash flows, particularly those that are several years in the future, and the fact that the method cannot easily take on board the attachment of probabilities to different estimates. Finally, it is a usual, although not an indispensable, part of the method to assume that all cash flows occur at the end of the year, and this too is a potential source of errors.

With easy access to computers, it is now possible to calculate a whole range of NPVs corresponding to worst-case and best-case scenarios as well as those expected, so to some extent some of the problems mentioned above can be lessened.

Test your understanding 12

A company has a cost of capital of 8%. The future cash flows of a project, excluding the initial investment amount, when discounted at 8% have a present value of $450,000. Which one of the following statements is correct?

A $450,000 is the extra value that would be added onto the business if it undertakes the project.

B $450,000 is the maximum amount that the company should borrow if it wants to make a profit on the project.

C $450,000 is the maximum that the company should invest today into the project for the project to be worthwhile.

D $450,000 is the profit on the project, expressed in present value terms.

7 Annuities

An **annuity** is an arrangement by which cash is received or paid in a series of constant annual amounts. The length of time during which the annuity is paid can either be until the death of the recipient or for a guaranteed minimum term of years, irrespective of whether the annuitant is alive or not. In other types of annuity, the payments are deferred until sometime in the future, such as the retirement of the annuitant.

When two or more annuities are being compared, they can cover different time periods and so their net present values become relevant. In your exam, you will be given the following formula for the NPV of a $1 annuity over n years at interest rate r, with the first payment 1 year after purchase.

$$\textbf{Annuity factor} = \frac{1-(1+r)^{-n}}{r}$$

To calculate the present value of an annuity cash flow:

PV = future cash flow × annuity factor

There is also a cumulative present value table available in the exam where you can look up values of the annuity factor for whole r values between 1% and 20% and whole years between 1 and 20.

e.g

Illustration 8 – Annuities

Let us revisit the last illustration:

A company can purchase a machine now for $10,000. The company accountant estimates that the machine will contribute $2,500 per annum to profits for five years, after which time it will have to be scrapped for $500.

Find the NPV of the machine using annuity discount factors if the interest rate for the period is assumed to be 5 per cent.

Solution

We can set out the calculations highlighting the annuity as follows:

After year	Total inflow ($)	Discount factor @ 5%	Present value ($)
0	(10,000)	1.000	(10,000)
1–5	2,500 per year	4.329 (W)	10,823
5	500	0.784	392
			1,215

This table gives the NPV as $1,215. Before we got $1,217, the difference being due to rounding.

(W) This figure can be obtained using the cumulative present value (annuity) table (which gives a figure of 4.329) or the formulae above (which gives a less rounded figure of 4.329476671). Unless told otherwise in the question, it won't matter which you use.

e.g

Illustration 9 – Annuities

An investor is considering two annuities, both of which will involve the same purchase price.

- Annuity A pays $5,000 each year for 20 years, while
- Annuity B pays $5,500 each year for 15 years.

Both start payment 1 year after purchase and neither is affected by the death of the investor.

Assuming a constant interest rate of 8 per cent, which is the better?

Solution

Using tables, the cumulative PV factors are 9.818 for A and 8.559 for B. This gives:

- PV of annuity A = 5,000 × 9.818 = 49,090
- PV of annuity B = 5,500 × 8.559 = 47,075

You will only be able to use the tables given in your exam if the period of the annuity is 20 years or less and if the rate of interest is a whole number. It is, therefore, essential that you learn to use the formula as well. You will notice that there is some loss of accuracy, due to rounding errors, when tables are used.

Using the above formula:

$$\text{Factor for the NPV of A} = \frac{1 - 1.08^{-20}}{0.08} = 9.818147$$

And so the NPV of A is:

$5,000 × 9.818147 = $49,090 (to the nearest $)

Similarly:

$$\text{Annuity factor for the NPV of B} = \frac{1 - 1.08^{-15}}{0.08} = 8.559479$$

And so the NPV of B is:

$5,500 × 8.559479 = $47,077 (to the nearest $)

From the viewpoint of NPVs, therefore, annuity A is the better choice. As we have already seen, however, there are two further considerations the investor may have. Assuming constant interest rates for periods of 15 or 20 years is speculative, so the NPVs are only approximations: they are, however, the best that can be done and so this point is unlikely to affect the investor's decision. More importantly, although any payments after the investor's death would go to their estate, some people may prefer more income 'up front' during their lifetime.

Unless the investor is confident of surviving the full 20 years of annuity A, they may prefer annuity B – especially as the two NPVs are relatively close to each other.

Test your understanding 13

A payment of $3,600 is to be made every year for seven years, the first payment occurring in one year's time. The interest rate is 8%. What is the PV of the annuity?

Test your understanding 14

A payment of $11,400 is to be made every year for 13 years, the first payment occurring in one year's time. The interest rate is 5%. What is the PV of the annuity?

Test your understanding 15

An annuity pays $12,000 at the end of each year until the death of the purchaser. Assuming a rate of interest of 6 per cent, what is the PV of the annuity if the purchaser lives for:

A 10 years; and

B 20 years after purchase?

In order to practise both methods, use the tables in (a) and the formula in (b).

Test your understanding 16

An investor is considering three options, only one of which she can afford. All three have the same initial outlay, but there are different income patterns available from each.

- Investment A pays $2,000 each year at the end of the next 5 years.
- Investment B pays $1,000 at the end of the first year, $1,500 at the end of the second year, and keeps growing by $500 per year until the final payment of $3,000 at the end of the fifth year.
- Investment C pays $4,000 at the end of the first year, $3,000 at the end of the second year, and $2,000 at the end of the third.

The investor estimates a constant rate of interest of 10 per cent throughout the next 5 years: which investment should she choose?

Test your understanding 17

Compare the following three potential investments, assuming the investor has a maximum of $15,000 to deploy, if the prevailing rate of interest is 11 per cent:

	Investment A	Investment B	Investment C
	$000	$000	$000
Initial outlay	14	14	12
Inflow at end of:			
Year 1	0	7	10
Year 2	6	7	8
Year 3	8	7	5
Year 4	10	7	5
Year 5	10	7	5
Year 6	10	7	5

None of the investments brings any income after year 6.

8 Perpetuities

Finally, there is the concept of **perpetuity**. As the name implies, this is the same as an annuity except that payments go on forever. it is therefore of interest to those who wish to ensure continuing payments to their descendants, or to some good cause. It must be recognised, however, that constant payments tend to have ever-decreasing value, owing to the effects of inflation and so some alternative means of providing for the future may be preferred.

To calculate the present value of a perpetuity cash flow:

PV = future cash flow × perpetuity factor.

Perpetuity factor = 1/r

This factor is not available on tables but is simple to calculate.

Test your understanding 18

Bob has won a competition that pays him $12,000 per annum for life, which upon his passing would then be payable to his descendants. Using an interest rate of 6%, calculate the present value of the income, assuming that this is effectively a perpetuity.

Advanced annuities and perpetuities

In all of the examples, we have assumed that the annuity or perpetuity cash flows start in Year 1 (T1). The use of annuity factors and perpetuity factors depend on this assumption.

It is possible that cash flows start **immediately (in year 0).** In this case, we have to adjust our calculations.

Illustration – Advanced annuity

A 5-year $600 annuity is starting today. Interest rates are 10%. Find the present value of the annuity.

Solution

If we consider the five receipts, this is essentially a standard 4-year annuity with an additional payment at T0. The present value could be calculated as follows:

	T_0		T_1	T_2	T_3	T_4
CF	600		600	600	600	600
	↓		↘	↓	↓	↙
PV	600	+	600 × 4-year 10% AF			

PV = 600 + (600 × 3.170) = 600 + 1,902 = $2,502

Remember from your NPV calculations, the discount factor for T0 = 1. Using this, the same answer can be found more quickly by ignoring the first cash flow and adding 1 to the 4 year AF:

PV = 600 × (1 + 3.170) = 600 × 4.17 = $2,502.

Illustration – Advanced perpetuity

A perpetuity of $2,000 is due to commence immediately. The interest rate is 9%. What is the PV?

Solution

This is essentially a standard perpetuity with an additional payment at T0. The PV could be calculated as follows:

T_0	T_1	T_2	T_3	T_4 ....
2,000	2,000 → ∞			

PV (2,000) + (2,000 × 9% perpetuity factor)

2,000 + (2,000 × (1 ÷ 0.09)) = $24,222.

Or by ignoring the first cash flow and adding 1 to the perpetuity factor:

$$2{,}000 \times \left(1 + \frac{1}{0.09}\right) = 2{,}000 \times 12.11 = \$24{,}222$$

Delayed annuities and perpetuities

In the last example, the cash flows started at T0. It is also possible that the cash flows are delayed and start later than T1.

Illustration – Delayed annuity

What is the PV of $200 received each year for four years, starting in three years' time, if the discount rate is 5%?

Solution

Consider the cash flows:

T0	T1	T2	T3	T4	T5	T6
			200	200	200	200

Here, we can use the normal 4 year annuity factor, but this will only discount the series of cash flows back to one time period before they started, i.e. time period 2. This means that the resulting figure now needs to be discounted for a further 2 years. As it is now a single figure, the 2 year discount factor (rather than annuity factor) should be used.

The calculation to get the time period 0 value (present value) is therefore:

$200 × (4 year annuity factor at 5%) 3.546 × (2 year discount factor at 5%) 0.907 = **$643**

Illustration – Delayed perpetuity

What is the PV of a $300 perpetuity due to commence in year 2? Assume an interest rate of 6%.

Solution

Taking the same approach as for the annuity, using the perpetuity factor ($1/r = 1/0.06$) will discount the cash flows back to time period 1, so they will need to be further discounted by 1 year ($1.06^{-1} = 0.943$) to get to a time period 0 figure:

$300 × 1/0.06 × 0.943 = **$4,715**

Test your understanding 19

A payment of $3,600 is to be made each year. The interest rate is 8%. What is the PV of the annuity if:

(a) There are seven payments and the first payment is made immediately?

(b) There are seven payments and the first payment is made in five years' time?

(c) The payments are made into perpetuity, starting immediately?

(d) The payments are made into perpetuity, starting in 3 years' time?

9 Internal rate of return

We have seen that if the NPV is positive, then it means that the project is more profitable than investing at the discount rate, whereas if it is negative, then the project is less profitable than a simple investment at the discount rate.

For most projects, the NPV falls as the discount rate increases. When the NPV becomes zero we have a breakeven discount rate, defined as **the internal rate of return (IRR)** of the project.

This now gives us two ways of appraising an investment:

1 Accept if NPV > 0 as this means the project will increase shareholder wealth

2 Accept if actual discount rate < project IRR, as this means we should have a positive NPV.

Calculating IRR

The internal rate of return (IRR) is the discount rate at which the NPV is zero. It is obtained generally by a trial and error method as follows.

1 find a discount rate at which the NPV is small and positive

2 find another (larger) discount rate at which the NPV is small and negative

3 use linear interpolation between the two to find the point at which the NPV is zero.

Illustration 10 – IRR

Find the IRR for the following project.

Time	Cash flow ($000)
0	(80)
1	40
2	30
3	20
4	5

The question offers no guidance as to what discount rates to try, so we will select 5 per cent randomly. Since 5 per cent turns out to give a positive NPV, we now randomly select 10 per cent in the hope that it will give a negative NPV.

Time	Cash flow $000	PV (5%) $000	PV (10%) $000
0	(80)	(80.000)	(80.000)
1	40	38.095	36.364
2	30	27.211	24.793
3	20	17.277	15.026
4	5	4.114	3.415
Net present value:		6.697	(0.402)

We can now use either (a) a graphical method or (b) a calculation based on proportions.

(a) **Graphical method**

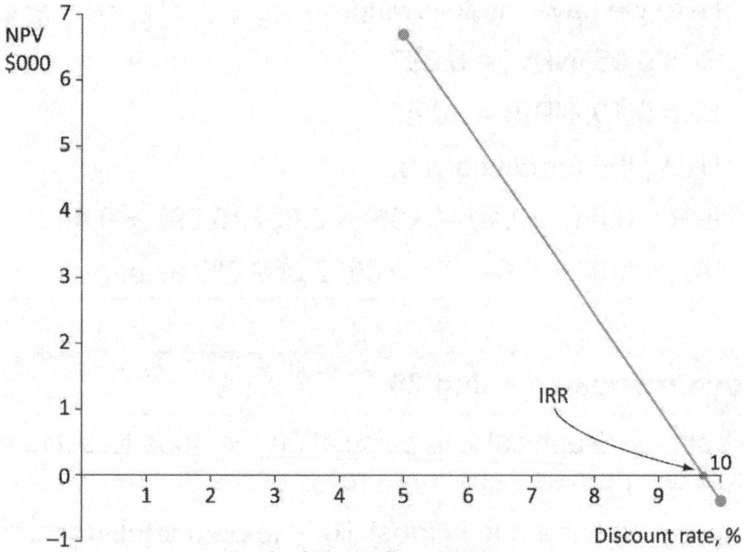

Graph of NPV to discount rate

From the graph, the estimated IRR is 9.7 per cent.

(b) **Calculation method using proportions**

The NPV drops from 6.697 to –0.402, that is, a drop of 7.099, when the discount rate increases by 5 percentage points (from 5 to 10 per cent).

NPV will therefore drop by 1 when the discount rate increases by 5/7.099 = 0.7043 percentage points.

The NPV will reach zero if, starting at its 5 per cent level, it drops by 6.697.

This requires an increase of 6.697 × 0.7043 = 4.7 percentage points in the discount rate.

Hence, the IRR (the discount rate at which NPV is zero) is 5 + 4.7 = 9.7 per cent.

Calculation method using formula

In general, if you have calculated two NPVs (NPV1 and NPV 2) for two discount rates (R1 and R2 respectively), then the IRR will be given by the formula:

$$R_1 + (R_2 - R_1) \times \frac{NPV_1}{NPV_1 - NPV_2}$$

The formula is provided in the exam.

This formula works whether or not one of the NPVs is positive and one negative, or both are negative or both are positive, so don't bother having a third guess if the first two don't give a positive and negative NPV.

The main calculation aspect to be careful with is if either of the NPVs is negative.

Here we have the following:

$R_1 = 0.05$, $NPV_1 = 6.697$

$R_2 = 0.10$, $NPV_2 = -0.402$

Using the formula gives:

IRR = 0.05 + (0.10 – 0.05) × 6.697/(6.697 + 0.402)

IRR = 0.05 + 0.0472 = 0.0972 or 9.7% as before.

Test your understanding 20

Use both the graphical and calculation methods to estimate the IRR for the following project, and interpret your result.

The calculation method is most likely to be useful in your assessment.

Time	Cash flow ($000)
0	(100)
1	50
2	50
3	20

10 Terminal values and sinking funds

Instead of being asked to calculate a present value for a series of cash flows spread over many different time periods, you may be asked to calculate a **terminal value**.

This simply means that instead of discounting all the cash flows to the present day and adding them up they should all be compounded to the end of the project and added up.

Illustration 11 – Terminal values

An investor invests \$3,000 initially and then \$1,800 at the end of the first, second and third years, and finally \$600 at the end of the fourth year. If interest is paid annually at 6.5 per cent, find the value of the investment at the end of the fifth year.

Solution

The diagram shows when the investments and evaluation take place.

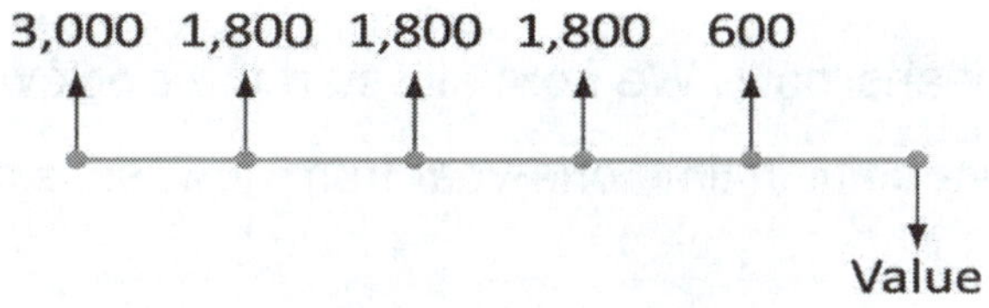

The \$3,000 is invested for 5 years and grows to:

$$\$3{,}000 \times 1.065^5 = \$4{,}110.26$$

The three sums of \$1,800 are invested for 4, 3 and 2 years, and grow in total to:

$$\$1800 \times (1.065^4 + 1.065^3 + 1.065^2) = \$6{,}531.55$$

Finally, the \$600 is invested for just 1 year and grows to:

$$\$600 \times 1.065 = \$639$$

The total value at the end of 5 years is \$11,280.81.

A **sinking fund** is a special type of investment in which a constant amount is invested each year, usually with a view to reaching a specified value at a given point in the future. Questions need to be read carefully in order to be clear about exactly when the first and last instalments are paid.

Illustration 12 – Sinking funds

Suppose a company needs to replace a machine costing \$50,000 in 6 years' time. To achieve this it will make six annual investments, starting immediately, at 5.5 per cent.

Find the value of the annual payment.

Solution

To ensure you have understood the question it is always worth drawing a timeline diagram showing, in this case the payments (denoted by P) and asset replacement:

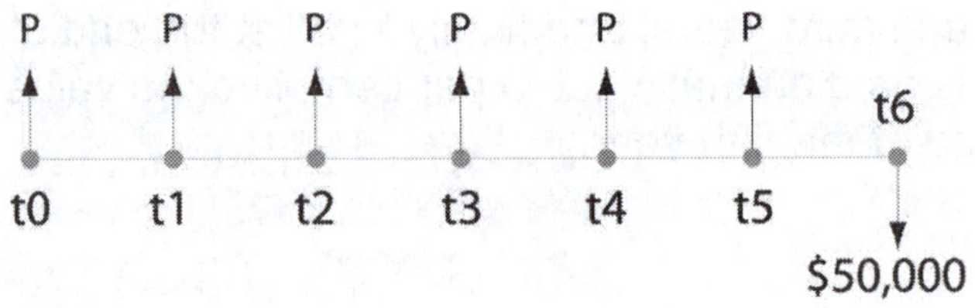

Note:

- t0 means 'now'. We normally start the clock with the first cash flow.
- t1 is a point in time one year from now, so is at the end of the first year.
- t2 is a point in time two years from now, etc.

The first investment grows for 6 years and its final value is $P(1.055)^6$. The second amounts to $P(1.055)^5$, the third to $P(1.055)^4$, etc. until the sixth, which amounts to only $P(1.055)^1$.

We thus need to solve the following

$\$50,000 = P(1.055)^6 + P(1.055)^5 + P(1.055)^4 + P(1.055)^3 + P(1.055)2 + P(1.055)$

$\$50,000 = P(1.055^6 + 1.055^5 + 1.055^4 + 1.055^3 + 1.055^2 + 1.055)$

$\$50,000 = P \times 7.267$, giving

$P = \$50,000/7.267 = \$6,880$ per annum (to the nearest \$)

Test your understanding 21

Three annual instalments of \$500 are to be paid, starting immediately, at 4.9 per cent per annum.

Find the value of the investment **immediately after** the third instalment.

A sinking fund may be used in relation to interest-only mortgages. The borrower pays the interest on the mortgage during the mortgage term, but does not pay off any capital. Instead, a separate investment is set up and regular deposits into the investment are made, with the aim of reaching an investment value by the end of the mortgage term that is enough to pay off the full capital amount.

Test your understanding answers

Test your understanding 1

The interest rate in the formula needs attention: it is assumed that r is a proportion, and so, in this case, we must convert r = 8 per cent into a proportion:

$r = 0.08$

Also, we have

$P = 5{,}000$ and $n = 5$

So

$V = P(1 + r \times n) = 5{,}000(1 + 0.08 \times 5) = 5{,}000 \times 1.4 = 7{,}000$

Thus, the value of the investment will be $7,000.

Test your understanding 2

A $r = 0.05$, $n = 5$, $P = 20{,}000$:

$V = 20{,}000(1 + 0.25) = \$25{,}000$

B $r = 0.06$, $n = 3$, $P = 50{,}000$:

$V = 50{,}000(1 + 0.18) = \$59{,}000$

C $r = 0.01$, $n = 6 \times 4 = 24$, $P = 30{,}000$:

$V = 30{,}000(1 + 0.24) = \$37{,}200$

Test your understanding 3

A The only part of this type of calculation that needs particular care is that concerning the interest rate. The formula assumes that r is a percentage expressed as a decimal, and so, in this case:

$r = 0.08$

In addition, we have $P = 5{,}000$ and $n = 5$, so:

$V = P(1 + r)^5 = 5{,}000 \times (1 + 0.08)^5 = 5{,}000 \times 1.469328 = \$7{,}346.64$

Thus, the value of the investment will be $7,346.64.

It will be noted that compound interest gives higher values to investments than simple interest.

B With slight modifications, the basic formula can be made to deal with compounding at intervals other than annually. Since the compounding is done at 6-monthly intervals, 4 per cent (half of 8 per cent) will be added to the value on each occasion. Hence, we use r = 0.04. Further, there will be ten additions of interest during the five years, and so n = 10. The formula now gives:

$V = P(1 + r)^{10} = 5{,}000 \times 1.04^{10} = \$7{,}401.22$

Thus, the value in this instance will be $7,401.22.

In a case such as this, the 8 per cent is called a nominal annual rate, and we are actually referring to 4 per cent per 6 months.

Test your understanding 4

A $r = 0.05, n = 5, P = 20{,}000$

$V = 20{,}000(1.05)^5 = \$25{,}525.63$

B $r = 0.06, n = 3, P = 50{,}000$

$V = 50{,}000(1.06)^3 = \$59.550.80$

C $r = 0.01, n = 6 \times 4 = 24, P = 30{,}000$

$V = 30{,}000(1\ .01)^{24} = \$38{,}092.04$

Test your understanding 5

We have, for option A, P = 20,000; n = 10 × 4 = 40; r = 0.015 and so:

$V = 20{,}000\ (1 + 0.015)^{40} = \$36{,}280.37$

For option B, P = 20,000; n = 10 × 2 = 20; r = 0.032 and so:

$V = 20{,}000\ (1 + 0.032)^{20} = \$37{,}551.21$

Hence, option B is the better investment.

In this case, P = 20,000 was given but it is not necessary to be given an initial value because $1 can be used instead.

Test your understanding 6

A For $1, value at the end of 1 year = $1 \times 1.03^2 = 1.0609$. Hence, the effective annual rate is 6.09 per cent.

B For $1, value at the end of 1 year = $1 \times 1.02^4 = 1.0824$. Hence, the effective annual rate is 8.24 per cent.

C For $1, value at the end of 1 year = $1 \times 1.01^{12} = 1.1268$. Hence, the effective annual rate is 12.68 per cent.

Test your understanding 7

Over 5 years, the value has increased by $250, which is a 25% increase on the starting value of $1,000

Step 1 – add 1 to the value as a decimal = 1.25

Step 2 – there is 1/5 of 5 years in an annual period so take to the power of 1/5 (or 0.2):

$1.25^{1/5} = 1.0456$

Step 3 – take 1 off the calculated value = 0.0456, or 4.56%

Alternatively:

$V = P(1 + r)^n$

$\$1,250 = \$1,000 \times (1 + r)^5$

$\$1,250/\$1,000 = 1.25$

$1.25 = (1 + r)^5$

$1.25^{1/5} = 1 + r = 1.0456$

giving an effective annual rate of 4.56%

Test your understanding 8

The annual ratio = 1.2 = monthly ratio^{12}

A Add 1 to annual rate = 1.5

$1/12^{th}$ of a year in a monthly period so take to the power of 1/12:

$1.2^{1/12} = 1.0153$

Take 1 off the calculated value = 0.0153, or 1.53 per cent.

B Using the monthly figure to start:

Add 1 to the monthly rate = 1.0153

9 months in a nine month period so take to the power of 9:

$1.0153^9 = 1.1464$

Take 1 off the calculated value = 0.1464, or 14.64 per cent.

Test your understanding 9

A Discount factor at 9 per cent for 6 years = 1.09^{-6} = 0.596 (or use tables)

PV = $12,000 × 0.596 = $7,152

B Discount factor at 14 per cent for 8 years = 1.14^{-8} = 0.351 (or use tables)

PV = $90,000 × 0.351 = $31,590

C Discount factor at 6.3 per cent for 5 years = 1.063^{-5} = 0.737 (have to use calculator)

PV = $80,000 × 0.737 = $58,960

D Discount factor at 10 per cent for 4.25 years = $1.10^{-4.25}$ = 0.667 (have to use calculator)

PV = $50,000 × 0.667 = $33,350

Test your understanding 10

Year	Cash flow $	DF at 6%	PV $
0	(25,000)	1.000	(25,000)
1	6,000	0.943	5,658
2	10,000	0.890	8,900
3	8,000	0.840	6,720
4	7,000	0.792	5,544
			1,822

The NPV of the project is positive at $1,822. The project should therefore be accepted.

Test your understanding 11

Time	A $000	Discount factor	PV $000	
0	(35)	1.000	(35.00)	
1	(10)	0.943	(9.43)	
2	20	0.890	17.80	
3	30	0.840	25.20	
4	40	0.792	31.68	
Net present value:			30.25	(i.e. $30,250)

Time	B $000	Discount factor	PV $000	
0	(55)	1.000	(55.00)	
1	0	0.926	–	
2	15	0.857	12.86	
3	25	0.794	19.85	
4	35	0.735	25.73	
Net present value:			3.44	(i.e. $3,440)

Both investments have positive NPVs and so both are worthwhile.

Test your understanding 12

C

The $450,000 is the present value of the future cash flows of the project. Investing anything up to $450,000 today would give a positive total NPV. Investing exactly $450,000 today would lead to an NPV of $0 and the project would just be worthwhile (as it would return exactly 8% and cover its funding costs). NPV calculations use cash flows rather than profits, so answers B and D are not relevant. As the initial investment amount has not been included in the $450,000 figure, the extra value added onto the business would be the $450,000 less the initial investment value, so answer A is incorrect.

Test your understanding 13

Using the formula:

$$\frac{1-(1+r)^{-n}}{r} = \frac{1-1.08^{-7}}{0.08} = 5.206$$

$3,600 × 5.206 = $18,741.60

Note that the AF could have been taken straight from the tables.

Test your understanding 14

Using the formula:

$$\frac{1-(1+r)^{-n}}{r} = \frac{1-1.05^{-13}}{0.05} = 9.394$$

$11,400 × 9.394 = $107,091.60

Note that the AF could have been taken straight from the tables.

Test your understanding 15

A If n = 10 and rate is 6 per cent, from tables the annuity factor is 7.360:

PV = $12,000 × 7.360 = $88,320

B If n = 20, from the formula:

$$\frac{1-(1+r)^{-n}}{r} = \frac{1-1.06^{-20}}{0.06} = 11.4699$$

$12,000 × 11.4699 = $137,639

Test your understanding 16

From tables, the cumulative present value factor for a constant inflow at 10 per cent for 5 years is 3.791; hence the NPV of investment A is

$2,000 × 3,791 = $7,582

The other two investments do not involve constant inflows, and so the PVs for individual years have to be summed.

Year (end)	PV factor	Investment B Inflow ($)	PV ($)	Investment C Inflow ($)	PV ($)
1	0.909	1,000	909	4,000	3,636
2	0.826	1,500	1,239	3,000	2,478
3	0.751	2,000	1,502	2,000	1,502
4	0.683	2,500	1,707.50	–	–
5	0.621	3,000	1,863	–	–
			7,220.50		7,616

In summary, the NPVs of investments A, B and C are $7,582, $7,220.50 and $7,616, respectively.

The investor should choose C as it has the highest NPV.

Test your understanding 17

Time	Discount factor	A $000	PV $000	B $000	PV $000	C $000	PV $000
0	1.000	(14)	(14.000)	(14)	(14,000)	(12)	(12.000)
1	0.901	0	0.000	7	–	10	9.010
2	0.812	6	4.872	7	–	8	6.496
3	0.731	8	5.848	7	–	5	–
4	0.659	10	6.590	7	–	5	–
5	0.593	10	5.930	7	–	5	–
6	0.535	10	5.350	7	29.61	5	12.590
Net present values:			14.590		15.617		16.096

In the case of B we have multiplied 7 by the cumulative PV (annuity) factor for 6 years at 11 per cent, giving 7 × 4.231 = 29.617.

For C we have subtracted the 2-year cumulative PV (annuity) factor from the 6-year factor and then multiplied the result by 5.

All the investments are worthwhile since they have positive NPVs. Investment C costs the least initially and yet has the highest NPV and so is to be preferred.

Test your understanding 18

For a perpetuity of $12,000 per annum, discounted at 6 per cent, the present value is $12,000/0.06 or $200,000.

You can check this easily. At 6 per cent, the interest on $200,000 is $12,000 per annum, so the annuity can be paid indefinitely without touching the capital.

Test your understanding 19

(a) An advanced annuity of seven years of $3,600 at 8%. Ignore the first payment and add 1 to the 6 year annuity factor at 8%.

$3,600 × (1 + 4.623) = $20,243

(b) A delayed annuity of seven years of $3,600 at 8% starting at T5. Discount the value using the seven year annuity factor and then discount using a 4 year discount factor.

$3,600 × 5.206 × 0.735 = $13,775

(c) An advanced perpetuity of $3,600 at 8%. Add one to the perpetuity factor.

$3,600 × (1 + 1/0.08) = $48,600

(d) A delayed perpetuity of $3,600 at 8% starting at T3. Discount using the perpetuity factor and then discount using a 2 year discount factor.

$3,600 × 1/0.08 × 0.857 = $38,565

Test your understanding 20

Time	Cash flow $000	PV (5%) $000	PV (15%) $000
0	(100)	(100.000)	(100.000)
1	50	47.619	43.478
2	50	45.351	37.807
3	20	17.277	13.150
Net present value:		10.247	(5.565)

A Graphical method

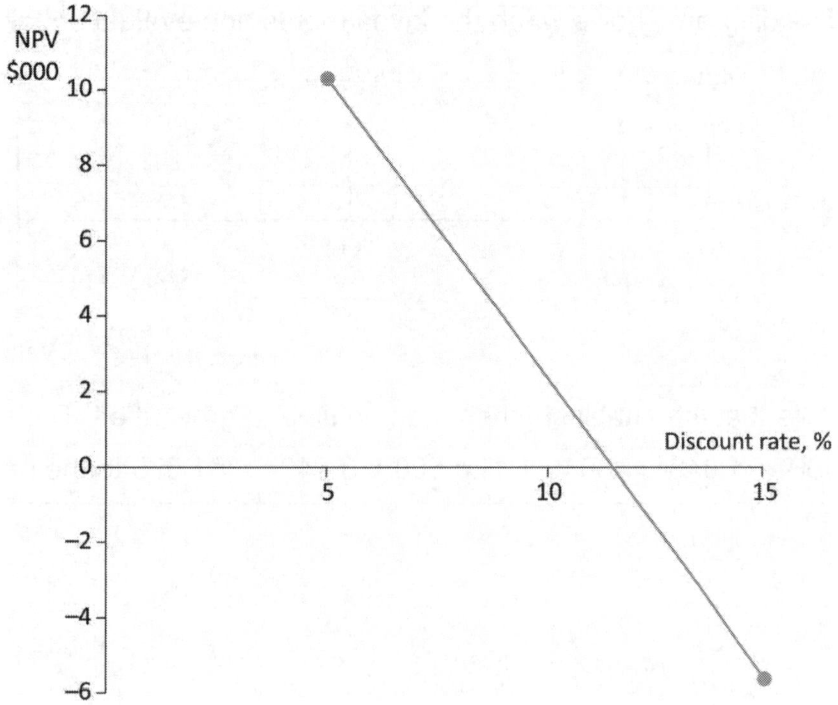

From the graph, the estimate of the IRR is 11.5 per cent.

B Using proportions:

The NPV drops by 10.247 + 5.565 = 15.812 when discount rate increases by 10 percentage points.

The NPV will drop by 1 ($000) when discount rate increases by 10/15.812 = 0.6324 percentage points.

For IRR, NPV must drop by 10.247, which requires an increase in the discount rate of 10.247 × 0.6324 = 6.5 percentage points.

Hence, the IRR = 5 + 6.5 = 11.5 per cent.

Alternatively, **using the formula***:*

$R_1 = 0.05$, $NPV_1 = 10.247$

$R_2 = 0.15$, $NPV_2 = -5.565$ Using the formula gives

IRR = 0.05 + (0.15 – 0.05) × 10.247/(10.247 + 5.565)

IRR = 0.05 + 0.0648 = 0.1148 or 11.5% as before.

Test your understanding 21

The diagram shows when the investments and evaluation take place:

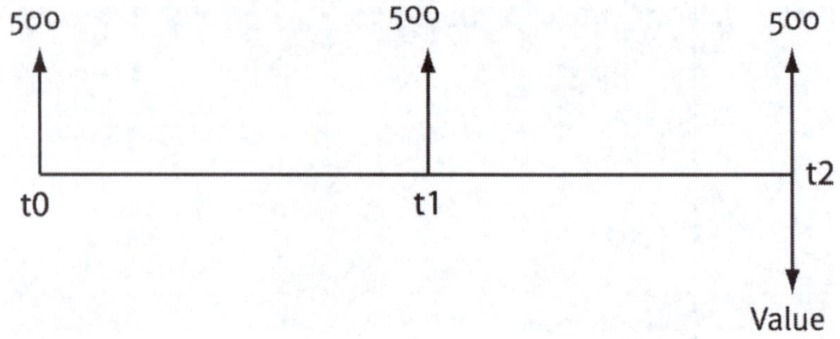

Note that the final instalment has no time to grow at all. The value is:

$500 \times (1.049^2 + 1.049 + 1) = 500 \times 3.1494 = \$1,575$ to the nearest $

Chapter

8

Informational Context of Business I: Summarising and Analysing Data

Chapter learning objectives

On completion of their studies, students should be able to:

- explain the difference between data and information and the characteristics of good information
- identify relevant data from graphs, charts and diagrams: bar charts, scatter diagrams, histograms, and ogives.

1 Introduction

Data, when first collected, is often not in a form that conveys much information. In this chapter we look at ways in which raw data can be collated into more meaningful formats, looking at some pictorial representations of data that provides convenient ways of communicating them to others.

2 Data and information

Immediately after collection, in what is often termed its raw form, data is not very informative. We cannot learn about the situation from it or draw conclusions from it.

After it has been sorted and analysed, data becomes **information** that, it is to be hoped, is understandable and useful.

The word data means facts. Data consists of numbers, letters, symbols, raw facts, events and transactions which have been recorded but not yet processed into a form which is suitable for making decisions.

Information is data which has been processed in such a way that it has meaning to the person who receives it.

e.g

Illustration 1 – Data and information

In management accounting, the accounting system records a large number of facts (data) about materials, times, expenses and other transactions.

These facts are then classified and summarised to produce information in the form of accounts, which are organised into reports designed to help management to plan and control the firm's activities.

Test your understanding 1

What, if any, is the difference between data and information?

A They are the same

B Data can only be figures, whereas information can be facts or figures

C Information results from sorting and analysing data

D Data results from obtaining many individual pieces of information

3 Characteristics of good information

Information is provided to management to assist them with planning, controlling operations and making decisions. Management decisions are likely to be better when they are provided with better quality information. The attributes of good information can be identified by the '**ACCURATE**' acronym as shown below:

A. Accurate

- The degree of accuracy depends on the reason why the information is needed.
- For example, reports may show figures to the nearest dollar or nearest thousand dollars for a report on the performance of different divisions.
- Alternatively, when calculating the cost of a unit of output, managers may want the cost to be accurate to the nearest cent.

C. Complete

- Managers should be given all the information they need, but information should not be excessive.
- For example, a complete control report on cost variances should include all standard and actual costs necessary to understand the variance calculations.

C. Cost effective

- The value of information should exceed the cost of producing it.
- Management information is valuable, because it assists decision making.
- If a decision backed by information is different from what it would have been without the information, the value of information equates the amount of money saved/earned as a result.

U. Understandable

- Use of technical language or jargon must be limited. For example, accountants must always be careful about the way in which they present financial information to non-financial managers.

R. Relevant

- The information contained within a report should be relevant to its purpose.
- Redundant parts should be removed.
- In the context of responsibility accounting, information about costs and revenues should be reported to the manager responsible, who is in a position to control them.

A. Authoritative

- Information should be trusted and provided from reliable sources so that the users can have confidence in their decision making.

T. Timely

- Information should be provided to a manager in time for him/her to make decisions based on that information.

E. Easy to use

- Information should be accessible via the appropriate channels of communication (verbally, via a report, a memo, an email etc.).

Test your understanding 2

Which of the following is NOT a characteristic of good information for a product price list?

A All products included

B Products listed in alphabetical order

C Prices rounded to the nearest $100

D Shows current prices

4 Bar charts

Bar charts are a simple way of representing actual data pictorially, subject to the following rules:

- Distances against the vertical axis are measurements and represent numerical data.
- Horizontal distances have no meaning. There is no horizontal axis or scale, there are only labels.

Bar charts are very useful for making comparisons between different data items, data sets and so on.

Illustration 2 – Bar charts

A company trades in five distinct geographical markets. In the last financial year, its turnover was:

	$m
Europe	59.3
Asia	61.6
South America	10.3
North America	15.8
Africa	9.9
Total	156.9

We can display these turnover figures as a bar chart.

Solution

To draw this chart, it is simply a matter of drawing five vertical 'bars', with heights to represent the various turnover figures, and just labels for regions in the horizontal direction.

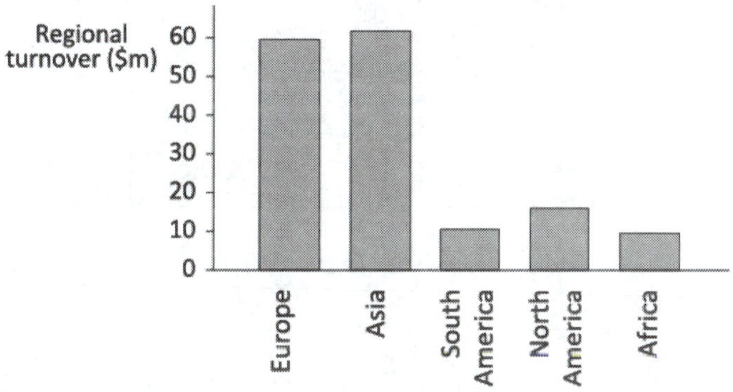

Using this chart it is easy to see, for example, that revenue is highest in Asia.

There are a number of variations on such a basic bar chart, used to display more data or more complex data. An example will show just one.

e.g

Illustration 3 – Bar charts continued

A rival company to the one mentioned earlier trades in the same five geographical markets. Its turnover in the last financial year was:

	$m
Europe	60.2
Asia	69.0
South America	11.1
North America	18.0
Africa	8.8
Total	167.1

We can display the turnover figures for both companies on a single chart.

There are at least two types of bar chart which can be used here: a multiple bar chart and a compound (or component or stacked) bar chart:

(a) Multiple

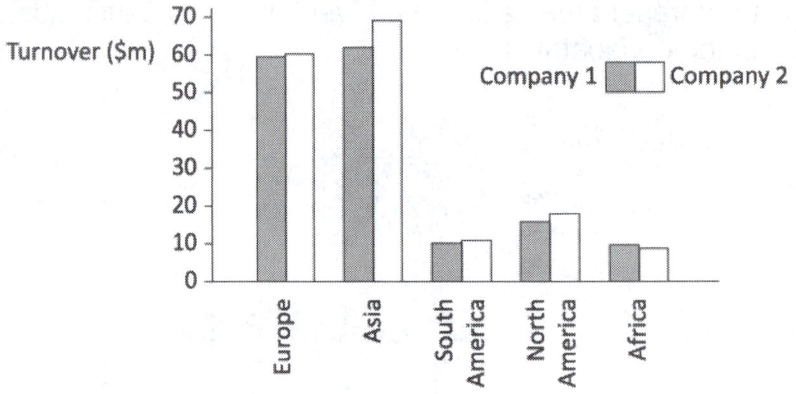

(b) Compound

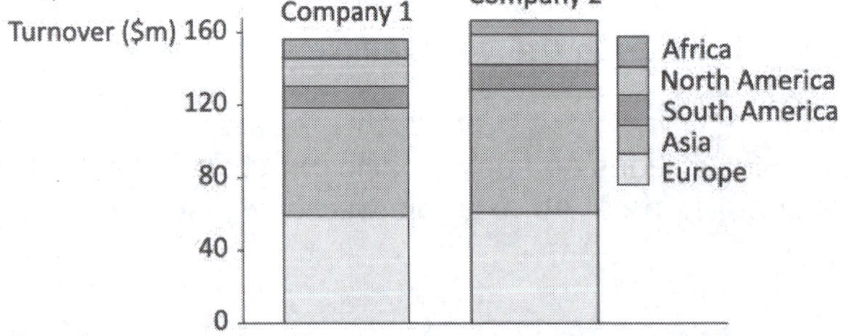

The multiple bar chart readily displays how well the two companies have performed in each market, but not so clearly in total. Conversely, the relative total performance of the two companies can be seen easily from the compound bar chart, but not so the breakdown by region.

Test your understanding 3

The following are percentage distributions of household income in two regions:

Income ($000)	*Region A*	*Region B*
0–10	25	15
10–20	30	29
20–30	32	38
30–40	10	9
40 or more	3	9
Total	100	100

Display the data by the following bar charts:

A region A by a simple bar chart

B region A by a compound bar chart

C both regions by a multiple bar chart

The following information is relevant to the next 4 TYUs.

	Number of pies sold			
Pie flavourings	*2013*	*2014*	*2015*	*2016*
Chocolate	240	305	290	360
Toffee	120	135	145	210
Apple	70	105	125	190
Banana	30	35	40	35

Test your understanding 4

The following compound bar chart illustrates the 2013 section of the above data. What are the heights of the four horizontal lines in the bar?

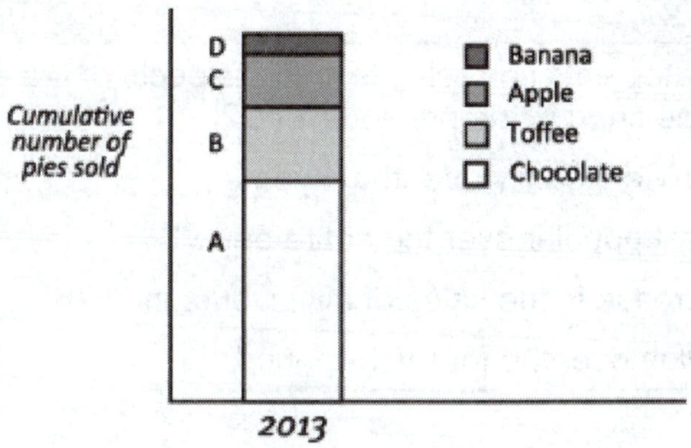

Test your understanding 5

Which of the following statements correctly describes an aspect of the data which is illustrated by the 2013 bar?

A In 2013, chocolate sold more than all the other flavours put together.

B Sales rose from 2013 to 2014.

C The popularity of banana increased very little over the 4 years.

D In 2013, toffee was less popular than apple.

Test your understanding 6

The data may be illustrated by the following chart. What type of chart is it?

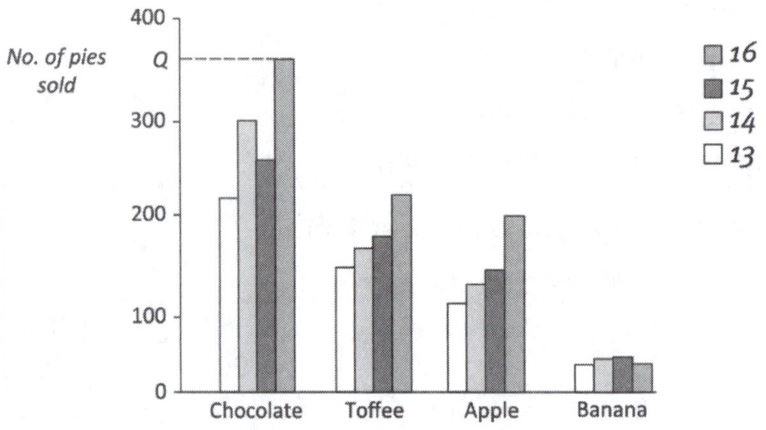

A Multiple bar chart

B Simple bar chart

C Histogram

D Component bar chart

Test your understanding 7

Which of the following statements correctly describe aspects of the data which are illustrated by the chart in the previous TYU?

A Sales of chocolate rose steadily over the 4 years.

B Banana was the least popular over the entire period.

C There was a big increase in the sales of all flavours in 2016.

D Total sales have fallen over the four-year period.

5 Scatter diagrams

A scatter diagram is a visual way of determining if there might be a relationship between two variables.

Two variables are said to be correlated if they are related to one another, or, more precisely, if changes in the value of one tend to accompany changes in the other.

For example, if children take higher vitamin C supplements, does that result in higher intelligence or is there no relationship between the two?

Illustration 4 – Scatter diagrams

A company is investigating the effects of its advertising on sales. Consequently, data on monthly advertising and sales in the following month are collated to obtain:

Advertising expenditure in month ($000)	*Total sales in following month* ($000)
1.3	151.6
0.9	100.1
1.8	199.3
2.1	221.2
1.5	170.0

Plot these data on a scatter diagram.

Solution

Since the company is interested in how advertising affects sales, it is clear that sales should be the dependent variable, **y**, and advertising the independent, **x**.

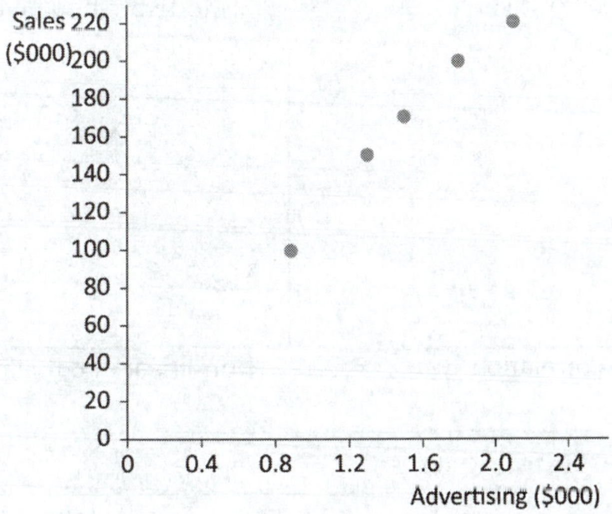

Scatter diagram

The five pairs of data points are marked as points on the graph.

The scatter diagram seems to show a case where the two variables are related to one another. Further, the relationship seems to be of an approximately **linear nature**: it is an example of linear correlation. Since the approximation is so good, and the points are close to a straight line, we talk of strong linear correlation.

Finally, as the gradient of the 'line' is upward sloping – i.e. positive – it shows positive linear (or direct) correlation.

A scatter diagram can reveal a range of different types and degrees of correlation:

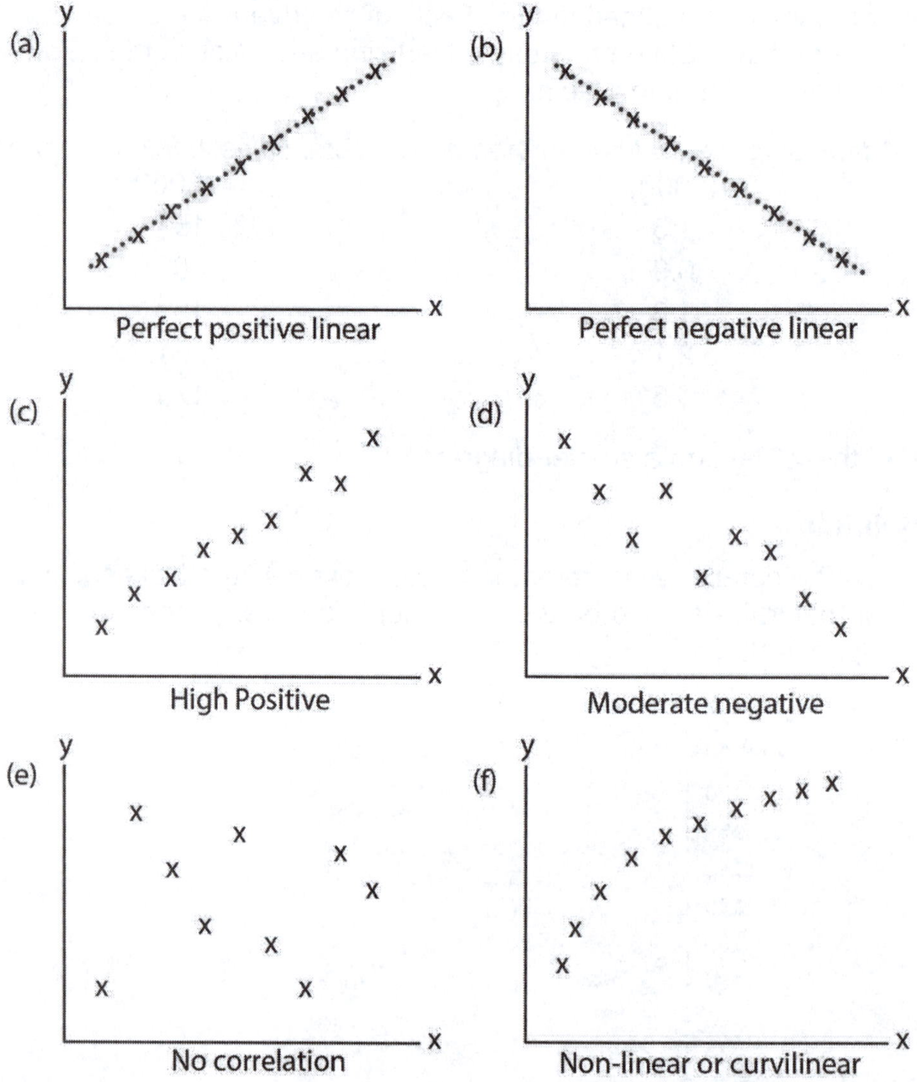

Test your understanding 8

From your own experience, try to think of pairs of variables that might have the different degrees of correlation, from weak to strong and from negative to positive.

Test your understanding 9

A company owns six sales outlets in a certain city. The sales last year of one of its key products is given below, together with the sizes of each outlet.

Outlet	*Floor space* m^2	*Sales of L* *'000 units*
A	75	22.4
B	60	21.1
C	108	29.6
D	94	27.1
E	92	27.0
F	130	36.9

The company is investigating the effects of outlet size on sales.

Plot a scatter diagram of sales of L against size of outlet.

6 Histograms and ogives

In this section we look at diagrammatic representations of frequency and cumulative frequency distributions.

Histograms

When looking at bar charts, you know that frequency is represented by the height of a block. With histograms the frequency is represented by the **area** of a block or rectangle.

More specifically, a histogram is a diagram consisting of rectangles whose area is proportional to the frequency of a variable and whose width is equal to the class interval. The x-axis is the variable being measured and the y-axis is the corresponding frequency.

Consider the following illustration.

Illustration 5 – Histograms

In order to assist management negotiations with the trade unions over piecework rates, the management services department of a factory is asked to obtain information on how long it takes for a certain operation to be completed. Consequently, the members of the department measure the time it takes to complete 30 repetitions of the operation, at random occasions during a month. The times are recorded to the nearest tenth of a minute.

19.8	21.3	24.6	18.7	19.1	15.3
20.6	22.1	19.9	17.2	24.1	23.0
20.1	18.3	19.8	16.5	22.8	18.0
20.0	21.6	19.7	25.9	22.2	17.9
21.1	20.8	19.5	21.6	15.6	23.1

Represent this data as a histogram.

Solution

First, we need to obtain a frequency distribution.

The frequency distribution is obtained by tallying the number of values in a certain range or class. The choice of classes is somewhat arbitrary, but should be such that they are neither too narrow, which would result in most of the frequencies being zero, nor too wide, which would produce only a small number of classes and thereby tell us little. As a rough guide, between four and twelve groups are often used.

Time (minutes)	*Tally*	*Frequency*
15-under 17	III	3
17-under 19	IIIII	5
19-under 21	IIIII IIIII	10
21-under 23	IIIII II	7
23-under 25	IIII	4
25-under 27	I	1

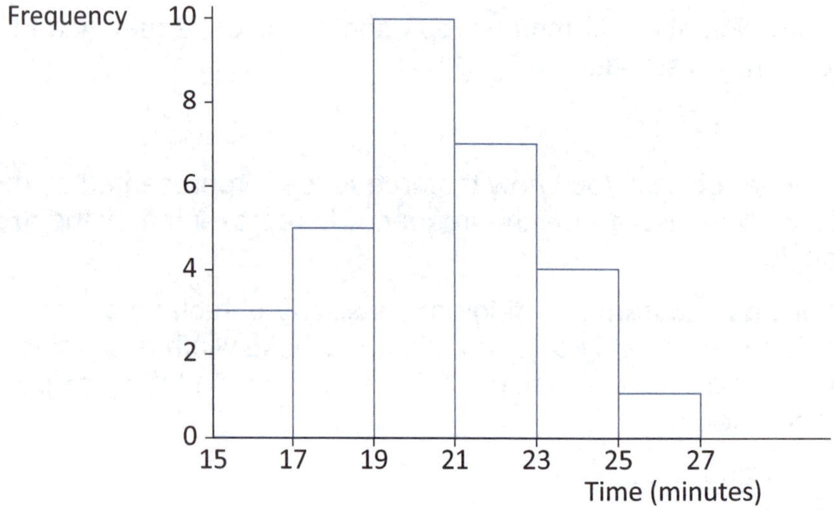

At first glance this may look no different from what we have seen before. However, if we were to look at examples with uneven class sizes, we would see that representing frequency by height alone can be misleading and a switch to areas (histograms) gives a fairer representation of the underlying data. Histograms with uneven class sizes are not part of the syllabus.

Ogives

An ogive is a graph of cumulative frequency distributions.

Cumulative frequencies are the number of data values up to – or up to and including – a certain point. They can easily be compiled as running totals from the corresponding frequency distribution.

Illustration 6 – Ogives

Draw an ogive for the data in Illustration 4.

Solution

The cumulative frequency distribution is

Time (minutes) (less than)	*Cumulative frequency*
15	0
17	3
19	8
21	18
23	25
25	29
27	30

This gives the following ogive

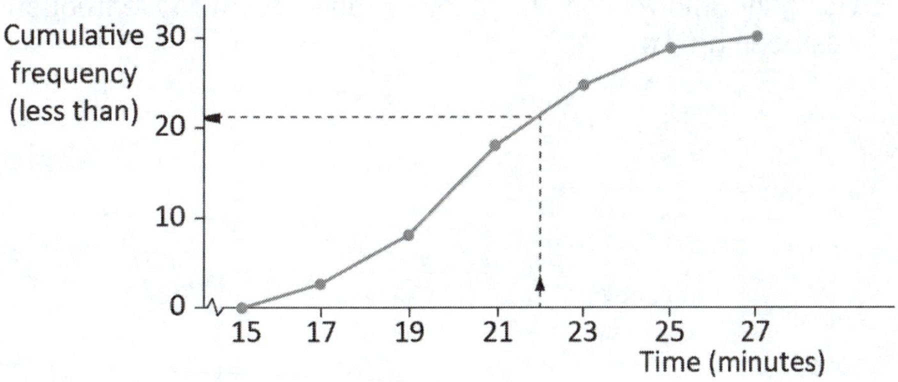

Note:

The horizontal axis has been started at 15 rather than 0 to make it easier to read. Having part of the axis missing like this is known as a broken scale.

Test your understanding 10

A cumulative frequency distribution of weekly wages is as follows:

Weekly wage	Cumulative frequency
Less than $150	45
Less than $200	125
Less than $300	155
Less than $400	170
Less than $600	175

A How many were paid less than $300?

B How many were paid more than $200?

C How many were paid between $200 and $300?

The following information is relevant to the next 2 TYUs.

The managers of a sales department have recorded the number of successful sales made by their 40 telesales persons for one week.

Suppose the frequency distribution and cumulative frequencies were as follows:

Sales	Frequency	Cumulative frequency
0 and under 10	0	0
10 and under 15	7	7
15 and under 20	16	23
20 and under 25	13	36
25 and under 30	4	40

Sales persons who achieve fewer than twenty sales are required to undertake further training.

Test your understanding 11

Using this information, the following ogive (cumulative frequency graph) has been drawn.

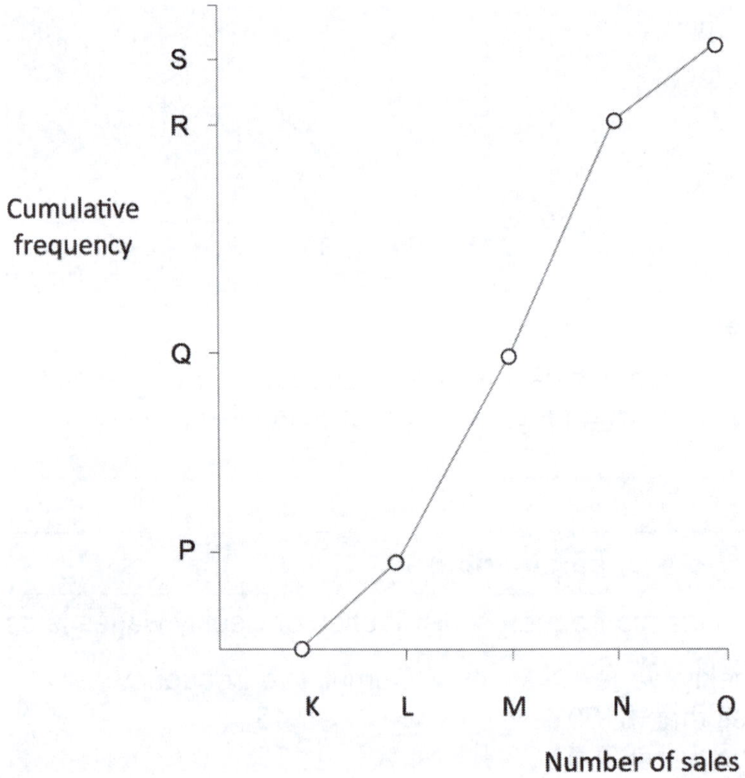

Find the values corresponding to the letters K–S.

Test your understanding 12

In the distribution given in the previous TYU, what percentage of the sales force sold less than 20?

A 40.0%

B 50.0%

C 57.5%

D 69.6%

At present, you cannot be asked to draw charts during a computer-based assessment. Exam questions therefore take the form of labelling charts, calculating particular values, selecting a type of chart appropriate to particular data and drawing conclusions from charts.

In later exams, you may have to interpret charts, for example as part of a case study exam.

Test your understanding answers

Test your understanding 1

C

The two terms are frequently used synonymously but strictly speaking they mean different things. Data is obtained from a survey and is turned into information by sorting and analysis. Both data and information can comprise either facts or figures.

Test your understanding 2

C

All products included means the price list is complete. Being listed in alphabetical order means the list should be easy to use. Showing current prices means the information is relevant to purchasers. Rounding prices to the nearest $100 is unlikely to be accurate enough for a purchaser.

Test your understanding 3

(a)

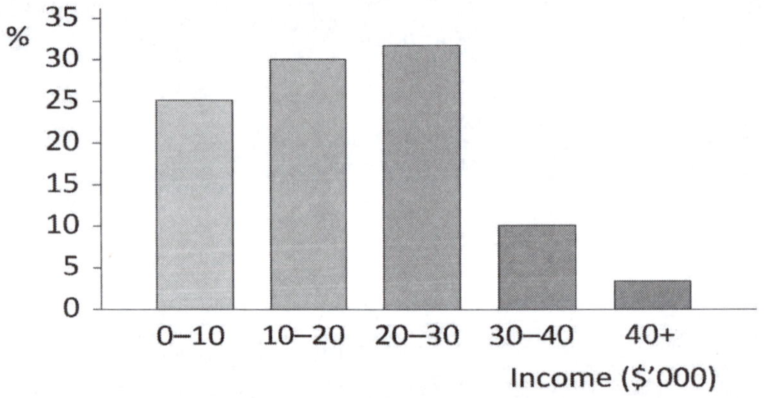

Simple bar chart for Region A

(b) It is easiest to first calculate cumulative frequencies:

Income ($000)	Region A	Cumulative%
0–10	25	25
10–20	30	55
20–30	32	87
30–40	10	97
40 or more	3	100
Total	100	

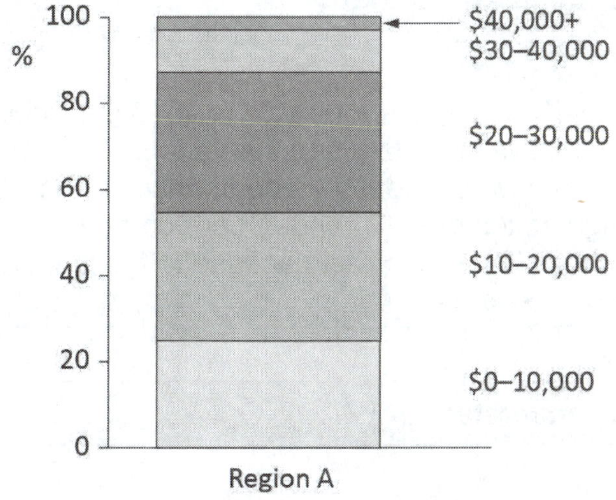

Compound bar chart for Region A

(c)

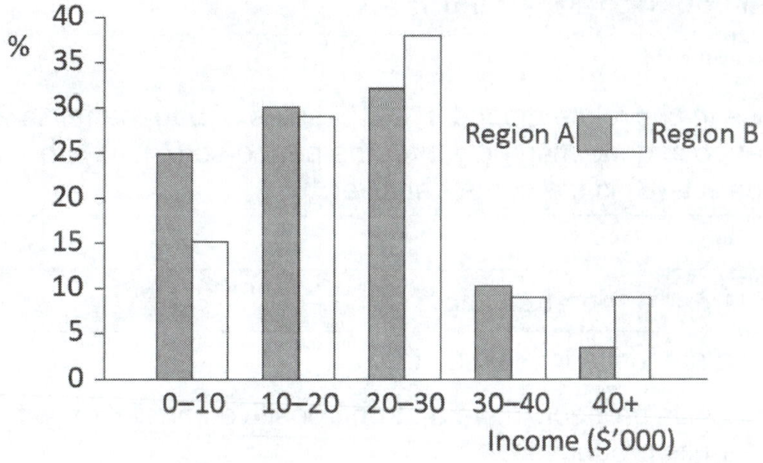

Multiple bar chart

Test your understanding 4

Chocolate on its own gives a bar height of 240. Putting a bar for toffee on top of this raises the height by a further 120, to a total of 360. The 70 added by apple raises the height to 430 and finally banana takes it up a further 30 to give an overall bar height of 460.

Answers:

A 240

B 360

C 430

D 460

Test your understanding 5

A

The bar clearly shows the total sale in 2013 and additionally enables us to see the relative importance of the various fillings. Without the bars for the other years we cannot make comparisons from one year to the next so, although statements (B) and (C) are correct they cannot be deduced from the chart. (D) is incorrect because toffee is more popular than apple. The correct answer is (A).

Test your understanding 6

A

Multiple bar chart showing sales of pies.

Test your understanding 7

B

Sales in chocolate dipped in 2015, sales of banana fell in 2016 and total sales rose quite markedly over the period so (A), (C) and (D) are all incorrect. (B) is the correct answer.

Test your understanding 8

These are just some examples:

- costs probably have a strong positive correlation with the number of units produced
- number of deaths on the roads probably has a middling positive correlation with traffic levels
- the level of street crime is often thought to relate to the level of visible policing, so the correlation would be negative but probably not strong
- a strong negative correlation would probably be found if almost any measure of bodily function, such as the condition of the heart, were compared with age in adults, although the graph is unlikely to be perfectly linear.

Test your understanding 9

We are investigating the effect of size on sales, so sales must be the dependent variable.

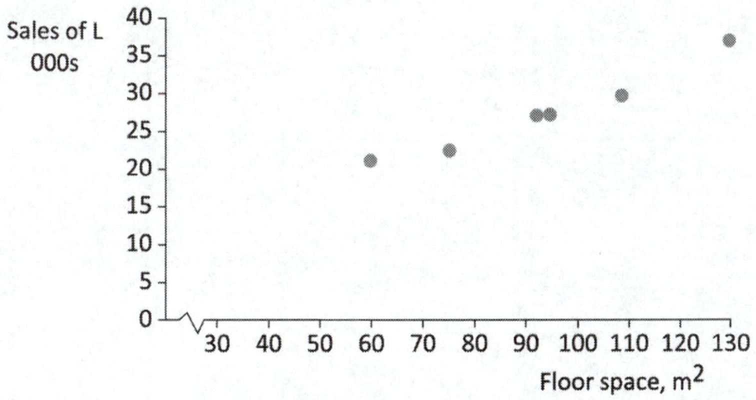

The scatter diagram indicates that there is a positive linear correlation between outlet size and sales: larger outlets have higher sales figures.

Test your understanding 10

A	155 were paid less than $300.
B	50 were paid more than $200.
C	30 were paid between $200 and $300.

Test your understanding 11

In a cumulative frequency diagram, cumulative frequencies are plotted (vertically) on the upper limits of the corresponding intervals (horizontally). The cumulative frequency of the very bottom limit (of 10 in this case) is always zero.

K	10
L	15
M	20
N	25
O	30
P	7
Q	23
R	36
S	40

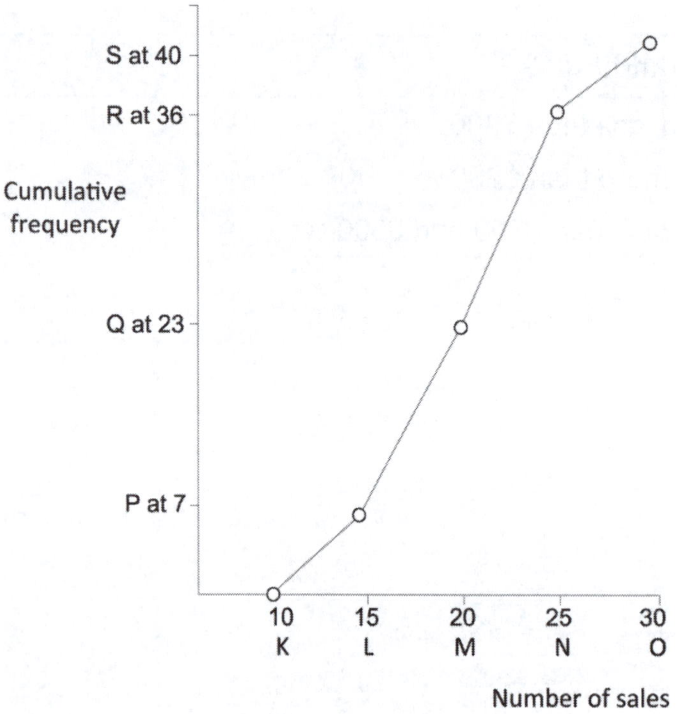

Test your understanding 12

C

Twenty-three people out of the sales force of 40 made less than 20 sales so the percentage is 100 × 23/40 = 57.5.

Chapter

9

Macroeconomic and Institutional Context III: Index Numbers

Chapter learning objectives

On completion of their studies, students should be able to:

- calculate indices for price inflation and national income growth using either base or current weights and use indices to deflate a series.

1 Introduction

Index numbers measure how a group of related commercial quantities vary, usually over time.

For example, suppose you wanted to know how UK companies had fared during 2017. One way of answering this would be to look at the share prices of companies listed on the UK Stock Exchange and compare the prices at the start and end of the year.

However, this would very time consuming, particularly if a large number of companies were chosen. A simpler approach would be to look at one of many Stock Exchange indices.

For example, the Financial Times 100 shares index (FTSE 100) incorporates the values of the shares of the 100 largest companies listed on the UK Stock Exchange. As such, any movement in this figure shows us quickly how larger businesses performed.

- At 1st January 2021 FTSE 100 index was 6,461
- At 1st January 2022 FTSE 100 index was 7,385
- Overall, the average change in value during 2021 of the UK's 100 largest companies was an increase of ((7,385 – 6,461) / 6,461) 14.3%.

As we shall see, most well-known index numbers are averages, but they have the extra property that they relate the quantities being measured to a fixed point or base period.

2 Definitions

If a series of values relating to different times are all expressed as a percentage of the value for a particular time, they are called index numbers with that time as the base.

$$\text{Index number} = \frac{\text{Value in any given year}}{\text{Value in base year}} \times 100$$

We shall generally refer to years but monthly data might have a particular month as base and so forth, so strictly speaking we should say 'time point' rather than 'year'.

e.g **Illustration 1**

Express the following data with 2016 as the base:

Year	2016	2017	2018	2019	2020
Value	46	52	62	69	74

Solution

We have to express each value as a percentage of the value for 2016. That means we must divide each by the 2016 value (i.e. by 46) and multiply by 100.

For example, the index for 2018 will be (62/46) × 100 = 135. The full set of figures is as follows:

Year	2016	2017	2018	2019	2020
2016 = 100	100	113	135	150	161

A few points of note:

- The base year did not have to be the first of the series. We could have chosen any year.
- Expressions such as '2016 = 100' tell us that the associated values are index numbers with base 2016.
- The index number for the base year (2016 in this case) will always be 100.
- We have rounded to the nearest whole number simply to avoid cluttering the text, while you get used to the idea of index numbers. In fact, they could be expressed to any degree of accuracy.

3 Interpretation of index numbers

An index of 113 tells us that there has been a 13 per cent increase since the base year.

In Illustration 1, we can see that values increased by 13 per cent from 2016 to 2017, by 35 per cent over the 2 years from 2016 to 2018, by 50 per cent over 3 years and by 61 per cent over the 4 years 2016–2020.

It is essential to realise that the percentage changes always refer back to the base year. It is not possible to derive the percentage increase from one year to the next by subtracting index numbers.

e.g

Illustration 2

Find the percentage increase from 2019 to 2020 for the data in Illustration 1.

Solution

$$\frac{161}{150} \times 100 = 107.3$$

Therefore, the percentage increase is 7.3 per cent.

If we were to subtract the index numbers, we would get 161 – 150 = 11 points, which is clearly not the same as 11%.

To derive the percentage increase from year A to year B, the easiest method is to index the year B figure with base year A and then subtract 100.

If values have declined, the index number will be less than 100, and when you interpret them by subtracting 100, the resulting negative tells you there has been a decline. For example, an index of 94 means there has been a decline of 6% (94 –100 = – 6) since the base year.

Finally, some index numbers become very large, like the FT100 index mentioned earlier. A 6,000 level means that there has been a 5,900% increase in share prices since the base year – not a very meaningful interpretation, even to those of us who are quite numerate. A much better interpretation is that share prices are now 60 times what they were in the base year.

Hence, there are two ways of interpreting an index number:

- subtracting 100 gives the percentage increase since the base year
- dividing by 100 gives the ratio of current values to base-year values.

Test your understanding 1

Year	2014	2015	2016	2017	2018	2019	2020
Profits ($ m)	1.2	1.5	1.8	1.9	1.6	1.5	1.7

A Express the profits figures above as index numbers with:

(i) base 2014

(ii) base 2017.

B Interpret both the index numbers for 2018.

C Find the percentage increase from 2019 to 2020.

D Interpret the index number 2,500 with 2012 = 100.

Test your understanding 2

Profits have been as follows ($m):

2016	2017	2018	2019	2020
4.1	3.7	3.5	3.8	3.9

When converted to index numbers with base 2016, the index for 2020 is

A 95

B 105

C 20.2

D 5

4 Choice of base year

Although a particular base may be satisfactory for several years, it becomes less meaningful as time passes, as the base comparison point becomes more and more out of date. Eventually it is necessary to shift to a new base. This is called rebasing.

The only requirements of a suitable base year are, first, that it should be a fairly typical year. For example, if prices are being indexed then a year should be chosen in which prices were neither especially high nor especially low. Second, it should be sufficiently recent for comparisons with it to be meaningful. For example, it might be useful to know that production had changed by a certain percentage over the last year or two or perhaps over 10 years, but an index with a base of, say, 50 years ago may not be very relevant.

It is also the case, as we shall see shortly, that many index numbers span a wide range of popular goods and, reflecting what people actually buy, they are very different now from 20 or 30 years ago. The base year has to move in order to keep up with the composition of index numbers to some extent.

5 Change of base year

If possible, you should return to the original data and recalculate the index numbers with the new base year. However, if only the index numbers are available, they can be indexed as if they were the original data. The only problem in using already rounded data (such as the calculated index numbers) as your start point is that sometimes rounding errors may build up. The effect of this may be negligible. As the following example shows, changing the base using index numbers instead of raw data can give very good results.

e.g

Illustration 3

Staffing levels in a particular business have been as follows:

Year	2012	2013	2014	2015	2016	2017	2018	2019	2020
Staff	8	9	9	12	20	22	24	25	27

(a) Express the data as index numbers with base 2012.

(b) Using the original data, change the base to 2017.

(c) Using the index with base 2012, change the base to 2017 and compare your results with those in part (b).

Express your answers to one decimal place throughout.

Solution

Year	2012	2013	2014	2015	2016	2017	2018	2019	2020
Staff	8	9	9	12	20	22	24	25	27
2012 = 100	100.0	112.5	112.5	150.0	250.0	275.0	300.0	312.5	337.5
2017 = 100	36.4	40.9	40.9	54.5	90.9	100.0	109.1	113.6	122.7
2017 = 100	36.4	40.9	40.9	54.5	90.9	100.0	109.1	113.6	122.7

The second index has been obtained from the original data, by dividing by 22 and multiplying by 100. The third index has been obtained from the 2011 = 100 index numbers by dividing by 275 and multiplying by 100. As you can see, the results are identical when rounded to one decimal place in this case.

Test your understanding 3

The following index numbers have base 2010. Recalculate them with base 2017.

Year	2016	2017	2018	2019	2020
2010 = 100	129.0	140.3	148.5	155.1	163.2

Interpret the two index numbers for 2020, with bases 2010 and 2017.

Test your understanding 4

Which of the following statements about the base year is/are correct?

A The base year has to be changed from time to time.

B The base year is fixed and cannot be changed.

C The base year should be one in which there were important changes regarding the variable being measured.

D The base year should be the one in which the variable being measured took its lowest value.

6 Combining series of index numbers

When a series of index numbers is subject to a change of base or perhaps a small change of composition, you will find in the series a year with two different index numbers, and the change of base will be shown in the series. The technique involved in combining two series into a single one is called splicing the series together.

Illustration 4

The price index below changed its base to 2018 after many years with base 2005. Recalculate it as a single series with base 2018. By how much have prices risen from 2015 to 2020?

Year	Price index
	(2005 = 100)
2015	263
2016	271
2017	277
2018	280
	(2018 = 100)
2019	104
2020	107

Solution

The index numbers from 2019 onwards already have 2018 = 100, so nothing need be done to them. What we have to do is to change the base of the original series, so it too is 2018. In this series the value for 2018 is 280, so we must divide the index numbers for 2015–18 by 280 and multiply by 100:

Year	Price index	Price index	
	(2005 = 100)	(2018 = 100)	
2015	263	94	= 100 × (263/280)
2016	271	97	= 100 × (271/280) etc.
2017	277	99	
2018	280	100	
	(2018 = 100)		
2019	104	104	
2020	107	107	

Now that we have a single series spanning both 2015 and 2020, we can compare the two years directly.

$$100 \times \frac{107}{94} = 114$$

So, prices have risen by 14 per cent from 2015 to 2020.

You may notice that we rounded to the nearest whole number in this example. This is because the original index numbers had plainly been rounded to the nearest whole number and at best, we can hope that our results will be accurate to that same extent. You cannot acquire increased accuracy in the course of calculating.

Test your understanding 5

The following price index has undergone a change of base in 2017. Splice the two series together with base 2017.

Year	Price index (2007 = 100)
2014	141
2015	148
2016	155
2017	163

Year	Price index (2017 = 100)
2018	106
2019	110
2020	116

7 Relative price indices

The notation commonly used for the construction of index numbers is as follows: the subscripts '0' and '1' are used, respectively, for the base year and the year under consideration, usually called the current year. Hence, for any given item:

P_0 = price in base year　　P_1 = price in current year

Q_0 = quantity in base year　　Q_1 = quantity in current year

$V_0 = P_0Q_0$ = value in the base year　　$V_1 = P_1Q_1$ = value in current year

where value (V) means the total expenditure on the item (price × quantity), and other sorts of weights are denoted by w.

For a given item, the **price index** = 100 × (P_1/P_0), but quite often we work with the ratio called the **price relative** = P_1/P_0 and leave the multiplication by 100 to the end of the calculation.

The usual formula for a relative price index is therefore:

$$\text{Relative price index} = \frac{\Sigma[w \times (P_1/P_0)]}{\Sigma w} \times 100$$

The weights could be base-year quantities (i.e. Q_0) or values (i.e. P_0Q_0), or current-year quantities or values (i.e. Q_1 or P_1Q_1), or they could simply be decided on some other basis such as the weighting of exam marks.

The index will be called base-weighted or current-weighted, depending on whether it uses base or current weights.

The formula is not provided in the exam.

e.g

Illustration 5

A grocer wishes to index the prices of four different types of tea, with base year 1995 and current year 2021. The available information is as follows:

	1995		2021	
	Price ($)	Quantity (crates)	Price ($)	Quantity (crates)
Type	P_0	Q_0	P_1	Q_1
A	0.89	65	1.03	69
B	1.43	23	1.69	28
C	1.29	37	1.49	42
D	0.49	153	0.89	157

Calculate the **base-weighted** relative **price index** using as weights **(a) quantities**; and **(b) values** (i.e. revenue for each item).

Solution

	Price relative (Rel) P_1/P_0	Base year quantity (Q_0)	Base year value (V_0) $P_0 \times Q_0$	Rel × Q_0	Rel × V_0
A	1.157	65	57.85	75.21	66.93
B	1.182	23	32.89	27.19	38.88
C	1.155	37	47.73	42.74	55.13
D	1.816	153	74.97	277.85	136.15
Total		278	213.44	422.99	297.09

Base-weighted relative price indices are:

Weighted by quantity: $$\frac{\Sigma(\text{Rel} \times Q_0)}{\Sigma Q_0} \times 100 = \frac{422.99}{278} \times 100 = 152.2$$

Weighted by value: $$\frac{\Sigma(\text{Rel} \times V_0)}{\Sigma V_0} \times 100 = \frac{297.09}{213.44} \times 100 = 139.2$$

The first index tells us that prices have risen on average by 52 per cent; the second that they have risen by 39 per cent. Why might this be so?

The really big price rise is D's 82 per cent. The size of the index will be very strongly influenced by the weight given to D. In the first case, the quantity 153 is bigger than all the other quantities put together. D gets more than half of the total weight and so the index strongly reflects D's price rise and is very high. However, when we use value for weighting, D's value is only about one-third of the total because its price is low, so the price index is rather smaller.

Test your understanding 6

Using the data of the previous Illustration, calculate the current-weighted relative price index with weights given by (a) quantities; and (b) values.

8 Choice of base weighting or current weighting

- In general, current weighting will seem better because it remains up to date.
- In particular, current-weighted indices reflect shifts away from goods subject to high price rises (as their quantities will be lower in recent periods).
- Base-weighted indices do not do this and hence exaggerate inflation.
- However, current quantities can be very difficult to obtain – some considerable time may elapse after a year ends before a company knows what quantity it sold, whereas base quantities are known and remain steady for the lifetime of the index.
- So, current-weighted price indices are usually much more costly and time-consuming to calculate than are base-weighted ones.
- The stability of base weights means that the index for each year can be compared with that of every other year, which, strictly speaking, a current-weighted index cannot as the base comparison point changes each year.
- There can be no general guidance on the choice: it depends on the resources available and on the degree to which prices and quantities are changing. The only other consideration is that, as always, you must compare like with like. The retail price index (RPI), as we shall see, is a current-value-weighted relative index weighted by (almost) current values, and that method of construction should be used if possible if comparison with the RPI is a major function of the index being constructed.

9 Quantity indices

Although it is the most important and most frequently encountered, price is not the only financial factor measured by index numbers. Quantity indices constitute another category. They show how the amounts of certain goods and commodities vary over time or location. They are of importance when one is considering changes in sales figures, volumes of trade and so on.

When considering price indices, quantities emerged as the best weighting factor. Here, the converse is true: prices are considered the most appropriate weights when calculating quantity indices.

A **relative** quantity index will take the form:

$$\frac{\Sigma[w \times (Q_1/Q_0)]}{\Sigma w} \times 100$$

An **aggregate** quantity index will take the form:

$$\frac{\Sigma wQ_1}{\Sigma wQ_0} \times 100$$

where in both cases the weights could be prices, either base year or current, or values or some other measure of the importance of the items. P_0, P_1, Q_0 and Q1 have the same meanings as earlier in this chapter.

The calculation of quantity indices and their application involve no new arithmetical techniques, as the following example illustrates.

These formulae are not given in the exam.

Test your understanding 7

A company manufactures three products, A, B and C, and the quantities sold in 2019 and 2020 were as follows:

Product	Quantity sold		Weights
	2019	2020	
A	7	10	85
B	12	15	68
C	25	25	45

Find the index of the quantity sold in 2020 with 2019 as a base using the weights given by using the relatives method.

Test your understanding 8

In general, the relative sizes of current-weighted and base-weighted price indices are as follows:

A more or less equal.

B current-weighted bigger than base-weighted.

C base-weighted bigger than current-weighted.

D no regular pattern exists.

Test your understanding 9

Which of the following is an advantage of base-weighting?

A The index remains up to date.

B The index is easy to calculate.

C The index gives relatively high results.

D The index is comparable with the RPI.

10 Inflation

One of the most common areas indices are used is in measuring and dealing with inflation.

Terminology

When describing cash flows it is important to clarify whether inflation is included in the figures.

- 'Money' cash flows include predicted inflation and other price rises – they are the actual cash flows that take place. If I am awarded a 3% pay rise, then my gross salary will increase by 3% in money terms.
- 'Real' cash flows have had general inflation taken out of them. If general inflation is 3% per annum, then a 3% pay rise leaves me no better off in real terms – I cannot buy any more goods than before. If inflation is only 2% then I am approximately 1% better off in real terms (Note: this is a simplification).

Some payments are 'index linked', meaning that they automatically increase in line with inflation. (Strictly speaking, they increase in line with a specific index used to measure inflation.)

Measuring UK inflation

The Retail Prices Index (RPI) was the UK's main indicator of inflation before 2003. Since then, the Government has focused policy on the Consumer Prices Index (CPI), although RPI figures are still widely quoted and used. Like the RPI, the CPI measures the average change from month to month in the prices of consumer goods and services. However, it differs in the particular households it represents, the range of goods and services included, and the way the index is constructed.

The most useful way to think about both the CPI and RPI indices is to imagine a 'shopping basket' containing those goods and services on which people typically spend their money. As the prices of the various items in the basket change over time, so does the total cost of the basket. Movements in the CPI and RPI indices represent the changing cost of this representative shopping basket.

In principle, the cost of the basket should be calculated with reference to all consumer goods and services purchased by households, and the prices measured in every shop or outlet that supplies them. In practice, both the CPI and RPI are calculated by collecting a sample of prices for a selection of representative goods and services in a range of UK retail locations. Currently, around 120,000 separate price quotations are used every month in compiling the indices, covering some 650 representative consumer goods and services for which prices are collected in around 150 areas throughout the UK.

Within each year, the RPI and CPI are calculated as fixed quantity price indices – only the prices of goods affect the index from month to month.

However, the contents of the baskets of goods and services and their associated weights are updated annually. This is important in helping to avoid potential biases in consumer price indices that might otherwise develop over time, for example, due to the development of entirely new goods and services, or the tendency for consumers to substitute purchases away from those particular goods and services for which prices have risen relatively rapidly.

For example, over recent years the basket has been amended to include items in growing markets such as coffee pods and re-usable bottles, whereas items in declining markets such as CD-ROMs (superseded by memory sticks and drives) and sat navs (superseded by use of mobile phone navigation aids or built in car navigation systems) have been removed.

One major source of information comes from the diaries filled in by people taking part in the Office of National Statistics (ONS) 'Expenditure and Food Survey', a continuous survey of over 6000 households each year.

Adjusting for inflation

There are many situations, business and other, where it is important to make adjustments for inflation.

For example, a company may wish to adjust its revenue figures to reveal the real change in sales, or an employee may wish to adjust his/her salary to hopefully reveal a real increase in income and purchasing power. The Government and many employers often use inflation as a guide to pay increases and taxation changes.

In your later exams, you may need to adjust for inflation when calculating net present values for capital investment projects, or allow for inflation when comparing numbers in different years.

e.g

Illustration 6

An inflation index and an index for a company's wages are given below:

Year	2018	2019	2020
Inflation index	110	114	119
Wages index	100	106	109

Determine what has happened to wages in real terms between 2018 and 2020 (you do not have to look at each year separately).

Solution

To compare two sets of index numbers, it is often useful to rebase both sets of figures to the same base. Here rebasing the inflation figures to 2018 will enable the index numbers to be compared directly:

Year	2018	2019	2020
Inflation index (rebased to 2018)	100	103.6	108.2
Wages index	100	106	109

This shows that wages have gone up by 9% over the two years while inflation by 8.2%. To get a wages index in real terms we can then divide the wages index by the inflation index.

Year	2018	2019	2020
Inflation index (rebased to 2018)	100	103.6	108.2
Wages index (money terms)	100	106.0	109.0
Wages index (real terms)	100	102.3	100.7

Overall wages have increased in real terms by 0.7%.

Test your understanding 10

At the start of a year, the CPI stood at 340. At that time, a certain person's index-linked pension was $4,200 per annum and she had $360 invested in an index-linked savings bond. At the start of the following year, the CPI had increased to 360. To what level would the pension and the bond investment have risen?

Test your understanding 11

Use the data given below to compare average earnings from 2017 to 2020.

	Average weekly earnings (male manual workers, 21 years+)	CPI (January 1994 = 100)
2017	$83.50	201.1
2018	$96.94	235.6
2019	$113.06	271.9
2020	$125.58	303.7

Test your understanding 12

The following are the annual salaries of trainee accountants employed by a particular firm over the period 2015 – 2020, and the corresponding values of the CPI with base 2014.

Year	Salary ($)	CPI
2015	18,100	106.9
2016	18,600	115.2
2017	19,200	126.1
2018	19,700	133.5
2019	20,300	138.5
2020	20,900	140.7

A Express the salaries at constant 2015 prices.

B Index the results with 2015 = 100.

C Comment on your results.

Test your understanding 13

How are the weights obtained for the retail price index? They are:

A The quantity of the item that the average household bought.

B The amount the average household spent on the item.

C The quantity of the items that were sold by a sample of retail outlets.

D The expenditure on the item at a sample of retail outlets.

Test your understanding answers

Test your understanding 1

		Year	2014	2015	2016	2017	2018	2019	2020
A	(i)	2014 = 100	100	125	150	158	133	125	142
	(ii)	2017 = 100	63	79	95	100	84	79	89

B The index of 133 means there has been a 33 per cent increase in profits from 2014 to 2018. The index of 84 means that profits in 2018 are 16 per cent below their level in 2017.

C 100 × (1.7/1.5) = 113 so there has been a 13 per cent increase from 2019 to 2020.

D An index of 2,500 means that values now are 2,500/100 = 25 times their value in the base year, 2012.

Test your understanding 2

A

$$\text{Index} = \frac{3.9}{4.1} \times 100 = 95 \text{ (to the nearest whole number)}$$

Test your understanding 3

Divide through by 140.3 and multiply by 100:

Year	2016	2017	2018	2019	2020
2017 = 100	91.9	100	105.8	110.5	116.3

The index of 163.2 tells us that values in 2020 were 63.2 per cent higher than in 2010; the index of 116.3 tells us that they were 16.3 per cent higher than in 2017.

Test your understanding 4

The correct answer is (A). A base year will be fixed for several years but will eventually have to be changed to keep it relevant. The base year should be a very typical year in which there are no big changes or specially high or low values in the variable.

Test your understanding 5

Year	Price index (2007 = 100)	Price index (2017 = 100)
2014	141	86.5
2015	148	90.8
2016	155	95.1
2017	163	100
	(2017 = 100)	
2018	106	106
2019	110	110
2020	116	116

The technique used in this example is quite generally applicable. Regardless of which year you eventually want as base, the first step in splicing together two index number series should always be to take as the new overall base the year in which the base changes. (2017 in this example).

Test your understanding 6

As before, we need the price relatives, which have already been calculated. This time, however, they will be multiplied first by Q_1 and second by the value Q_1P_1.

Note: Unrounded values used to calculate Q, Rel column and V, × Rel column.

The calculations are as follows:

	Q1	Rel (P_1/P_0)	V1 = P_1Q_1	Q_1 × Rel	V_1 × Rel
A	69	1.157	71.07	79.85	82.25
B	28	1.182	47.32	33.09	55.92
C	42	1.155	62.58	48.51	72.28
D	157	1.816	139.73	285.16	253.80
Total	296		320.70	446.61	464.25

(a) Using Q_1 as weights, the price index is:

$$\frac{\Sigma(\text{Rel} \times Q_1)}{\Sigma Q_1} \times 100 = \frac{446.61}{296} \times 100 = 150.9$$

(b) Using V_1 as weights, the price index is:

$$\frac{\Sigma(\text{Rel} \times V_1)}{\Sigma V_1} \times 100 = \frac{464.25}{320.7} \times 100 = 144.8$$

Can you explain these further index numbers, compared with the ones we got using base weighting? Here they are in table form:

	Base-weighted	Current-weighted
Weighted by quantity	152.2	150.9
Weighted by value	139.2	144.8

Although the quantity of D purchased has dropped a little, presumably because of its high price rise, it still remains the cheapest and most popular brand. In fact, using quantities, it still accounts for over half the total weight. So its price index continues to be high, albeit slightly smaller than with base weighting.

The opposite has occurred with values. Although the quantity of D purchased has dropped, this is more than compensated by its increase in price and so it has increased its proportion of the total value (from 35 to 44 per cent). Consequently, the current-value-weighted index increasingly reflects D's big price rise and so is greater than the base-value-weighted index.

Test your understanding 7

Product	Q_1/Q_0	w	w × (Q_1/Q_0)
A	1.4286	85	121.4
B	1.25	68	85
C	1	45	45
Total		198	251.4

$$\text{Relative quantity index} = 100 \times \frac{251.4}{198} = 127.0$$

Test your understanding 8

C

Base-weighted index numbers do not reflect the fact that customers buy less of items that are subject to high price rises. They subsequently exaggerate inflation and tend to be greater than current-weighted index numbers.

Test your understanding 9

B

Base-weighted indices do not remain up to date, and since the RPI is current-weighted they are not really comparable. Base-weighted indices do exaggerate inflation but this is not an advantage. However, they are easy to calculate since the same weights are used year after year and this is an advantage.

Test your understanding 10

First of all, the CPI has risen by 20 from 340. As a percentage, this is

$$\frac{20}{340} \times 100 = 5.88\%$$

The pension and the investment, being index-linked, would increase by the same percentage. The pension thus increases by 5.88% of $4,200 = $247 (nearest $), and the investment by 5.88% of $360 = $21.17. Hence, at the start of the year in question, the pension would be $4,447 per annum, and the investment would stand at $381.17.

Test your understanding 11

The value of the CPI in 2017 shows that average prices were 2.011 times higher than in January 1994. The purchasing power of $1 will therefore have decreased by this factor in the time. A 2017 wage of $83.50 was therefore 'worth'

$$\frac{83.50}{2.011}$$

in January 1994. This is known as the real wage, at January 1994 prices. Applying this process to all the figures, we obtain:

		Real wages, January 1994 prices
2017		$41.52
2018	96.94/2.356 =	$41.15
2019		$41.58
2020		$41.35

The average wages of this section of society can thus be seen not to have changed appreciably in real terms over this time period. The apparent rises in wages have been almost exactly cancelled out by similarly sized price rises.

Test your understanding 12

A Each value must be multiplied by

$$\frac{\text{2015 CPI}}{\text{CPI of year in Q}} = \frac{106.9}{\text{CPI of year in Q}}$$

B (Each adjusted salary will then be divided by the 2015 salary and multiplied by 100. The results are:

Year	Salary ($)	CPI	Salary at 2015 prices	Index 2015 = 100
2015	18,100	106.9	18,100	100
2016	18,600	115.2	17,260	95
2017	19,200	126.1	16,277	90
2018	19,700	133.5	15,775	87
2019	20,300	138.5	15,668	87
2020	20,900	140.7	15,879	88

C The real salary paid to trainees, which tells us what they can purchase with their salary, has fallen steadily until 2020 when it increased a little. The decline over the entire 5-year period is 12 per cent.

We should hasten to add that this is an imaginary firm!

The CPI is not the only index used in deflation, particularly if there is a more suitable index available. For instance, an exporting company interested in its real level of profits might well deflate its actual profit figures by an index of export prices.

Test your understanding 13

B

The expenditure per $1,000 spent by the average household is given by the Family Expenditure Survey. The quantity bought would not be applicable because the household may only have one car and lots of baked beans, but the car is more significant than the beans. (C) would not be appropriate for the same reason. It might be possible to use a system similar to (D) but this is not the method used.

Chapter

10

Informational Context of Business II: Inter-relationships between variables

Chapter learning objectives

On completion of their studies, students should be able to:

- describe the principal business applications of big data and analytics
- demonstrate the relationship between data variables: correlation coefficient and the coefficient of determination
- prepare a trend equation using either graphical means or regression analysis.

1 Introduction

This chapter examines the **strength** and **nature** of the relationship between two sets of figures.

For example

- How **strong** is the link between advertising spend and sales revenue in our industry? Is advertising a key driver of sales or a minor one?

  To explore the strength of the relationship between two sets of figures we will look at the subject of **correlation**.

- What is the **nature** of this relationship? Can we quantify it by determining an equation linking sales and advertising? If we can do this, then we could use such an equation to help forecast future sales.

  This will involve us looking at the subject of **regression**.

These two concepts are linked – regression may give us an equation to use for forecasting but correlation will tell us how useful the equation is.

The chapter also introduces the concept of big data. Some data analysis has become very complex due to the nature of the fast flowing world we now live in. Businesses may require substantial storage space to hold the data and algorithms may be needed to help interpret it.

2 Big data and analytics

Big data is called 'big' for a reason –terabytes and terabytes of information flow into companies every day. Regular data becomes 'big data' when it is large enough that it cannot be easily processed using conventional methods. With this volume, spreadsheets are of little use; they lack flexibility and scalability. However, once processed, big data can be very valuable.

With the use of skilled workers and analytics software, large volumes of data may be analysed that may otherwise be untapped by conventional business intelligence programmes. Thus, big data can be turned into useful information that can help companies make more informed business decisions.

How is this relevant to today's businesses?

There are three specific ways in which big data can lead to better products/ services and a better user experience – when viewed with context:

- Big data allows businesses to expand their knowledge of their customers and develop products/services that are best suited to their needs.
- Big data gives businesses a deeper understanding of how their customers behave, allowing them to connect with customers on a more meaningful level.
- Big data can help boost marketing activities, since it provides businesses with a chance to analyse customer behaviour on multiple channels and understand when the customer is most likely to buy products/services.

Potential pitfalls that can trip up businesses on big data analytics initiatives include a lack of internal analytic skills and the high cost of hiring experienced analytics professionals. The amount of information that is typically involved, and its variety, can also cause data management issues, involving data quality and consistency as well as gdpr (general data protection regulation) issues.

e.g

Illustration 1 – Big data and analytics

The airline industry

It is the big data era in the airline industry, which in many ways was one of its earliest participants.

Airlines are awash with data, much of it unstructured. Only recently have airlines been able to use big data techniques to solve, among other objectives, how to recognise and enhance customer value and how to cultivate high-value customers.

Airlines have always been very good at collecting data, but they haven't always been good at using it. Now that the costs of storing and processing data have dropped – even as airlines collect more and more of it – it is becoming easier for a company to act on it. At United Airlines, roughly a terabyte of customer data is floating around at any given time within its systems. 'We don't keep it all' says the company's vice president of e-commerce. 'We have to be selective about what we grab. For the data that is selected, a real-time decision engine does the crunching to turn it into something useful.'

The airline looks at who the customer is and his/her propensity to buy certain products. More than 150 variables about that customer – prior purchases and previous destinations among them – are now assessed in real time to determine an individual's likely actions, rather than an aggregated group of customers.

It is similar story at Southwest Airlines, which is using big data to determine which new customer services to implement. They use aggregated, anonymous data to promote products, services and featured offers to customers on multiple channels, devices and websites. They say that 'by observing and looking into customer behaviours and actions online, we are better suited to offer our travellers the best rates and experiences possible. We also use big data to support the evolving relationships with our customers.'

Another area in which the effects of big data technology are visible is in the handling of customers' luggage. Delta Airlines say 'we have over a number of years invested millions of dollars in baggage tracking.' Through the use of hand-held baggage scanners used at passenger check-in, the airline has a vast amount of tracking data available and one of the things they realised in 2013 was that 'customers would benefit from having that information'. For this reason, Delta was the first major airline to launch an application allowing customers to track their bags from their mobile devices and the free app has been downloaded more than 11 million times.

Supermarkets

You might not be surprised to learn data collection and analysis are playing an integral part in the retail strategies that are more involved and subtle than a raw fight on price alone.

Technology, or more precisely the vast amount of big data that grocery retailers can now collect on our spending and shopping habits and analyse, has certainly grown to play a more critical role in their quest for market share and price supremacy.

Pricing is very data intensive and has a number of elements to it. The real battle is not on price matching but instead on using price as a means to build trust and ultimately loyalty with customers. To that aim, the ultimate challenge facing supermarkets is how to integrate data from a whole host of areas – from competitive market information from third party providers, loyalty card data and a single view of each customer's transactions across an entire rage of channels – to offer personalised promotions on the right products to the right customers at the right time.

Tesco plc, the British supermarket chain, is currently the second most profitable retailer in the world with outlets in twelve countries. Tesco was one of the first companies to embrace, and benefit from, big data analytics. Back in 1995, Tesco introduced the Club card, its own loyalty scheme. Most competitors used it only as a means to target discounts and coupons and so quickly abandoned the scheme as unprofitable. Tesco, however, realised the value of the insight it would be getting into its customers' behaviours and now receives detailed data on two-thirds of all shopping baskets.

Tesco segmented customers into appropriate groups. This meant that they could be more targeted in the mailing of vouchers and coupons (the rate of coupon redemption shot up from 3% to 70%) but also that it could launch new product lines according to customer demands.

Using all this data Tesco started trying to convert the non-buyers.
E.g. finding that recent parents were spending their money elsewhere, they launched a Baby Club and ended up capturing 24% of the baby market.

Seeing that its analytics approach worked, Tesco started applying it to other fields also. One example is its optimised stock keeping system, which forecasts sales by product for each store based on historical sales and weather data. Through predictive analytics, Tesco manages to save a huge amount of stock that would otherwise expire and thus be wasted. In another instance, Tesco found that its management of the fridge and store temperatures was sub-optimal and thus enabled significant savings in energy costs.

Test your understanding 1

In which of the following situations would an analysis of big data be directly useful for a supermarket?

A Calculation of total sales for the year.

B Identifying trends in buying patterns of 18-40 year olds.

C Identifying slow moving product lines.

D Calculation of cost per store.

3 Pearson's correlation coefficient

The statistician Pearson developed a measure of the amount of linear correlation present in a set of pairs of data. Pearson's correlation coefficient, denoted r, is defined as:

$$r = \frac{n\Sigma xy - \Sigma x\Sigma y}{\sqrt{(n\Sigma x^2 - (\Sigma x)^2)(n\Sigma y^2 - (\Sigma y)^2)}}$$

where n is the number of data points (i.e. sample size).

This measure has the property of always lying in the range –1 to +1, where:

- **r = +1** denotes **perfect positive** linear correlation (the data points lie exactly on a straight line of positive gradient)
- **r = –1** denotes **perfect negative** linear correlation (again the data points lie on a straight line but with a negative gradient); and
- r = 0 denotes no linear correlation.

The strength of a correlation can be judged by its proximity to +1 or –1: the nearer it is (and the further away from zero), the stronger is the linear correlation. A common error is to believe that negative values of r cannot be strong. They can be just as strong as positive values except that values of y are decreasing as values of x increase.

The calculation of correlation coefficients can be useful in telling us how strongly two sets of data are related to each other – for instance factory costs in relation to production levels or sales volumes in relation to advertising spend – so that we can decide whether the data can be used to help us make good forecasts for the future.

e.g

Illustration 2 – Pearson's correlation coefficient

Evaluate Pearson's correlation coefficient for the data on sales and advertising spend in the table below, and interpret its value.

Advertising expenditure in month ($000)	Total sales in following month ($000)
1.3	151.6
0.9	100.1
1.8	199.3
2.1	221.2
1.5	170.0

Solution

With calculations involving summations, we facilitate the calculations by setting them out in columns:

x	y	x^2	y^2	xy
1.3	151.6	1.69	22,982.56	197.08
0.9	100.1	0.81	10,020.01	90.09
1.8	199.3	3.24	39,720.49	358.74
2.1	221.2	4.41	48,929.44	464.52
1.5	170.0	2.25	28,900.00	255.00
7.6	842.2	12.40	150,552.50	1,365.43

Using

$$r = \frac{n\Sigma xy - \Sigma x\Sigma y}{\sqrt{(n\Sigma x^2 - (\Sigma x)^2)(n\Sigma y^2 - (\Sigma y)^2)}}$$

Gives

$$r = \frac{(5 \times 1{,}365.43) - (7.6 \times 842.2)}{\sqrt{[(5 \times 12.4) - 7.6^2][(5 \times 150{,}552.5) - 842.2^2]}} = \frac{426.43}{\sqrt{4.24 \times 43{,}461.66}} = 0.993$$

The value of Pearson's correlation coefficient in this case is 0.993.

The arithmetic in such a calculation can be seen to be potentially very tedious. In the exam, it is more likely that you will be given the totals for x^2, y^2, etc. and asked to complete the calculation from the given data.

The value of the coefficient in this case is clearly very close to the value 1, indicating a very strong positive linear correlation.

Test your understanding 2

The following information relates to students' scores on final and mid-term examinations.

If $\Sigma x = 440$, $\Sigma y = 330$, $\Sigma x^2 = 17,986$, $\Sigma y^2 = 10,366$, $\Sigma xy = 13,467$ and $n = 11$, then the value of r, the coefficient of correlation, to two decimal places, is:

A 0.98

B 0.63

C 0.96

D 0.59

4 The coefficient of determination

We have already seen how Pearson's correlation coefficient allows us to discuss the strength of the relationship between two sets of figures. However, the interpretation of the figure is made slightly easier if we square the correlation coefficient, r, to give the coefficient of determination, r^2.

The **coefficient of determination, r^2**, gives the proportion of changes in y that can be explained by changes in x, assuming a **linear** relationship between x and y.

For example:

If the correlation coefficient were +0.7, say, then $r^2 = 0.49$ and we could state that 49% of the observed changes in y can be explained by the changes in x but that 51% of the changes must be due to other factors.

Spurious correlation

However, one must always watch out for 'spurious' correlation where there is a high value for the correlation coefficient but no direct 'cause and effect' relationship between the sets of data. Often a third 'hidden' factor is influencing both sets of data.

For example, suppose we assume that:

1 intelligent parents have intelligent children and that

2 intelligent parents give their children more vitamins.

A study examining the link between quantities of vitamins taken as children and intelligence would probably yield a high correlation, even if there was no scientific link between the two, because of this hidden third factor.

Test your understanding 3

If the Pearson correlation coefficient between x and y is + 0.9, which of the following is/are true?

A There is a strong linear relationship between x and y.

B y increases as x increases.

C Ninety per cent of the changes in y can be explained by the corresponding changes in x.

D The slope of the regression line of y on x is positive.

Test your understanding 4

Over a period of 12 months, in which monthly advertising expenditure ranges from $20,000 to $50,000, the correlation between monthly advertising expenditure and monthly sales is 0.8. Which of the following is/are true based on the information given?

A Higher sales are caused by higher expenditure on advertising.

B If advertising expenditure is increased to $100,000, sales will increase.

C Sixty-four per cent of the changes in sales from one month to the next can be explained by corresponding changes in advertising expenditure.

D A correlation coefficient derived from 24 months' data would be more reliable than that given above.

Interpreting correlation coefficients

In general, it is not always straightforward to interpret a value of r. Although it would be inappropriate for the purpose of this text to go into detailed theory, it must be noted that the sample size (n) has a crucial effect: the smaller the value of n, the 'easier' it is for a large value of r to arise purely by accident.

Very rough guidelines are that, with a sample of ten data points, a minimum correlation of about 0.6 is needed before you can feel confident that any sort of linear relationship holds. With twenty data points, the minimum correlation needed is about 0.4.

Extrapolation is a further danger in the interpretation of r. If your x-values range from 0.9 to 2.1, then r = 0.993 tells you that there is a near-perfect linear relationship between x and y in that range. However, you know nothing at all about the relationship outside that range. It may or may not continue to be linear. The process of drawing conclusions outside the range of the data is called extrapolation. It often cannot be avoided but it leads to unreliable conclusions.

It is possible that an apparently high correlation can occur accidentally or spuriously between two unconnected variables. There is no mathematical way of checking when this is the case, but common sense can help. In the case under discussion, it seems plausible that sales and the advertising spend are connected, and so it would seem reasonable to assume that this is not an accidental or spurious correlation.

More importantly here, two variables can be correlated because they are separately correlated to a hidden third variable. The size of the region could well be such a variable: larger regions would tend to have larger sales figures and the management of larger regions would tend to have larger advertising budgets. It is therefore possible that this high correlation coefficient may have arisen because the variable 'sales' is highly correlated with size of region, advertising expenditure is highly correlated with size of region, but sales and advertising spend are not themselves directly connected.

Even if this third variable effect is not present, we still cannot conclude that y depends on x. The strong correlation lends support to the assumption that this is so, but does not prove it. Correlation cannot be used to prove causation.

Test your understanding 5

The correlation between x and y is 0.85. This means that:

A x is 85 per cent of y.

B y is 85 per cent of x.

C there is a strong relationship between x and y.

D there is a weak relationship between x and y.

Test your understanding 6

If the correlation coefficient between consumption expenditure and disposable income is 0.8, what is the coefficient of determination?

A 0.64

B 89

C 20.8

D 0.4

Test your understanding 7

If the coefficient of determination from a set of data is 85 per cent, which of the following statements would be correct?

A When temperature increases by 1°C, sales increase by 85 per cent.

B When temperature increases by 1°C, sales increase by 15 per cent.

C On 85 per cent of days, it is possible to accurately predict sales if an accurate prediction of temperature exists.

D 85 per cent of the changes in sales from one day to the next can be explained by corresponding changes in temperature.

5 Rank correlation: Spearman's coefficient

There are occasions when the degree of correlation between two variables is to be measured but one or both of them is not in a suitable quantitative form.

For example if a student comes top in their mathematics exam, does that mean they will also come top in their economics exam? Here we are interested in their rank rather than their absolute mark.

In such circumstances, Pearson's coefficient cannot be used, but an alternative approach – rank correlation – might be appropriate. The most common measure of this type is Spearman's rank correlation coefficient, R:

$$R = 1 - \frac{6\Sigma d^2}{n(n^2 - 1)}$$

where d denotes the difference in ranks, and n the sample size.

The arithmetic involved in calculating values of this coefficient is much easier than that for Pearson's coefficient, as the following example illustrates.

Illustration 3 – Rank correlation, R

As part of its recruitment procedures, a company awards applicants ratings from A (excellent) to E (unsatisfactory) for their interview performance, and marks out of 100 for a written test. The results for five interviewees are as follows.

Interviewee	Interview grade	Test score
a	A	60
b	B	61
c	A	50
d	C	72
e	D	70

Calculate the Spearman's rank correlation coefficient for this data, and comment on its value.

Solution

In order to apply the formula, the grades and scores are ranked, with the best scores given a rank of 1. Notice how interviewees a and c share the best interview grade. They therefore share the ranks 1 and 2 to give 1.5 each.

Interviewee	Rank of interview grade	Rank of test score	d	d^2
a	1.5	4	–2.5	6.25
b	3	3	0	0.00
c	1.5	5	–3.5	12.25
d	4	1	3	9.00
e	5	2	3	9.00
				36.50

Hence:

$$R = 1 - \frac{6\Sigma d^2}{n(n^2 - 1)} = 1 - \frac{6 \times 36.50}{5(25 - 1)} = -0.825$$

The high negative value (near to –1) indicates that interview grades and test scores almost totally disagree with each other – good interview grades go with the lowest test scores and vice versa. This should concern the company, as it may mean that one or both methods of judging applicants are faulty. The interpretation of R-values (and warnings!) is similar to that for r.

Note that it does not matter which way round the d figure is calculated and therefore whether d is negative or positive. This is because the figure is squared in the next step, removing any negative values.

Test your understanding 8

An expert was asked to rank, according to taste, eight wines costing below $4. Their rankings (with 1 being the worst taste and 8 the best) and the prices per bottle were as follows:

Sample $	Rank of taste	Price $
A	1	2.49
B	2	2.99
C	3	3.49
D	4	2.99
E	5	3.59
F	6	3.99
G	7	3.99
H	8	2.99

Calculate Spearman's rank correlation coefficient for the relationship between taste and price for this data (with the cheapest wine being ranked 1) and interpret your result. What result would you expect if the best-tasting wine were ranked 1 and the worst 8?

Test your understanding 9

If the correlation coefficient from a set of data measuring the relationship between temperatures on a particular day and sales values on that day is 0.95, which of the following statements would be correct?

A The positive sign tells us that there is a strong relationship between temperature and sales.

B The value of the correlation coefficient tells us that there is a strong linear relationship between temperature and sales.

C The value of the correlation coefficient tells us that for each increase of 1 degree in temperature, sales increase by 0.95 cartons.

D The value of correlation coefficient tells us that high temperatures cause high sales.

Which correlation coefficient to use?

Which correlation coefficient to use

If the data have already been ranked, there is no option but to use the rank correlation coefficient (R). Where actual values of x and y are given, Pearson's coefficient (r) should generally be used since information is lost when values are converted into their ranks. In particular, Pearson's coefficient must be used if you intend to use regression for forecasting (see later). The only advantages in converting actual data into ranks and using Spearman's coefficient are:

1 that the arithmetic is easier, but this is a minor point given computers and scientific calculators

2 that Spearman checks for a linear relationship between the ranks rather than the actual figures. If you simply want to confirm, say, that the variables increase together but have no concern about the linearity of the relationship, you might prefer to use the rank correlation coefficient.

6 Regression

The preceding sections give us a way of checking on whether it may be valid to assume that one variable, y, may depend on another, x. We now proceed to consider how, after making such an assumption, y can be forecast from x (for appropriate values of x). In other words, can we forecast factory spend values from knowledge of budgeted production levels or future sales volumes from budgeted advertising spend levels? This involves establishing an equation linking y and x of the form:

y = a function of x

For simplicity, we restrict our attention to instances of **linear** correlation. Thus, we are interested in situations where the dependence is in the form of a straight line. All linear equations can be arranged to conform to the same general format:

y = a + bx

where x and y are variables and y is dependent on the value of x, which is independent of y.

and a and b are numbers.

- "a" represents the point where the line cuts the y-axis (the intercept)
- "b" represents the gradient or slope of the line.

Graph of linear function y = a +bx

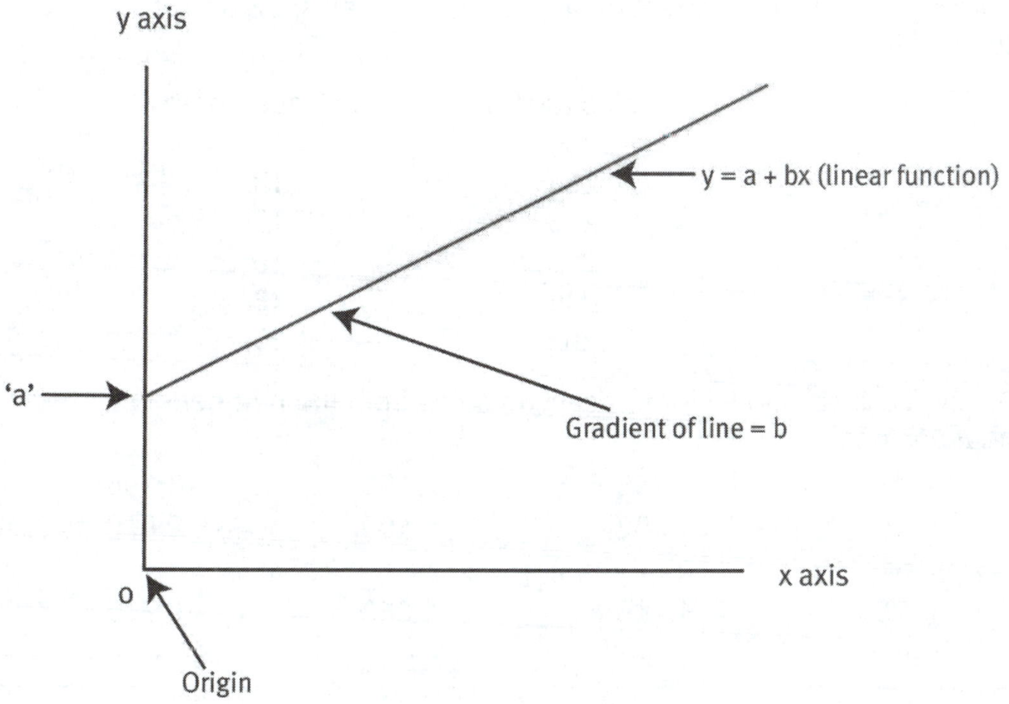

While this could be done by estimating the line using a scatter diagram, a formula-based method is quicker and involves less judgement.

7 Least-squares regression

Regression analysis finds the line of best fit computationally rather than by estimating the line on a scatter diagram. It seeks to minimise the distance between each point and the regression line.

The regression line has the equation:

$$y = a + bx$$

where:

$$\mathbf{b} = \frac{\mathbf{n\Sigma xy - (\Sigma x)(\Sigma y)}}{\mathbf{n\Sigma x^2 - (\Sigma x)^2}}$$

and

$$\mathbf{a = \bar{y} - b\bar{x}}$$

NB. $\bar{y} = \frac{\Sigma y}{n}$ and $\bar{x} = \frac{\Sigma x}{n}$

or in other words $\bar{y}$ and $\bar{x}$ are the mean (average) values of y and x.

The formulae are given in the exam but the descriptions of n, x, y, b and a are not.

e.g

Illustration 4 – Regression

A company has the following data on its sales during the last year in each of its regions and the corresponding number of salespersons employed during this time:

Region	Sales (units)	Salespersons
A	236	11
B	234	12
C	298	18
D	250	15
E	246	13
F	202	10

Develop a linear model for forecasting sales from the number of salespersons.

13	246	169	3,198
10	202	100	2,020
79	1,466	1,083	19,736

Solution

As we wish to forecast sales, we shall make this the dependent variable, y, and the number of sales persons the independent variable, x.

The next step is to evaluate the parameters a and b:

x	y	x^2	xy
11	236	121	2,596
12	234	144	2,808
18	298	324	5,364
15	250	225	3,750

Thus

$$b = \frac{(6 \times 19{,}736) - (79 \times 1{,}466)}{(6 \times 1{,}083) - 79^2} = \frac{2{,}602}{257} = 10.12$$

$$\bar{x} = \frac{79}{6} = 13.17$$

$$\bar{y} = \frac{1{,}466}{6} = 244.33$$

and so

$$a = 244.33 - (10.12 \times 13.17) = 111.05$$

Thus, the least-squares regression line in this case is

$$y = 111.05 + 10.12x$$

Interpreting a and b

In the equation of a straight line, y = a + bx, a is the intercept on the y-axis and b is the gradient or slope of the line. Expressed slightly differently, that means that a is the value of y when x = 0, and b is the increase in y for each unit increase in x.

The b-value of 10.12 tells us that each extra salesperson generates an extra 10.12 sales (on average), while the a-value of 111.05 means that 111.05 units will be sold if no salespeople are used.

Note: The latter conclusion may well be nonsensical because x = 0 is outside the range of the data, but we will return to this later.

Forecasting

Once the equation of the regression line has been computed, it is a relatively straightforward process to obtain forecasts.

For example, forecast the number of sales that would be expected next year in regions that employed (a) 14 salespersons; and (b) 25 salespersons.

Solution

As we have the 'best' line representing the dependence of sales on the number of salespersons, we shall use it for the forecasts. The values could be read off the line drawn on the scattergraph, but it is more accurate to use the equation of the line.

(a) The regression line is $y = 111.05 + 10.12x$ so, when $x = 14$:

$y = 111.05 + 10.12 \times 14 = 252.73$

Rounding this to a whole number, we are forecasting that 253 units will be sold in a region employing 14 salespersons.

(b) Substituting $x = 25$ into the formula:

$y = 111.05 + 10.12 \times 25 = 364.05$

Hence, the forecast is sales of 364 units in a region employing 25 salespersons.

Note: we will have more confidence with the forecast for 14 staff than we do for 25 staff as the latter is within the original range of measurements (between 10 and 18).

Limitations over the use of linear regression

Just because we have generated an equation of a straight line, it does not mean that it is useful for forecasting.

- Firstly, the actual relationship between the two sets of figures may not be linear. This can be investigated by calculating the coefficient of determination described earlier.

  For example, if $r^2 = 0.6$, then we can say that 60% of the variation in y can be explained using our regression line equation and variations in x. However, this means that 40% of the variation in y cannot be explained by our regression line equation.

- Secondly, even if we have a high level of correlation, this may be due to "spurious" correlation and the presence of other causal factors.

- Finally, we need to be careful using the regression line to make forecasts outside of the range of the original data ("extrapolation").

  For example, a straight line may be a reasonable reflection of the link between height and age of people between the ages of 10 and 16. However, if we use this to predict the height of a 90 year old, then we will probably predict that they should be 4m tall!

  Interpolation (forecasting within the established range of data) is more reliable than extrapolation.

Forecasting using the regression equation is a frequent exam question.

You will encounter regression analysis again in the later exam P1 Management Accounting.

Test your understanding 10

If the regression equation (in $'000) linking sales (y) and advertising expenditure (x) is given by y= 5,000 + 10x, forecast the sales when $100,000 is spent on advertising.

A $1,005,000

B $501,000

C $4m

D $6m

Test your understanding 11

In a forecasting model based on Y= a + bX, the intercept on the Y–axis is $234. If the value of Y is $491 and X is 20, then the value of the slope, to two decimal places, is:

A 224.55

B 212.85

C 12.85

D 24.85

Test your understanding 12

If the coefficient of determination is 0.49, which of the following is correct?

A y = 0.49x

B y = a +0.49x

C 49% of the variation in y can be explained by the corresponding variation in x

D 49% of the variation in x can be explained by the corresponding variation in y

Test your understanding 13

If the regression equation linking costs ($m) to number of units produced (000s) is *y* = 4.3 + 0.5*x*, which of the following is correct?

A For every extra unit produced, costs rise by $500,000.

B For every extra 1,000 units produced, costs rise by $500,000.

C For every extra 1,000 units produced, costs rise by $4.3m.

D For every extra unit produced, costs rise by $4,300.

Test your understanding 14

All of the following except one will adversely affect the reliability of regression forecasts. Which is the exception?

A Small sample

B Low correlation

C Extrapolation

D Negative correlation

Test your understanding 15

The regression equation $y = 50 - 2x$ has been obtained from fifteen pairs of x- and y-values, with the x-values ranging from 0 to 20. Which of the following is/are correct?

A When x = 0, y is estimated to be 25.

B y decreases by 2 whenever x increases by 1.

C The equation cannot be relied upon for x-values greater than 20.

D The correlation between x and y must be negative.

Test your understanding answers

Test your understanding 1

B

Calculating sales and costs and identifying slow moving inventory can be done using traditional accounting and warehousing systems. However, not until the stores are capturing more data about their shoppers will they be able to start identifying trends in relation to customer identifiers, such as age. This could be done through the use of loyalty cards.

Test your understanding 2

B

$$r = \frac{(11 \times 13{,}467) - (440 \times 330)}{\sqrt{(11 \times 17{,}986 - 440^2)(11 \times 10{,}366 - 330^2))}} = \frac{2{,}937}{\sqrt{4{,}246 \times 5{,}126}} = 0.63$$

Test your understanding 3

A True: the correlation is close to 1 in value.

B True: the correlation is positive.

C Untrue: the correct percentage would be 81.

D True: the correlation is positive.

Test your understanding 4

A Untrue based on this information. Causation cannot be deduced from high correlation.

B Untrue based on this information. We cannot be sure that the positive correlation will continue for advertising greater than $50,000.

C True.

D True.

Test your understanding 5

C

Correlation coefficients measure the strength of the linear relationship between two variables. They vary numerically between –1 and 1, being weak when close to 0 and strong when close to 1 or –1.

Test your understanding 6

A

The coefficient of determination is given by squaring the correlation coefficient. Often it is also multiplied by 100.

Test your understanding 7

(A), (B) and (C) are all incorrect because predictions cannot be made on the basis of the coefficient of determination.

Answer: (D).

Eighty-five per cent of the changes in sales from one day to the next can be explained by corresponding changes in temperature.

Test your understanding 8

Sample	Rank of taste	Rank of price	d	d^2
A	1	1	0	0
B	2	3	–1	1
C	3	5	–2	4
D	4	3	1	1
E	5	6	–1	1
F	6	7.5	–1.5	2.25
G	7	7.5	–0.5	0.25
H	8	3	5	25
				34.50

Hence

$$R = 1 - \frac{6\Sigma d^2}{n(n^2-1)} = 1 - \frac{6 \times 34.5}{8(64-1)} = 1 - \frac{207}{504} = 1 - 0.41 = 0.59$$

There seems to be some positive correlation between price and taste, with the more expensive wines tending to taste better. Given the sample size, the result is not really reliable and it cannot be extrapolated to wines costing more than $4. Had the taste rankings been allocated in the opposite order, the correlation would be negative indicating that the cheaper wines tasted worse.

Students often find this calculation difficult and it is worth running through it again if you had problems. Probably the most common errors are either forgetting to subtract from 1 or subtracting the numerator from 1 prior to dividing by the denominator.

Tied rankings can also be difficult. B, D and H all cost $2.99. Had they been marginally different they would have been ranked 2, 3 and 4. Since they are identical, they each have the rank of 3 (the **average** of 2, 3 and 4). Similarly, F and G share the ranks 7 and 8 by giving them an **average** 7.5 each.

The d column is obtained by subtracting rank of taste minus rank of price, but it would be equally correct the other way round.

Test your understanding 9

B

The positive sign tells us that as temperature rises, so do sales but it tells us nothing about the strength of the relationship. So (A) is incorrect.

The value of the correlation coefficient tells us that there is a strong linear relationship between temperature and sales (B) but it cannot prove cause and effect, so (D) is wrong. Equally, it doesn't enable us to estimate likely changes in sales corresponding to known changes in temperature and hence (C) is incorrect.

Test your understanding 10

D

y = 5,000 + 10x, and x = 100 when advertising is $100,000.

Hence y = 5,000 + 10 × 100 = 6,000 (in $000). Hence, sales forecast is $6m.

A is wrong because x = 100,000 has been used and the units of y ignored.

B In (B) 5,000 + 10 has been calculated before multiplication by 100 and in

C the 10x has been wrongly subtracted.

Test your understanding 11

C

$$Y = a + bX$$
$$491 = 234 + 20b$$
$$257 = 20b$$
$$12.85 = b$$

Test your understanding 12

C

The coefficient of determination gives the percentage of the variation in y which can be explained by the regression relationship with x. Answers (A) and (B) are confusing this with the actual regression equation, while answer (D) has x and y the wrong way round.

Test your understanding 13

B

In the equation y = a + bx, if x increases by one unit, y will increase by b units. In this case, if x increases by 1 unit, y increases by 0.5 units, which translates into production increasing by 1,000 units and costs by $500,000. All the other answers have either confused a and b or confused the units of x and y.

Test your understanding 14

D

It is the strength of the correlation but not its sign that influences the reliability of regression forecasts. Correlation can be negative but still very strong so (D) is the exception. Small samples, low correlation and extrapolation all tend to give unreliable forecasts.

Test your understanding 15

A	Incorrect: when x = 0, y = 50 – 0 = 50
B	Correct
C	Correct
D	Correct

Chapter

11

Informational Context of Business III: Forecasting

Chapter learning objectives

On completion of their studies, students should be able to:

- demonstrate trends and patterns in time series graphs, using appropriate techniques
- identify the components of a time series model
- prepare a trend equation using either graphical means or regression analysis
- understand seasonal variations using both additive and multiplicative models and explain when each is appropriate
- calculate predicted values, given a time series model
- identify the limitations of forecasting models.

1 Introduction

In the last chapter, we looked at linear regression as a method for forecasting. However, one limitation of this was that we only incorporated one causal factor (shown as the independent variable, x). In reality, forecasting scenarios are more complex than this.

Time series analysis is one approach to forecasting more complex scenarios.

2 Components and models of time series

There are considered to be four components of variation in time series:

- the trend, T
- the seasonal component, S
- the cyclical component, C; and
- the residual (or irregular, or random) component, R.

The **trend** in a time series is the general, overall movement of the variable over time, with any sharp fluctuations largely smoothed out. It is often called the underlying trend, and any other components are considered to occur around this trend.

The **seasonal** component accounts for the regular variations that certain variables show at various times of the year. Thus, a newly formed ice-cream manufacturing company may have sales figures showing a rising trend. Around that, however, the sales will tend to have peaks in the summer months and troughs in the winter months. These peaks and troughs around the trend are explained by the seasonal component.

The **cyclical** component explains much longer-term variations caused by business cycles. For instance, when a country's economy is in a slump, most business variables will be depressed in value, whereas when a general upturn occurs, variables such as sales and profits will tend to rise. These cyclical variations cover periods of many years and so have little effect in the short-term.

The **residual** component is that part of a variable that cannot be explained by the factors mentioned above. It is caused by random fluctuations and unpredictable or freak events, such as a major fire in a production plant. If the first three components are explaining the variable's behaviour well, then, subject to rare accidents, the irregular component will have little effect.

The four components of variation are assumed to combine to produce the variable in one of two ways: thus, we have two mathematical models of the variable. In the first case there is the **additive** model, in which the components are assumed to add together to give the variable, Y:

$$\mathbf{Y = T + S + C + R}$$

The second, **multiplicative**, model considers the components as multiplying to give Y:

$$Y = T \times S \times C \times R$$

Note that, in the additive model, all components are in the same units as the original variable. In the multiplicative model, the trend is in the same units as the variable and the other three components are just multiplying factors.

Inflation and growth can erode the validity of the figures used in an additive model, so most firms use the multiplicative approach.

e.g

Illustration 1

Suppose we have a monthly sales figure of $21,109.

Additive model

Thus, under the additive model, the figure might be explained as follows:

- the trend might be $20,000
- the seasonal factor: + $1,500 (the month in question is a good one for sales, expected to be $1,500 over the trend)
- the cyclical factor: – $800 (a general business slump is being experienced, expected to depress sales by $800 per month); and
- the residual factor: + $409 (due to unpredictable random fluctuations).

The model gives:

$$Y = T + S + C + R$$

$$Y = \$20{,}000 + \$1{,}500 + (-\ \$800) + \$409$$

$$Y = \$21{,}109$$

Multiplicative model

The multiplicative model might explain the same sales figures as:

- trend: $20,000
- seasonal factor: 1.10 (a good month for sales, expected to be 10 per cent above the trend)
- cyclical factor: 0.95 (a business slump, expected to cause a 5 per cent reduction in sales); and
- residual factor: 1.01 (random fluctuations of 1 per cent).

The model gives:

$$Y = T \times S \times C \times R$$

$$Y = \$20{,}000 \times 1.10 \times 0.95 \times 1.01$$

$$Y = \$21{,}109$$

Test your understanding 1

The component parts of a time series model are:

A the trend

B the cyclical component

C the seasonal component

D the residual component.

Associate each of the following with the appropriate component.

P The impact of a strike.

Q An economic cycle of ups and downs over 5 years.

R A long-term increase of 5 per cent per annum.

S An increase in sales over Christmas.

Test your understanding 2

In a time series analysis using the multiplicative model, at a certain time actual, trend and seasonal values are 523, 465 and 1.12 respectively.

Assuming there is no cyclical element to be incorporated, find the residual element at this point.

A 1.2597

B 56.88

C 1.0042

D 51.7857

3 Establishing the underlying trend

There are many ways of forecasting time series variables. Within the BA1 syllabus, you need to be aware of two methods for determining the trend.

1 If we assume a linear trend, then we can determine the trend line using linear regression

2 For situations where the assumption of a linear trend is not reasonable, then the alternative is to use moving averages (which can also be used for linear trends).

Both of these will be used in this chapter.

e.g

Illustration 2 – McNamee

The following table gives the quarterly sales figures for McNamee, a small company, for the last 3 years.

	Time period	Sales $000
20X2	quarter 1 (t = 1)	42
	quarter 2 (t = 2)	41
	quarter 3 (t = 3)	52
	quarter 4 (t = 4)	39
20X3	quarter 1 (t = 5)	45
	quarter 2 (t = 6)	48
	quarter 3 (t = 7)	61
	quarter 4 (t = 8)	46
20X4	quarter 1 (t = 9)	52
	quarter 2 (t = 10)	51
	quarter 3 (t = 11)	60
	quarter 4 (t = 12)	46

Forecast the 20X5 quarterly values of the **trend** in the series.

Solution

Note that the figures we are given are actual figures and will include seasonal variations. We need to strip out these variations to find the trend and then roll that trend forward for the four quarters of 20X5.

Let us look at a graph of the data (ignore the trend line for now):

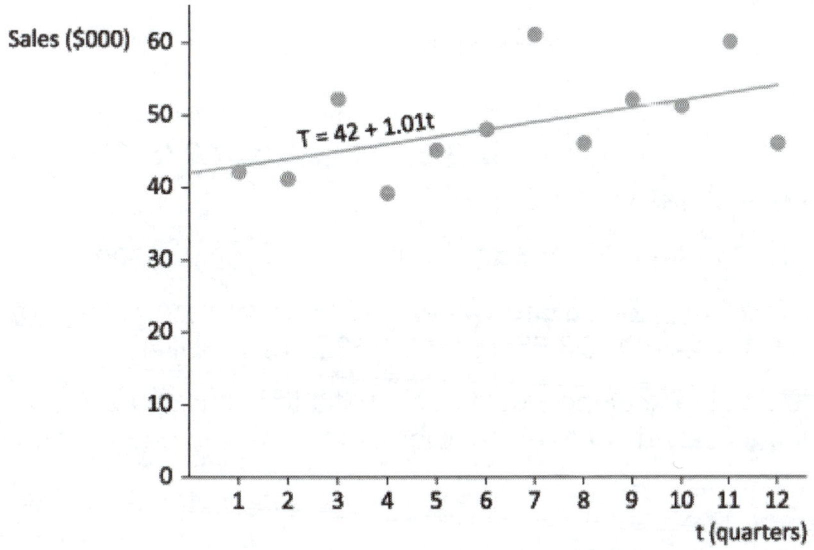

This is a time series graph, showing that the company's sales are following an upward trend, of a more or less linear shape, and that there is a definite seasonal pattern:

- each third quarter is a peak; and
- each fourth quarter is a trough.

This means that we can calculate a trend using regression analysis and that there will be seasonal variations around that trend.

Note that the twelve quarters for which we have data have been numbered from one to twelve, for ease of reference. If we perform a regression analysis on this data (with t as our x values and T as our Y values), we produce the equation:

$T = 42.0 + 1.01t$

If you like, you can use the regression techniques from the previous chapter to calculate the b value of 1.01 and the a value of 42.0 from the sales data to prove that the above equation is correct.

T therefore represents the linear trend value for sales ($'000) and t is the number of the quarter (20X2, quarter 1: t = 1, and so on). This trend line has been superimposed on the graph.

The process of calculating the trend, whether by regression or by moving averages (see later), is often described as 'smoothing the data'. As you can see from the above graph, the original ups and downs of the data have been smoothed away, leaving an upward linear trend.

To forecast the trend values for 20X5, we just need to put the appropriate quarterly t value into the trend equation. As the t values increase by 1 each quarter and the last quarter of 20X4 had a value of 12, we start with a value of 13 in the first quarter of 20X5:

20X5, quarter 1:	t = 13, giving
	$T = 42.0 + 1.01 \times 13 = 55.1$ ($000)
20X5, quarter 2:	t = 14, so
	$T = 42.0 + 1.01 \times 14 = 56.1$ ($000)
20X5, quarter 3:	t = 15:
	$T = 42.0 + 1.01 \times 15 = 57.2$ ($000)
20X5, quarter 4:	t = 16:
	$T = 42.0 + 1.01 \times 16 = 58.2$ ($000)

The 20X5 quarterly **trend** values, in $000s, are therefore forecast to be Q1 55.1, Q2 56.1, Q3 57.2 and Q4 58.2, respectively.

Note that these alone would not constitute accurate forecasts for 20X5 sales, as they do not yet incorporate the anticipated seasonal variations.

Test your understanding 3 – Bates

Bates has the following sales results for the last 4 years for product B, broken down by quarter.

Sales of article B (000 units)

	Q1	Q2	Q3	Q4
20X3	24.8	36.3	38.1	47.5
20X4	31.2	42.0	43.4	55.9
20X5	40.0	48.8	54.0	69.1
20X6	54.7	57.8	60.3	68.9

(Note: a number of the TYUs in this chapter relate to this data.)

Required

(a) Look at the data. What sort of trend and seasonal pattern do you expect to emerge from the analysis of this data?

(b) Use the regression equation T = 28.54 + 2.3244t to forecast the trend in sales for the four quarters of 20X7. Assume that t rises by 1 each quarter and the value at Q4 20X6 was 16.

Test your understanding 4

The regression equation of a linear trend is given by T = 43 + 5.9t where the time t = 1 in the first quarter of 2011 and the value of t rises by 1 each quarter.

Estimate the trend for the fourth quarter of 2015, giving your answer correct to three significant figures.

4 Forecasting seasonal components

Up to now, we have not had to concern ourselves with the choice of model. Since the nature of the seasonal component is so different in the two models, we now have to make a choice.

- The **multiplicative** model is usually considered the better, because it ensures that seasonal variations are assumed to be a constant proportion of the sales.
- The **additive** model, in contrast, assumes that the seasonal variations are a constant amount, and thus would constitute a diminishing part of, say, an increasing sales trend.

Because there is generally no reason to believe that seasonality does become a less important factor, the multiplicative model is adopted more frequently. In exam questions, you will be told which model to use.

The arithmetic involved in computing seasonal components can be time consuming but is simple. Assuming there are no cyclical or residual variations:

Multiplicative model: Actual value Y = T × S and therefore S = Y / T

Additive model: Actual value Y = T + S and therefore S = Y – T

For forecasting purposes, the same degree of seasonality is assumed to continue into the future, and so the historical seasonal components are simply projected unaltered into the future.

Note that when looking at existing data, the actual data represents the Y values, but when forecasting into the future, Y represents the forecast numbers.

e.g

Illustration 3 – McNamee (continued)

Using the multiplicative model, calculate the seasonal components from the sales data and trend of Illustration 2.

Solution

As we are using the multiplicative model, for each quarter we can calculate the seasonal variation as S = Y / T, which means we need to calculate the trend (T) value first (using T = 42.0 + 1.01t as determined in illustration 1). Here are the first and last calculations in detail. Have a go at the remaining calculations yourself.

First

- For Q1 20X2, when t = 1, T = 42.0 + (1.01 × 1) = 43.01
- S = Y/T = 42 / 43.01 = 0.9765

Last

- For Q4 20X4, when t = 12, T = 42.0 + (1.01 × 12) = 54.12
- S = Y/T = 46 / 54.12 = 0.8500

The complete set of ratios, arranged by quarter, is:

	Quarter 1	Quarter 2	Quarter 3	Quarter 4
20X2	0.9765	0.9314	1.1548	0.8471
20X3	0.9564	0.9988	1.2431	0.9185
20X4	1.0178	0.9789	1.1297	0.8500
Total	2.9507	2.9091	3.5276	2.6156
Mean	0.9836	0.9697	1.1759	0.8719

Note that within each quarter, the seasonal variation values are different but close to each other. This is to be expected. To simplify the data, we calculate an average seasonal variation per quarter, shown in the 'Mean' line of the table.

These figures show that, on average in the past, quarter 1 sales have been (0.9836) 98 per cent (approximately) of the trend, quarter 2 sales (0.9697) 97 per cent of the trend, and so on.

We will assume that these seasonal variations will continue into 20X5 and beyond, so we can now use them to help make our forecasts.

Tidying up the seasonal adjustments

In the multiplicative model, the seasonal components should cancel out over a year, meaning that if you add them together, they should add up to a value of 4 (an average of 1 each). To do this we first add them up to see how far away they are from a total of 4:

Total = 0.9836 + 0.9697 + 1.1759 + 0.8719 = 4.0011

There is a surplus 0.0011 in our total, which needs to be removed. If we take this surplus and divide by 4, we get the amount that each seasonal adjustment should be reduced by:

0.0011 / 4 = 0.0003 (to four decimal places)

Deduct this value from each of the seasonal variations and you get:

Q1 0.9833, Q2 0.9694, Q3 1.1756 and Q4 0.8716

The numbers now add up to 3.9999, but this is close enough to 4.

Note: if you are asked to use the additive model rather than the multiplicative model, the method is very similar:

- Calculate the trend values for the data given
- Calculate the seasonal variations as S = Y – T
- Average the seasonal variations
- Tidy up the seasonal variations, **which for the additive model should add up to zero.**

Test your understanding 5 – Bates (continued)

Using the original sales data and the regression line calculated for Bates

T = 28.54 + 2.3244 × t,

find the seasonal component (S) as the arithmetic mean of Y/T for each quarter, where Y denotes the actual sales and T the trend given by the regression equation.

Adjust your average seasonal variations so that they add to 4.

Test your understanding 6

In the additive model, four seasonal components initially calculated as +25, –54, –65 and +90 are to be adjusted so that they total zero.

Calculate the values of the adjusted seasonal components, giving your answers to the nearest whole number.

5 Producing the final forecast

So far, we haven't considered the final two components of variation, C and R. Isolating the cyclical component (C) of time series has proved to be a controversial area in economics and statistics. There is no consensus on an approach to the problem. Also, as we have already mentioned, cyclical variations have little effect in the short-term. For these reasons, we shall omit the factor C from our calculations.

The residual component is by nature unpredictable. The best that we can do is to hope that any random fluctuations are small and that no freak events occur, so that the factor R has no overall effect.

Therefore, instead of the multiplicative model $Y = T \times S \times C \times R$, we will use $Y = T \times S$ and for the additive model, instead of $Y = T + S + C + R$, we will use $Y = T + S$

e.g

Illustration 4 – McNamee (continued)

In the illustration used so far, forecast the sales during 20X5.

Solution

In illustration 2, we found the forecast trend values (T) for 20X5:

Q1 55.1, Q2 56.1, Q3 57.2, Q4 58.2

In illustration 3, we found the quarterly seasonal variations (S):

Q1 0.9833, Q2 0.9694, Q3 1.1756, Q4 0.8716

Now we combine these to calculate our forecast Y figures. As we have been using the multiplicative model, the formula is:

$Y = T \times S$

20X5 quarter 1: Y $= 55.1 \times 0.9833 = 54.18$

20X5 quarter 2: Y $= 56.1 \times 0.9694 = 54.38$

20X5 quarter 3: Y $= 57.2 \times 1.1756 = 67.24$

20X5 quarter 4: Y $= 58.2 \times 0.8716 = 50.73$

The forecast sales for the four quarters of 20X5, in $000s, are thus Q1 54.18, Q2 54.38, Q3 67.24 and Q4 50.73

Note that in our original data, each third quarter was a peak and each fourth quarter a trough. Our forecast for 20X5 matches this pattern.

Test your understanding 7 – Bates (continued)

Using the results of TYUs so far that relate to Bates, forecast the sales of B for the four quarters of 20X7 using the seasonal variations to two decimal places.

Test your understanding 8

Based on the last fifteen periods, where x is the period number, the underlying trend of sales is:

345.12 – 1.35x

If the sixteenth period has a seasonal factor of –23.62, assuming an additive forecasting model, then the forecast for that period, in whole units, is:

A 300

B 343

C 347

D 390

Test your understanding 9

Based on twenty past quarters, the underlying trend equation for forecasting is: y = 23.87 + 2.4x, where x is the quarter number. If quarter 21 has a seasonal factor of 1.08, using a multiplicative model, then the forecast for the quarter, in whole units, is:

A 75

B 80

C 83

D 85

6 Seasonal adjustment

Seasonal adjustment is the process of deseasonalising the data, or stripping out the seasonal variations to calculate the trend.

We have already done this in illustration 2 as part of calculating our forecasts, but sometimes it is useful on its own, to allow us to look at data without seasonal distortions.

In the multiplicative model, the calculation is T = Y / S

In the additive model, the calculation is T = Y – S

Effectively, the **seasonally adjusted figure is an estimate of the trend**.

Illustration 5 – McNamee (continued)

McNamee, the company in our illustrations, reports sales of $50,000 during the fourth quarter of a certain year. **Seasonally adjust this figure**.

Solution

We saw earlier that the seasonal component for the fourth quarter in this series is 0.8716. As we have been using the multiplicative model, our calculation is T = Y / S:

$$\frac{\$50,000}{0.8716} = \$57,365$$

we see that the seasonally adjusted sales for the quarter in question are $57,365.

Test your understanding 10 – Bates (continued)

Bates has forecast sales of $60,000 in the first quarter of a year.

Seasonally adjust this figure using the seasonal adjustment figure that was calculated to two decimal places.

7 Moving average trends

When calculating the trend, regression analysis is only useful if the trend is assumed to be linear. Moving average calculations can be used whether the trend is linear or not.

By calculating average figures over the period in which the seasonal variations apply, we can strip out those variations to isolate the trend. The average figures that we calculate are the estimates of the underlying trend figures.

If we believe the seasonal variations repeat every fourth set of data, we will use a 4-point moving average. If the variations repeat every third set of data, we use a 3-point moving average, and so on.

The technique can be long winded but simple to apply.

Illustration 6 – Three point moving average

To calculate a three point moving average, lay out the data in order, such as in the first three columns of the table below. Then, add the first 3 numbers together and divide by 3. Then, add numbers 2-4 together and divide by 3, then numbers 3-5 and so on. The average that you calculate should be placed in the centre of the 3 numbers used to calculate it, so the first average will be placed against the second number, as follows:

		Actual sales (Y)	Moving average (T)
20X2	Jan-Apr	15	
	May-Aug	13	15
	Sep-Dec	17	20
20X3	Jan-Apr	30	25
	May-Aug	28	30
	Sep-Dec	32	35
20X4	Jan-Apr	45	40
	May-Aug	43	45
	Sep-Dec	47	

Example calculations:

First average: (15 + 13 + 17) / 3 = 15

Second average: (13 + 17 + 30) / 3 = 20

Third average: (17 + 30 + 28) / 3 = 25

Once the seasonal variations have been stripped out through averaging, you can see that there is a straightforward underlying trend. Every four months, the trend is that sales increase by 5. This trend was almost impossible to see just by looking at the raw data in the actual sales column.

Note that you cannot calculate an average for the first or last point of data, due to the requirement to use the current number and the numbers from the periods before and after to calculate an average for a particular period.

Once we have the trend figures, we can use the same methods as earlier to calculate the seasonal variations – the question will tell you whether to use the multiplicative or additive method. Once the seasonal variations are known, you will be able to produce forecasts by rolling the trend and the seasonal variations forward.

To illustrate a four point moving average, we will look at the McNamee data from the previous illustrations.

When the moving average data is based on an **even** number, there is an extra step to the calculations; otherwise, the average (trend) data that we calculate will be between two periods, which is no use for forecasting.

e.g

Illustration 7 – McNamee

For McNamee Ltd, the company in our illustrations, the trend repeats every four quarters, so we need to calculate a four-point moving average.

This means starting from the first data point and use the first four numbers. Then we move down one point and use numbers 2-5, then 3-6 and so on until we reach the end of the data.

Instead of calculating the average directly, we first simply total the numbers, as shown in the 'Four-quarterly total' column. Note that these totals sit between quarters. For instance, the first number is centred between quarters 2 and 3.

The next step is to produce an eight quarterly total by taking the numbers in the 'Four-quarterly total' column and adding them in pairs. So 174 + 177 becomes 351, with the 351 placed in the centre of the two numbers used to calculate it, meaning it sits on the Q3 row. Then move down one number and add 177 + 184 to give 361, which sits against the Q4 row. This means that all the figures in the 'Centred eight quarterly total' column now sit against individual quarters rather than between them.

Now we can calculate the average. As we've added four numbers and then added two sets of four together, we must divide by 8 to get the average. This gives us the numbers in the 'Moving average (T)' column.

Solution

		Sales ($000) (Y)	Four-quarterly total	Centred eight-quarterly total	Moving average (T)
20X2	Q1	42			
	Q2	41			
			174		
	Q3	52		351	43.88
			177		
	Q4	39		361	45.13
			184		
20X3	Q1	45		377	47.13
			193		
	Q2	48		393	49.13
			200		
	Q3	61		407	50.88
			207		
	Q4	46		417	52.13
			210		
20X4	Q1	52		419	52.38
			209		
	Q2	51		418	52.25
			209		
	Q3	60			
	Q4	46			

As you can see, it is much more long winded to calculate moving averages when the seasonal variations rotate on an even numbered basis. However, the end result is the same – a set of trend figures with the seasonal variations stripped out, also known as deseasonalised or seasonally adjusted figures.

Test your understanding 11 – Bates (continued)

Using the data for Bates, repeated below, calculate the trend for the sales of article B as a centred four-point moving average.

Sales of article B (000 units)

	Q1	Q2	Q3	Q4
20X3	24.8	36.3	38.1	47.5
20X4	31.2	42.0	43.4	55.9
20X5	40.0	48.8	54.0	69.1
20X6	54.7	57.8	60.3	68.9

Test your understanding 12 – McNamee (continued)

Using the data for the company McNamee in the illustrations:

A find the seasonal components from the new trend values calculated in illustration 7, assuming the multiplicative model

B forecast sales for the four quarters of 20X5 (use the following trend values for Q1-Q4 20X5: 51.8, 51.6, 51.5 and 51.4)

C deseasonalise fourth-quarterly sales of $50,000.

Test your understanding 13 – Bates (continued)

Using the data for Bates in the TYUs to date:

A evaluate the seasonal component for each quarter based on the moving average trend obtained in TYU11

B forecast the sales of B for the four quarters of 20X7 using trend forecasts of 66.7, 68.8, 70.9 and 73.0.

8 Forecasting limitations

Care must be taken when placing reliance on the forecasts calculated. For data that was not strongly correlated in the first place, the forecasts will not necessarily be very reliable. Any time that data is being extrapolated rather than interpolated, the results will also be less reliable. Changing operational conditions may mean that two sets of data that were strongly correlated in a previous time period may become less so over time. External forces, such as inflation or the forecast being made during a boom or recession, should also be taken into account when making predictions. Any assumptions made in terms of linear relationships or on the cyclical nature of seasonal variations may not hold true. Unexpected (residual) variations will also affect the accuracy of any forecasts.

Therefore, those who use the results of the regression analysis, correlation analysis and moving average calculations to produce forecasts should be made aware of these limitations, so that they do not overly rely on the figures.

You will revisit forecasting in the P1 Management Accounting exam.

Test your understanding answers

Test your understanding 1

The component parts of a time series model are:

A	The trend	R
B	The cyclical component	Q
C	The seasonal component	S
D	The residual component	P

Test your understanding 2

C

In the full multiplicative model Y = T × S × C × R, so if we can ignore cyclical elements (a common simplification in exam questions), this reduces to give:

$$Y = T \times S \times R$$

R = Y/(T × S) = 523/(465 × 1.12) = 1.0042 (to four decimal places).

Note: In A the Y = T ratio has been multiplied by 1.12 instead of divided, while in both B and D the additive model has been used.

Test your understanding 3 – Bates

A For every quarter, each year shows an increase in sales, so an increasing trend is expected. Also, there is a regular seasonal pattern with a steady increase in sales from Q1 to Q4.

B In 20X7, t takes values 17–20, giving trend forecasts as follows:

Q1	t = 17	T = 28.54 + 2.3244 × 17 = 68.0548
Q2	t = 18	T = 28.54 + 2.3244 × 18 = 70.3792
Q3	t = 19	T = 28.54 + 2.3244 × 19 = 72.7036
Q4	t = 20	T = 28.54 + 2.3244 × 20 = 75.028

Test your understanding 4

In the fourth quarter of 2015, t = 20, so

T = 43 + 5.9 × 20 = 161.

Test your understanding 5 – Bates (continued)

Year	Quarter	t	T	Sales, Y	Y/T
20X3	1	1	30.8644	24.8	0.8035
	2	2	33.1888	36.3	1.0937
	3	3	35.5132	38.1	1.0728
	4	4	37.8376	47.5	1.2554
20X4	1	5	40.1620	31.2	0.7769
	2	6	42.4864	42.0	0.9886
	3	7	44.8108	43.4	0.9685
	4	8	47.1352	55.9	1.1860
20X5	1	9	49.4596	40.0	0.8087
	2	10	51.7840	48.8	0.9424
	3	11	54.1084	54.0	0.9980
	4	12	56.4328	69.1	1.2245
20X6	1	13	58.7572	54.7	0.9310
	2	14	61.0816	57.8	0.9463
	3	15	63.4060	60.3	0.9510
	4	16	65.7304	68.9	1.0482

Year	Q1	Q2	Q3	Q4	
20X3	0.8035	1.0937	1.0728	1.2554	
20X4	0.7769	0.9886	0.9685	1.1860	
20X5	0.8087	0.9424	0.9980	1.2245	
20X6	0.9310	0.9463	0.9510	1.0482	
Total	3.3201	3.9710	3.9903	4.7141	Total
Average	0.8300	0.9928	0.9976	1.1785	3.9989
+ adj.	0.0003	0.0003	0.0003	0.0003	0.0012
Comp.	0.8303	0.9931	0.9979	1.1788	4.0001

Quite a few rounding errors will have built up by now, so do not worry if your results differ a little from these.

To two decimal places, the seasonal components are

0.83 0.99 1.00 1.18

Test your understanding 6

Start by adding the seasonal components together:

25 – 54 – 65 + 90 = –4.

To sum to zero we thus need to add 4 in total, equivalent to adding 1 to each component.

- First = 25 + 1 = 26
- Second = –54 + 1 = –53
- Third = –65 + 1 = –64
- Fourth = 90 + 1 = 91.

Test your understanding 7 – Bates (continued)

The model is Y = T × S so the forecast sales (Y) in '000 units are given by multiplying the trend forecasts (T) calculated in TYU3 by the seasonal factors (S) calculated in TYU5.

Using a regression equation and seasonal components to forecast is a very common assessment question.

Forecast trend	68.0548	70.3792	72.7036	75.028
Seasonal	0.83	0.99	1.00	1.18
Forecast sales	56.5	69.7	72.7	88.5

Test your understanding 8

A

For the sixteenth period, put x = 16:

Trend = 345.12 – (1.35 × 16) = 323.52

Forecast is 23.62 below the trend:

Forecast = 323.52 – 23.62 = 299.9 = 300 (to nearest unit).

Test your understanding 9

B

Trend forecast = 23.87 + 2.4 × 21 = 74.27

Forecast = trend × seasonal factor

= 74.27 × 1.08

= 80

Test your understanding 10 – Bates (continued)

The seasonal adjustment for the first quarter, as calculated in TYU5, is 0.83.

The seasonally adjusted figure in a multiplicative model is calculated as T = Y / S

T = 60,000 / 0.83 = 72,289 units.

Seasonal adjustment is another common exam question.

Test your understanding 11 – Bates (continued)

Year	Quarter	Sales (Y)	Four-point moving total	Eight-point moving total	Four-point moving ave. trend (T)
20X3	1	24.8			
	2	36.3			
			146.7		
	3	38.1		299.8	37.4750
			153.1		
	4	47.5		311.9	38.9875
			158.8		
20X4	1	31.2		322.9	40.3625
			164.1		
	2	42.0		336.6	42.0750
			172.5		
	3	43.4		353.8	44.2250
			181.3		
	4	55.9		369.4	46.1750
			188.1		

20X5	1	40.0		386.8	48.3500
			198.7		
	2	48.8		410.6	51.3250
			211.9		
	3	54.0		438.5	54.8125
			226.6		
	4	69.1		462.2	57.7750
			235.6		
20X6	1	54.7		477.5	59.6875
			241.9		
	2	57.8		483.6	60.4500
			241.7		
	3	60.3			
	4	68.9			

Test your understanding 12 – McNamee (continued)

A First of all, in order to find S-values, we have to compute the individual values of Y ÷ T, and tabulate and average them as before.

For example 20X2 quarter 3 = 52 ÷ 43.88 = 1.1851.

		Sales ($000) (Y)	Moving average (T)	Seasonal variation (S)
20X2	Q1	42		
	Q2	41		
	Q3	52	43.88	1.1851
	Q4	39	45.13	0.8642
20X3	Q1	45	47.13	0.9548
	Q2	48	49.13	0.9770
	Q3	61	50.88	1.1989
	Q4	46	52.13	0.8824
20X4	Q1	52	52.38	0.9927
	Q2	51	52.25	0.9761
	Q3	60		
	Q4	46		

Tabulated by quarter:

	Quarter 1	Quarter 2	Quarter 3	Quarter 4
20X2			1.1851	0.8642
20X3	0.9548	0.9770	1.1989	0.8824
20X4	0.9927	0.9761		
Total	1.9475	1.9531	2.3840	1.7466
Mean	0.9738	0.9766	1.1920	0.8733
Add up the mean figures to see if they add up to 4. They total to 4.0157 Therefore we must adjust the figures down by (0.0157 / 4) = 0.0039				
Adjustment	-0.0039	-0.0039	-0.0039	-0.0039
Seasonal variation	0.9699	0.9727	1.1881	0.8694

B Trend (T) figures, in $000s, given in the question:

Q1 51.8, Q2 51.6, Q3 51.5 and Q4 51.4

Seasonal variations (S) calculated in part A:

Q1 0.9699, Q2 0.9727, Q3 1.1881, Q4 0.8694

As we are using a multiplicative model, Y = T × S

20X5 quarter 1: Y = 51.8 × 0.9699 = 50.24

20X5 quarter 2: Y = 51.6 × 0.9727 = 50.19

20X5 quarter 3: Y = 51.5 × 1.1881 = 61.19

20X5 quarter 4: Y = 51.4 × 0.8694 = 44.69

C The deseasonalised figure is an estimate of the trend. For the multiplicative model, this is calculated as T = Y / S

T = $50,000 and S (calculated in part A) is 0.8694

T = Y / S = $50,000 / 0.8694 = $57,511

Test your understanding 13

Calculating the seasonal multiplier as Y/T from the answers in TYU11 and arranging these values according to their quarters gives:

	Q1	Q2	Q3	Q4	
20X3			1.017	1.218	
20X4	0.773	0.998	0.981	1.211	
20X5	0.827	0.951	0.985	1.196	
20X6	0.916	0.956			
Total	2.516	2.905	2.983	3.625	Total
Average	0.839	0.968	0.994	1.208	4.009
–	0.002	0.002	0.002	0.002	0.008
Comp.	0.837	0.966	0.992	1.206	4.001

Rounding to two decimal places gives seasonal components of:

0.84   0.97   0.99   1.21

Forecast for 20X7

	Q1	Q2	Q3	Q4
Trend	66.70	68.80	70.90	73.00
Seasonal variation	0.84	0.97	0.99	1.21
Sales	56.028	66.736	70.191	88.33

Hence the sales forecasts for the four quarters of 20X7 are (in '000 units):

56   67   70   88

Chapter

12

Mock Assessment

Chapter learning objectives

This section is intended for use when you have completed your study and initial revision. It contains a complete mock assessment.

This should be attempted as an exam conditions, timed mock. This will give you valuable experience that will assist you with your time management and examination strategy.

1 Mock Assessment

Subject BA1

Fundamentals of Business Economics

Instructions: attempt all 60 questions

Time allowed 2 hours

Do not turn the page until you are ready to attempt the assessment under timed conditions

Mock Assessment 1 – Questions

Test your understanding 1

Hammer, a listed company, is evaluating four projects with the following details:

Project	**A**	**B**	**C**	**D**
NPV at a discount rate of 10% ($)	10,000	12,000	(5,000)	7,000
ROCE	12%	5%	13%	10%

Given the directors wish to maximise shareholder wealth, which project should be undertaken?

A Project A

B Project B

C Project C

D Project D

Test your understanding 2

Quest's weekly costs (C) were plotted against production levels (p) for the last 50 weeks and a regression line C = 1,000 + 2.50p was found, where C is measured in $ and p in units.

Which of the following would this denote?

A fixed costs are $1,250

B variable costs are $1,250 per unit

C fixed costs are $1,000; variable costs are $2.50 per unit

D fixed costs are $250; variable costs are $1,000 per unit

Test your understanding 3

The 'agency problem' refers to which of the following situations?

A Shareholders acting in their own short-term interests rather than the long-term interests of the company

B A vocal minority of shareholders expecting the directors to act as their agents and pay substantial dividends

C Companies reliant upon substantial government contracts such that they are effectively agents of the government

D The directors acting in their own interests rather than the shareholders' interests

Test your understanding 4

Since the end of World War II, it has been the stated policy of most developed countries to eliminate protectionism through free trade policies enforced by international treaties and organisations such as the World Trade Organisation.

All of the following statements, relating to trade protection, are true except which one?

A Import quotas tend to reduce prices

B Trade protection tends to reduce consumer choice

C Trade protection tends to reduce exports

D Tariffs tend to reduce competition

Test your understanding 5

Which one of the following would result from the setting of a maximum price for a product that is above the equilibrium price?

A Supply would outstrip demand

B Demand would outstrip supply

C The demand curve would shift to the left

D No effect

Test your understanding 6

The market capitalisation of Palermo has been increasing steadily over the past 12 months. All of the following would be expected to raise share values except which one?

A An announcement of higher than expected profits

B A reduction in corporation tax

C A rise in interest rates

D A rise in share prices on overseas stock markets

Test your understanding 7

The ... (i) in a company are all those who have an interest in the strategy and behaviour of the ... (ii) .... Their interest may not always coincide with those of the ... (iii) .... who are principally interested in ... (iv) .... The task of .... (v) .... is to attempt to reconcile these conflicting interests.

Read the above passage and indicate where each of the following words should be placed in the passage.

A Management

B Shareholders

C Stakeholders

D Company

E Profits

Test your understanding 8

If a person's disposable income rises by 10% from $2,000 per month and their consumption rises by 8.75% from $1,600 per month, what is their marginal propensity to consume?

A 0.7

B 0.875

C 1.4

D 11.4

Test your understanding 9

In a histogram in which one class has a frequency of 112 and a bar height of 32, what height would the bar be for a class of equal width with a frequency of 28?

A 8

B 16

C 49

D 98

Test your understanding 10

Enjoyaball currently sells 10,000 units of its children's outdoor activity sets per month at $10 per unit and the demand for its product has a price elasticity of –2.5, a rise in the price of the product to $11 will do which of the following?

A raise total revenue by $7,250

B reduce total revenue by $17,500

C reduce total revenue by $25,000

D raise total revenue by $37,500

Test your understanding 11

How much does FGH Co need to be invested now at 5% to yield an annual income of $4,000 in perpetuity?

A $80,000

B $90,000

C $100,000

D $120,000

Test your understanding 12

A UK oil company that judges that its shareholders' best interests are served by minimising its expenditure on measures to ensure that its plant and pipelines do not damage the environment is likely to be met with which of the following reactions?

A applause by all the major stakeholders in the company

B criticism by major investors in the company

C support by the media

D support by the UK government

Test your understanding 13

If an indirect tax is imposed on a good or service, which of the following will result?

A The price will rise by an amount equal to the tax

B The producer decides on how much of the tax to pass on to the customer

C The price rise will be smaller the greater is the price elasticity of demand

D The price rise will be greater the smaller is the price elasticity of supply

Test your understanding 14

The following is a list of possible sources of market failure.

(i) Externalities

(ii) Monopoly power

(iii) Public goods and services

(iv) Merit goods

(v) Lack of knowledge

For each of the following cases, indicate which one of the above sources of market failure matches the case given:

A Businesses fail to properly train their employees because they fear that they will move to other firms after their training.

B There is a failure to provide efficient street cleaning services because it is impossible for the service providers to ensure that all who benefited from the services paid for them.

Test your understanding 15

The introduction of a national minimum wage will lead a business to reduce its number of employees most when which of the following is the case?

A the demand for its final product is price elastic

B wage costs are a small proportion of total costs

C there is a low degree of substitutability between capital and labour

D the supply of substitute factors of production is price inelastic

Test your understanding 16

All of the following are examples of where externalities are likely to occur except which one?

A A business providing training schemes for its employees

B Government expenditure on vaccination programmes for infectious diseases

C Attending a concert given by a government funded orchestra

D Private motorists driving cars in city centres

Test your understanding 17

If the demand curve for Good A shifts to the left when the price of Good B rises, we may conclude which of the following?

A the goods are substitutes

B Good A is an inferior good

C the goods are complements

D the demand for Good A is price elastic

Test your understanding 18

The recession phase of the trade cycle will normally be accompanied by all of the following except which one?

A A rise in the rate of inflation

B A fall in the level of national output

C An improvement in the trade balance

D A rise in the level of unemployment

Test your understanding 19

Exchange rates are determined by supply and demand for currencies in the foreign exchange market. State whether each of the following would be part of the supply of a country's currency or part of the demand for that country's currency.

Statement	Supply	Demand
Payments for imports into the country.		
Inflows of capital into the country.		
Purchases of foreign currency by the country's central bank.		

Test your understanding 20

A table has five rows showing exam results and three columns showing schools in a town. Which of the following charts could be used to show the data?

(i) A multiple bar chart

(ii) A simple bar chart

(iii) A component bar chart

A (i) and (ii) only

B (i) and (iii) only

C (ii) only

D All of the above

Test your understanding 21

If banks are required to keep a reserve assets ratio of 10% and also wish to keep a margin of liquid reserves of 10%, by how much would deposits ultimately rise by if they acquire an additional $1000 of reserve assets?

A $10,000

B $5,000

C $1,000

D $500

Test your understanding 22

If a commercial banks reallocates some of its assets from less profitable to more profitable ones, which of the following will result?

A the bank's liquidity will be increased

B the safety of the bank's assets will be increased

C the bank's liquidity will be decreased

D the liquidity and safety of the bank's assets will be unaffected

Test your understanding 23

In the modern world most of the world's currencies are floating. Under a regime of floating exchange rates, which one of the following would lead to a rise in the exchange rate for a country's currency?

A a shift in the country's balance of payments current account towards a surplus

B a rise in interest rates in other countries

C an increasing balance of trade deficit

D the central bank buying foreign exchange on the foreign exchange market

Test your understanding 24

In December, unemployment in the region of Hareville is 423,700. If the seasonal factor using an additive time series model is + 81,500, what is the seasonally adjusted level of unemployment to the nearest whole number?

A 342,200

B 505,200

C 345,316

D 519,877

Test your understanding 25

An inflation index and index numbers of XYZ's sales ($) for the last year are given below.

Quarter:	1	2	3	4
Sales ($) index:	109	120	132	145
Inflation index	100	110	121	133

Which of the following statements relate to 'real' sales, i.e. adjusted for inflation?

A approximately constant keeping up with inflation

B growing steadily and not keeping up with inflation

C growing steadily and keeping ahead of inflation

D falling steadily and not keeping up with inflation

Test your understanding 26

Other things being equal, all of the following would lead to a rise in share prices for a company except which one?

A A rise in interest rates

B A reduction in corporation tax

C A rise in company profits

D A decline in the number of shares in issue

Test your understanding 27

A producer has a price inelastic supply curve for its product. State whether each of the following effects would occur (yes/no) if the firm experienced an increase in demand for its product.

Effects	Yes	No
Sales volume would increase.		
The volume of supply would increase.		

Test your understanding 28

Australia is currently experiencing low real interest rates. The effects include all of the following except which one?

A Credit based sales will tend to be high

B Nominal costs of borrowing will always be low

C Business activity will tend to increase

D Investment will be encouraged

Test your understanding 29

Last year, the government of Country A increased its budget deficit significantly. This is likely to lead to which of the following reactions?

A Increase in the level of withdrawals from the economy

B Decrease in the equilibrium level of national income

C Increase in aggregate demand in the economy

D Decrease in the level of employment in the economy

Test your understanding 30

For a given set of goods, the price index is 104. Which of the following statements is/are correct about average prices?

A Prices have risen by 104 per cent

B Prices are now 1.04 times their base year value

C Prices have risen by 4 per cent

D Prices have risen by 96 per cent

Test your understanding 31

Identify the correct word or phrase in the following to complete each of the following statements.

(i) Internal economies of scale can only be obtained when the industry/company/market increases in size.

(ii) Diseconomies of scale occur when the business becomes inefficient/technically outdated/too large and, in consequence, costs begin to rise.

Test your understanding 32

The following diagram shows the aggregate demand curve (AD) and the aggregate supply curve (AS) for an economy:

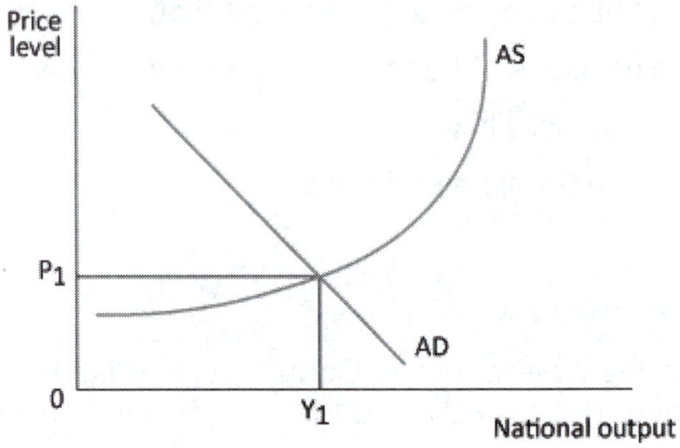

With reference to the diagram:

A ………… supply shock would shift the ………… curve to the left and cause the rate of inflation to increase. However the level of .... would fall.

Use the following words and phrases to fill in the gaps in the above passage.

positive

aggregate demand

negative

aggregate supply

national output

Test your understanding 33

With reference to PESTEL analysis, which of the following are sources of political risk?

(i) Rising nationalisation

(ii) Competing religious groups

(iii) Newly created international alliances

A (i) and (ii) only

B (i) and (iii) only

C (i) only

D All of the above

Test your understanding 34

In November, unemployment in a region is 238,500. If the seasonal component using an additive time series model is –82,000, what is the seasonally adjusted level of unemployment to the nearest whole number?

Test your understanding 35

All of the following will encourage the process of the globalisation of production except which one?

A Reductions in international transport costs

B Higher levels of tariffs

C Reduced barriers to international capital movements

D Increased similarity in demand patterns between countries

Test your understanding 36

A luxury men's outerwear retailer has a constant (flat) trend in its sales, and is subject to quarterly seasonal variations as follows:

Quarter	Q1	Q2	Q3	Q4
Seasonality	+50%	+50%	–50%	–50%

Assuming a multiplicative model for the time series and that unit sales in Q2 were 240, predicted unit sales for the next quarter, Q3, will be closest to:

A 60

B 80

C 120

D 160

Test your understanding 37

If the coefficient of determination between output and production costs over a number of months is 89 per cent, which of the following comments is correct?

A 89 per cent of the variation in production costs from one month to the next can be explained by corresponding variation in output

B Costs increase as output increases

C The linear relationship between output and costs is very weak

D An increase of 100 per cent in output is associated with an increase of 89 per cent in costs

Test your understanding 38

Carrera is a high-end soft drink manufacturer. Flavour X is a crucial ingredient in their recipes. Four years ago, Flavour X cost $5 per kg and the price index most appropriate to the cost of Flavour X stood at 150. The same index now stands at 430.

To the nearest $0.10, what is the best estimate of the current cost of Flavour X per kg?

A $1.70

B $9.30

C $14.30

D $21.50

Test your understanding 39

Identify which of the following statements about the balance of payments is true and which is false.

Statement	True	False
(i) A deficit on a country's balance of payments current account can be financed by a surplus of invisible earnings.		
(ii) Flows of profits and interest on capital appear in the Capital Account.		
(iii) Flexible exchange rate systems should, in principle, prevent persistent current account imbalances.		
(iv) Current account deficits tend to worsen in periods of rapid economic growth.		

Test your understanding 40

Which of the following economic conditions is likely to lead to demand-pull inflation?

A A worsening balance of payments and a rising exchange rate

B An increase in Government spending and firms operating at full capacity

C Increased monopoly power in goods and labour markets

D An increase in interest rates and a rise in the world price of oil

Test your understanding 41

The correlation coefficient for ten pairs of x and y values, with x ranging from \$500 to \$700, is calculated to be 0.79, and the regression equation is y = 620 + 4.3x. Which two of the following are correct?

A When x = \$600, the estimate of y = 3,200

B When x = \$550, the estimate of y from the regression equation is likely to be reliable

C When x = 0, the estimate of y from the regression equation is likely to be reliable

D When x increases by \$1, y increases by 0.79

Test your understanding 42

All of the following are benefits that all countries, such as France, gain when adopting a single currency, such as the Euro, except which one?

A Reduced transactions costs

B Increased price transparency

C Lower interest rates

D Reduced exchange rate uncertainty

Test your understanding 43

For each of the following events, indicate whether the direct effect of each on an economy would raise inflation, reduce inflation or leave the rate of inflation unaffected. Assume that the economy is close to full employment.

Event	Raise inflation	Lower inflation	Leave inflation unchanged
(i) A rise (appreciation) in the exchange for the country's currency.			
(ii) A significant increase in the money supply.			
(iii) A rise in business expectations leading to an increase in investment.			

Test your understanding 44

If the exchange rate for a country's currency were to rise (appreciate), would the following prices rise, fall or remain unchanged as a direct result?

Price	Rise	Fall	Remain unchanged
Domestic price of imported goods.			
Foreign price of imported goods.			

Test your understanding 45

Abacus has arranged a 10-year lease, at an annual rent of $8,000. The first rental payment has to be paid immediately and each lease payment is a year apart.

What is the present value of the lease at 12 per cent?

A $50,624

B $53,200

C $45,200

D $65,288

Test your understanding 46

What type of relationship would there likely be between the cost of electricity for a firm and overall factory production levels?

A perfect positive linear

B perfect negative linear

C high positive

D low negative

Test your understanding 47

Which of the following would be expected to lead to a fall in the value of £ sterling against the US dollar?

(i) A rise in US interest rates

(ii) A rise in UK interest rates

(iii) Intervention by the Bank of England to buy sterling

A (i) only

B (ii) only

C (i) and (iii)

D (ii) and (iii)

Test your understanding 48

Tobacco advertising is virtually banned in all marketing communication forms in many countries around the world. This can be explained as an influence of which of the following?

A technological environment

B legal environment

C economic environment

D ecological environment

Test your understanding 49

Two wine tasters ranked eight bottles of wine as follows:

Wine	A	B	C	D	E	F	G	H
Taster X	3	7	1	8	5	2	4	6
Taster Y	3	8	2	7	4	1	5	6

Find Spearman's rank correlation coefficient for this data, giving your answer to three decimal places.

Test your understanding 50

A boiler supplier offers a 7 year contract with an annual charge of $13,000 at each year end. If the discount rate is 10 per cent, what is the present value of the contract, giving your answer to the nearest $?

A $63,284

B $91,316

C $91,000

D $79,885

Test your understanding 51

Sales figures for Radiow are given as 547,000 but after seasonal adjustment using a multiplicative model they are only 495,000. What is the seasonal component for the particular season, to 3 d.p.?

A 1.224

B 0.905

C 1.105

D 0.683

Test your understanding 52

The internal rate of return (IRR) can be described as:

1 The breakeven discount rate for a project.

2 The rate at which the present value of the future cash inflows for a project is equal to the initial cash outflow.

3 The rate of profit earned from taking on a project.

Which of the above statements are correct?

A 1 and 2

B 1 and 3

C 2 and 3

D 3 only

Test your understanding 53

X Ltd is currently selling a product at a price of $60 with a resulting demand of 20,000 units per annum. Due to competitive pressure, the company is considering dropping the price to $48. It is hoped that this will boost sales to 21,000 units per annum.

What is the price elasticity of demand, to 2 decimal places, calculated using the average arc method?

A –0.08

B –0.20

C –0.22

D –0.25

Test your understanding 54

A company based in the UK acquires 50% of its resources in the UK and the other 50% from suppliers in Continental Europe (the Eurozone countries). It sells nearly all its output to North America. It is strategically exposed to the risk of a rise in the value of the euro, and to a fall in the value of the dollar against sterling. What is the term for this type of currency exposure?

A Transaction

B Translation

C Economic

D Strategic

Test your understanding 55

State whether each of the following statements is true or false.

Statements	True	False
If the demand curve for Good A shifts to the right when the price of Good B falls we can conclude that A and B are substitute goods.		
If the demand for a good is price inelastic, a fall in its price will leave sales volume unchanged and total revenue reduced.		

Test your understanding 56

Match the following situations to the definitions given below:

Situations	Definition
The emission of dangerous fumes from car exhausts.	
Premature death of consumers of tobacco.	

Definitions

A Positive externality in consumption

B Negative externality in consumption

C Negative externality in production

D None of the above

Test your understanding 57

Show what you would expect to happen to the following economic indicators in the boom phase of the trade cycle in the economy.

Indicators	Rise	Fall	Remain unchanged
The rate of inflation.			
The rate of unemployment.			

Test your understanding 58

In comparison to forward contracts, which of the following are true in relation to futures contracts?

(i) They are more expensive

(ii) They are only available in a small amount of currencies

(iii) They are less flexible

(iv) They are probably an imprecise match for the underlying transaction

A (i), (ii) and (iv) only

B (ii) and (iv) only

C (i) and (iii) only

D All of the above

Test your understanding 59

'There is a risk that the value of our foreign currency denominated assets and liabilities will change when we prepare our accounts.'

To which type of risk does the above statement refer?

A Translation risk

B Economic risk

C Transaction risk

D Interest rate risk

Test your understanding 60

With reference to PESTEL analysis, which of the following statements is true?

A One form of political risk is government measures to improve the competitiveness of national companies

B Political risk is confined to less developed countries

C A tax increase is never the result of political forces and can therefore not be considered a political risk

D All of the above

Test your understanding answers

Test your understanding 1

B

As it has the highest NPV.

Test your understanding 2

C

Fixed costs are $1,000; variable costs are $2.50.

Test your understanding 3

D

Directors, who are placed in control of resources that they do not own and are effectively agents of the shareholders, should be working in the best interests of the shareholders. However, they may be tempted to act in their own interests, for example by voting themselves huge salaries. The background to the agency problem is the separation of ownership and control – in many large companies the people who own the company (the shareholders) are not the same people as those who control the company (the board of directors).

Test your understanding 4

A

Import quotas will tend to reduce the level of competition in the market, leading to higher prices for consumers.

Test your understanding 5

D

As the new price is a maximum above the current equilibrium, there would be no effect. If it had been set below the equilibrium then demand would outstrip supply.

Test your understanding 6

C

Asset prices, such as those of shares, and interest rates are inversely related.

Test your understanding 7

The **stakeholders** in a company are all those who have an interest in the strategy and behaviour of the **company**. Their interest may not always coincide with those of the **shareholders** who are principally interested in **profits**. The task of **management** is to attempt to reconcile these conflicting interests.

Test your understanding 8

A

Change in income = $2,000 × 10% = $200

Change in consumption = $1,600 × 8.75% = $140

MPC = change in consumption/change in income

MPC = $140/$200 = 0.7

Test your understanding 9

A

112/32 = 3.5. The frequency is 3.5 times the bar height.

28/3.5 = 8

Test your understanding 10

B

With a PED of –2.5, the quantity demanded will proportionately change 2.5 times as much as the price when the price is changed.

A rise in price from $10 to $11 is a 10% change, so the demand will fall (because the PED is negative) by 25% to 7,500 units.

Old revenue = 10,000 × $10 = $100,000. New revenue = 7,500 × $11 = $82,500, a fall of $17,500.

Test your understanding 11

A

A real life example of this is a pension. In other words, you are living off the interest and the capital remains.

PV = 1/interest rate

$4,000 × (1/0.05) = $80,000

Test your understanding 12

B

The modern view is that being socially responsible can offer business benefits. This is particularly true of the oil industry where major UK and US companies have attracted very substantial criticism as a result of an apparent failure to adequately protect the environment from oil spills.

Test your understanding 13

C

Initially, for the same price the producer will receive a lower income as some of the sales value is now passed on to the tax authorities.

An indirect tax is paid by the consumer so the producer does not decide how much is passed on to the consumer.

However, the producer may choose to raise the price in order to sustain their income levels. How much they choose to raise the price by will depend on the price elasticity of demand. The greater it is, the more a price rise will compromise their overall revenue and so would lead the supplier to consider a smaller price rise.

A smaller price elasticity of supply would mean that a change in price doesn't affect the level of supply that much.

Test your understanding 14

(a) (i) Externalities

(b) (iii) Public goods and services

Test your understanding 15

A

The business has a choice of either reducing its costs or passing the cost increase onto the consumer. If the product is price elastic then increasing the price to cover the cost increase will compromise the business's revenue from the product, so the business would be encouraged to look instead to cutting the wage cost by reducing the number of employees.

Test your understanding 16

C

(A) would lead to other businesses benefitting from better-trained staff once those staff have moved jobs. (B) would mean that even unvaccinated individuals would benefit from lower instances of the disease. (D) would lead to negative pollution externalities.

Test your understanding 17

C

A shift to the left means a drop in demand at the same price level. Raising the price of good B would normally lead to a contraction of demand for good B. if demand for good A also falls but without a price change then it is probably bought in conjunction with good B, i.e. it is a complementary good.

Test your understanding 18

A

Test your understanding 19

Statement	Supply	Demand
Payments for imports into the country.	X	
Inflows of capital into the country.		X
Purchases of foreign currency by the country's central bank.	X	

Test your understanding 20

B

A simple bar chart could not hold this amount of information.

Test your understanding 21

B

The bank wishes to keep a cash ratio of 20% (or 0.2). Using the credit multiplier this means that cash deposits will multiply by 1/0.2 = 5 times. Therefore $1,000 of extra assets would be multiplied to $5,000.

Test your understanding 22

C

Assets that are more profitable tend to be less liquid and vice versa. For instance, a long-term bond will tend to have a higher yield than a short-term one but cash is tied up for longer.

Test your understanding 23

A

A rise in the exchange rate can be caused by an increase in demand for the currency or a decrease in supply. If the balance of payments starts to shift towards a surplus it means that exports are increasing and/or imports are decreasing. If exports are increasing then demand for the home currency will rise. If imports are decreasing then the supply of the home currency will fall. Either way the shift will tend to push the exchange rate up.

Test your understanding 24

A

In the additive model, value Y= trend T + seasonal S. The seasonally adjusted value estimates the trend Y – S = 423,700 – 81,500 = 342,200 in this case.

The errors were: in B, adding instead of subtracting S, and in C and D, getting confused with the multiplicative model and multiplying or dividing by 0.81500.

Test your understanding 25

A

Quarter	'Real' sales
1	(109/100) × 100 = 109.0
2	(120/110) × 100 = 109.1
3	(132/121) × 100 = 109.1
4	(145/133) × 100 = 109.0

The 'real' series is approximately constant and keeping up with inflation.

Test your understanding 26

A

The price of shares is determined by demand and supply. (B) and (C) would raise the demand for shares and (D) would reduce the supply. However, a rise in interest rates would reduce the demand for shares as alternative investments have become more attractive.

Test your understanding 27

Effects	Yes	No
Sales volume would increase.	X	
The volume of supply would increase.		X

Test your understanding 28

B

Low interest rates encourage borrowing and therefore spending and investment and they discourage savings. The nominal rate of interest is dependent on both the real rate and the inflation rate. So if inflation is high then even at low real rates the nominal rate will be high.

Test your understanding 29

C

A budget deficit (when government spending is greater than government income from tax receipts) is designed to boost aggregate demand in the economy. Government spending is an injection into the circular flow.

Test your understanding 30

B and C

An index of 104 means that prices have risen by 4 per cent, which in turn means that current values are 1.04 times their values in the base year, on average.

Test your understanding 31

(i) Company. Internal economies arise from the advantages of large scale production within the business.

(ii) Too large. Diseconomies of scale occur when a business becomes too big, the others can occur in a business of any size.

Test your understanding 32

A **negative** supply shock would shift the **aggregate supply** curve to the left and cause the rate of inflation to increase. However the level of **national output** would fall.

Test your understanding 33

D

All are sources of political risk.

Test your understanding 34

Answer: 320,500

The additive model is A = T + S and seasonal component provides an estimate of T = A – S = 238,500 – (–82,000) = 238,500 + 82,000.

Test your understanding 35

B

Tariffs are a method of protectionism with the aim of reducing imports. This will hinder globalisation rather than encourage it.

Test your understanding 36

B

Multiplicative model forecast = T × S

Sales last quarter 240(Q2)

Seasonality for Q2 = +50% S = 150

Trend = (240/150) × 100 = 160 for Q3

Seasonality = –50% S = 50

Forecast = 160 × (50/100) = 80

Test your understanding 37

A

A coefficient of determination between output and production costs tells us that 89 per cent of the variation in production costs from one month to the next can be explained by corresponding variation in output. It also tells us that the linear relationship between output and costs is very strong (not weak, as in C). Only a positive correlation can tell us that costs increase as output increases and we cannot assume this form the coefficient of determination.

Test your understanding 38

C

The cost of flavour X was \$5 when the index was 150. This means that the cost of \$5 is 150% of the base cost. The base cost always has an index of 100, so from this information we could calculate the base cost as \$5 / 150 × 100 = \$3.33.

As the index is now 430, this means that the current cost is now 430% of the base cost and we can calculate this as \$3.33 × 430 / 100 = \$14.32, which is \$14.30 to the nearest \$0.10

Test your understanding 39

Statement	**True**	**False**
(i) A deficit on a country's balance of payments current account can be financed by a surplus of invisible earnings.		X
(ii) Flows of profits and interest on capital appear in the Capital Account.		X
(iii) Flexible exchange rate systems should, in principle, prevent persistent current account imbalances.	X	
(iv) Current account deficits tend to worsen in periods of rapid economic growth.	X	

Test your understanding 40

B

Increases in government spending tend to raise aggregate demand. If firms are operating at full capacity then they will struggle to increase output (at this point, the price elasticity of supply will be low). The consequence of this is an increase in the equilibrium price.

Test your understanding 41

A Correct

B Correct

C Incorrect: x = 0 is outside the range of the data

D Incorrect: when x increases by 1, y increases by 4.3 from the regression equation

Test your understanding 42

C

Having a single currency would not have a direct impact on interest rates. Countries within the single currency zone would have a single central bank and individual countries may therefore lose control of the setting of interest rates applicable in their country.

Test your understanding 43

Event		**Raise inflation**	**Lower inflation**	**Leave inflation unchanged**
(i)	A rise (appreciation) in the exchange for the country's currency.		X	
(ii)	A significant increase in the money supply.	X		
(iii)	A rise in business expectations leading to an increase in investment.	X		

Test your understanding 44

Price	**Rise**	**Fall**	**Remain unchanged**
Domestic price of imported goods.		X	
Foreign price of imported goods.			X

Test your understanding 45

A

Present value = $8,000 + present value of an annuity of $8,000 for 9 years at 12 per cent.

Present value = $50,626

Test your understanding 46

C

High positive. It is unlikely to be perfect as there may be other factors that impact the cost, such as price rises and people accidentally leaving lights on overnight.

Test your understanding 47

A

A rise in US interest rates is likely to prompt a flow of funds from UK to US increasing the relative demand (and value) of the dollar, meaning a corresponding relative fall in value of sterling.

Test your understanding 48

B

Regulation falls under the legal aspect of PESTEL. It could also be linked to the political aspect if the regulation is politically motivated.

Test your understanding 49

	A	B	C	D	E	F	G	H
d	0	–1	–1	1	1	1	–1	0
d2	0	1	1	1	1	1	1	0

$\Sigma d^2 = 6; n = 8$

$$\text{Rank correlation} = 1 - \frac{6 \times \Sigma d^2}{n(n^2 - 1)}$$

$$= 1 - \frac{6 \times 6}{8 \times 63} = 0.929$$

Test your understanding 50

A

The supplier's maintenance contract is a year end annuity of $13,000 per year. Discounting at 10 per cent and using the cumulative discount factor table gives a present value of $13,000 × 4.868 = $63,284.

Test your understanding 51

C

Seasonally adjusted value (T) = actual value (Y)/seasonal component (S).

So seasonal component = actual value divided by seasonally adjusted value = Y/T = 547/495 = 1.105.

Test your understanding 52

A

Statements 1 and 2 are correct. IRR is calculated using cash flows rather than profits so statement 3 is incorrect.

Test your understanding 53

C

- Percentage change in price = ($60 – $48)/$54 = –22.22%
- Percentage change in demand = (21,000 – 20,000)/20,500 = +4.878%
- PED = (+4.878)/(–22.22) = –0.2195 = –0.22

Test your understanding 54

C

Economic exposures are strategic exposures to currency risk. An economic exposure gives rise to transaction exposures. In this example, transaction exposures will arise whenever the company buys supplies in the euro zone for payment in euros and whenever it sells to customers in the US for payment in dollars.

Test your understanding 55

Statements	True	False
If the demand curve for Good A shifts to the right when the price of Good B falls we can conclude that A and B are substitute goods.		X
If the demand for a good is price inelastic, a fall in its price will leave sales volume unchanged and total revenue reduced.		X

As good A sees an increase in demand (demand curve shifts to the right) when the price of another good falls, the goods are complementary goods rather than substitutes. The price fall of good B expands demand for good B and, as the products are complementary and bought together, demand for good A increases even though its own price has not changed.

If good A were a substitute for good B, demand for A would decrease (demand curve shifts to the left) when the price of good B falls as more people are encouraged to switch from A to B even though the price of A has not changed.

To be price inelastic means that demand will change by a lower percentage than the price when the price changes. A price fall will lead to an increase in demand that is a smaller percentage than the reduction in price and therefore to a reduction in revenue (demand × price). To see no change at all in demand, the good would have to be perfectly price inelastic.

Test your understanding 56

Situations	Definition
The emission of dangerous fumes from car exhausts.	B
Premature death of consumers of tobacco.	D

Test your understanding 57

Indicators	Rise	Fall	Remain unchanged
The rate of inflation.	X		
The rate of unemployment.		X	

Test your understanding 58

D

All these statements are true of futures contracts, when compared to forward contracts.

Test your understanding 59

A

Translation risk.

Test your understanding 60

A

One form of political risk is government measures to improve the competitiveness of national companies. The other statements are false.

A

B

C

D

E

M

N

O

P

Q

R

S

T

U

V

W

Y

THIS IS A FLAP.
FOLD THIS PAGE OUT.

Robert Browning

The Laboratory

ANCIEN RÉGIME

This tells us that the poem is set in France, in the days when they had a monarchy.

I

Now that I, tying thy glass mask tightly,
May gaze thro' these faint smokes curling whitely,
As thou pliest thy trade in this devil's-smithy—
Which is the poison to poison her, prithee?

She wears a mask for safety.

She knows what she's doing is evil.

II

He is with her, and they know that I know
Where they are, what they do: they believe my tears flow
While they laugh, laugh at me, at me fled to the drear
Empty church, to pray God in, for them! —I am here.

She's paranoid that she's a laughing stock — this makes her more determined to get revenge.

The whole poem is in rhyming couplets.

III

Grind away, moisten and mash up thy paste,
Pound at thy powder,—I am not in haste!
Better sit thus, and observe thy strange things,
Than go where men wait me and dance at the King's.

The way she describes making the poison shows her violent feelings — she'd like to do these things to her rival.

Their lives are based around the Royal Court.

IV

That in the mortar—you call it a gum?
Ah, the brave tree whence such gold oozings come!
And yonder soft phial, the exquisite blue,
Sure to taste sweetly,—is that poison too?

She wants to know how the poison is made, and where the ingredients come from.

The poison is precious to her.

The colour of the poison is beautiful to her.

V

Had I but all of them, thee and thy treasures,
What a wild crowd of invisible pleasures!
To carry pure death in an earring, a casket,
A signet, a fan-mount, a filigree basket!

There's no doubt about what she wants to happen.

The potions are rare and valuable.

She gets carried away with excitement, listing all the things she can think of that could hold poison.

VI

Soon, at the King's, a mere lozenge to give,
And Pauline should have just thirty minutes to live!
But to light a pastile, and Elise, with her head
And her breast and her arms and her hands, should drop dead!

There's a dark humour here — usually people would use these to make things better.

The idea of killing excites her.

Robert Browning

VII

Quick—is it finished? The colour's too grim!
Why not soft like the phial's, enticing and dim?
Let it brighten her drink, let her turn it and stir,
And try it and taste, ere she fix and prefer!

She has the whole plan worked out, down to the smallest details.

She's worried there's not enough poison.

VIII

What a drop! She's not little, no minion like me!
That's why she ensnared him: this never will free
The soul from those masculine eyes,—say, 'no!'
That to pulse's magnificent come-and-go.

She says her lover's mistress trapped him. Maybe she thinks this justifies her own violence.

Respectful way of describing life — but she wants to end it.

IX

For only last night, as they whispered, I brought
My own eyes to bear on her so, that I thought
Could I keep them one half minute fixed, she would fall
Shrivelled; she fell not; yet this does it all!

Graphic description of death.

X

Not that I bid you spare her the pain;
Let death be felt and the proof remain:
Brand, burn up, bite into its grace—
He is sure to remember her dying face!

She wants the mistress to suffer — she wants absolute revenge.

She takes pleasure in the cruelty of what she's doing.

XI

Is it done? Take my mask off! Nay, be not morose;
It kills her, and this prevents seeing it close:
The delicate droplet, my whole fortune's fee!
If it hurts her, beside, can it ever hurt me?

She's so keen to see the poison, she risks removing her protective mask.

The poison is her most prized possession, possibly her only one.

XII

Now, take all my jewels, gorge gold to your fill,
You may kiss me, old man, on my mouth if you will!
But brush this dust off me, lest horror it brings
Ere I know it—next moment I dance at the King's!

She spends everything she has on the poison.

She's delighted that the poison is ready.

POEM DICTIONARY

thy — your
thou — you
pliest — carry out
smithy — workshop
prithee — please
mortar — a small bowl
whence — from where
yonder — over there
phial — a small bottle
thee — you
signet — a seal on a ring
filigree — delicate ornamental metal
lozenge — a tablet or pill
pastile — a substance burnt to clean the air
ere — before
minion — a small, weak person

The Village Schoolmaster

This poem is about the old schoolmaster of a village school. He was a rather strange bloke — he was bad-tempered and a bit frightening, but also very intelligent and skilful. Although the poet doesn't say it outright, it seems that the people in the village thought he was a bit of an oddball.

You've Got to Know What Happens in the Poem

Lines 1-12 — The poet points out a place in the countryside where a village school was. Then we hear about how strict the schoolmaster was — he was often in a bad mood and the pupils were scared of him.

Lines 13-24 — Then the poet says how clever the schoolmaster was. He had loads of different skills. The villagers were amazed by how much he knew — although they didn't seem to like him very much.

Learn About the Three Types of Language

1) INTIMIDATING LANGUAGE — The way the schoolmaster looked and acted makes him seem scary and unpleasant. The children were afraid of his temper, and laughed at his rubbish jokes to avoid getting on the wrong side of him.
2) LANGUAGE ABOUT EDUCATION — The schoolmaster had all sorts of skills and knowledge. The villagers were amazed at how much he knew.
3) MYSTERY — He was an outsider and a loner. The people in the village didn't know much about him and seemed to think he was a bit odd, rather than respecting him.

Remember the Feelings and Attitudes in the Poem

"Today, children, you're going to learn about how great I am."

1) FEAR — The children were scared of the schoolmaster.
2) FASCINATION — The villagers were fascinated by the schoolmaster, but they didn't respect him very much (lines 23-24).
3) MOCKERY — The poet seems to mock the school master — he creates an impression of him being a pompous show-off (although he doesn't openly say this).

Think About Your Feelings and Attitudes to the Poem

1) Pick 2 words or phrases that stand out to you. If none stand out, just pick 2 unusual words or phrases.
2) Write these 2 words or phrases down. Then write about how they make you feel. If they don't make you feel anything, don't worry — just make something up, as long as it's not too stupid.

EXAMPLE The description of the schoolmaster as having "The day's disasters in his morning face" makes him sound scary and intimidating. I wouldn't want to have him as my headteacher.

Themes — characters, closing couplets, memory...

Compare 'The Village Schoolmaster' with other poems on the same themes: characters (Ulysses p.26-27 and 'Kid' p.60-61), closing couplets ('Havisham' p.36-37 and 'I've made out a will' p.64-65) and memory ('We Remember Your Childhood Well' p.46-47 and 'Homecoming' p.56-57).

The Laboratory

Key Poem

This poem's set in France, back in the days when posh people lived at the King's Court. The woman's at a drug shop to get some poison so she can kill her lover's mistress and some other women who she reckons are after her lover. Seems a trifle extreme...

You've Got to Know What Happens in the Poem

Lines 1-4	The woman talks to the chemist while he mixes the poison in his workshop.
Lines 5-8	Her lover is with another woman and they think she's at church crying — but she's not.
Lines 9-20	She watches the chemist and says how lovely the poisons look. She wants all of them.
Lines 21-24	She plans to poison two other women called Pauline and Elise at the King's Court.
Lines 25-28	She tells the chemist to make the poison brighter, to make her lover's mistress drink it.
Lines 29-32	She says there's not enough poison to kill the mistress — she's too big and strong.
Lines 33-40	Last night, she felt she could kill the mistress by looking at her. She wants her to die painfully.
Lines 41-48	She's so grateful to the chemist she offers to kiss him. Now she's off to use the poison.

Learn About the Three Types of Language

1) VIOLENT LANGUAGE — She's absolutely merciless about taking her revenge. She wants the mistress's death to be horrible and painful, and violent thoughts are never far from her mind.
2) IMAGERY — For all her nastiness, she can be quite eloquent with her descriptions.
3) OBSESSIVE LANGUAGE — She gives up all her wealth and possessions for the poison — nothing else matters to her. She gets very excited when she thinks about revenge.

Remember the Feelings and Attitudes in the Poem

Ice with your poison, I mean drink?

1) OBSESSION — She's obsessed with the thought of getting revenge.
2) SINGLE-MINDEDNESS — revenge is all that matters to her.
3) IMMORALITY — She knows what she's doing is wrong, but she doesn't care.

She wants to kill the mistress just to get revenge on her lover for being unfaithful — pretty twisted really.

Think About Your Feelings and Attitudes to the Poem

1) Pick 2 words or phrases that stand out to you. If none stand out, just pick 2 unusual words or phrases.
2) Write these 2 words or phrases down. Then write about how they make you feel. If they don't make you feel anything, don't worry — just make something up, as long as it's not too stupid.

EXAMPLE I am horrified by the line "He is sure to remember her dying face!". She wants her lover to see his mistress when she dies, which is a very sick way of getting revenge on him.

Themes — evil, danger, characters...

Compare 'The Laboratory' with other poems on the same themes: evil ('Education for Leisure' p.48-49), danger ('Hitcher' p.66-67) and characters ('Havisham' p.36-37, 'Salome' p.42-43 and 'Those bastards in their mansions' p.62-63).

Gerard Manley Hopkins

Gerard Manley Hopkins (1844-1889) was born in Stratford, Essex. He studied Classics at Balliol College, Oxford, and was a famous Victorian poet. He became a Jesuit priest and concentrated on teaching and preaching for several years, before resuming his writing.

Inversnaid

This darksome burn, horseback brown,
His rollrock highroad roaring down,
In coop and in comb the fleece of his foam
Flutes and low to the lake falls home.

A windpuff-bonnet of fawn-froth
Turns and twindles over the broth
Of a pool so pitchblack, fell-frowning,
It rounds and rounds Despair to drowning.

Degged with dew, dappled with dew
Are the groins of the braes that the brook treads through,
Wiry heathpacks, flitches of fern,
And the beadbonny ash that sits over the burn.

What would the world be, once bereft
Of wet and of wildness? Let them be left,
O let them be left, wildness and wet;
Long live the weeds and the wilderness yet.

Repetition of how dark the stream is.

Alliteration of "c" sounds makes the stream sound rough.

The water sounds melodic.

Continual motion, like a whirlpool.

Alliteration and repetition shows that there's dew all around.

The tree is motionless but alive.

Uses a rhetorical question to appeal to the reader's emotions.

Alliteration of "r" sounds reminds us of the roar of water.

The bubbles of the stream are described like they're a person's or animal's hair.

The froth is like a hat on the water.

Hostile and unwelcoming.

The stream moves like a person walking.

Repetition creates a passionate, emotional feel.

"W" sounds are repeated throughout this verse.

POEM DICTIONARY
burn — stream
coop — an enclosed area
comb — the top of a wave
fawn — light greyish-brown colour
fell — fiercely
degged — sprinkled
braes — hills
flitches — cuttings
bereft — deprived

Inversnaid

This poem is about a burn (stream) flowing through a rugged, unspoilt area of Scotland. The area is wild and beautiful, and the poet wants it to stay that way. Don't we all, Gerard...

You've Got to Know What Happens in the Poem

Lines 1-4 A dark-coloured stream flows down into a lake.

Lines 5-8 The stream sounds dark and angry.

Lines 9-12 There's dew on the hills, some wild plants, and an ash tree by the river.

Lines 13-16 The poet says we should leave beautiful places like this as they are.

Learn About the Three Types of Language

1) SOUND EFFECTS — There's loads of alliteration to create the effect of the fast flow of water. There's also plenty of rhyming, assonance and onomatopoeia (see glossary, p.92) to help us feel like we can really hear the sounds of the country. These effects add to the rugged, natural feel.
2) PERSONIFICATION — The burn is described as if it's a person. This allows the poet to make it sound angry and fierce, and also strong and admirable.
3) EMOTIONAL LANGUAGE — The poet feels passionately that places like this should be left alone. He seems to be worried that the growth of towns and cities means there are fewer and fewer unspoilt areas of countryside.

Remember the Feelings and Attitudes in the Poem

Something's not right...

1) DANGER — The stream seems fierce and dangerous.
2) BEAUTY — The whole area is beautiful, rugged and unspoilt.
3) PRESERVATION — The poet wants this place to stay as it is. He believes it would be terrible if beautiful, natural places like this didn't exist anymore.

Think About Your Feelings and Attitudes to the Poem

1) Pick 2 words or phrases that stand out to you. If none stand out, just pick 2 unusual words or phrases.
2) Write these 2 words or phrases down. Then write about how they make you feel. If they don't make you feel anything, don't worry — just make something up, as long as it's not too stupid.

EXAMPLE When the poet asks "What would the world be, once bereft / Of wet and wildness?", it makes me sad. I live in a city, a long way from anywhere like the place the poet describes, and I think it is a pity that so many people grow up without knowing places like this.

Themes — imagery, mood, language effects...

Compare this poem with other poems on the same themes: imagery ('Sonnet' p.34-35 and 'Homecoming' p.56-57), mood ('Elvis's Twin Sister' p.38-39 and 'November' p.58-59) and language effects ('Sonnet 130' p.20-21 and 'Stealing' p.50-51).

John Clare

John Clare (1793-1864) was the son of a Northampton labourer. He left school at 11 and educated himself after that. For most of his life he lived in rural Northamptonshire. He is famous for writing poems about life in the country, although he also wrote about politics, the environment, corruption and poverty.

Sonnet

I love to see the summer beaming forth
And white wool sack clouds sailing to the north
I love to see the wild flowers come again
And Mare blobs stain with gold the meadow drain
And water lilies whiten on the floods
Where reed clumps rustle like a wind shook wood
Where from her hiding place the Moor Hen pushes
And seeks her flag nest floating in bull rushes
I like the willow leaning half way o'er
The clear deep lake to stand upon its shore
I love the hay grass when the flower head swings
To summer winds and insects happy wings
That sport about the meadow the bright day
And see bright beetles in the clear lake play

Repetition emphasises his feelings.

The colour of wool suggests the purity and cleanliness of the soft, fluffy clouds.

Yellow and white enforce the brightness of early summer.

Trees around the lake make it seem alive and healthy.

Natural and unspoilt.

The insects are playful and fun-loving.

Alliteration enforces the idea of brightness.

The whole scene is shining brightly.

Using "gold" instead of yellow is an idealistic way of seeing it.

Suggests there's a light, pleasant breeze.

Rhyming couplets throughout the poem.

Gentle movement.

Brightness continues to the end of the poem.

The poem finishes on a light-hearted, carefree note.

POEM DICTIONARY

sonnet — a poem with 14 lines
Mare blobs — buttercups
Moor Hen — a bird that lives on ponds
flag — type of leaf
bull rushes — plants that grow in ponds
o'er — over

Sonnet

This is a good old-fashioned poem about how lovely summer in the countryside is. It's a really idealistic poem — the poet talks about all the best things in summer, like pretty flowers, trees and meadows (and ignores things like hayfever and another dull series of Big Brother).

You've Got to Know What Happens in the Poem

Lines 1-4 The poet describes how much he likes the lovely summer, with the lovely clouds floating over the lovely flowers in the lovely meadow.

Lines 5-10 Lilies and reeds grow in the lake. A bird swims across the water. The poet says how great the willow trees on the banks are.

Lines 11-14 He says he loves the way the grass and flowers blow in the wind, and cheery little insects skip about on the surface of the lake.

Learn About the Two Types of Language

1) VISUAL LANGUAGE — Nature is in full bloom. The sun is out, the fields are golden — even the beetles are bright...
2) PEACEFULNESS — The countryside is quiet and calm. The flowers are swaying in the gentle breeze. The insects are just messing around and not stinging anyone. It's a very idealistic poem.

There's no punctuation in the poem. This helps the poet to create one big image, made up of all the different things he describes.

Remember the Feelings and Attitudes in the Poem

Ah, the glorious British summer of 2004.

1) LOVE — He loves the summer and the natural scenery.
2) TRANQUILLITY — He feels relaxed and at peace.
3) HAPPINESS — Overall, he's just dead happy that it's summer and he's in the countryside. Bless.

Think About Your Feelings and Attitudes to the Poem

1) Pick 2 words or phrases that stand out to you. If none stand out, just pick 2 unusual words or phrases.
2) Write these 2 words or phrases down. Then write about how they make you feel. If they don't make you feel anything, don't worry — just make something up, as long as it's not too stupid.

EXAMPLE The phrase "summer beaming forth" reminds me of the long summer holidays when I was really young. The whole world seemed to be bright and blooming, and this poem brings back the happy, relaxed feelings of that time for me.

Themes — language effects, mood, imagery...

You could compare 'Sonnet' with other poems on the same themes: language effects ('The Eagle' p.24-25 and 'Anne Hathaway' p.40-41), mood ('Inversnaid' p.32-33) and imagery ('Before You Were Mine' p.44-45 and 'My father thought it bloody queer' p.54-55).

Key Poem

Havisham

Carol Ann Duffy was born in 1955 in Glasgow. She studied philosophy at the University of Liverpool, and in 1996 began lecturing in poetry at Manchester Metropolitan University. As well as writing poetry, she has also written plays.

Havisham

Beloved sweetheart bastard. Not a day since then
I haven't wished him dead. Prayed for it
so hard I've dark green pebbles for eyes,
ropes on the back of my hands I could strangle with.

Spinster. I stink and remember. Whole days
in bed cawing Nooooo at the wall; the dress
yellowing, trembling if I open the wardrobe;
the slewed mirror, full-length, her, myself, who did this

to me? Puce curses that are sounds not words.
Some nights better, the lost body over me,
my fluent tongue in its mouth in its ear
then down till I suddenly bite awake. Love's

hate behind a white veil; a red balloon bursting
in my face. Bang. I stabbed at a wedding-cake.
Give me a male corpse for a long slow honeymoon.
Don't think it's only the heart that b-b-b-breaks.

Her feelings are a confused mix — the tender love she would have had for him as a husband, and her violent bitterness at being rejected.

She's become so hardened by her hatred that she can't see clearly.

She's so angry she could use her veins to strangle him.

She's disgusted with herself too.

She screams like an animal.

She becomes more reflective here, wondering how she's become so messed up.

This shows us how long she's been wearing it.

She recognises how irrational and savage she's become.

Even her dreams end violently.

In her fantasies, the man is seen as an object, not a person.

The veil usually hides a blushing bride, but here it masks her hatred.

Could be a sign of a wedding party — a metaphor for her dreams of married bliss being cruelly dashed.

Any man will do — she wants revenge on men in general.

Usually a happy time, but here it's connected with death and revenge.

Could mean that her mind has also broken, or that she wants to break the entire body of a man.

POEM DICTIONARY
spinster — a woman who's never married
cawing — making the sound of a crow
slewed — twisted sideways, lopsided
puce — a deep red or purple colour
fluent — flowing or speaking smoothly

Havisham

Key Poem

Miss Havisham was a character in "Great Expectations" by Charles Dickens. She was jilted on her wedding day and ended up a bit mad, staying in her wedding dress for years with the rotting cake in her room. In this poem, Duffy describes her feelings. It's a tad bitter and twisted, this one...

You've Got to Know What Happens in the Poem

Lines 1-4 — Havisham's dead angry. She wants to kill the man who jilted her.

Lines 5-9 — She describes the weird things she does — like staying in bed all day screaming, and always wearing her old, manky wedding dress.

Lines 9-12 — She says she sometimes dreams there's a man in bed with her, then wakes up abruptly.

Lines 12-16 — She tells us that she stabbed the cake, but really wants to stab a man.

Learn About the Three Types of Language

1) VIOLENT LANGUAGE — Havisham's hell-bent on revenge. She wants to take out her anger on a man — but settles for stabbing the wedding-cake instead.
2) REFLECTIVE LANGUAGE — There are signs that she hasn't always been a nutter. At times she reflects on how she's become like she is, and we see a more sensitive side to her.
3) WEDDING-RELATED LANGUAGE — There are plenty of images of weddings — but instead of being signs of love and happiness, they come to stand for Havisham's bitterness and violent streak.

Remember the Feelings and Attitudes in the Poem

"I could murder a slice of cake..."

1) ANGER — Havisham is really really really really angry — at the man who jilted her, and also at men in general.
2) BITTERNESS — She's very very very bitter about it too. She wants to get revenge.
3) SADNESS — She's also unhappy — she uses her violent feelings to cover up the fact that she's actually very upset and vulnerable because she was dumped on her big day.

Havisham is totally obsessed by what's happened to her. She can't think about anything else, even though it happened years ago.

Think About Your Feelings and Attitudes to the Poem

1) Pick 2 words or phrases that stand out to you. If none stand out, just pick 2 unusual words or phrases.
2) Write these 2 words or phrases down. Then write about how they make you feel. If they don't make you feel anything, don't worry — just make something up, as long as it's not too stupid.

EXAMPLE When Havisham describes herself "trembling if I open the wardrobe", I feel sorry for her. She's so scared of what she has become that she can't even bear to look at herself in the mirror.

Themes — mood, strong emotions and the first person...

Compare 'Havisham' with other poems about the same themes: mood ('Tichborne's Elegy p.14-15), strong emotions ('Those bastards in their mansions' p.62-63 and 'The Affliction of Margaret' p.10-11) and use of the first person ('Kid' p.60-61 and 'Ulysses' p.26-27).

Elvis's Twin Sister

Elvis's Twin Sister

Are you lonesome tonight? Do you miss me tonight?

Elvis is alive and she's female: Madonna

In the convent, y'all,
I tend the gardens,
watch things grow,
pray for the immortal soul
of rock 'n' roll.

They call me
Sister Presley here.
The Reverend Mother
digs the way I move my hips
just like my brother.

Gregorian chant
drifts out across the herbs
Pascha nostrum immolatus est ...
I wear a simple habit,
darkish hues,

a wimple with a novice-sewn
lace band, a rosary,
a chain of keys,
a pair of good and sturdy
blue suede shoes.

I think of it
as Graceland here,
a land of grace.
It puts my trademark slow lopsided smile
back on my face.

Lawdy.
I'm alive and well.
Long time since I walked
down Lonely Street
towards Heartbreak Hotel.

This colloquial greeting reveals her background. She's from the southern USA, like her brother.

She leads a simple, peaceful life.

Sounds like a typical religious activity, but the next line makes the link with Elvis.

This name combines both aspects of her personality.

Humorous image of Elvis's sexy movements in a convent. The use of the slang word "digs" also seems comically out of place.

Peaceful religious singing contrasts with Elvis's rock 'n' roll.

A hymn sung at Easter — religion is central to her life.

She has the usual basic clothes and possessions of a nun. They're functional, not fashionable.

A similarity with her brother — but she wears them because they're practical, rather than because they're fashionable.

She loves the convent as Elvis loved his home — but maybe the name is more appropriate here, as she's found happiness.

Another famous Elvis characteristic — but his sister's smile is genuine, not just a trademark.

Slang way of saying "lord" humorously links the religious and rock 'n' roll parts of her background.

This refers to the rumours that "Elvis lives".

Places from Elvis songs. Heartbreak and loneliness are things of the past now.

POEM DICTIONARY

convent — a place where nuns live
Gregorian chant — a religious style of singing in harmony
habit — a dress worn by a nun
hues — shades, colours
wimple — a piece of cloth that a nun wears around her head
rosary — religious beads
Graceland — the home of Elvis Presley

Elvis's Twin Sister

The poet imagines that Elvis Presley has a twin sister who's living as a nun (in real life Elvis didn't have a sister). She's happier than her brother was, suggesting that a simple life will bring you more happiness than wealth and fame can bring. If only we could persuade Will Young to be a monk...

You've Got to Know What Happens in the Poem

Lines 1-10 — Elvis's imaginary sister talks about her simple, peaceful life as a nun. She hints at her similarity in appearance to Elvis (lines 8-10).

Lines 11-20 — She describes the religious singing that rings out around the convent. She says she wears simple, practical clothes.

Lines 21-30 — She's really happy at the convent — she's left her sadness behind.

Learn About the Three Types of Language

1) ELVIS REFERENCES — Lots of famous aspects of Elvis's life (like his songs, looks and clothes) are used to reinforce the idea that the nun is just like him — she's just chosen a different way of life.
2) RELIGIOUS LANGUAGE — The simple clothes and religious lifestyle of the nuns contrast with the flamboyant life that Elvis led. This emphasises the differences between the choices they have made.
3) HUMOUR — The idea of a nun looking and acting like Elvis is pretty funny when you think about it. It adds a light-hearted touch to the poem.

Remember the Feelings and Attitudes in the Poem

1) CONTENTMENT — Elvis's sister is happy living her simple life.
2) HUMOUR — There's a light-hearted feel to the poem — the idea of a nun looking and acting like Elvis is quite comical.
3) SIMPLICITY — The poet could be suggesting that you'll be happier if you lead a simple life than if you go after fame and money.

Think About Your Feelings and Attitudes to the Poem

1) Pick 2 words or phrases that stand out to you. If none stand out, just pick 2 unusual words or phrases.
2) Write these 2 words or phrases down. Then write about how they make you feel. If they don't make you feel anything, don't worry — just make something up, as long as it's not too stupid.

EXAMPLE When Elvis's sister says "The Reverend Mother / digs the way I move my hips", it makes me laugh. The idea of a nun moving like Elvis is comical in itself, but by using the word "digs", Duffy makes it sound like the Reverend Mother is attracted to Elvis's sister just like a fan might be attracted to Elvis. This is funny because nuns are supposed to be well-behaved and more serious than that.

Themes — characters, the first person and imagery...

Compare 'Elvis's Twin Sister' with other poems about the same themes: strong characters ('Salome' p.42-43 and 'My Last Duchess' p.22-23), use of the first person ('My father thought it bloody queer' p.54-55 and 'The Song of the Old Mother' p.8-9) and imagery ('Kid' p.60-61 and 'Sonnet' p.34-35).

Key Poem

Anne Hathaway

Anne Hathaway

'Item I gyve unto my wife my second best bed ...'

(from Shakespeare's will)

The bed we loved in was a spinning world
of forests, castles, torchlight, clifftops, seas
where he would dive for pearls. My lover's words
were shooting stars which fell to earth as kisses
on these lips; my body now a softer rhyme
to his, now echo, assonance; his touch
a verb dancing in the centre of a noun.
Some nights, I dreamed he'd written me, the bed
a page beneath his writer's hands. Romance
and drama played by touch, by scent, by taste.
In the other bed, the best, our guests dozed on,
dribbling their prose. My living laughing love –
I hold him in the casket of my widow's head
as he held me upon that next best bed.

This is how she remembers it, rather than the "second best bed".

She feels that he took her to romantic, exciting places — it's like being in a fairytale.

Shows their love was rare and magical.

She feels they existed in his imagination — their life was a fantasy.

Other people speak in boring prose — not beautiful poetry like Shakespeare.

She felt safe and secure with him.

This seems ironic now — it doesn't feel second best to Anne.

Her experiences with Shakespeare were everything to her.

She sees their love as a hidden treasure.

Their bodies fit together, like a rhyming couplet.

He injected life and movement into her.

She feels like she's become part of a work of fiction.

Sounds ordinary and dull, contrasting with what happened in Anne's bed.

Alliteration.

His resting place is inside her head.

POEM DICTIONARY

prose — normal writing or speech (not poetry)

casket — coffin

Anne Hathaway

Key Poem

In this poem, Duffy writes as Shakespeare's wife, Anne Hathaway. Like many love poems written by Shakespeare himself, it's a sonnet — a kind of poem with 14 lines. The poem's about what went on in the "second best bed" that Shakespeare left Anne in his will.

You've Got to Know What Happens in the Poem

Lines 1-7 Anne describes her memories of the bed. She associates it with fond memories of her passionate love with Shakespeare. She compares his love to the words in his poems.

Lines 8-10 She seems to see their love as one of Shakespeare's plays.

Lines 11-14 Their guests' time in the better bed seems inferior to the love between Anne and Shakespeare. She says she'll always remember the love between them in that bed (lines 13-14).

Learn About the Two Types of Language

1) ROMANTIC LANGUAGE — There are some quite traditional romantic metaphors. This shows how precious and amazing Anne's time with Shakespeare was. Some of Anne's language reminds us of Shakespeare's own poetry, or speeches from his plays.

2) REFERENCES TO PLAYS AND POEMS — She compares the way Shakespeare loved her to his writing methods. Poetic techniques like rhyming and assonance are mentioned. Their love was so intense that it seemed poetic — Anne felt like she was in a play, rather than the real world.

Remember the Feelings and Attitudes in the Poem

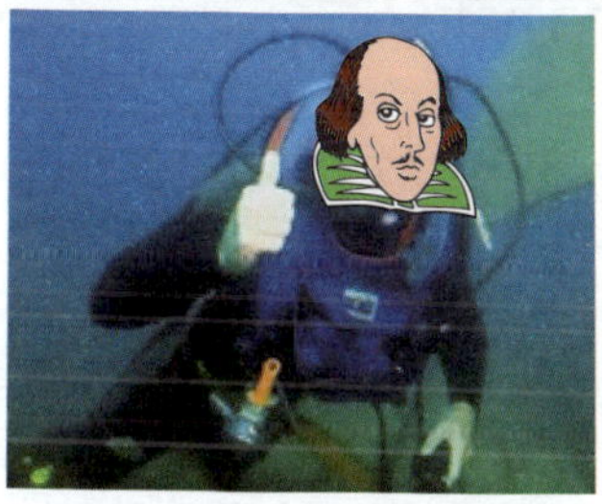

1) FONDNESS — Anne has fond memories of Shakespeare.
2) EXCITEMENT — She's excited just remembering what it was like being with him.
3) FANTASY — She feels like they were in their own world, where everything seemed magical, like a fantasy.

Think About Your Feelings and Attitudes to the Poem

1) Pick 2 words or phrases that stand out to you. If none stand out, just pick 2 unusual words or phrases.
2) Write these 2 words or phrases down. Then write about how they make you feel. If they don't make you feel anything, don't worry — just make something up, as long as it's not too stupid.

EXAMPLE I think it's really beautiful when Anne says "My lover's words / were shooting stars". It reminds me of how excited I feel when I read my boyfriend's love letters.

Themes — love, memory and closing couplets...

Compare 'Anne Hathaway' with other poems about the same themes: love ('Mother, any distance...' p.52-53 and 'On my first Sonne' p.6-7), memory ('We Remember Your Childhood Well' p.46-47 and 'My Last Duchess' p.22-23) and a closing couplet ('Sonnet 130' p.20-21).

Salome

Salome

I'd done it before
(and doubtless I'll do it again,
sooner or later)
woke up with a head on the pillow beside me – whose? –
what did it matter?
Good-looking, of course, dark hair, rather matted;
the reddish beard several shades lighter;
with very deep lines around the eyes,
from pain, I'd guess, maybe laughter;
and a beautiful crimson mouth that obviously knew
how to flatter ...
which I kissed ...
Colder than pewter.
Strange. What was his name? Peter?

Simon? Andrew? John? I knew I'd feel better
for tea, dry toast, no butter,
so rang for the maid.
And, indeed, her innocent clatter
of cups and plates,
her clearing of clutter,
her regional patter,
were just what needed –
hungover and wrecked as I was from a night on the batter.

Never again!
I needed to clean up my act,
get fitter,
cut out the booze and the fags and the sex.
Yes. And as for the latter,
it was time to turf out the blighter,
the beater or biter,
who'd come like a lamb to the slaughter
to Salome's bed.

In the mirror, I saw my eyes glitter.
I flung back the sticky red sheets,
and there, like I said – and ain't life a bitch –
was his head on a platter.

She's only slightly regretful — which is shocking when we realise what she's actually done.

Sounds like she's having a light-hearted chat with a friend.

The pain is more recent than we realise.

The coldness hints at what we find out later — he's dead.

Biblical names suggest the link with Salome.

Suggests she's well-off.

She complains about minor problems like being hungover, but doesn't seem bothered about the man she's killed.

Without knowing who he is, she assumes he's violent.

She makes her connection to Salome clear — we expect the worst now.

Black humour — she doesn't tell us that there isn't a body attached to the head.

At first we think this means his hair is thick or tangled — but it could actually be matted with blood.

Sounds natural and normal here — but the colouring is really from blood stains.

Rhyming, here and in other verses, makes her sound in control — she didn't do it by accident.

We think this means she's been drinking. But it turns out to have a more literal, violent meaning.

Common, everyday sayings suggest she's a normal person with normal problems.

Light-hearted expression.

Christian image of innocence which contrasts with the previous line — now he's the victim.

An evil look before she reveals the truth.

Sarcastically pretends to be bothered — she doesn't seem to really care about what she's done.

The poem finishes with a shocking revelation. But even here, her tone is calm.

POEM DICTIONARY

Salome — Biblical woman who tricked Herod into giving her the head of John the Baptist on a plate
crimson — a deep red colour
pewter — a kind of metal, made up mainly of tin
platter — a large dish for food

Salome

This poem's pretty grim. The woman in the poem wakes up after a one-night stand, after getting drunk the night before. She regrets it and says she needs to stop doing this sort of thing. Then it turns out she's cut the bloke's head off. Nice.

You've Got to Know What Happens in the Poem

Lines 1-14 — The character in the poem wakes up with a man's head on the pillow next to her. She can't remember who he is.

Lines 15-23 — She calls for her maid, who enters making loads of noise.

Lines 24-32 — She says she needs to cut out her unhealthy habits and get rid of the man in her bed.

Lines 33-36 — She pulls the sheets back, and we realise there's nothing there but his severed head.

Learn About the Three Types of Language

1) DOUBLE MEANINGS — Some of the language in the poem can be read in a different way after finding out that she's actually killed the man, rather than just sleeping with him. There's some black humour in the double meanings — they're both horrible and funny at the same time.
2) CASUAL LANGUAGE — The woman describes the incident as if it's just a normal event. Her casual tone is really shocking when we realise the full horror of what she'd done.
3) BIBLICAL REFERENCES — The poem is set in the modern day, but there are references to religious stories which connect what happens to the story of Salome.

Remember the Feelings and Attitudes in the Poem

"More blood, ma'am?"

1) CASUALNESS — At first, the woman seems vaguely regretful — but we soon start to realise that she's not all that bothered.
2) NASTINESS — We see her evil side at the end of the poem.
3) PRIDE — She even seems quite proud of killing the man — she seems to enjoy letting us think she's only slept with him, before dramatically revealing the truth at the end of the poem.

Think About Your Feelings and Attitudes to the Poem

1) Pick 2 words or phrases that stand out to you. If none stand out, just pick 2 unusual words or phrases.
2) Write these 2 words or phrases down. Then write about how they make you feel. If they don't make you feel anything, don't worry — just make something up, as long as it's not too stupid.

> **EXAMPLE** The line "I flung back the sticky red sheets" makes me feel sick. I find it disgusting that she could be lying there in a bed drenched in blood, talking calmly about chopping off a man's head.

Themes — evil, irony and characters...

Compare 'Salome' with other poems about the same themes: evil ('Hitcher' p.66-67 and 'The Last Duchess' p.22-23), irony ('Tichborne's Elegy' p.14-15 and 'The Man He Killed' p.16-17), and character ('Havisham' p.36-37 and 'The Laboratory' p.30-31).

Key Poem — Before You Were Mine

The first 3 verses each start with a reminder of the distance in time between the poet's birth and her mum's youth and fun.

The poet talks directly to her mum.

Before You Were Mine

I'm ten years away from the corner you laugh on
with your pals, Maggie McGeeney and Jean Duff.
The three of you bend from the waist, holding
each other, or your knees, and shriek at the pavement.
Your polka-dot dress blows round your legs. Marilyn.

I'm not here yet. The thought of me doesn't occur
in the ballroom with the thousand eyes, the fizzy, movie tomorrows
the right walk home could bring. I knew you would dance
like that. Before you were mine, your Ma stands at the close
with a hiding for the late one. You reckon it's worth it.

The decade ahead of my loud, possessive yell was the best one, eh?
I remember my hands in those high-heeled red shoes, relics,
and now your ghost clatters toward me over George Square
till I see you, clear as scent, under the tree,
with its lights, and whose small bites on your neck, sweetheart?

Cha cha cha! You'd teach me the steps on the way home from Mass,
stamping stars from the wrong pavement. Even then
I wanted the bold girl winking in Portobello, somewhere
in Scotland, before I was born. That glamorous love lasts
where you sparkle and waltz and laugh before you were mine.

Her mother's life was fun before she was born.

Compares her mother with Marilyn Monroe — she was glamorous and desirable.

There could be a hint of jealousy here.

Her mum was the centre of attention, with exciting opportunities.

She used to belong to herself, not someone else.

Her mum wasn't scared of the consequences of enjoying herself.

The poet was a demanding baby.

The glamour is a thing of the past, and won't return.

Sounds like something a parent would say to their child, but here it's the other way around.

Alliteration stresses her mum's defiance and energy.

Contrasts with "the right walk home" (line 8). Maybe she's made the wrong choice in life.

Repeating this emphasises the difference between then and now.

Emphasises that the poet's birth was the turning point in her mum's life.

She was bright, energetic and fun-loving.

As a child, the poet wanted what she couldn't have — her birth meant that her mum couldn't be a "bold girl" any more.

Before You Were Mine

Key Poem

The poet talks to her mother about the ten years before the poet's birth. She imagines her mum led a fun-filled, carefree life. But that all changed when she became a mother, and her child took her freedom away. The poet wants the happy, fun-loving girl, but realises she only exists in the past.

You've Got to Know What Happens in the Poem

Lines 1-5 The poet describes her mum having fun with friends. She compares her with Marilyn Monroe.

Lines 6-11 Her mum stayed out late dancing, not put off by being told off by her own mother. The poet says that her mother was happiest during the ten years before she was born.

Lines 12-15 The poet remembers glimpses of her mum's fun-loving past from when she was a child.

Lines 16-20 She remembers her mum teaching her to dance. She wanted her to be like this more often, but realises that she was only really fun-loving and glamorous before she was born.

Learn About the Three Types of Language

1) EXCITING LANGUAGE — There are loads of words and phrases which describe how exciting, fun and glamorous the poet's mum's life was before the poet was born.
2) POSSESSIVE LANGUAGE — It seems that when the poet was born, she took control of her mum, and her mum couldn't be free any more. The idea of breaking free from your parents is turned on its head, with the child stopping the parent from having fun.
3) LANGUAGE ABOUT TIME — There's a very clear division between the time before the poet was born and the time after she was born, when her mum's glamorous life came to an abrupt end.

Remember the Feelings and Attitudes in the Poem

Not to be confused with Marilyn Manson.

1) ADMIRATION — The poet admires her mum's headstrong, rebellious approach to life.
2) NOSTALGIA — She wishes her mum was still fun-loving and carefree.
3) SELF-CRITICISM — The poet seems to criticise herself for taking away her mum's freedom (line 11).

Think About Your Feelings and Attitudes to the Poem

1) Pick 2 words or phrases that stand out to you. If none stand out, just pick 2 unusual words or phrases.
2) Write these 2 words or phrases down. Then write about how they make you feel. If they don't make you feel anything, don't worry — just make something up, as long as it's not too stupid.

EXAMPLE When the poet says "I wanted the bold girl winking in Portobello", it makes me sad. She seems to admire the happy, rebellious side of her mother more than the responsible parent side, but the poet knows that she is the very reason for the change in her mother's lifestyle.

Themes — parent/child, getting older, imagery...

Compare 'Before You Were Mine' with other poems about the same themes: parent/child relationships ('My father thought it bloody queer' p.54-55), getting older ('Mother, any distance' p.52-53) and imagery ('Homecoming' p.56-57 and 'Kid' p.60-61).

We Remember Your Childhood Well

The poem starts on a defensive note. We know they wouldn't say this if there hadn't been an accusation.

The memories are entirely negative.

We Remember Your Childhood Well

Nobody hurt you. Nobody turned off the light and argued
with somebody else all night. The bad man on the moors
was only a movie you saw. Nobody locked the door.

Your questions were answered fully. No. That didn't occur.
You couldn't sing anyway, cared less. The moment's a blur, a *Film Fun*
laughing itself to death in the coal fire. Anyone's guess.

Nobody forced you. You wanted to go that day. Begged. You chose
the dress. Here are the pictures, look at you. Look at us all,
smiling and waving, younger. The whole thing is inside your head.

What you recall are impressions; we have the facts. We called the tune.
The secret police of your childhood were older and wiser than you, bigger
than you. Call back the sound of their voices. Boom. Boom. Boom.

Nobody sent you away. That was an extra holiday, with people
you seemed to like. They were firm, there was nothing to fear.
There was none but yourself to blame if it ended in tears.

What does it matter now? No, no, nobody left the skidmarks of sin
on your soul and laid you wide open for Hell. You were loved.
Always. We did what was best. We remember your childhood well.

This refers to the child murders on the Lancashire moors in the 1960s.

Suggests the person was trapped.

They make it as vague as possible, to try to confuse the person and cover up the truth.

They say that it was the child's choice. This seems unlikely as they don't let that person get a word in now.

They use images of happiness to cover up the painful truth.

At least they're honest here — they were in charge.

Sounds sinister and controlling.

The voices were loud and angry.

They even tell the person what their own feelings and opinions were.

The denials now sound very forceful.

Suggests the pain of the person's childhood still affects him/her now.

They shift all the guilt and responsibility onto the child.

The person feels that what happened in their childhood ruined the rest of their life.

They insist that their version of events is more accurate than the person whose childhood is being discussed.

POEM DICTIONARY
Film Fun — a magazine about films

We Remember Your Childhood Well

In this poem, the people speaking deny that anything bad happened in someone's childhood (possibly their son or daughter). The child seems to have claimed he or she was abused, but we never hear that side of the story, so we can only guess what happened from what the people denying it say.

You've Got to Know What Happens in the Poem

Lines 1-3	The people speaking deny the claim that the person they're speaking to was abused as a child.
Lines 4-6	There are more denials. They say the child was never really bothered about singing.
Lines 7-9	They deny forcing the child to go somewhere. They say the child wanted to go, and enjoyed it.
Lines 10-12	Aggressively, they say that they're the only ones who can remember what really happened.
Lines 13-18	They again deny sending the child away. They tell the child that it was his/her own fault if anything bad happened. They claim they treated the child well.

Learn About the Three Types of Language

1) DENIAL — We don't hear the accusations, but the denials give us clues as to what they are. There's a defensive tone right from the start — we can tell the people speaking are covering something up.
2) AGGRESSION — The tone becomes more threatening as the poem goes on. The people speaking find it more and more difficult to pretend to be pleasant, and in the end resort to threats and guilt trips.
3) PAIN and FEAR — The childhood memories are confused and scary. The fact that we don't find out exactly what happened increases the sense of fear in the poem. Past events seem to have caused lasting pain to the person, even after growing up.

Remember the Feelings and Attitudes in the Poem

1) CRUELTY — There's a cruel, sinister feel to the poem.
2) SUSPICION — We suspect that bad things happened to the child, but the people speaking are trying to cover up the truth.
3) GUILT — They even try to make the victim feel that what happened was his/her fault.
4) PAIN — There's a real sense of pain and sadness — it seems that the person's life has been ruined by the events in his/her childhood (lines 16-17).

Think About Your Feelings and Attitudes to the Poem

1) Pick 2 words or phrases that stand out to you. If none stand out, just pick 2 unusual words or phrases.
2) Write these 2 words or phrases down. Then write about how they make you feel. If they don't make you feel anything, don't worry — just make something up, as long as it's not too stupid.

> **EXAMPLE** When the people in the poem say "There was none but yourself to blame if it ended in tears", I feel angry. Trying to make someone feel guilty for something that happened when they were a child is an extremely cruel thing to do.

Themes — mood, attitudes towards others, memory...

Compare 'We Remember Your Childhood Well' to other poems about the same themes: mood ('Hitcher' p.66-67, 'The Little Boy Lost' and 'The Little Boy Found' p.12-13), attitudes towards other people ('My Last Duchess' p.22-23) and memory ('Homecoming' p.56-57).

Education for Leisure

Note: This poem won't be named in any questions in the June 2009 exam.
You can write about it if the question asks you to use a poem by Carol Ann Duffy, but doesn't say which one.
It won't be in the anthology after the June 2009 exam.

Education for Leisure

Today I am going to kill something. Anything.
I have had enough of being ignored and today
I am going to play God. It is an ordinary day,
a sort of grey with boredom stirring in the streets.

I squash a fly against the window with my thumb.
We did that at school. Shakespeare. It was in
another language and now the fly is in another language.
I breathe out talent on the glass to write my name.

I am a genius. I could be anything at all, with half
the chance. But today I am going to change the world.
Something's world. The cat avoids me. The cat
knows I am a genius, and has hidden itself.

I pour the goldfish down the bog. I pull the chain.
I see that it is good. The budgie is panicking.
Once a fortnight, I walk the two miles into town
for signing on. They don't appreciate my autograph.

There is nothing left to kill. I dial the radio
and tell the man he's talking to a superstar.
He cuts me off. I get our bread-knife and go out.
The pavements glitter suddenly. I touch your arm.

He/she is motivated by the need for attention.

Wants to be grand and powerful.

Not a very impressive achievement.

He/she breathes on the mirror. He/she thinks even this shows talent.

Very arrogant. There's nothing to back this claim up.

He/she blames others for their own failures.

Pathetic and darkly humorous attempt at being powerful.

Sounds Biblical — trying to live up to the intention of playing God.

Sounds disappointed.

More rejection. "Cuts" seems to give the character the idea of getting the knife.

Excitement contrasts with line 4.

Matter-of-fact tone is chilling.

Alliteration adds to the irritable feeling.

He/she felt excluded because they couldn't understand it.

Another boast — but it seems he/she hasn't achieved anything.

This ambitious claim contrasts with what he/she actually does.

Scaring the pets is a comically poor attempt at being powerful.

The character thinks he/she deserves to be recognised.

Suggests the character is famous and popular, but we know this isn't true.

Purposeful, violent tone.

Now he/she threatens the reader.

POEM DICTIONARY
signing on — registering for unemployment benefit

Education for Leisure

The person in this poem is a bit disturbed. Fed up of feeling bored and ignored, he/she goes on a killing spree, starting with animals. Then they go outside with a knife, presumably to kill people, although we don't find out exactly what happens then. I just read a book when I'm bored...

You've Got to Know What Happens in the Poem

Lines 1-4 The character in the poem is bored and restless, so he/she decides to kill something.

Lines 5-7 The character kills a fly, which makes him/her think about how he/she felt excluded at school.

Lines 8-14 The character claims to be a genius and is determined to prove it.
He/she enjoys the power of killing the pets in the house.

Lines 15-20 The character is annoyed that no-one recognises or respects him/her.
He/she gets a knife and goes outside.

Learn About the Three Types of Language

1) VIOLENT LANGUAGE — The person in the poem kills everything they can find in the house, then goes outside to continue the killing spree. The really shocking thing about the violence is the character's calm tone — as if he/she is describing normal and reasonable behaviour.
2) BOASTFUL LANGUAGE — The character seems really arrogant. Loads of the sentences begin with "I", showing how self-obsessed the character is.
3) LANGUAGE OF REJECTION — The character feels rejected and excluded. He/she wants to be well-known instead of ignored, and the mindless violence is his/her way of trying to be recognised.

Remember the Feelings and Attitudes in the Poem

"Uh-oh..."

1) RESENTMENT — The character resents the way people ignore him/her.
2) GRIM DETERMINATION — He/she is determined to make their mark on the world, by showing how powerful he/she is.
3) CALMNESS — He/she is very laid back about all the killing.
4) ENJOYMENT — He/she enjoys the sense of power they get from killing.

Clearly the character has lost the plot — he/she thinks killing the fish is a sign of genius, and seems ready to kill anyone just to get attention.

Think About Your Feelings and Attitudes to the Poem

1) Pick 2 words or phrases that stand out to you. If none stand out, just pick 2 unusual words or phrases.
2) Write these 2 words or phrases down. Then write about how they make you feel. If they don't make you feel anything, don't worry — just make something up, as long as it's not too stupid.

EXAMPLE When the person in the poem says "I touch your arm", it sends a chill down my spine. At this point it seems that, now he/she has run out of animals to kill, he/she will kill anyone they find, starting with the reader.

Themes — danger, death, the first person...

Compare 'Education for Leisure' with other poems about the same themes: danger ('Stealing' p.50-51 and 'Those bastards in their mansions' p.62-63), death ('Hitcher' p.66-67 and 'The Man He Killed' p.16-17) and use of the first person ('Kid' p.60-61 and 'The Laboratory' p.30-31).

Key Poem

Stealing

Note: This is only a key poem for exams from 2010 onwards.

Stealing

The most unusual thing I ever stole? A snowman.
Midnight. He looked magnificent; a tall, white mute
beneath the winter moon. I wanted him, a mate
with a mind as cold as the slice of ice
within my own brain. I started with the head.

Better off dead than giving in, not taking
what you want. He weighed a ton; his torso,
frozen stiff, hugged to my chest, a fierce chill
piercing my gut. Part of the thrill was knowing
that children would cry in the morning. Life's tough.

Sometimes I steal things I don't need. I joy-ride cars
to nowhere, break into houses just to have a look.
I'm a mucky ghost, leave a mess, maybe pinch a camera.
I watch my gloved hand twisting the doorknob.
A stranger's bedroom. Mirrors. I sigh like this – *Aah.*

It took some time. Reassembled in the yard,
he didn't look the same. I took a run
and booted him. Again. Again. My breath ripped out
in rags. It seems daft now. Then I was standing
alone amongst lumps of snow, sick of the world.

Boredom. Mostly I'm so bored I could eat myself.
One time, I stole a guitar and thought I might
learn to play. I nicked a bust of Shakespeare once,
flogged it, but the snowman was strangest.
You don't understand a word I'm saying, do you?

Alliteration creates a sense that the character feels passionate about the snowman.

Suggests he/she feels emotionally frozen.

The split rhyme emphasises excitement as well as the sharp coldness.

This metaphor suggests the narrator spoils things, and also that he/she feels dead like a ghost.

Realises how pointless and silly it sounds.

More slang words.

Realises that he/she isn't making any sense.

It sounds like the character in the poem is responding to a question the reader has asked.

The snowman is unable to communicate, like the character in the poem.

Rhyming makes these 2 words seem connected, suggesting the narrator's dead emotions.

Seems to be boasting here.

Offhand comment — doesn't care about the effects on other people.

Use of slang shows the character's casual approach to theft.

Sounds both threatening and forlorn — the character's life is lonely and unreal.

The character's actions have a violent and destructive result on his/her own body.

Self-destructive and pointless.

POEM DICTIONARY
reassembled — put back together
bust — a statue of someone's head and shoulders

Stealing

Key Poem

The rather strange character in the poem remembers stealing a snowman. Then he/she describes stealing lots of other things because he/she was bored. The dirty tea-leaf.

You've Got to Know What Happens in the Poem

Lines 1-10 — The character in the poem remembers stealing a snowman at night, bit by bit. This seems to have been for company, and also to make the children who made it cry.

Lines 11-15 — The character describes stealing cars, cameras and other things — and getting a thrill from it.

Lines 16-20 — The character couldn't put the snowman back together properly — so he/she destroyed it.

Lines 21-25 — The character says he/she steals because of boredom, but can't seem to explain it properly.

Learn About the Three Types of Language

1) CONVERSATIONAL LANGUAGE — It feels like the character is talking directly to us. His/her chatty tone of voice shows how casual he/she is about stealing.
2) SIMILES and METAPHORS — There's also some quite descriptive language, which contrasts with the normally down-to-earth tone. It's as if his/her real feelings are struggling to come out.
3) SOUND EFFECTS — The irregular rhymes, sometimes between words on the same line, and alliteration draw the reader's attention to certain combinations of words.

Remember the Feelings and Attitudes in the Poem

1) ENTHUSIASM — At the start of the poem, the thief is enthusiastic about explaining why he/she steals things.
2) BOREDOM — By the end, loneliness and boredom take over.
3) FRUSTRATION — He/she is frustrated and angry when destroying the snowman.
4) FUTILITY — At the end, he/she feels the whole attempt to explain it is futile.

Think About Your Feelings and Attitudes to the Poem

1) Pick 2 words or phrases that stand out to you. If none stand out, just pick 2 unusual words or phrases.
2) Write these 2 words or phrases down. Then write about how they make you feel. If they don't make you feel anything, don't worry — just make something up, as long as it's not too stupid.

EXAMPLE The statement "better off dead than giving in, not taking / what you want" makes me angry with the person in the poem. He/she is trying to come across as bold and decisive, but this sentence really shows how selfish the character is, not thinking about anyone but him/herself.

Themes — attitudes towards others, danger, language...

Compare 'Stealing' with other poems about the same themes: attitudes towards others ('November' p.58-59 and 'Hitcher' p.66-67), danger ('Education for Leisure' p.48-49 and 'Those bastards in their mansions' p.62-63) and language effects ('The Laboratory' p.30-31 and 'Kid' p.60-61).

Key Poem

Mother, any distance

Simon Armitage was born in 1963 in Huddersfield, West Yorkshire. As well as poetry, he's also written four stage plays, and writes for TV, film and radio. He studied at Leeds University and he now teaches at Manchester Metropolitan University.

from **Book of Matches**

Mother, any distance greater than a single span
requires a second pair of hands.
You come to help me measure windows, pelmets, doors,
the acres of the walls, the prairies of the floors.

You at the zero-end, me with the spool of tape, recording
length, reporting metres, centimetres back to base, then leaving
up the stairs, the line still feeding out, unreeling
years between us. Anchor. Kite.

I space-walk through the empty bedrooms, climb
the ladder to the loft, to breaking point, where something
has to give;
two floors below your fingertips still pinch
the last one-hundredth of an inch ... I reach
towards a hatch that opens on an endless sky
to fall or fly.

He addresses her directly. It's like a personal message to her.

Double meaning — a "span" is a measurement, but it could also mean "life-span".

Holding the start of the tape measure could stand for her thinking back to when he was born.

Without his mother, even the walls and floors seem daunting.

He moves upwards and away from his mother.

They have to let go of their shared history.

He feels free to fly away. His mother will keep him from getting carried away.

Being on his own is like an adventure on a different planet.

They have to sever their ties at some point.

She's now only a small part of his life.

She won't let go completely.

He feels there's no limit to the opportunities open to him. They can't be measured like the walls.

Suggests he's "flying the nest". He doesn't know if he'll succeed or fail.

POEM DICTIONARY
pelmets — boards or material above a window which hide the curtain rail

Mother, any distance

Key Poem

In this poem, the poet is moving out of his mum's house. But he still needs her to help measure things in his new house, and this becomes a metaphor for how he can always turn to her for support if he needs to. Like when his laundry needs doing, probably...

You've Got to Know What Happens in the Poem

Lines 1-4 — The poet's mother comes to the house he's moving into, to help measure walls and other things.

Lines 5-8 — She holds the end of the tape measure while he walks away to measure things. This makes him think about how she's always looked after him — but now she has to let him go.

Lines 9-15 — The poet is looking forward to being independent, but he's also a bit scared by it. He doesn't know if he'll succeed without his mum or not, but she'll always be there for him if he needs her.

Learn About the Two Types of Language

1) LANGUAGE ABOUT MEASUREMENT — Measurements and distances are an extended metaphor in this poem. They represent the poet's changing relationship with his mother. They were once close, but they are now becoming more distant.
2) LANGUAGE ABOUT MOVEMENT — Walking around his own house is like exploring a new world. He feels ready to "fly" away from his mum (lines 13-15), but she seems ready to catch him when he falls (lines 12-13).

Remember the Feelings and Attitudes in the Poem

1) EXCITEMENT — The poet is excited about being independent in his new life.
2) FEAR — He's also worried by the thought of being on his own.
3) ACCEPTANCE — He accepts that his mother will always be a part of his life.
4) APPRECIATION — He seems to appreciate that he can turn to her if he needs her.

Think About Your Feelings and Attitudes to the Poem

1) Pick 2 words or phrases that stand out to you. If none stand out, just pick 2 unusual words or phrases.
2) Write these 2 words or phrases down. Then write about how they make you feel. If they don't make you feel anything, don't worry — just make something up, as long as it's not too stupid.

EXAMPLE When the poet says "I space-walk through the empty bedrooms", I feel both excited and nervous for him. This line shows that breaking free from his mother is a big adventure for him, but also that he is now on his own in the big wide world.

Themes — parent/child relationships, getting older, imagery

Compare 'Mother, any distance...' with other poems about the same themes: parent/child relationships ('Before You Were Mine' p.44-45 and 'The Affliction of Margaret' p.10-11), getting older ('Kid' p.60-61) and imagery ('Anne Hathaway' p.40-41 and 'I've made out a will' p.64-65).

My father thought it bloody queer

from Book of Matches

My father thought it bloody queer,
the day I rolled home with a ring of silver in my ear
half hidden by a mop of hair. 'You've lost your head.
If that's how easily you're led
you should've had it through your nose instead.'

And even then I hadn't had the nerve to numb
the lobe with ice, then drive a needle through the skin,
then wear a safety-pin. It took a jeweller's gun
to pierce the flesh, and then a friend
to thread a sleeper in, and where it slept
the hole became a sore, became a wound, and wept.

At twenty-nine, it comes as no surprise to hear
my own voice breaking like a tear, released like water,
cried from way back in the spiral of the ear. *If I were you,*
I'd take it out and leave it out next year.

The word "queer" could mean "odd" — but it could also mean his dad thinks the earring looks gay.

Could suggest he was drunk when he got his ear pierced.

His scruffy hair-do shows he's trying to be a rebel.

Bulls are led around by a nose-ring — his dad says he got the earring because his mates told him to get one.

Could mean either "You've gone mad" or "I can't even see your head any more."

As well as not having the courage to do it, the word "nerve" suggests he couldn't take the pain.

Sounds violent and painful.

This shows that it bled, and also suggests it made him cry with the pain — not very rebellious.

He's just inflicted an unnecessary injury on himself.

Remembering his dad's reaction upsets him.

He remembers his voice breaking as a teenager. It's also breaking now, with emotion.

This is a common saying, but here it has a more literal meaning — in a way he has become his father.

It's not entirely clear who he's talking to here. But by saying the same things as his dad, it seems the poet has come to see things the same way his dad did.

This description suggests his emotions being bottled up, then suddenly flooding out.

POEM DICTIONARY
sleeper — a stud to stop a pierced ear from closing up

My father thought it bloody queer

The poet describes a time when he was a teenager and got his ear pierced. His dad wasn't impressed, and his attempt to be a rebel seemed a bit stupid. Now he's grown up, he hears himself saying the same things his dad said. Now where's my pipe...

You've Got to Know What Happens in the Poem

Lines 1-5	The poet remembers coming home after getting his ear pierced. His dad took the mickey out of him and said it was stupid.
Lines 6-11	The poet says that he didn't have the courage to pierce his own ear, so he got a jeweller to do it. Afterwards, his ear went all sore and bled. Awww...
Lines 12-15	Now the poet's grown up, his dad's comments still upset him. He says the same things his dad used to say.

Learn About the Three Types of Language

1) DESCRIPTIVE LANGUAGE — The poet's scruffy appearance when he comes home with the earring shows that he's a typical teenager. This makes him seem predictable and conventional — not rebellious as he thought at the time.
2) AMBIGUOUS LANGUAGE — A lot of the words and phrases in this poem are ambiguous — they look like they have one meaning, then when you read them again they mean something else.
3) PAINFUL LANGUAGE — The poet describes two kinds of pain — physical pain from having his ear pierced, and emotional pain when he remembers his dad's reaction and how stupid he felt.

Remember the Feelings and Attitudes in the Poem

"Father, I want to be a doctor."

1) AMUSEMENT — The poet's descriptions of his funny appearance suggest he's amused when he remembers the incident.
2) REGRET — But he's upset and regretful when he remembers how stupid he felt after his dad's comments about the earring.
3) AGREEMENT — At the end of the poem, he seems to have come round to his dad's point of view — he now says the same kind of things to kids that his dad said to him.

Think About Your Feelings and Attitudes to the Poem

1) Pick 2 words or phrases that stand out to you. If none stand out, just pick 2 unusual words or phrases.
2) Write these 2 words or phrases down. Then write about how they make you feel. If they don't make you feel anything, don't worry — just make something up, as long as it's not too stupid.

> **EXAMPLE** When the poet says "It took a jeweller's gun / to pierce the flesh", it makes me wince with pain. It sounds like a horrible and pointless thing to put yourself through, just to try and look cool.

Themes — parent/child relationships, getting older, memory

Compare 'My father thought it...' with other poems about the same themes: parent/child relationships ('Before You Were Mine' p.44-45 and 'On my first Sonne' p.6-7), getting older ('Kid' p.60-61 and 'Mother, any distance...' p.52-53) and memory ('We Remember Your Childhood Well' p.46-47).

Key Poem

Homecoming

Homecoming

This applies to the whole poem — the poet wants to make you think.

This suggests the trust exercise and the jacket are related in some way.

These words suggest a lack of control.

Think, two things on their own and both at once.
The first, that exercise in trust, where those in front
stand with their arms spread wide and free-fall
backwards, blind, and those behind take all the weight.

The jacket seems vivid and colourful — unlike the darkness and uncertainty of most of the memories in the poem.

He's saying the mother's perfect, but this could be sarcastic.

This usually means just to have a good go at doing something, but the following lines make it sound more violent.

Colloquial — this sounds like someone talking.

The second, one canary-yellow cotton jacket
on a cloakroom floor, uncoupled from its hook,
becoming scuffed and blackened underfoot. Back home
the very model of a model of a mother, yours, puts
two and two together, makes a proper fist of it
and points the finger. Temper, temper. Questions
in the house. You seeing red. Blue murder. Bed.

Here, colours represent strong words and emotions.

This gives us a clue — it seems that the poet is talking to someone about something that happened before they met.

Mysterious image. You can't make out any features of this person.

Usually this would sound protective, but the darkness makes us uncertain.

This could be well-meaning or threatening.

Then midnight when you slip the latch and sneak
no further than the call-box at the corner of the street;
I'm waiting by the phone, although it doesn't ring
because it's sixteen years or so before we'll meet.
Retrace that walk towards the garden gate; in silhouette
a father figure waits there, wants to set things straight.

We don't know if these are his arms and ribs, or those of the person he's talking to.

You have to make your own interpretation here, like in the poem as a whole.

This reminds us of the trust exercise at the start.

These ribs are pleats or seams. These arms are sleeves.
These fingertips are buttons, or these hands can fold
into a clasp, or else these fingers make a zip
or buckle, you say which. Step backwards into it
and try the same canary-yellow cotton jacket, there,
like this, for size again. It still fits.

This could mean that the person hasn't changed.

POEM DICTIONARY
silhouette — a dark, shadowy figure

Homecoming

Key Poem

This is a pretty confusing poem because it's not very clear exactly what's happening. There are some hazy memories of people sneaking about and getting told off. A yellow jacket is described, which seems to be a metaphor for people changing over time.

You've Got to Know What Happens in the Poem

Lines 1-4 The poet describes an exercise where people learn to trust someone.

Lines 5-11 A yellow jacket lies on the floor somewhere getting trampled on. Then someone, probably a young woman, gets told off by their mum for doing something wrong.

Lines 12-17 The same person sneaks off again, this time to a phone box. A dark figure waits by a gate.

Lines 18-23 The different parts of the yellow jacket are described as if they're parts of someone's body. It seems that the person hasn't changed much, because the jacket still fits.

Learn About the Three Types of Language

1) AMBIGUOUS LANGUAGE — Lots of the images and description in the poem are ambiguous — we're not sure what they mean. This is often deliberate — it's supposed to make us stop and think about what the poet means.
2) COLOUR — Most of the images in the poem are dark and shadowy, reinforcing the vague and uncertain nature of the poem. The bright yellow colour of the jacket stands out.
3) METAPHORICAL LANGUAGE — The yellow jacket becomes a metaphor, possibly for behaviour or personality. The jacket still fits, so maybe the person the poet is talking to hasn't changed much.

Remember the Feelings and Attitudes in the Poem

"Err, hello, police? I'm being stalked by a poet..."

1) ANGER — The mother (lines 8-10) is very angry with her child.
2) TENSION — We don't know how the "father figure" is going to "set things straight" (line 17).
3) UNCERTAINTY — The poet wants us to make our own minds up about what the jacket stands for. We have to make the connections between the different things he describes.

Don't worry if you find this poem really confusing. You don't have to completely understand it — as long as you can make some interesting points about it.

Think About Your Feelings and Attitudes to the Poem

1) Pick 2 words or phrases that stand out to you. If none stand out, just pick 2 unusual words or phrases.
2) Write these 2 words or phrases down. Then write about how they make you feel. If they don't make you feel anything, don't worry — just make something up, as long as it's not too stupid.

EXAMPLE The line "a father figure waits there, wants to set things straight", makes me worry about the safety of the person in the poem. The way this person has to sneak around suggests he or she is afraid of someone, making the father figure's intentions sound menacing and dangerous.

Themes — memory, imagery and mood...

Compare 'Homecoming' with other poems about the same themes: memory ('Before You Were Mine' p.44-45 and 'We Remember Your Childhood Well' p.46-47), imagery ('Havisham' p.36-37 and 'Tichborne's Elegy' p.14-15) and mood ('Elvis's Twin Sister' p.38-39).

November

The year moves to its end, like the old people's lives.

Blunt statement that they can't ignore the sad truth of what's happening.

Double meaning — "it's the right time", and also "time has done this to these people".

Their whole bodies have stopped working properly.

John's physically and emotionally broken by the experience.

The darkness and run-down buildings surround them.

Inside and outside their minds, as well as the normal meanings.

There's only a brief flicker of light.

November

We walk to the ward from the badly parked car
with your grandma taking four short steps to our two.
We have brought her here to die and we know it.

You check her towel, soap and family trinkets,
pare her nails, parcel her in the rough blankets
and she sinks down into her incontinence.

It is time John. In their pasty bloodless smiles,
in their slack breasts, their stunned brains and their baldness,
and in us John: we are almost these monsters.

You're shattered. You give me the keys and I drive
through the twilight zone, past the famous station
to your house, to numb ourselves with alcohol.

Inside, we feel the terror of the dusk begin.
Outside we watch the evening, failing again,
and we let it happen. We can say nothing.

Sometimes the sun spangles and we feel alive.
One thing we have to get, John, out of this life.

Hints at the distress that the poet and John are feeling.

Uneven rhythm echoes her tiny steps.

They're "wrapping up" her life.

Strong image of her physical helplessness.

They will end up like this too. The matter-of-fact tone contrasts with the shocking word "monsters".

The fading light represents the knowledge that they too are getting older.

They're helpless to stop the ageing process and death.

Tries to take something positive out of the day's events.

POEM DICTIONARY

pare — trim

incontinence — not being able to control bodily functions, like going to the toilet

twilight — fading light after sunset

twilight zone — a run-down industrial area

November

The poet writes about taking the grandmother of a person called John to live in a nursing home. The poet and John both know she won't be coming out again. The poet writes as if he's talking to John, and describes their sad thoughts on the journey back.

You've Got to Know What Happens in the Poem

Lines 1-6 The poet and John help John's grandma settle in at the home. She seems weak and helpless.

Lines 7-9 Other old people in the home are described. They are pale and seemingly lifeless.

Lines 10-15 The poet and John go home. They feel really depressed, watching the night draw in.

Lines 16-17 The poet says that we should make the most of the chances we get to live.

Learn About the Three Types of Language

1) DECAY — There are lots of images of things breaking down, e.g. the health of the old people. The title of the poem suggests the approaching cold weather, and reinforces the idea that the old people are in the autumn years of their lives.
2) INEVITABILITY — The poem is written in the present tense, as if it's happening now. This emphasises that growing old and dying is inescapable and inevitable — it's bound to happen eventually.
3) DARKNESS — The daylight fades away during the poem, suggesting the gradual approach of death. The gloomy setting also represents the poet's and John's depressed thoughts.

Remember the Feelings and Attitudes in the Poem

1) HORROR — The poet is horrified by the state of the old people.
2) FEAR — He's depressed and frightened by the thought of the same thing happening to him and everyone else (line 13).
3) HELPLESSNESS — He feels helpless to prevent an equally horrible end to his own life (line 15).

The poet and John are emotionally exhausted at the end of the poem — they have to "numb" their pain with drink.

Think About Your Feelings and Attitudes to the Poem

1) Pick 2 words or phrases that stand out to you. If none stand out, just pick 2 unusual words or phrases.
2) Write these 2 words or phrases down. Then write about how they make you feel. If they don't make you feel anything, don't worry — just make something up, as long as it's not too stupid.

EXAMPLE I find the poet's comment, "we are almost these monsters", very shocking. Describing old people as "monsters" makes them sound totally inhuman and disgusting. Also the fact that he is "almost" like them suggests the poet will inevitably end up the same way.

Themes — death, attitudes to others, strong emotions...

Compare 'November' to other poems on the same themes: death ('Tichborne's Elegy' p.14-15 and 'Ulysses' p.26-27), attitudes towards other people ('Salome' p.42-43 and 'The Man He Killed' p.16-17) and strong emotions ('Havisham' p.36-37 and 'On my first Sonne' p.6-7).

Key Poem

Kid

Title suggests Batman and Robin could stand for a father and his son.

Alliteration emphasises sarcasm and contempt.

His tone is bitter when he describes how he was deserted.

The cliché of "letting the cat out of the bag" is changed slightly.

Combines the phrases "playing ball" and "ball boy" to stress how he used to do whatever Batman wanted.

Rhyme and rhythm make these words reflect his new strength and energy.

Imagines Batman eating basic, disgusting food on his own.

Robin enjoys patronising Batman.

Kid

Batman, big shot, when you gave the order
to grow up, then let me loose to wander
leeward, freely through the wild blue yonder
as you liked to say, or ditched me, rather,
in the gutter ... well, I turned the corner.
Now I've scotched that 'he was like a father
to me' rumour, sacked it, blown the cover
on that 'he was like an elder brother'
story, let the cat out on that caper
with the married woman, how you took her
downtown on expenses in the motor.
Holy robin-redbreast-nest-egg-shocker!
Holy roll-me-over-in-the-clover,
I'm not playing ball boy any longer
Batman, now I've doffed that off-the-shoulder
Sherwood-Forest-green and scarlet number
for a pair of jeans and crew-neck jumper;
now I'm taller, harder, stronger, older.
Batman, it makes a marvellous picture:
you without a shadow, stewing over
chicken giblets in the pressure cooker,
next to nothing in the walk-in larder,
punching the palm of your hand all winter,
you baby, now I'm the real boy wonder.

Batman claimed he was giving Robin his freedom.

Robin felt scared and alone.

First sign that he's beginning to take control.

Batman was supposed to catch criminals, but these phrases make it sound like he's the criminal.

These lines combine Robin's "holy" catchphrase with tabloid-headline style scandals.

Normal clothes show he's grown up and he's living in the real world now.

Robin was always inferior — but without him, Batman's alone.

Gloats about Batman's loneliness and frustration.

Robin was always called the "boy wonder", but now it has new meaning — Robin's in charge now.

POEM DICTIONARY

leeward — towards the wind
scotched — put an end to
caper — a crime in a comic or film
on expenses — paid for by work
doffed — got rid of
giblets — the guts and insides of a chicken

Kid

Key Poem

This poem uses the superhero Batman and his sidekick Robin to stand for a young person who's been deserted by the person who was supposed to look after him. Now "Robin" is taking revenge, by showing that "Batman" wasn't such a hero after all. Holy poetry anthology!

You've Got to Know What Happens in the Poem

Lines 1-5 — Robin (the narrator) is angry that Batman left him to fend for himself when he wasn't ready. But now Robin's taking control of his life.

Lines 6-13 — Robin takes pleasure in revealing what Batman was really like. He wasn't a father figure to Robin as people had thought — he was taking out a married woman and claiming the money back from work.

Lines 14-18 — Robin says he's not going to be Batman's sidekick any more. He's grown up, got rid of his silly costume and got some proper clothes.

Lines 19-24 — Robin imagines Batman falling on hard times, and gloats when he pictures him struggling.

Learn About the Three Types of Language

1) LANGUAGE ABOUT LONELINESS — At first Robin describes his own loneliness, but by the end of the poem it's Batman who's on his own, in Robin's imagination at least.
2) CLICHÉS — There are a lot of commonly-used phrases and clichés, but they often merge together or end in an unexpected way. A lot of these phrases come from the Batman comics.
3) BITTERNESS and SARCASM — Robin's bitter and annoyed that everyone thinks Batman was so great. This is what makes him determined to get revenge by revealing the truth about him.

Remember the Feelings and Attitudes in the Poem

"I'm a bat, man."

1) ANGER — Robin is angry and bitter that Batman deserted him.
2) DEFIANCE — But he feels more confident now — he's defiant when he says he's "turned the corner".
3) PRIDE — Robin's proud of his new-found independence.
4) PLEASURE — He enjoys dishing the dirt on Batman, and takes pleasure from the idea of Batman being sad and alone.

Think About Your Feelings and Attitudes to the Poem

1) Pick 2 words or phrases that stand out to you. If none stand out, just pick 2 unusual words or phrases.
2) Write these 2 words or phrases down. Then write about how they make you feel. If they don't make you feel anything, don't worry — just make something up, as long as it's not too stupid.

EXAMPLE When the Robin character says "I'm not playing ball boy any longer", I admire his determination. He feels very badly treated by "Batman", but instead of wallowing in self-pity, he has done something about it. I think that shows a lot of courage and self-belief.

Themes — getting older, memory and characters...

Compare 'Kid' with other poems about the same themes: getting older ('My father thought it...' p.54-55 and 'Mother, any distance...' p.52-53), memory ('Before You Were Mine' p.44-45 and 'My Last Duchess' p.22-23) and characters ('The Village Schoolmaster' p.28-29).

Those bastards in their mansions

He's totally open about his hatred for rich people.

Makes them sound whingeing and pathetic.

They think he's sneaky.

He imagines breaking into their homes.

He sees revolution as dramatic and heroic — he seems to think it's a pretty good idea.

The upper class seem very distant and different to him.

They want to contain and suppress him, to avoid a revolution.

This sounds sinister, like he's waiting for his opportunity.

from **Book of Matches**

Those bastards in their mansions:
to hear them shriek, you'd think
I'd poisoned the dogs and vaulted the ditches,
crossed the lawns in stocking feet and threadbare britches,
forced the door of one of the porches, and lifted
the gift of fire from the burning torches,

then given heat and light to streets and houses,
told the people how to ditch their cuffs and shackles,
armed them with the iron from their wrists and ankles.

Those lords and ladies in their palaces and castles,
they'd have me sniffed out by their beagles,
picked at by their eagles, pinned down, grilled
beneath the sun.

Me, I stick to the shadows, carry a gun.

Suggests wealth and privilege, and this is what he really seems to hate.

Double meaning — "vault" means jump over, but it also suggests the rich people's money.

Another stereotype of rich houses. He suggests the ditches are there to keep him out.

Stereotype of poverty.

Suggests ordinary people are imprisoned by the rich.

Stereotype that the upper class all hunt animals. He says they want to hunt him down in the same way.

His intentions are far more brutal and less subtle than they imagined.

This poem has references to the story of Prometheus. In Greek mythology, Prometheus stole fire from the gods to give to mankind. As a punishment, he was chained to a rock where an eagle tore at his liver.

POEM DICTIONARY
britches — trousers worn to the knee or just below
beagles — a breed of dog used for hunting

Those bastards in their mansions

The person in this poem has really got it in for rich people. He says they treat him like he's trying to start a revolution. Turns out he's just lurking in the shadows. With a gun. So that's all right then.

You've Got to Know What Happens in the Poem

Lines 1-6	The person in the poem has a go at rich people. He says they treat him like he's a criminal.
Lines 7-9	He denies causing poor people to revolt — though it sounds like he'd like to.
Lines 10-13	He says that the rich want to hunt him down and imprison him.
Line 14	Rather than doing any of the things he's suspected of, he's waiting for his chance to strike.

Learn About the Three Types of Language

1) STEREOTYPES — His descriptions of rich and poor people are simplified and exaggerated — he sees the rich as living in big mansions, and imagines they in turn have a stereotyped image of the poor. He uses these stereotypes to emphasise how different they are to ordinary, working class people.
2) REVOLUTIONARY LANGUAGE — He sees ordinary, poor people as being oppressed by the rich. He says he hasn't been trying to start a revolution, i.e. getting the poor to take power from the rich. But the way he describes revolution suggests he actually thinks it would be a good thing.
3) AGGRESSIVE LANGUAGE — He has a lot of violent, aggressive feelings towards rich people. He describes the violent things he's been accused of, but denies they're true — until the last line.

Remember the Feelings and Attitudes in the Poem

"Go stop revolution, Rover."

1) RESENTMENT — The person in the poem hates rich people.
2) OPPRESSION — He says the rich oppress ordinary people — they control them with force.
3) INDIGNATION — He's angry about the things he's been wrongly accused of.
4) REVENGE — He wants to have his revenge on rich people.

Think About Your Feelings and Attitudes to the Poem

1) Pick 2 words or phrases that stand out to you. If none stand out, just pick 2 unusual words or phrases.
2) Write these 2 words or phrases down. Then write about how they make you feel. If they don't make you feel anything, don't worry — just make something up, as long as it's not too stupid.

EXAMPLE When the person in the poem says "I stick to the shadows, carry a gun", it makes me feel both worried and excited. Having a gun shows he's plotting something very violent, which I find disturbing. But the way he waits in the shadows means we don't know when or how he will do it.

Themes — danger, attitudes to others and strong emotions

Compare 'Those bastards in their mansions' with other poems on the same themes: danger ('Education for Leisure' p.48-49 and 'Stealing' p.50-51), attitudes towards other people ('Hitcher' p.66-67) and strong emotions ('The Song of the Old Mother' p.8-9).

I've made out a will

from Book of Matches

I've made out a will; I'm leaving myself
to the National Health. I'm sure they can use
the jellies and tubes and syrups and glues,
the web of nerves and veins, the loaf of brains,
and assortment of fillings and stitches and wounds,
blood – a gallon exactly of bilberry soup –
the chassis or cage or cathedral of bone;
but not the heart, they can leave that alone.

They can have the lot, the whole stock:
the loops and coils and sprockets and springs and rods,
the twines and cords and strands,
the face, the case, the cogs and the hands,

but not the pendulum, the ticker;
leave that where it stops or hangs.

Humorously says his insides must be useful.

Rhyming adds to the light-hearted tone.

The exact amount reminds us of the will theme.

Could mean ribcage, or that people are trapped by their bodies' limitations.

Sounds like his body's a shop, and the parts are goods.

Here the poet describes his body like it's a car engine, with lots of complicated parts.

Returns to the theme of a will, but leaves the heart where it is instead of leaving it to someone.

We expect him to say he's leaving valuable items, but instead he leaves his body.

Cockney rhyming slang — loaf of bread = head.

His body is far from perfect.

Light-heartedly describes the deep colour of blood.

Reminds us of the saying "Your body is a temple" — you should look after it.

Blunt tone makes his feelings clear.

The body is just clothing — it's not important.

The body is described like a clock.

Reminds us of the heart's regular beat, and also that life is ticking away.

The poem ends on the serious subject of death.

POEM DICTIONARY
bilberry — a dark blue fruit
chassis — the frame of a car
sprockets — wheels on a chain

I've made out a will

The poet has written a will — but instead of saying who he's leaving his possessions to, he says he's leaving his body to the NHS. It's quite humorous, but has a serious point — he says the NHS can have everything but his heart, which is the only part of his body that's important to him.

You've Got to Know What Happens in the Poem

Lines 1-8	The poet describes all the different things in his body, in a disgusting but comical way. He says the National Health Service can have everything apart from his heart.
Lines 9-12	He compares his body to an engine (line 10), clothes (line 11) and a clock (line 12).
Lines 13-14	The poem ends on a more serious note, by reminding us of the suddenness of death.

Learn About the Three Types of Language

1) LANGUAGE RELATED TO WILLS — There are a few little phrases thrown in which give the poem the feel of a will. This reinforces the theme of the poem.
2) HUMOROUS LANGUAGE — There are quite a lot of funny descriptions, even though they're often about pretty disgusting things like blood and guts. This allows the poet to talk about death, which could be a pretty depressing subject, in a light-hearted way.
3) METAPHORICAL LANGUAGE — The body is described as if it's various different things, such as an engine, a clock and a cathedral. This helps the poet give a certain impression of the body and its different parts.

Remember the Feelings and Attitudes in the Poem

Anyone for jelly?

1) HUMOUR — The poet has a light-hearted attitude towards his body.
2) FEARLESSNESS — He's not bothered about the prospect of death.
3) SENTIMENTALITY — He has an emotional attachment to his heart.

The poet's feelings about his heart could refer to its connection to love — although he doesn't say this outright.

Think About Your Feelings and Attitudes to the Poem

1) Pick 2 words or phrases that stand out to you. If none stand out, just pick 2 unusual words or phrases.
2) Write these 2 words or phrases down. Then write about how they make you feel. If they don't make you feel anything, don't worry — just make something up, as long as it's not too stupid.

EXAMPLE I find the poet's description of "the jellies and tubes and syrups and glues" in his body sickening. It's a very unpleasant way of describing what people's bodies are made of.

Themes — death, imagery and the first person...

Compare 'I've made out a will' with other poems about the same themes: death ('November' p.58-59 and 'Tichborne's Elegy' p.14-15), imagery ('Havisham' p.36-37 and 'Sonnet 130' p.20-21) and use of the first person ('Education for Leisure' p.48-49 and 'Homecoming' p.56-57).

Key Poem

Hitcher

Hitcher

I'd been tired, under
the weather, but the ansaphone kept screaming:
One more sick-note, mister, and you're finished. Fired.
I thumbed a lift to where the car was parked.
A Vauxhall Astra. It was hired.

I picked him up in Leeds.
He was following the sun to west from east
with just a toothbrush and the good earth for a bed. The truth,
he said, was blowin' in the wind,
or round the next bend.

I let him have it
on the top road out of Harrogate – once
with the head, then six times with the krooklok
in the face – and didn't even swerve.
I dropped it into third

and leant across
to let him out, and saw him in the mirror
bouncing off the kerb, then disappearing down the verge.
We were the same age, give or take a week.
He'd said he liked the breeze

to run its fingers
through his hair. It was twelve noon.
The outlook for the day was moderate to fair.
Stitch that, I remember thinking,
you can walk from there.

The narrator is trying to get away from stress at work.

Before he kills the hitcher, the killer himself hitches a lift.

The narrator's problems come to him via modern technology — the hitcher lives a simpler life.

Rhyming words emphasise pressure from work.

Romantic image of travelling.

The hitcher is relaxed and dreamy, unlike the narrator.

The violence is shocking because it comes suddenly — there's no build-up to it.

He hits the hitcher repeatedly — it's a savage, sustained attack.

Sounds like he's boasting.

Pretends he's being considerate.

Disturbing image, but his matter-of-fact tone suggests he's not bothered by it.

Another connection between him and the hitcher, but it doesn't matter to him.

Makes fun of the hitcher's dreamy attitude.

Could be a play on words — the hitcher will need a few stitches if he's still alive.

The rhyming here shows the narrator is more relaxed than at the start of the poem.

POEM DICTIONARY
Krooklok — metal device used to prevent car theft

Hitcher

Key Poem

The chap in this poem isn't an awfully nice fella. He picks up a hitch-hiker — ok so far — then duffs him up, chucks him out of his car while it's still going and leaves him for dead. And the moral of the story is: if you're in Leeds, get the bus.

You've Got to Know What Happens in the Poem

Lines 1-5 — The narrator was feeling under pressure as he hitched a lift to the car he'd hired.

Lines 6-10 — He describes picking a hitch-hiker up, and the easy-going lifestyle the hitcher was leading.

Lines 11-18 — He tells us he beat up the hitcher while he was still driving, then pushed him out of the car.

Lines 19-25 — He jokes that the weather's nice so the hitcher can walk the rest of the way.

Learn About the Four Types of Language

1) CONTRASTS — The simple, relaxed life of the hitcher contrasts with the stress the narrator feels.
2) VIOLENT LANGUAGE — The narrator describes quite graphically how he attacked the hitcher. His descriptions are particularly shocking because of the casual tone of voice he uses.
3) FLIPPANT REMARKS — He makes some pretty flippant comments and sick jokes about the assault. He makes fun of the hitcher for his easy-going lifestyle.
4) LINKS — There are some similarities between the narrator and the hitcher.

Remember the Feelings and Attitudes in the Poem

1) STRESS — At the start of the poem, the narrator feels irritable, ill and under pressure.
2) DETACHMENT — His matter-of-fact tone shows he doesn't feel bad about what he does.
3) JEALOUSY — He envies the hitch-hiker's relaxed lifestyle and hates him for it.
4) SPITE — His nasty joke at the end suggests he takes a sick pleasure from killing the hitch-hiker.

Think About Your Feelings and Attitudes to the Poem

1) Pick 2 words or phrases that stand out to you. If none stand out, just pick 2 unusual words or phrases.
2) Write these 2 words or phrases down. Then write about how they make you feel. If they don't make you feel anything, don't worry — just make something up, as long as it's not too stupid.

EXAMPLE When the narrator describes the hitcher "bouncing off the kerb, then disappearing down the verge", I feel shocked. This is a horrible image. Even though he knows he has probably killed the hitcher, the narrator describes it as if it is a perfectly normal sight.

Themes — mood, evil and attitudes towards other people...

Compare 'Hitcher' with other poems about the same themes: mood ('Havisham' p.36-37 and 'Education for Leisure' p.48-49), evil ('My Last Duchess' p.22-23 and 'The Laboratory' p.30-31) and attitudes towards other people ('The Song of the Old Mother' p.8-9 and 'Stealing' p.50-51).

Death

Death is something people feel emotional about — so it's a good theme for poetry.

1) The death of a loved one causes grief and a sense of loss.
2) Everyone dies — it's something we need to prepare for.
3) Deaths caused by war, crime or execution can seem an unnecessary waste of life.

Some Poets write about Killing and Murder

Education for Leisure (Pages 48-49)

1) The poet writes from the point of view of a psychopath who's planning to "kill something".
2) The character usually has a dull life — feeling "ignored" and suffering from "boredom".
3) The character gets obsessed with the power of killing. It makes their life feel more exciting. They imagine themselves as a "genius" and a "superstar".
4) At the end of the poem, the character seems to threaten the reader: "I touch your arm."

Note: This poem won't be named in any questions in the June 2009 exam. You can write about it if the question asks you to use a poem by Carol Ann Duffy, but doesn't say which one. It won't be in the anthology after the June 2009 exam.

The Man He Killed (Pages 16-17)

1) In this poem, a soldier talks about a man he killed during a battle. He points out the irony that if he had met the man in other circumstances, they might have been friends.
2) He imagines that the man he killed was rather like himself. He might have only enlisted in the army because he was unemployed and needed a job. Even though officially the man was his "foe", there wasn't necessarily anything bad about him.
3) The poem points out how foolish and wasteful the killing in war is: "You shoot a fellow down / You'd treat if met where any bar is".

Death can be Depressing

On my first Sonne (Pages 6-7)

1) The poet expresses the grief he feels over the loss of a child: "Farewell, thou child of my right hand, and joy".
2) The poet tries to find something positive in his son's death — that at least the boy has escaped many of life's troubles and old age.
3) He pays tribute to his son by saying he was "his best piece of poetrie" — his best work. He vows never to love anything so much again, in case he loses it.

November (Pages 58-59)

1) Seeing the old people in the home makes the poet think about his own death.
2) The old people appear to be very close to death — their "pasty bloodless smiles" and "stunned brains" suggest that some parts of their bodies are already dead.
3) The thought of death depresses the poet — "we feel the terror of the dusk begin."
4) But at the end he says, "sometimes the sun spangles", and this makes him determined to get as much out of life as possible before he dies.

This topic's a bit bleak...

Other poems which talk about death are: 'Tichborne's Elegy' (p.14-15), 'The Laboratory' (p.30-31), 'Salome' (p.42-43) and 'Hitcher' (p.66-67). They fall into two camps — 1) poets feeling awful about people dying in real life, and 2) poets writing from the point of view of a crazed killer.

Parent/Child Relationships

Family arguments — a great source of poetic inspiration.

1) The parent/child relationship is central to most people's lives.
2) Parent/child relationships often change as people grow older.
3) Some children struggle for independence from their parents.

Parents Find it Hard to Let Go

Mother, any distance (Pages 52-53)

1) The person in this poem is moving into his own house. He's becoming independent from his mum.
2) His mum helps him measure things. The tape measure, "unreeling / years between us", becomes a metaphor for all their shared memories and history.
3) His mother finds it difficult to let go of him completely: "your fingertips still pinch / the last one-hundredth of an inch".
4) At the end, he faces up to life without his mum. He's ready "to fall or fly".

The Affliction of Margaret (Pages 10-11)

1) The woman in the poem hasn't heard from her son for 7 years.
2) We see the mother's anguish at not knowing whether her son is dead or alive.
3) She's desperate to hear from him, whatever has happened to him: "Oh find me, prosperous or undone!"
4) She describes her son as if he's almost perfect: "He was among the prime in worth."
5) She dearly loves her son, but we don't find out how he feels about her.

Children's Views of their Parents Change Over Time

My father thought it bloody queer (Pages 54-55)

1) The poet remembers his father's anger and sarcasm when he "rolled home with a ring of silver" in his ear. He was hurt and upset by his father's reaction.
2) When the earring became sore and painful, he started to realise his father might have been right.
3) Now the poet's older, he finds himself giving the same advice as his father did: "*If I were you, / I'd take it out and leave it out next year.*"

Parents make Sacrifices for their Children

Before You Were Mine (Pages 44-45)

1) The poet imagines her mother as a glamorous young woman in the 1950s, looking and behaving like "Marilyn".
2) She likes to think of her mother as a bit of a rebel who put pleasure first. She imagines her staying out late, not caring that she would get "a hiding" when she came home.
3) She remembers as a child, playing with her mum's high-heeled shoes, "relics" of her frivolous past, and her mum teaching her to "*Cha cha cha*" on the way back from Church.
4) She realises the sacrifices her mother's made since her birth. With the "loud, possessive yell" of a young baby, she took over her mum's life. Her mum no longer had time to go out and have a good time.

Everyone starts off as a squalling baby...

Other poems which describe parent/child relationships are 'On my first Sonne' (p.6-7), 'We Remember Your Childhood Well' (p.46-47) and 'Kid' (p.60-61).

Danger

Some people are scared by danger — others get a kick out of it.

1) Danger can arise from the natural environment, e.g. storms, earthquakes and floods.
2) Danger can also be caused by people — through aggression and violence.
3) Some people find danger and risk-taking exciting (we don't endorse this attitude...).

People can Find Themselves in Dangerous Situations

The Little Boy Lost and The Little Boy Found (Pages 12-13)

1) The little boy is helpless on his own — "the mire was deep".
2) The danger is averted when God appears, "like his father in white".
3) Blake uses the story to make his moral clear — he says we're lost without God.

Patrolling Barnegat (Pages 18-19)

1) The poem describes a small band of watchmen patrolling the beach during a fierce storm.
2) The storm is described as very powerful: "Waves, air, midnight, their savagest trinity lashing". It is an uncontrollable part of nature: "Wild, wild the storm".
3) The storm is dangerous — out to sea the watchmen wonder if they can see a wrecked ship: "is that a wreck? is the red signal flaring?".

Some Poets write about Dangerous People

Hitcher (Pages 66-67)

1) The poem is written from the point of view of a murderer who kills a hitch-hiker.
2) At first, the murderer sounds like an ordinary man. He moans about everyday things: "I'd been tired, under / the weather".
3) Then as the story unfolds, it becomes clear that the murderer is a dangerous criminal. He's planned the murder in advance, hiring a car to do the murder in.
4) The hitch-hiker is unaware of the danger he's in. He talks happily to the murderer about his life and aspirations: "The truth, / he said, was blowin' in the wind".
5) The murder is brutal and shocking, especially because the murderer himself doesn't seem shocked by it: "I let him have it / on the top road out of Harrogate".

Danger and Risk-Taking can be Exciting

Stealing (Pages 50-51)

1) The poem is written from the point of view of a young thief.
2) There isn't any point to the thief's law-breaking: "I steal things I don't need. I joy-ride cars / to nowhere".
3) The only reason the thief does it is for the "thrill" — they describe the excitement they feel from standing in "A stranger's bedroom. Mirrors. I sigh like this — *Aah*."
4) When they're not stealing, the thief feels bored: "Mostly I'm so bored I could eat myself."

People do strange things for kicks...

This is a bit of a grim topic: people being frightened and getting hurt. If you want more of this doleful stuff, then have a look at these poems: 'The Laboratory' (p.30-31), 'Education for Leisure' (p.48-49) and 'Those bastards in their mansions' (p.62-63).

Attitudes Towards Other People

Poems are often about the poets' attitudes and feelings towards other people. Sometimes their attitude towards others is very positive and warm, other times it's very nasty indeed...

1) Some poets write about positive attitudes and feelings towards other people.
2) Some poets write about negative or violent attitudes towards other people.
3) Sometimes poets write about their attitudes towards other people changing.

Poems can be about Positive Attitudes towards Others

Anne Hathaway (Pages 40-41)

1) The poem is written from the point of view of Shakespeare's wife, remembering her dead husband.
2) Her attitude towards him is very loving and affectionate. She describes him as "my living laughing love", as if he is still alive. The word "laughing" emphasises how much she enjoyed his company.
3) She has fond memories of how he made her feel. She describes how spending time with him was like going to a magical land: "a spinning world / of forests, castles, torchlight".
4) Even now he's dead, she won't forget him: she carries the memories in "the casket of my widow's head".

Poems can portray Negative Attitudes towards Others

Those bastards in their mansions (Pages 62-63)

1) The character in the poem hates rich, upper class "bastards".
2) He has a stereotyped view of them — "Those lords and ladies in their palaces and castles".
3) He sees rich people as bullies who would "have me sniffed out by their beagles".
4) He also suggests that they're a bit paranoid and pathetic, as they "shriek" about him breaking into their houses.

Kid (Pages 60-61)

1) The Robin character hates Batman because he "ditched" him when Robin still needed him.
2) Robin thinks other people had a false impression of Batman. Robin says he's "scotched that 'he was like a father / to me' rumour" and shown everyone what Batman's really like.
3) Robin sees Batman as selfish and irresponsible for neglecting him. He also sees him as immoral — he was taking a married woman "downtown on expenses in the motor".
4) At the end of the poem, Robin portrays Batman as a loser, living on his own eating rubbish: "you without a shadow, stewing over / chicken giblets in the pressure cooker".

"Mad, moi?"

The Laboratory (Pages 30-31)

1) The woman in the poem feels really angry towards her lover and his new mistress. She thinks they've made a fool of her: "they laugh, laugh at me".
2) She's intent on revenge and wants to use poison to kill the mistress in a painful way: "Let death be felt and the proof remain". Through killing his mistress, she hopes to hurt her lover as well: "He is sure to remember her dying face!"
3) She is excited about the idea of killing and getting revenge. She feels no guilt about what she is doing.

Anger, resentment, love, lust, hate, jealousy, contempt...

Poems which show characters' attitudes towards other people include: 'Stealing' (p.50-51), 'Hitcher' (p.66-67) and 'The Song of the Old Mother' (p.8-9).

Love

There are a few poems on the good old-fashioned theme of love in this anthology, but not many of them are romantic. Some of them are about love between people in families, some of them describe love of nature, or even love of crime...

1) Some poets write about romantic love.
2) Poets also write about family love, e.g. between mother and son.
3) Some poets write about their love of nature, or a particular place or pastime.

Some Poems are about Romantic Love

Sonnet 130 (Pages 20-21)

1) This poem is a sonnet (it's 14 lines long). Sonnet form is often used for love poetry.
2) In the first part of the poem, Shakespeare goes against the reader's expectations of a love sonnet. He's pretty rude about his mistress, e.g. he says her "eyes are nothing like the sun", her hair is like "black wires" and her breath "reeks".
3) On line 9, he says "I love to hear her speak". This is the first hint that he does love his mistress.
4) In the last two lines, the tone changes. Shakespeare declares that his mistress is just as wonderful as any woman who's praised with silly compliments: "I think my love as rare / As any she belied with false compare."

Anne Hathaway (Pages 40-41)

1) This poem is a sonnet, a traditional form for a love poem.
2) Anne Hathaway describes the love between her and her husband Shakespeare, before he died.
3) The love between them was almost too good to be true. Anne uses romantic, magical words to describe it: "my lover's words / were shooting stars".
4) She says their love was "Romance / and drama played by touch, by scent, by taste" — their love was so passionate she felt as if they were characters in one of her husband's plays.

Some Poems are about Love of Places or Nature

Sonnet (Pages 34-35)

1) The poet describes how much he loves the countryside in summer.
2) He starts three lines with the phrase "I love" which emphasises his feelings.
3) He describes the countryside in a very positive way, using words like "beaming", "happy" and "bright" to show how much he likes it.

Inversnaid (Pages 32-33)

1) The poet describes a place with wild, natural scenery, with a "darksome burn" rolling through the hills.
2) In the final stanza, the poet makes an appeal for places like this to be left alone. He loves the "wilderness" and wants it to survive.

"Who cares about boys? I love shrubbery..."

Some Poets love Wolverhampton Wanderers...

The poems in this anthology are pretty bleak — there aren't many about love. Other poems you could look at are: 'On my first Sonne' (p.6-7), 'The Affliction of Margaret' (p.10-11), 'Mother, any distance' (p.52-53), and... no, that's it.

Memory

Many poems are based around memories — of people, events and feelings.

1) Memories can be associated with many different feelings, e.g. pride, shame, joy or anger.
2) People sometimes block out bad memories.
3) Memories can be unreliable — you might remember things differently to how they actually happened.

Memories can be Unreliable and Confusing

Homecoming (Pages 56-57)

1) This poem is deliberately ambiguous. It encourages the reader to "Think" in the first line, and then presents a series of images, many of which seem to be from the past. The clearest story is about a mother getting angry with her child — the child goes to bed angry and then sneaks off at night.
2) The poem plays around with time. The poet says he's there the night the person sneaks out, but there isn't any contact between them "because it's sixteen years or so before we'll meet."
3) The poet says the person should "Retrace that walk towards the garden gate". This suggests the homecoming of the poem's title. Maybe the child who sneaked away is returning home as an adult.
4) The end of the poem suggests that the person is going back to their old life and the character they used to be. An old yellow jacket seems to symbolise the person's old life. The poet encourages them to step back into it: "It still fits."

We Remember Your Childhood Well (Pages 46-47)

1) This poem is about someone telling someone else that his or her memories are wrong.
2) It seems likely that there is a reason why the memories are being denied — perhaps to cover up mistreatment or abuse that happened in the past.
3) The memories are only hinted at, which makes us think the worst about what happened, e.g. the phrase "Nobody forced you" sounds really sinister.

The Village Schoolmaster (Pages 28-29)

1) The poet points out the "straggling fence" next to where the school was. This makes him remember the schoolmaster.
2) The schoolmaster was "a man severe" — he doesn't sound particularly friendly. But he had bags of knowledge and a wide range of skills.
3) Memories of the schoolmaster are unclear in places, e.g. the poet says "the story ran that he could gauge", suggesting no-one was quite sure about him.
4) The schoolmaster seems mysterious — he "Amazed the gazing rustics".

Some Memories inspire Pride and Affection

Ulysses (Pages 26-27)

1) Ulysses has returned to his home of Ithaca after years spent away. He finds normal life boring and wants to return to travelling and adventure.
2) Ulysses has strong memories of the glory of his former life. He remembers the "drunk delight of battle" and all that he has "seen and known".
3) In the past, he became famous and had an impact on events. He says, "I am a part of all that I have met".
4) He's proud of his former achievements. Memories of his past glory inspire him to go travelling again: "I cannot rest from travel: I will drink / Life to the lees".

"Give me a sword and I'll show you a thing or two."

I remember it well...

"Memories, like the corners of my mind..." How does the rest of that song go? Ah well. Another poem which deals with memories is 'Before You Were Mine' (p.44-45). And don't forget it.

Evil

Evil is a good subject for poems because it's dramatic and extreme.

1) Some characters seem to kill just for fun.
2) Others become obsessed with revenge, and will do anything to get it.
3) Some characters appear quite normal, but give us little glimpses that they're not quite the ticket.

Some Characters are Openly Evil

The Laboratory (Pages 30-31)

1) The woman in this poem suspects her husband or lover has been unfaithful to her.
2) She's determined to get revenge by poisoning the other woman.
3) She's very nasty — she's prepared to murder the other woman just to get her own back on her lover. She sounds pleased when she says "He is sure to remember her dying face!"

Hitcher (Pages 66-67)

1) The killer plans the murder in advance — he's arranged a hire car for it.
2) His attitude to the killing is shocking — he sounds calm when he describes it, rather than angry or worked up. This suggests it might not be the first time he's done this.
3) The nature of the violence is barbaric — he headbutts him, then hits him "six times with the krooklok / in the face". He seems to enjoy watching the hitcher "bouncing off the kerb".
4) He callously mocks the hitcher's attitude after attacking him: "He'd said he liked the breeze / to run its fingers / through his hair." He seems to think that the hitcher's lifestyle is reason enough to attack him.

Some Characters Gradually Reveal their Evil Side

My Last Duchess (Pages 22-23)

1) The Duke is showing a guest a portrait of his dead wife. He seems pleasant and polite.
2) But we gradually realise there's something fishy about him. He starts to criticise the Duchess for the way she acted: "her looks went everywhere".
3) The Duke says the Duchess treated him no better than anyone else — he seems really jealous.
4) He sounds sinister when he tells his guest: "I gave commands; / Then all smiles stopped together." This makes it sound like he murdered his wife just because he didn't like her flirting with other men.

Salome (Pages 42-43)

1) The woman in this poem has cut off a man's head.
2) She seems mildly regretful at first, but we think this is because she's slept with a stranger.
3) When it turns out she's actually beheaded the man, we see what she's said in a different context. She says she'd "done it before" and she'll "do it again" — she's a serial murderer.
4) She can't remember who the man is: "a head on the pillow beside me – whose? – / what did it matter?" This suggests that she kills randomly, rather than having anything in particular against her victims.

I call him "Mini-Simon-Armitage"...

Yep, this anthology's certainly got a dark side. Other poems about evil are: 'Havisham' (p.36-37) and 'Education for Leisure' (p.48-49). But remember — don't have nightmares.

Getting Older

This theme falls into two camps: poems about growing up, and poems about ageing.

1) Growing up and becoming independent from your parents can be a difficult time.
2) Growing old and realising you've not got much time left can be depressing.

Growing Up can be a Difficult Time

Mother, any distance (Pages 52-53)

1) The character in this poem is moving into a new house for the first time.
2) He asks his mum to help him measure the new house. His mum stands at the bottom of the stairs holding a tape measure as her son walks up the stairs, holding the other end.
3) This situation is used as a metaphor for the character gaining independence from his mum. The tape measure represents the bond between them. For a long time, his mother keeps hanging onto the end of the tape measure ("your fingertips still pinch / the last one-hundredth of an inch") — this represents the way she is clinging on to her son.
4) There comes a point when the character needs to let go of the tape measure, because it won't stretch any further. He realises that he has to take risks for himself: "to fall or fly" without his mum there to help him.

Kid (Pages 60-61)

1) The character in this poem feels that he was let down by the person who was supposed to look after him when he was young.
2) He says he was given "the order / to grow up" — expected to be independent before he was ready.
3) The character says he's now grown up and made a success of himself: "now I'm taller, harder, stronger, older." But he's still bitter about his experience of adolescence.

Growing Old Isn't Much Fun Either

Ulysses (Pages 26-27)

1) Ulysses has returned home as a hero after ten years travelling back from the Trojan war.
2) He's bored of being "an idle king" though, and wants to continue his adventures until he dies.
3) He knows he's not as strong and fit as he used to be, and he's aware that death isn't far away. But this doesn't put him off — he tells his crew that he is still "strong in will".
4) Ulysses isn't prepared to just fade away as he gets older. He wants to "drink / Life to the lees".

November (Pages 58-59)

1) The poet finds the old people depressing to look at — their "pasty bloodless smiles" make them seem almost dead already.
2) He realises that he and John will soon be old too — "we are almost these monsters".
3) The thought of growing old scares him witless — "we feel the terror of the dusk begin."
4) He knows there's nothing he can do to avoid getting old and dying, but says it's important to make the most out of the times when "we feel alive".

"Oh no! I'm going to die!"

This page is dedicated to Adrian Mole Aged 13 and ¾...

Other poems about getting older are: 'Before You Were Mine' (p.44-45) and 'My father thought it bloody queer' (p.54-55). That's it for poets' ideas, attitudes and feelings. Phew.

Strong Emotions

Poets often show strong emotions in their poems — either their own emotions, or those of the people they are writing about. Strong emotions are things like love, hate, anger, jealousy and joy.

1) Poems are often about personal subjects, which the poet has strong emotions about.
2) Poems about difficult situations often contain strong emotions, e.g. poems about death or danger.
3) Poets can show strong emotions through the language they use to write about a subject.
4) When a poet writes about strong emotions, it can make the reader think about times when they felt the same way. It often increases the connection the reader feels to the poem.

Poems about Difficult Situations show Strong Emotions

On my first Sonne (Pages 6-7)

1) The poet loved his son and was very proud of him — he calls him his "best piece of poetrie".
2) He's devastated by his son's death, but he's also grateful for the time he had with him — "Seven yeeres tho'wert lent to me and I thee pay."
3) Jonson sees life as painful. He suggests people are better off dead, as they don't have to suffer the pain of getting old — he asks: "why / Will man lament the state he should envie?"

Tichborne's Elegy (Pages 14-15)

1) This poem was written as the poet was waiting for his execution in the Tower of London.
2) The poet feels huge sadness and bitterness about his coming execution.
3) Throughout the poem, he keeps pointing out the bitter irony of his situation: even though he is young and healthy, his life is coming to an end: "My fruit is fallen, and yet my leaves are green".
4) He feels angry about the way his life is going to be wasted. Instead of being able to enjoy his life, it's going to be cut short: "My prime of youth is but a frost of cares."

Poems can Include Mixed Emotions

Havisham (Pages 36-37)

1) Havisham has very strong mixed emotions about the man who jilted her, calling him "Beloved sweetheart bastard".
2) She's extremely angry and bitter, and wants to "strangle" him.
3) It's years since he rejected her, but she can't let go — "I stink and remember." She's obsessed.
4) Behind all the violence, she's also very unhappy, wondering "who did this / to me?"
5) She also desperately wants him to be there, and has sexual fantasies about "the lost body".

November (Pages 58-59)

1) This poem describes an elderly woman being taken to a care home. The poet feels guilty about putting the woman into care: "We have brought her here to die and we know it."
2) The poet's feelings about the elderly people in the care home are mixed.
3) On the one hand, the poet seems repulsed by the elderly people, describing them as almost inhuman. For example, he describes their "pasty bloodless smiles" and their "stunned brains".
4) But the poet can also empathise with the elderly people — he can imagine growing old himself, and realises it's only a matter of time before he ends up in the same situation.
5) He sounds frightened and depressed by old age, and the fact that he can do nothing to stop it happening. Nightfall is used as a metaphor for old age: "we let it happen. We can say nothing."

Strong emotions are dramatic and compelling...

Poems are often about personal or dramatic events — no wonder they're emotional.
'The Affliction of Margaret' (p.10-11) and 'Kid' (p.60-61) are also good examples of this theme.

Use of the First Person

If the poet writes in the first person, they use words like "I" and "me", rather than "she" and "him."

1) Writing in the first person allows the poet to use their voice directly.
2) This allows them to talk about their personal thoughts and feelings.
3) The first person lets us see things from the poet or character's point of view.

Writing in the First Person can Express Personal Feelings

Anne Hathaway (Pages 40-41)

1) The poet imagines Anne Hathaway's feelings after her husband dies.
2) The use of the first person makes the poem sound loving and tender — for example when she says, "My lover's words / were shooting stars" and "My living laughing love".
3) Using the first person emphasises how personal the poem is. It's about memories of a relationship — the kind of stuff other people wouldn't know about.

My father thought it bloody queer (Pages 54-55)

1) The poet uses the first person to show the physical pain he felt from having his ear pierced, and the emotional pain caused by his father's reaction.
2) He says he hadn't dared to "drive a needle through the skin". This shows he wasn't very courageous about it, and makes his attempt to be rebellious look a bit silly.
3) He shows that his father's mocking reaction still bothers him, as he describes "my own voice breaking like a tear" when he finds himself saying the same things his dad said to him.

Sonnet (Pages 34-35)

1) This poem is about how much the poet loves the countryside in summer.
2) Three lines of the poem start with "I love" which emphasises his feelings.

Writing in the First Person can be Persuasive

The Man He Killed (Pages 16-17)

1) This poem makes a point about the barbarity and foolishness of war — how people who could be friends kill each other because they are on different sides.
2) Hardy writes in the first person from the point of view of a soldier who has fought in a war. This increases the impact of the message because the character is speaking from personal experience.
3) Using the first person makes it sound as if the character is talking directly to the reader: "I shot him dead because – / Because he was my foe". This makes the poem more compelling and persuasive.

The Song of the Old Mother (Pages 8-9)

1) The message of the poem is about how harsh life is for many old people.
2) The poet writes in the first person, from the point of view of an old woman.
3) The character of the woman talks directly to the reader about her situation. She describes her list of chores, starting early "in the dawn" and not stopping till the "stars" are out. She contrasts this with the "idleness" of young people.
4) The poem gives a voice to a character who would usually be ignored.

The first person lets the poet speak directly to the reader...

'Stealing' (p.50-51) and 'Mother, any distance' (p.52-53) also use the first person. It makes a big difference to the effect of a poem, as it lets the poet talk personally — poems like 'The Man He Killed' would lose a lot of impact if it was just "he" or "she" instead of "I".

Characters

Most poets write about people — apart from the nature-loving, obsessed-with-potatoes brigade.

1) Many poems are about a particular character — their personality, actions and emotions.
2) The characters in a poem can be real or completely made-up.
3) Sometimes the main character is the poet themselves.
4) Often an important character isn't actually present in the poem — they're just talked about by the other characters.

Characters can be Portrayed Negatively

Kid (Pages 60-61)

1) The poem is addressed to a character who was a father-figure to the poet in his childhood.
2) The poet says that he hero-worshipped this character but was badly let down by him — ditched "in the gutter".
3) Even now the poet is older, he's still bitter about the way he was treated. He enjoys thinking about the character being unhappy and alone: "punching the palm of your hand all winter".
4) He refers to the character sarcastically as "Batman, big-shot". He used to think the character was a big hero, but it turned out he was much more ordinary.

Havisham (Pages 36-37)

1) The character in this poem is based on a character called Miss Havisham, in Charles Dickens' novel "Great Expectations". She was jilted on her wedding day and went a bit crazy.
2) In the poem, she has extremely violent thoughts about the bloke who rejected her, but she's also desperate for him to come back. She's obsessed with the rejection she suffered.
3) We can see her confusion in the opening line, when she calls him "Beloved sweetheart bastard."
4) Overall, she's very bitter and violent — her grim request of "a male corpse for a long slow honeymoon" shows she's lost control.

Sometimes a Key Character is Absent

The Affliction of Margaret (Pages 10-11)

1) In this poem, a woman called Margaret worries about what has happened to her son who disappeared seven years ago. Even though we never meet the son, he is an important character in the poem.
2) Margaret's opinion of her son is very loving and positive. She says that he was "among the prime in worth, / An object beauteous to behold".
3) There are hints though, that her son wasn't perfect. She says, "if things ensued that wanted grace, / As hath been said, they were not base". This suggests that other people didn't like his behaviour — but Margaret still defends him.

My Last Duchess (Pages 22-23)

1) In the poem, a rich man looks at a painting of his dead wife and describes what she was like.
2) The character of the dead wife is described in a lot of detail — but all through the eyes of her husband, who had her killed. We never hear her side of the story.
3) The husband says his wife made him angry because she favoured everyone with her smiles and blushes, rather than saving them for him. There is a suggestion that she was unfaithful to him: "she liked whate'er / She looked on, and her looks went everywhere."

Characters are just the people in a poem...

Other poems with interesting characters include: 'Ulysses' (p.26-27), 'The Village Schoolmaster' (p.28-29), 'Salome' (p.42-43), 'Education for Leisure' (p.48-49) and 'Hitcher' (p.66-67).

Imagery

The way a poet writes can make you form a picture in your head of what's being described — this is called "imagery". Two common forms of imagery are metaphors and similes (see glossary).

1) Imagery helps the reader imagine the situations, characters and emotions described in a poem.
2) Imagery often uses comparisons to describe something, e.g. "She ran like the wind."

Imagery can be used to Describe People

I've made out a will (Pages 64-65)

1) The poet gives a lot of fairly disgusting but humorous descriptions of the insides of his body.
2) The "jellies and tubes and syrups and glues" sound pretty horrible. They make it sound like his body is made up of food, with "bilberry soup" in his veins instead of blood.
3) The skeleton is described as "the chassis or cage or cathedral of bone" — this gives an idea of it being a big structure, like a car or a building.
4) In lines 9-12, the poet describes his body as if it's a shop, an engine, clothes and a clock. Describing his heart as "the pendulum, the ticker" gives the impression that when he dies, it'll just be like when a clock stops ticking.

Before

Before You Were Mine (Pages 44-45)

1) The poet uses imagery to describe the life her mother had, before she was born.
2) The images are quite nostalgic — her mum playing on a street corner, staying out late and dancing. These are things she wouldn't do in the same way again, once she settled down and had kids.
3) She uses glamorous language to describe her mother's younger self: "Marilyn", "fizzy, movie tomorrows", "high-heeled red shoes", "scent", "sparkle". This creates an image of a fun-loving young girl, full of ideals and dreams.

After

Some Poets use Imagery to Describe Places

Patrolling Barnegat (Pages 18-19)

1) The poet describes watchmen patrolling the beach during a fierce storm. He uses imagery to create a sense of how strong and frightening the storm is.
2) He describes the bad weather as if it is a violent, attacking force — e.g. "savagest trinity lashing".
3) The sound of the gale is described as if it's a person's voice: there's an "incessant undertone muttering" and sometimes it sounds like someone shrieking with "demoniac laughter".
4) He emphasises the gloominess of the scene with words like "midnight", "shadows" and "murk".

Inversnaid (Pages 32-33)

1) The poet describes a place he loves in the countryside. He makes an appeal for wild, natural places to be left as they are.
2) He builds up an image of the "darksome burn" in the first three verses. He emphasises the colours: the river is "horseback brown", the lake "pitchblack" and the froth on the lake "fawn".
3) He also describes the movement of the place: the river "roaring down" to the lake, the froth "turns and twindles" over the water, the brook "treads through" the hills.

Imagery is an important poetic device...

Most poems have a bit of imagery in. It's a useful way for a poet to give a particular impression of something. Examples include: 'Anne Hathaway' (p.40-41), 'Mother, any distance' (p.52-53), 'Homecoming' (p.56-57), 'The Eagle' (p.24-25), 'Ulysses' (p.26-27) and 'Sonnet' (p.34-35).

Closing Couplets

A closing couplet is the last two lines of a poem.

1) A closing couplet can sum up the poem as a whole.
2) A closing couplet can make a new or surprising point, giving the poem an unexpected conclusion.
3) Closing couplets can be set apart from the rest of the poem, and sometimes they rhyme.

Closing Couplets can Sum Up a Poem

The Village Schoolmaster (Pages 28-29)

1) The closing couplet seems to sum up the poem, by telling us how the villagers were baffled by how much the schoolmaster knew.
2) There is some uncertainty too. "Still the wonder grew" could mean that the villagers are impressed by the schoolmaster — but it might suggest that they aren't sure what to make of him. They seem amused by him, rather than in awe of him.

"Still the wonder grew"

I've made out a will (Pages 64-65)

1) The last two lines are separate from the rest of the poem. This emphasises the point they make.
2) The poem lists the parts of the poet's body that he's happy to leave to the NHS.
3) But the closing couplet says they can't have his heart — "not the pendulum, the ticker". The poet uses these two lines to make his wishes absolutely clear.

Closing Couplets can be Surprising

Sonnet 130 (Pages 20-21)

1) Shakespeare seems to be criticising his mistress, but the last two lines show he does love her really.
2) The closing couplet surprises the reader. It makes us look at the rest of the poem in a different way.
3) His love seems all the more genuine because he knows she's not perfect — "I think my love as rare / As any she belied with false compare."

November (Pages 58-59)

1) Most of this poem has a fairly depressing tone — the poet sees the old people in the home and they make him think about how his own death is unavoidable.
2) In the closing couplet, the poet is a bit more positive. He says "the sun spangles" — he sees a ray of light and feels more hopeful when he thinks of the times that "we feel alive".
3) The poet concludes that people should make the most out of opportunities when they come up — "One thing we have to get, John, out of this life."

Closing couplets leave a lasting impression on the reader...

Other poems with interesting closing couplets are: 'Anne Hathaway' (p.40-41), 'Salome' (p.42-43), 'Hitcher' (p.66-67), 'On my first Sonne' (p.6-7), 'The Song of the Old Mother (p.8-9) and 'Tichborne's Elegy (p.14-15). Remember to write about how they relate to the rest of the poem.

Irony

Irony can be funny, but it can also be tragic.

1) It's ironic when words are used in a sarcastic or comic way to imply the opposite of what they normally mean. People often do this to draw attention to something being funny or odd.
2) It's ironic when there is a big difference between what people expect or hope for and what actually happens.

Sometimes the Whole Poem is Ironic

Tichborne's Elegy (Pages 14-15)

1) The irony in this poem is that even though the poet is still young and healthy, his life is almost over because he is about to be executed: "My youth is spent, and yet I am not old".
2) Tichborne repeats this idea throughout the poem, with each line making clear the bitter irony of his situation: "And now I live, and now my life is done."

The Man He Killed (Pages 16-17)

1) The poet points out that the man he shot dead could have been his friend if they'd met in different circumstances.
2) It's ironic that, if they'd met "By some old and ancient inn", rather than being lined up opposite each other across a battlefield, they would have been having a drink together instead of shooting at each other.

Kid (Pages 60-61)

1) Robin sarcastically calls Batman a "big shot" — people used to think Batman was a big hero.
2) Now things have changed. Robin's the "real boy wonder" and Batman's lonely and poor — Robin pictures Batman "stewing over / chicken giblets in the pressure cooker".
3) It seems ironic that things have turned out this way, and Robin takes pleasure in pointing out this irony: "Batman, it makes a marvellous picture".

Irony Can Come Out at the End of the Poem

Salome (Pages 42-43)

1) This poem has lots of words which seem to have perfectly innocent meanings at first, but seem a lot more sinister when we find out what has actually happened at the end of the poem.
2) The man's "rather matted" hair and "crimson mouth" turn out to be like that because the woman has killed him — they're covered in blood.
3) The phrase "ain't life a bitch" is said ironically — the character doesn't really care about the dead man.

Those bastards in their mansions (Pages 62-63)

1) The character in the poem says he's innocent of all the things he's been accused of — he hasn't "poisoned the dogs", "crossed the lawns" or "given heat and light to streets and houses".
2) Rather than daringly stirring up a revolution, he says: "I stick to the shadows, carry a gun."
3) The irony is that he's actually planning something a lot more serious than the things he's denying. This irony only becomes clear in the last line of the poem.

Isn't it ironic...

Here are some other poems that have irony in them: 'Elvis's Twin Sister', (p.38-39), 'We Remember Your Childhood Well' (p.46-47), 'My father thought it bloody queer' (p.54-55), 'Hitcher' (p.66-67), 'My Last Duchess' (p.22-23) and 'The Laboratory' (p.30-31).

Language Effects

Language effects are the way the sounds of words in a poem are used to make a certain impression on the reader. Examples of language effects are alliteration, rhyme, assonance and onomatopoeia.

1) Language effects can create a mood or atmosphere in a poem.
2) Language effects can be useful for creating a vivid picture in the reader's mind of the place or person described in the poem.
3) Language effects can make a poet's feelings or opinions more forceful and convincing.

Language Effects Can be Used to Describe Nature

Patrolling Barnegat (Pages 18-19)

1) There's half-rhyme throughout the poem, with each line ending with a verb with an "-ing" ending. These are mostly words to do with the movement of the wind and sea, e.g. "lashing", "careering", and this creates a fearsome, unrelenting feel to the storm.
2) The poet uses onomatopoeic words to create the effect of the sounds of the storm, e.g. the vowel sounds of "hoarse roar" remind us of the deep rumbling sounds of a fierce storm.
3) Alliteration of hard "c" sounds in "combs careering" makes the sea sound rough and dangerous.

Inversnaid (Pages 32-33)

1) Alliteration in the phrase "rollrock highroad roaring" makes the reader think of the roar of the water flowing down over the stony bed of the stream.
2) The harsh alliteration of "in coop and in comb" adds to the impression of a rugged setting.
3) Rhyming couplets and a regular rhythm give the poem a natural and attractive feel.
4) In the last verse, the poet makes a point about how important it is to keep places like Inversnaid as they are. By repeating "w" sounds, the poet makes his point more effective, reminding us of the sounds of the countryside, like the wind blowing around the hills.

Language Effects Can be Used to Describe Feelings

Stealing (Pages 50-51)

1) The alliteration of "m" sounds in lines 2-4 creates an excited feel — the character is telling a story that they think is interesting.
2) The rhyming words in the poem show how the character sees certain things as being connected, e.g. "head" and "dead".
3) The irregularity of the rhyming shows how the character's thoughts jump about fairly randomly — he/she seems rather unstable.

Kid (Pages 60-61)

1) Every line in the poem rhymes or half-rhymes, e.g. "order", "wander", "yonder", "rather". This gives the poem a relentless feel, reflecting Robin's accusing, sometimes mocking tone.
2) The repeated, heavy rhythm in "taller, harder, stronger, older" emphasises how much Robin has changed. This adds to the aggressive, defiant feel.
3) Alliteration in "next to nothing" and "punching the palm" make Robin's vision of Batman's downfall seem more dramatic and hard-hitting.

Language effects make descriptions more memorable...

Think about the effect each poet is trying to create. You could write about the language effects in these poems: 'The Eagle' (p.24-25), 'Sonnet' (p.34-35), 'Salome' (p.42-43) and 'Those bastards in their mansions' (p.62-63).

Mood

Mood is the feel or atmosphere of a poem. There are loads of different kinds of mood, e.g. light-hearted, tense, comical, threatening.

1) Mood can be created by describing a particular setting.
2) Poets can create a certain mood by describing feelings — their own or other people's.
3) The mood can change from one part of a poem to another.

Mood can Come from the Situation

Sonnet (Pages 34-35)

1) The poet creates a peaceful, happy mood. The poem starts with "I love", so it starts on a positive note.
2) There are lots of idyllic countryside images, such as the "willow leaning half way o'er / The clear deep lake". These descriptions give the poem a tranquil feel.
3) There's plenty of colour too, which gives the feel of a bright, carefree summer's day.
4) The insects' "happy wings" and the description of the beetles playing make the scene seem carefree and natural.

Tichborne's Elegy (Pages 14-15)

1) The mood in this poem is sad, regretful and rather bitter.
2) Tichborne talks about how he's still young and fit, but his life will soon be over when he's executed. He seems bitter about his fate — "My feast of joy is but a dish of pain".
3) The poet constantly points out the bitter irony of his situation. The whole poem has a miserable, desperate tone.

Bitter, Chidiock?

Uncertainty can Create a Sinister Mood

We Remember Your Childhood Well (Pages 46-47)

1) This poem has an unpleasant, sinister mood. The person whose voice we hear makes a string of denials, suggesting that something very nasty has gone on in the past.
2) We don't hear directly what's being denied, which adds to the dark tone. The phrase "Nobody hurt you" hints at child abuse of some kind.
3) The person talking tries to confuse the person who's made the accusations — "The moment's a blur". This makes us distrust them, as they seem to be covering things up, and they don't offer clear explanations.
4) The mood becomes even bleaker at the end of the poem. The "skidmarks of sin" suggest how horrible the past events must have been.

Homecoming (Pages 56-57)

1) The first line sets the tone for a mysterious poem: "Think, two things on their own and both at once". The poet challenges us, as well as the woman he's talking to, to figure out how the "canary-yellow cotton jacket" and the trust exercise are related.
2) There's a tense mood in this poem, as it's difficult to work out exactly what's going on and how the things described in the poem are connected to each other.
3) There's also tension between the person the poet is talking to and her mother — "You seeing red. Blue murder. Bed."
4) The "silhouette" of a man who "wants to set things straight" seems threatening.

You'll probably never be in the mood for an exam...

Good poems to look at for this theme include: 'On my first Sonne' (p.6-7), 'The Affliction of Margaret' (p.10-11), 'Havisham' (p.36-37), 'Elvis's Twin Sister' (p.38-39) and 'Hitcher' (p.66-67).

Stage 1 — Planning

Before you write the essay, you've got to plan it. Spend ten minutes planning — that leaves you with fifty minutes for writing. Use this two-stage method to plan your essay:

A Read the Question Carefully and Underline Key Words

1) Read the question you've chosen a couple of times. The question will usually ask you how the poems show/present/use/convey the theme. Underline the theme and any other important words.
2) You have to compare four poems altogether. The question will give you the titles of one or two poems that you have to write about. You'll get some choice about which other poems you're going to compare. Pick poems which relate to the theme in the question.
3) Look up the poems you're going to write about in the copy of the Anthology you are given in the exam. Bend the corner over on those pages, so that you can find them again quickly.

EXAMPLE QUESTION

They want you to compare the poems.

The theme of this question is characters.

Question 1 Compare the ways characters are portrayed in *Havisham* by Carol Ann Duffy, *Kid* by Simon Armitage and two poems from the Pre-1914 Poetry Bank.

This bit tells you which poems to use in your answer.

B Spend 5-10 minutes Planning your Essay

Write a plan at the top of your answer paper — this will help you write a good essay. Just scribble stuff down, like in the example below. At the end of the exam, draw a neat line through your plan, so the examiner knows that it's rough work. Here's an example:

Plan: poems to write about: Ulysses, The Village Schoolmaster, Havisham, Kid
1) Intro about theme - characters
2) Structure
Ulysses: 4 verses, each shows diff emotion
Village: 1 verse, descriptions blend together
Havisham: verses flow into each other
Kid: similar to Village Schoolmaster
3) Language
Ulysses: frustrated, heroic
Village: nostalgic, mysterious
Havisham: aggressive, confused
Kid: vengeful, sarcastic
4) Attitudes and Feelings
Ulysses: boredom, pride, excitement
Village: respect, fear
Havisham: bitterness, loneliness
Kid: revenge
5) Conclusion - personal response:
Liked Ulysses because you see his human side

Planning is the basis of a good essay...

Always write a plan. It'll help you get your ideas in order, and write a well-structured essay. Once you've got a plan, you know what you're going to write — it will give you confidence.

THIS IS A FLAP.
FOLD THIS PAGE OUT.

Sample Essay — Death

Here's another example of a typical exam question — and how to answer it well...

A Here's an Exam-style Question about Death

Question 1 You should answer both (a) and (b).

(a) Compare how death is presented in *Hitcher* by Simon Armitage and one poem by Carol Ann Duffy.

(b) Compare how death is presented in *The Laboratory* by Robert Browning and one other poem from the Pre-1914 Poetry Bank.

B Here's an Example of a Plan for this Answer

Plan: poems to write about: Salome, Hitcher, The Man He Killed, The Laboratory

(a) 1) Intro about theme - death

2) Structure

Salome: Only reveals murder at end of poem, clues

Hitcher: Also starts off normal, then murder

3) Language

Sal: humour, casual tone, first person

Hit: contrast ordinary life / violence, humour, fp

4) Attitudes and Feelings

Sal: evil, pride in killing almost, bored of it

Hit: cold, distant, pride

5) Conclusion

Both show death from murderer's point of view.

(b) 1) Intro

2) Structure

Man he killed: short poem, message at end

Laboratory: long, 12 stanzas, scattered thoughts

3) Language

Man: colloquial, likeable, fp

Lab: melodramatic, excited, fp

4) Attitudes and Feelings

Man: irony, empathy

Lab: revenge, evil

5) Conclusion

Strong contrast

Here's an 'A' Grade Answer to the Question

1 Intro.

(a) Death is an emotional subject, often connected to feelings of grief, sadness and loss. The poems 'Salome' and 'Hitcher' are unusual in that they instead present death as mundane and humorous. Both poems are written in the first person, from the point of view of a murderer. These characters don't experience the usual emotions associated with death and are unrepentant about killing.

Treat each part of the question, (a) and (b), like a mini-essay.

2 Structure

The structures of the poems are important in the ways the poets present death. In both poems, we don't realise at first that the narrator is a murderer. In 'Salome' the implication is that the narrator has woken up after a drunken one night stand: "woke up with a head on the pillow beside me — whose — ?" Only in the last stanza is it revealed that she has beheaded the man. Likewise, in 'Hitcher' the narrator seems fairly ordinary at the start of the poem. The narrator describes feeling "tired, under / the weather". It is only in the third stanza that the reader suddenly realises that the narrator is a murderer.

Remember to relate the structure of the poems to the theme.

The key words in the question are highlighted in green.

3 Lang.

The way the poets use language to describe death is slightly different in 'Salome' and 'Hitcher'. In 'Salome', there is a humorous tone throughout the poem. The narrator's voice is lively and jokey, for example when she says the man she woke up next to was "Good-looking, of course". Even when she reveals the

Give examples and quotes from the poems to back up your points.

Sample Essay — Death

3 Language gruesome death, there is still a strong vein of black humour: "there, like I said – and ain't life a bitch – / was his head on a platter." The language used in 'Hitcher' is bleaker. This is partly because the murder is described in detail: hitting the man "six times with the krooklok / in the face". The black humour in the poem ("I let him have it / on the top road out of Harrogate") adds to the impact of the murder.

Try and write a similar amount about each poem — this will make sure your answer is balanced.

4 Attitudes The attitudes in the poems towards death are different. Salome shows an ambivalent attitude to death. She sounds almost bored with killing ("doubtless I'll do it again"), but she's also excited by it — her "eyes glitter" when she sees the blood and the dead man. In contrast, in 'Hitcher', the character's attitude towards death seems cold and unemotional. He seems to take pride in killing the man without losing control of the car: "didn't even swerve." The murder was premeditated as the character had hired a car. This contrasts with Salome, who killed drunkenly and impulsively.

Write about similarities and differences between the poems.

5 Conc. These poems both present death from the point of view of murderers. There is black humour and brutality in both poems. This makes them uneasy reading. I feel uncomfortable laughing at the humour in 'Hitcher', for example the phrase "I dropped it into third", because of the violence being described.

Include a conclusion for part (a).

1 Intro. (b) The poems 'The Man He Killed' and 'The Laboratory' present death in different ways. In 'The Man He Killed', a soldier describes killing a man in battle and the thoughts this stirred in him. In 'The Laboratory' a woman is planning a murder, possibly of her lover's new mistress.

Spend roughly half your time on (a) and half your time on (b).

2 Structure The structure of the poems relates to how death is presented. 'The Man He Killed' is a short poem, containing a simple message about the tragedy of war, summed up in its final stanza: "You shoot a fellow down / You'd treat if met where any bar is". In contrast, in 'The Laboratory', there are numerous stanzas. These visualise the character's excitable, easily distracted frame of mind as she prepares for the murder.

3 Lang. The poets also use language very differently to present death. The woman in 'The Laboratory' describes death in a cruelly melodramatic way: "He is sure to remember her dying face!". She asks lots of questions which makes her appear excited about the crime. In contrast, the character in 'The Man He Killed' uses plain language: "I shot at him as he at me". He killed in war, not out of malice.

Explain how the quotes you use help back up the point you're making.

4 Attitudes The attitudes to death contrast greatly between the two poems. The character in 'The Man He Killed', killed out of duty. He can empathise with the man he killed ("just as I"), and sees the irony that they might have been friends in different circumstances. The woman in 'The Laboratory' has a very different attitude to death; she is excited by the thought of getting her revenge and causing pain: "Let death be felt". It gives her a sense of power over the people she imagines "laugh" at her.

Using terms like "irony" and "empathy" correctly will impress the examiner.

5 Conc. In conclusion, there is a strong contrast in the way these two poems present death. 'The Man He Killed' is a moving poem with a peaceful message. The line "No other reason why" makes me feel sad; the soldiers pitted against each other are fighting for no reason other than they needed a job. On the other hand, 'The Laboratory' shows a malicious, vengeful view of death.

Say what your feelings are about the poems in the conclusion.

Sample Essay — Imagery

Some of the exam questions will be about poetic methods e.g. imagery, first person, character. Don't be scared off by these questions — you can still answer them by looking at the structure, language and feelings/attitudes in the poems.

A Here's an Exam-style Question about Imagery

Question 1 Compare how imagery is used to create vivid descriptions in *Anne Hathaway* by Carol Ann Duffy and one poem by Simon Armitage. Then go on to compare the ways imagery is used in two of the poems from the Pre-1914 Poetry Bank.

B Here's an Example of a Plan for this Answer

Plan: poems to write about: Anne Hathaway, Mother any distance, Sonnet, The Eagle

1) Intro about theme - imagery

2) Structure

Anne Hath: sonnet form, 14 lines/rhyming end couplet

Mother any dist: almost sonnet, uneven line lengths

3) Language

Anne: romantic images, metaphor of language for love

Moth: images holding tape, still anchoring son who is moving away

4) Attitudes and feelings

Anne: joy in memories, fondness

Mother: still loves mum, needs independence

then go on to compare pre-1914 poems:

2) Structure

Sonnet: sonnet form, rhyme, repetition 'I love'

Eagle: short, rhythm, rhyme

3) Language

Sonnet: colour / shine, detailed description

Eagle: simile 'thunderbolt', image power/height

4) Attitudes and feelings

Sonnet: joy, happiness in small things

Eagle: power, respect for nature

5) Conclusion for whole essay

Preferred Anne

Here's an 'A' Grade Answer to the Question

1 Introduction

Imagery is the way poets use language to create vivid descriptions of situations, events and even emotions. In 'Anne Hathaway' by Carol Ann Duffy, imagery is used to show the narrator's fond, happy memories of her relationship with her late husband: the images are romantic and blissful. In 'Mother, any distance...' by Simon Armitage, imagery is also used to show the relationship between two characters, in this case the narrator and his mother. The two pre-1914 poems, 'The Eagle' by Alfred Tennyson and 'Sonnet' by John Clare use imagery differently. They both use imagery to describe nature, creating a vivid sense of its beauty.

Establish why the theme is important

The key words in the question are highlighted in green.

2 Structure

'Anne Hathaway' is structured as a sonnet, with fourteen lines and a closing rhyming couplet. The sonnet form relates to the content and imagery in the poem: the narrator is describing her relationship with Shakespeare who was famous for his sonnets and breathtaking use of language. 'Mother, any distance...' also uses sonnet form as a basis for its structure, but changes and adapts it. For example, it isn't on the traditional fourteen lines, because the final phrase "to fall or fly" has been given its own line. This final phrase provides a strong image which sums up the feelings in the poem: it is given special emphasis by being put on its own.

This question asks for the Duffy/ Armitage poems to be compared first.

Sample Essay — Imagery

Both of these poems use language to create vivid imagery. In 'Anne Hathaway', there are romantic images, reminiscent of Shakespeare plays like 'Twelfth Night', to describe the couple's relationship: a fantasy world of "forest, castles, torchlight, clifftops, seas". Language is used as a metaphor for love: "my body now a softer rhyme / to his". The narrator uses this metaphor to show how in awe she was of the power of Shakespeare's writing. She imagines herself as a figment of his imagination: "I dream'd he had written me". 'Mother, any distance...' uses imagery to portray a different kind of relationship. The narrator describes walking up the stairs with a tape measure, with his mum holding the other end: "your fingertips still pinch / the last one-hundreth of an inch." There comes a point when he reaches the very top of the house, when she might have to let go. This image represents the narrator reaching a point in life where he needs to be independent from his mother and take risks: "to fall or fly."

Back up your points with quotes.

Compare the poets use of language.

The images in 'Anne Hathaway' and 'Mother, any distance...' are striking because they combine the everyday with the extraordinary. An old bed is described with the romance of "shooting stars" and "torchlight". A day spent measuring a new house is described in surreal terms: the "prairies of the floors" and a "space-walk". The poets' use of imagery emphasises how these ordinary objects and situations had special significance. 'Anne Hathaway' uses imagery to describe the uncommon joy the narrator associates with the bed: "The bed we loved in was a spinning world". In 'Mother, any distance...', the imagery shows the narrator's desire for independence. This feels strange and risky to him at first: "a hatch that opens on an endless sky".

Talk about how the poets use the theme to show feelings and attitudes.

The second part of this essay will compare the use of imagery in two pre-1914 poems: 'The Eagle' and 'Sonnet'. The structure of these poems relates to their use of imagery. 'The Eagle' is a very short poem, describing a single, striking image of an eagle perched on a crag before swooping on its prey. In a similar way, 'Sonnet' is quite a short poem with a single subject being described: the beauty of summer.

Be careful to leave time to write about all four essays.

The imagery used in 'The Eagle' emphasises the bird's power and authority. The eagle is described as high up, looking down on the world from his "mountain walls": even the sea seems small and insignificant from his perch. The bird is described as almost human: he has "crookèd hands" not claws. The simile of a "thunderbolt" is used to describe the awe-inspiring force of the bird as it swoops for prey. In 'Sonnet' John Clare also uses imagery to describe the beauty of nature. However, he focuses on a tamer, softer side of nature: "wild flowers", "wool sack clouds" and "hay grass". He uses language to create an image of happiness: "beaming forth", "sport about", "happy wings", "play". In both poems, colour is used to accentuate the beauty of the scene: the "azure" sea in 'The Eagle' and "stain with gold the meadow" in 'Sonnet'.

Explain the different methods the poet has used to create an overall image.

The imagery Tennyson uses in 'The Eagle' shows his feelings of respect for nature and the beauty of the world. He describes a natural environment of sea, cliffs and sun, untouched by humans. 'Sonnet' is different because it focuses on the poet's enjoyment of nature: he repeats the phrase "I love" three times in the poem, joyously affirming his reaction to the scene he is describing.

Keep comparing the poems all the way through.

All these poems use imagery to create vivid descriptions of their different subjects: love, growing up, nature's power and nature's beauty. I particularly like the way imagery is used to describe love in 'Anne Hathaway'. The phrase, "a verb dancing in the centre of a noun" describes the narrator's happiness in a witty and vibrant way.

Always put in a conclusion.

Sample Essay — Parent/Child Relationships

Read through this sample answer for some handy tips on how to write a fantastic essay. Key words have been highlighted in green — both in the question and the answer.

A Here's an Exam-style Question about Parent/Child Relationships

Question 1 Compare the ways parent/child relationships are presented in *Before You Were Mine* by Carol Ann Duffy and three other poems, one by Simon Armitage and any two from the Pre-1914 Poetry Bank.

B Here's an Example of a Plan for this Answer

Plan: poems to write about: Affliction of Margaret, On my first Sonne, My father, Before You Were Mine

1) Intro about theme - parent/child relationships

2) Structure
Affliction: each verse shows diff state of mind
First Sonne: one verse, sums up feelings
Before: each verse about diff time (ish)
My father: each verse about diff event (ish)

3) Language
Affliction: extreme words/metaphors show strong feelings
Sonne: gentler, calmer language
Before: conversational language shows empathy with mum
My father: colloquial language makes it sound normal

4) Attitudes and Feelings
Affliction: despair, sadness
First Sonne: sadness, acceptance, pride
Before: admiration, guilt
My father: pain

5) Conclusion - personal response:
I find On my first Sonne very moving
— "best piece of poetrie"

Here's an 'A' Grade Answer to the Question

1 Introduction

The relationship between a parent and a child can bring about any of a range of emotions. In 'The Affliction of Margaret', we see a parent's desperation at not hearing from her missing son in seven years, while in 'On my first Sonne', the poet bids farewell to his dead son. In 'Before You Were Mine', the poet describes the effect her own birth had on the lifestyle of her mother, whereas 'My father thought it bloody queer' describes a strained relationship between father and son.

Start by talking about the theme.

2 Structure

The differing structures of the poems affect their impact. Wordsworth's structure for 'The Affliction of Margaret' consists of eleven verses of seven lines each, one for each year her son has been missing. Each verse shows a different aspect of Margaret's desperation to hear from her child, e.g. in the first verse she appeals for him to "find me, prosperous or undone!"; in the second verse she recalls the doomed glimpses of hope she's had: "I catch at them, and then I miss". This gives the impression that her state of mind changes from day to day.

Always keep t[he] theme of the question in mi[nd] when you're talking about the structure [of] the poem.

The structure of 'On my first Sonne' is simpler than 'Affliction'. It consists of six rhyming couplets, making up just one verse in which Jonson, as a parent, pays tribute to his dead son. This makes the poem look like an inscription on a tombstone. Duffy's poem 'Before You Were Mine' also has a fairly regular structure, comprising four verses of five lines each, but with no regular rhyme scheme. Like 'Affliction', each verse describes a different thought, with the last verse describing the most recent thoughts.

Sample Essay — Parent/Child Relationships

Structure

2

The poem 'My father thought it bloody queer' by Armitage has a less regular structure than any of the three poems I have mentioned above. There are three verses, each with a different number of lines, and there is no regular rhyme scheme. As in 'The Affliction of Margaret' and 'Before You Were Mine', the effect of the verses is to separate the different ideas about the relationship between parent and child in the poem — the first verse describes his father's reaction to the earring, the second goes back to when he had his ear pierced, and the third describes how he now finds himself saying the same things as his father.

Talk about the effect created by the poems' structure.

There's only one part to this question, so compare all four poems throughout your essay.

Language

3

Each poet uses a different style of language to describe the parent/child relationship. In 'The Affliction of Margaret', there is a confused, obsessive style of language. Margaret often contradicts herself: "Neglect me! no I suffered long / from that ill thought". This shows her desperate state of mind. The language in 'On my first Sonne' is gentler and calmer. Jonson wants his son to "Rest in soft peace", and this expresses his tenderness towards his son and his acceptance that he has lost him.

Say how the kind of language used affects the theme.

'Before You Were Mine', on the other hand, uses conversational language to convey the idea that the poet is talking to her mother. Phrases such as "You reckon it's worth it" give the poem a personal feel and show that the poet is empathising with her mother. Similarly, 'My father' uses a conversational tone to show the relationship between son and father, although he does not address his parent directly. Colloquial phrases like "rolled home" give the poem a down-to-earth, everyday feel.

Use linking words and phrases like "similarly" and "in contrast".

Feelings and Attitudes

4

The attitudes towards parent/child relationships vary between the different poems. In 'Affliction', the breaking down of the relationship causes Margaret despair: the question "Was ever darkness like to this?" shows she cannot imagine a worse situation than the one she is in. Similarly, Jonson's feelings in 'On my first Sonne' are ones of sadness. However, the knowledge that his son is dead has allowed him to come to terms with what has happened; he says that perhaps death is the best state to be in, as his son has "scap'd worlds, and fleshes rage". He is also very proud of his son.

Remember to back up the points you make with relevant quotes.

Feelings about parent/child relationships in the post-1914 poems are less clear cut. In 'Before You Were Mine', the poet admires her mother's rebellious life before she was born: she calls her "Marilyn", which shows she sees her as glamorous. However, the poet seems to think her own birth deprived her mother of this exciting life, forcing her to be responsible. In 'My father', the parent/child relationship is strained, as the father mocks the child for his attempt at rebellion. Now he has grown up, the poet finds himself saying the same things as his father, but we can see that the memory of his father's reaction still hurts, as he describes "my own voice breaking like a tear".

Say how the feelings and attitudes in the poem are related to the theme.

Conclusion

5

All four of these poems take an interesting angle on the trials and tribulations of parent/child relationships. I feel that the most affecting is 'On my first Sonne'. I find this poem very moving, as Jonson bids a fond farewell to his son. He describes his son as his "best piece of poetrie", and I feel this is a beautiful way of showing the pride he had in his child.

Include a personal response to make the conclusion interesting.

Glossary

adjective	A word that describes something, e.g. "big", "fast", "annoying".
alliteration	Where words start with the same letter. It's often used in poetry to give a nice pattern to a phrase. E.g. 'Sally's slipper slipped on a slimy slug.'
ambiguity	Where a word or phrase has two or more possible meanings.
assonance	When words share the same vowel sound but the consonants are different. E.g. "Lisa had a piece of cheese before she went to sleep, to help her dream."
blank verse	Poetry that doesn't rhyme, usually in iambic pentameters.
colloquial	Sounding like everyday spoken language.
compound word	A word that is made up of two or more other words put together, e.g. "flame-red".
consonants	All the letters in the alphabet that aren't vowels.
contrast	When two things are described in a way which emphasises how different they are. E.g. a poet might contrast two different places or two different people.
dialect	Regional variation of a language. People from different places might use different words or sentence constructions. E.g. In some northern English dialects, people might say "Ey up" instead of "Hello".
empathy	When someone feels like they understand what someone else is experiencing and how they feel about it.
enjambement	When a sentence runs over from one line to the next.
iambic pentameter	This is a form of poetry that doesn't rhyme, but usually has a clear metre of ten syllables — five of them stressed, and five unstressed. The stress falls on every second syllable, e.g. "Coral is far more red than her lips' red."
imagery	Language that creates a picture in your mind.
irony	When words are used in a sarcastic or comic way to imply the opposite of what they normally mean. It can also mean when there is a big difference between what people expect and what actually happens.
language	The choice of words used. The language determines the effect the piece of writing will have on the reader, e.g. it can be emotive or persuasive.
layout	The way a piece of poetry is visually presented to the reader. E.g. line length, whether the poem is broken up into different stanzas, whether lines are arranged regularly or create some kind of visual pattern.
metaphor	A way of describing something by saying that it is something else, to create a vivid image. E.g. "His eyes were deep, black, oily pools."
metre	The arrangement of syllables to create rhythm in a line of poetry.
mood	The feel or atmosphere of a poem, e.g. humorous, threatening, eerie.
mythology	A collection of very old stories, often involving gods and heroes. Different cultures have their own mythologies.
narrator	The voice speaking the words that you're reading. E.g. a poem could be written from the point of view of a young child, which means the young child is the poem's narrator.

Glossary

oun	A word for a place, person or thing, e.g. "tree", "air", "Boris", "London".
nomatopoeia	A word that sounds like the thing it's describing. E.g. "buzz", "crunch", "bang", "pop", "ding".
ersona	A fictional character or identity adopted by a poet. Poets often create a persona so they can describe things from a different person's point of view, e.g. a male poet might use a female persona.
ersonification	A special kind of metaphor where you write about something as if it's a person with thoughts and feelings. E.g. "The sea growled hungrily."
honetic	When words are spelt as they sound rather than with their usual spelling. It's often used to show that someone's speaking with a certain accent.
hyme scheme	A regular system of rhyming words in a poem, e.g. in 'The Man He Killed', the 1st line of each verse rhymes with the 3rd, and the 2nd rhymes with the 4th.
hyming couplet	A pair of lines that are next to each other and whose final words rhyme.
hythm	When sentences or lines have a regular fixed pattern of syllables.
imile	A way of describing something by comparing it to something else, usually by using the words "like" or "as". E.g. "He was as pale as the moon," or "Her hair was like a bird's nest."
onnet	A type of poem with fourteen lines, and usually following a clear rhyme pattern. There are different popular patterns for sonnets. They will often have ten syllables a line, and end with a rhyming couplet.
tanza	A group of lines in a poem that often share the same rhythm pattern and have similar line lengths. Stanzas can also be called verses.
tereotype	An inaccurate, generalised view of a particular group of people. E.g. A stereotype of football fans might be that they're all hooligans.
tructure	The order and arrangement of a piece of writing. E.g. how the poem begins, develops and ends, whether it uses verses or not, whether it has a particular layout, etc.
yllable	A single unit of sound within a word. E.g. "all" has one syllable, "always" has two and "establishmentarianism" has nine.
ymbolism	When an object stands for something else. E.g. a candle might be a symbol of hope, or a dying flower could symbolise the end of a relationship.
syntax	The way a sentence is put together so that it makes sense.
heme	An idea or topic that's important in a piece of writing. E.g. a poem could be based on the theme of friendship.
verb	A word that describes something you do, e.g. "run", "talk", "hope".
vocabulary	All the words used in a piece of writing.
voice	The personality narrating the poem. Poems are usually written either using the poet's voice, as if they're speaking to you directly, or the voice of a character, e.g. an elderly man, or a horse.
vowels	Simple — the letters 'a', 'e', 'i', 'o' and 'u'.

Index

Index

The Publisher would like to thank:

Poets:

<u>Carol Ann Duffy</u> 'Elvis's Twin Sister', 'Anne Hathaway' and 'Salome' from *The World's Wife* (Picador Macmillan, 1999), © Carol Ann Duffy 1999, reprinted by permission of the publisher, Macmillan, London, UK.
'Education for Leisure' is taken from *Standing Female Nude* by Carol Ann Duffy published by Anvil Press Poetry in 1985.
'Stealing' is taken from *Selling Manhattan* by Carol Ann Duffy published by Anvil Press Poetry in 1987.
'Havisham' and 'Before You Were Mine' are taken from *Mean Time* by Carol Ann Duffy published by Anvil Press Poetry in 1993.
'We Remember Your Childhood Well' is taken from *The Other Country* by Carol Ann Duffy published by Anvil Press Poetry in 199C

<u>Simon Armitage</u> 'Hitcher', 'Those bastards in their mansions', 'My father thought it bloody queer', 'Mother', 'Kid', 'I've made out a will' and 'Homecoming' from *Selected Poems* (2001) all reprinted by permission of the publishers, Faber & Faber Ltd.
'November', Simon Armitage *ZOOM!* (Bloodaxe Books, 1989)

<u>William Butler Yeats</u> 'The Song of the Old Mother' published by permission of A.P. Watt Ltd. on behalf of Michael B. Yeats

Image sources:

<u>Image of Carol Ann Duffy</u> © Anvil Press

<u>Images of Ben Jonson, William Wordsworth, William Blake, John Clare, Thomas Hardy, Walt Whitman, Robert Browning, Alfred Lord Tennyson and Oliver Goldsmith</u> © Mary Evans Picture Library

<u>Images of William Butler Yeats and Gerard Manley Hopkins</u> © National Portrait Gallery, London

<u>Image of William Shakespeare</u> © Royal Shakespeare Company

<u>Image of Simon Armitage</u> © www.roderickfield.com

Every effort has been made to locate copyright holders and obtain permission to reproduce poems and images. For those poems and images where it has been difficult to trace the originator of the work, we would be grateful for information. If any copyright holder would like us to make an amendment to the acknowledgements, please notify us and we will gladly update the book at the next reprint. Thank you.